THE MALLEABILITY OF INTELLECTUAL STYLES

Intellectual styles are individuals' preferred ways of using the abilities that they possess. The extent to which one can change his or her intellectual style is a question of interest to both researchers and the general public. This book presents the first comprehensive and systematic review of existing research on the malleability of intellectual styles. By critically analyzing research findings derived from both cross-sectional and longitudinal investigations performed over the past seven decades, Li-fang Zhang demonstrates that intellectual styles can be modified through both socialization and purposeful training. Professor Zhang elucidates the heuristic value of these findings for the development of adaptive intellectual styles in both academic and nonacademic settings. She proposes further avenues of research that might advance scholarly understanding of the nature of and the potential for modifying intellectual styles.

Li-fang Zhang is Professor of Psychology and Education in the Faculty of Education at The University of Hong Kong. She is the coauthor of five books, including the award-winning monograph *The Nature of Intellectual Styles* (2006). Professor Zhang has also published works on such diverse research areas as creativity, giftedness, personality, student development, teacher education, higher education, multicultural education, and the academic profession.

The Malleability of Intellectual Styles

LI-FANG ZHANG

The University of Hong Kong

CAMBRIDGE
UNIVERSITY PRESS

32 Avenue of the Americas, New York NY 10013-2473, USA

Cambridge University Press is part of the University of Cambridge.

It furthers the University's mission by disseminating knowledge in the pursuit of education, learning and research at the highest international levels of excellence.

www.cambridge.org
Information on this title: www.cambridge.org/9781107096448

© Li-fang Zhang 2013

This publication is in copyright. Subject to statutory exception and to the provisions of relevant collective licensing agreements, no reproduction of any part may take place without the written permission of Cambridge University Press.

First published 2013

A catalogue record for this publication is available from the British Library

Library of Congress Cataloguing in Publication data
Zhang, Li-fang.
The malleability of intellectual styles / Li-fang Zhang.
 pages cm
Includes bibliographical references and index.
ISBN 978-1-107-09644-8 (hard covers : alk. paper)
1. Cognitive styles. 2. Learning, Psychology of. I. Zhang, Li-fang. II. Title.
BF311.Z45 2014
153–dc23   2013013588

ISBN 978-1-107-09644-8 Hardback
ISBN 978-1-107-50757-9 Paperback

Cambridge University Press has no responsibility for the persistence or accuracy of URLs for external or third-party internet websites referred to in this publication, and does not guarantee that any content on such websites is, or will remain, accurate or appropriate.

To Ashley, my beloved daughter

Contents

Preface		page ix
Acknowledgments		xi

PART I. BACKGROUND

1	Motivation for This Book	3
	Identity Issues	5
	Controversial Issues Concerning the Nature of Intellectual Styles	10
	Why This book	16
	About This Book	18
2	Key Style Models and Measures	20
	Integrative Style Models	20
	Individual Style Models/Constructs and Measures	24
	Closing Remarks	46

PART II. EMPIRICAL EVIDENCE: CROSS-SECTIONAL STUDIES

3	Gender and Intellectual Styles	49
	Gender-Role Socialization: Theoretical Perspectives and Research	51
	Setting Parameters: Literature Search Procedures and Results	53
	Gender Differences in Intellectual Styles: Research Evidence	56
	Conclusions, Limitations, and Implications	80
4	Culture and Intellectual Styles	87
	Culture and Theoretical Models of Culture	87
	The Conceptual Links between Culture and Intellectual Styles: A Hypothesis	90
	Literature Search Procedures and Results	92
	Culture and Intellectual Styles: Empirical Evidence	93

	Summary: General Findings Across the Six Models	115
	Limitations and Implications	116
5	Academic Discipline and Intellectual Styles	120
	Literature Search Procedures and Results	121
	Research Findings	123
	Conclusions and Implications	155
6	Occupation and Intellectual Styles	158
	Literature Search Procedures and Results	158
	Research Findings	159
	Conclusions and Implications	184

PART III. EMPIRICAL EVIDENCE: LONGITUDINAL STUDIES

7	Longitudinal Studies with Interventions	189
	Literature Search Procedures and Results	189
	Research Findings	192
	Limitations and Conclusions	247
8	Longitudinal Studies without Interventions	250
	Setting Boundaries: Literature Search Procedures and Results	250
	Research Findings	251
	Conclusions, Limitations, and Future Research	280

PART IV. CONCLUDING REMARKS

9	Evaluation, Future Directions, and Implications	287
	What the Existing Literature Says	288
	Limitations and Research Agenda	289
	General Implications for Education and Beyond	295

Epilogue	301
Appendix	303
References	315
Author Index	355
Subject Index	365

Preface

Why is it that a student can be considered dumb by one teacher but smart by another? How is it possible that a student can fail a multiple-choice test but excel at an individual project? How can one explain the fact that a teacher can be evaluated very highly by one group of students but very poorly by another? How could an individual be considered mediocre in one organization but a great asset in another?

There are a number of possible explanations for these and many other similar situations. One is that people have different intellectual styles, and the same individual may deploy different intellectual styles in different environments. Intellectual styles – an umbrella term for such constructs as cognitive styles, learning styles, teaching styles, and thinking styles – refer to people's preferred ways of processing information and dealing with tasks. Like abilities and personalities, styles significantly affect human performance. However, styles are neither abilities nor personalities; rather, they are at the interface between abilities and personalities (Sternberg, 1997). Styles can be ability-based and personality-based (Sternberg, Grigorenko, & Zhang, 2008), but they are still styles.

The purpose of this book is to address the nature of intellectual styles, particularly as it relates to the issue of style malleability, through delineating and integrating major relevant conceptual and empirical work. Research findings obtained from longitudinal and experimental investigations along with those derived from cross-sectional studies are systematically presented and critically analyzed. The thrust of this book is that people's intellectual styles can change – both as a function of socialization and as a result of training. Specifically, this book has three objectives. The first is to facilitate a good understanding of how the major bodies of literature documented in the past seven decades converge to support the argument that people's intellectual styles are more dynamic than static. The second is to discuss the implications of the research findings for both academic (e.g., schools and universities) and nonacademic settings (e.g., government and industry). The third objective of this book is to stimulate further research on the malleability of intellectual styles through suggesting ideas for future research programs.

This book is aimed at graduate students and upper-division undergraduate students as well as academics who wish to do research in the field of intellectual styles and its related academic fields. These related fields of inquiry include the following: applied psychology, clinical psychology, cognitive psychology, consulting psychology, cross-cultural psychology, developmental psychology, differential psychology, educational psychology, industrial/organizational psychology, educational administration and policy making, general education, teacher education, higher education, multicultural education, institutional administration and management, curriculum design and instruction, business management, health sciences, student development, career counseling, marriage counseling, school counseling, anthropology, cultural and ethnic studies, sociology, information technology, and liberal studies.

Although this book is intended for the audiences mentioned in the preceding paragraph, practitioners, educational and noneducational, should also be interested in reading this book not only because they will find the research evidence for style modifiability intriguing, but also because they will find the discussion on the practical implications of the research findings for education and beyond useful. Indeed, anyone who is interested in understanding how to develop effective intellectual styles should find this book helpful.

Finally, four technical aspects of the book should be noted. First, the literature search for this book was conducted using the PsycINFO Database (1940 to 2011). Second, in the case of several style constructs, the same style construct has historically been assigned different names, so these names are used interchangeably in this book to refer to the same style construct. For example, Holland's (1973) construct of personality-based style is referred to as career interest type, career interest style, career personality type, and career personality style. Another example is that both "personality style" and "personality type" are used to refer to Jung's (1923) concept of personality-based style. Third, the studies reviewed in Part II of this book are broadly referred to as "cross-sectional studies"; some are actually "one-shot" investigations. Fourth and lastly, the expressions "college" and "university" carry the same meaning, both referring to higher educational institutions, and the phrases "business world," "business settings," and "nonacademic settings" are used interchangeably.

Acknowledgments

Many people have contributed enormously to the publication of this book. I should especially like to express my deep gratitude to Robert J. Sternberg, my mentor for more than two decades, for his unflagging encouragement and support and for having set a superb example for me on my journey to pursue excellence. Dr. Sternberg has played a vital role in shaping my professional standards, values, and ways of thinking throughout the years. My sincere thanks also go to those people, both in Hong Kong and around the world, many of whom I have never met, who have strongly supported me in so many different ways at various stages of my academic career.

I am grateful to all the scholars in the field of intellectual styles and its allied academic disciplines, particularly my coauthors/editors and contributors to my edited books, whose work has been critical to the development of my thinking and research on the nature of intellectual styles. My special thanks go to Chen Chen, Jieqiong Fan, Gloria Yi-ming Kao, Leonidas Kyriakides, Chi-ho Lau, Ruby Tai, Yu-chu Yeh, Lin Yong, and Tak-ming Yu for their generous sharing of unpublished research findings.

I sincerely thank my PhD students, Sanyin Cheng, Bing Li, Ruby Tai, Qiuzhi Xie, and Lin Yong, for their capable assistance in finding some of the research materials used in this book. I am particularly indebted to Jieqiong Fan, who has given me unfailing support throughout my writing of this book – not only in terms of assisting in literature searches, but also with respect to locating many types of hard-to-find information. Jieqiong's competent and conscientious aid has been invaluable to me in writing this book.

I am immensely grateful to my colleagues and students at The University of Hong Kong, who have created the congenial work environment in which I have been pursuing my academic career for more than 16 years. I am also greatly indebted to The University of Iowa, Yale University, Tufts University, Columbia University, The George Washington University, University of Cambridge,

Harvard University, Seton Hall University, University of Nebraska-Lincoln, University of California-Berkeley, University of Geneva, and the National Training Center for Foreign Affairs of the U.S. Department of State for having provided me with tremendous intellectual stimulation over the years.

I sincerely thank Adebowale Akande, Allan Bernardo, Chen Chen, Guohai Chen, Meng Deng, Weiqiao Fan, Hong Fu, Yunfeng He, Paul Higgins, Jiafen Huang, Rongjin Huang, Ben Jiao, Lizhen Jing, Mark Mason, Baden Nima, Gerard A. Postiglione, David Watkins, Qiufang Wen, Yau-ho Paul Wong, Guohong Wu, Shengquan Sam Ye, Lili Zhang, Minxuan Zhang, Chang Zhu, and Xinhua Zhu for their kind facilitation of data collection over the years. I am also very grateful to the tens of thousands of research participants whose engagement in my research over the years has made it possible for me to achieve a good understanding of the role of intellectual styles in many domains of human learning, performance, and development.

I deeply appreciate the constructive feedback given by the anonymous reviewers of the book proposal and those of the book manuscript. My very special thanks go to Simina Calin for contracting the book, as well as to my Cambridge University Press editors, Eve Mayer and David Repetto; my production editor, Josh Penney; my project manager, Rishi Gupta of Aptara; and my copy editor, Fred Goykhman of PETT Fox, Inc., for their steadfast support in the process of turning the manuscript into a published book. My sincere thanks also go to Claudia Chan, Gileb Koo, Samsom Liu, and Fanny Wong for their very competent and patient assistance in the preparation of the book and to Catherine Liu and Stanley Shum for their many years of support as research assistants. I owe an equally tremendous debt to my family and friends, who have strongly supported me throughout the years.

Financial support for this work over the years came in part from the Committee on Research and Conference Grants, the Wu Jieh-Yee Education Research Fund, and the Sik Sik Yuen Education Research Fund, administered by The University of Hong Kong. The work was also partially funded by the General Research Fund, administered by the University Grants Council of the Hong Kong Special Administrative Region, the People' Republic of China.

PART I

BACKGROUND

1

Motivation for This Book

In 2008, one and a half months before their presidential campaign, the Republican presidential candidate John McCain and the Democratic candidate Barack Obama reacted very differently to the most serious U.S./world economic crisis since the Great Depression that preceded World War II. While McCain officially suspended his campaign to return to Washington, DC, on September 24, reportedly to deal with the financial crisis, and suggested that the debate scheduled for that Friday be rescheduled, Obama not only rejected the proposal for the rescheduling, but also carried out his campaign as planned. When asked by reporters about this, Obama responded by saying that presidents need to deal with more than one issue at a time. More than one month later (October 29, 2008), when former president Bill Clinton joined then-Senator Obama at a rally in Florida five days before the general election, Clinton, praising Obama's way of dealing with the financial crisis, revealed that when McCain abruptly suspended his campaign to go back to Washington, Obama was making phone calls (to Bill Clinton, Hillary Clinton, and others), trying to understand the situation before making a decision as to what to do. Obama ended up winning the election.

One way of viewing what happened is in terms of the different thinking styles of the two presidential candidates. According to Sternberg's (1997) theory of mental self-government, McCain was using a monarchic thinking style, dealing with one issue at a time. Obama, on the other hand, was using a hierarchical style, dealing with several issues, but perceiving one, in this case the presidential debate, as the most important issue at the time. Such different ways of dealing with the financial crisis are what Kagan (1965) might call acting impulsively, in the case of McCain, and acting reflectively, in the case of Obama. Similar situations abound in other walks of life as well. What we see in a campaign, we see every day in the behavior of more ordinary people. In a more general sense, ways of reacting to a situation such as that of McCain are referred to in this book as Type II intellectual styles, which include what Sternberg calls the monarchic thinking style, what Kagan calls the impulsive style, and many other styles that denote a norm-favoring tendency and demonstrate more conventional and more rigid ways of dealing with tasks. In contrast, ways of handling a situation such as that of Obama are referred to as Type I intellectual styles, which include what Sternberg calls the hierarchical thinking style, what Kagan calls the reflective style, and many other styles that suggest a creativity-generating tendency and new ways of handling tasks.

"Intellectual style" – a term that encompasses all style constructs, with or without the root word "styles" – refers to people's preferred ways of processing information and handling tasks. Different scholars tend to adopt their own favored style terms, both in their writings and in the speeches they deliver. Examples of these terms are "cognitive style," "learning style," "thinking style," "mind style," "mode of thinking," and "teaching style." Recently, a consensus seems to have been reached (Zhang, Sternberg, & Rayner, 2012a) that all style labels can be best represented by what Zhang and Sternberg (2005) called "intellectual styles" in their "Threefold Model of Intellectual Styles" (see Chapter 2 in this book).

Can people's intellectual styles be changed? Founded on a systematic body of empirical evidence, this book focuses on examining style malleability. It will be argued that intellectual styles can be changed, both by virtue of people's natural socialization in different situations and as a result of training. Before reading the evidence concerning style malleability, readers might wish to have some general background information on the field of styles. To those readers who are already familiar with the literature on intellectual styles, I apologize for having to spend the best part of the first two chapters introducing background work on styles.

It is commonly acknowledged that the field of intellectual styles does not have a unified history and interrelated philosophical and theoretical foundations. Similarly, it is widely accepted that it was Gordon Allport (1937) who introduced the notion of styles to psychology when he compared "styles of life" to a way of identifying unique personality types or types of behaviors. A complete historical account of the various philosophical-theoretical foundations of the field is, of course, well beyond the scope of this chapter; proper historical treatments of the field can be found in a number of publications (e.g., Dember, 1964; Kagan & Kogan, 1970; Messick, 1994; Moskvina & Kozhevnikov, 2011; Nielsen, 2012; Rayner & Riding, 1997; Vernon, 1973; Zhang & Sternberg, 2006). Furthermore, the impact of these historical issues on research activities in the field has been recounted in great depth elsewhere (e.g., Rayner, Zhang, & Sternberg, 2012; Zhang, Sternberg, & Rayner, 2012b).

The aim of this chapter is to situate the theme of this book – style malleability – within the larger context of the major research activities in the field of intellectual styles. The chapter does this by discussing issues that tend to be confusing not only to the general public but also to researchers in the field and to practitioners who are interested in applying the notion of styles to their work. These issues include the main difficulties that have led to the lack of identity of the style construct (or broadly, the lack of identity of the field of styles) and long-term controversial issues surrounding the nature of intellectual styles. Ultimately, the chapter explains why there is an urgent need for a book on the malleability of intellectual styles.

Specifically, the remainder of this chapter is divided into four parts. The first describes three major difficulties that present challenges to the identity of the field of intellectual styles. The second describes three long-standing controversial issues in the field. The third explains why it is critical that evidence for style modifiability be provided immediately. The final part of this chapter lays out the structure of the book.

Identity Issues

In 2012, Zhang, Sternberg, and Rayner (2012b) noted that until recently, the field of intellectual styles has been searching for its identity within the larger context of education, psychology, and business literatures, largely owing to three major related difficulties. These are difficulties in: (1) distinguishing styles from abilities/intelligences and personality; (2) finding a common language and a common conceptual framework for the style construct; and (3) establishing a link between the field of styles and other allied fields.

Distinguishing Style from Ability/Intelligence and Personality

One identity issue that the field of styles has been constantly facing is the difficulty in differentiating styles from abilities/intelligences on the one hand and from personality on the other. Such a difficulty has arisen from the fact that some of the earlier theories proposed styles that could not be shown to be "pure" style constructs (Sternberg, 2001). This lack of uniqueness has led many to question the need for a distinctive area of research on styles, and resulted in a severe reduction in styles research during the 1970s. At the same time, this identity crisis has triggered much discourse on the relationships of styles to abilities/intelligences and to personality.

Discussion concerning the intricate relationships of style to ability/intelligence and personality is best manifested in relation to Witkin's construct of field dependence/independence (FDI, also widely known as psychological differentiation), commonly recognized as the pioneering style construct in the field. With respect to its relationship to ability, some scholars (e.g., Jones, 1997a; Richardson & Turner, 2000; Zigler, 1963) have contended that FDI should not be regarded as a style construct because of the essential role that intelligence plays in individuals' performance on tests of FDI. In fact, even now, more than five decades after the establishment of Witkin's theory of psychological differentiation and after the theory has already generated tens of thousands of research programs, some scholars still reject the notion that field dependence/independence is a style construct. For example, at the turn of the 21st century, Richardson and Turner (2000) elaborated at length why FDI should be regarded as analytical ability. The central argument for their position is that the measures of FDI too often fail to show discriminant validity from conventional intelligence tests.

Other scholars, however, despite acknowledging that individuals' performance on the FDI tests does correlate with intellectual tasks that require disembedding, especially visual disembedding, have strongly argued that the FDI construct plays a unique role in accounting for individual differences (e.g., Dubois & Cohen, 1970; Jones, 1997b; Satterly, 1976; Spotts & Mackler, 1967; Stuart, 1967; Weisz, O'Neill, & O'Neill, 1975). In this regard, Kagan and Kogan (1970) astated that given the evidence that the FDI indices only negligibly clustered with verbal comprehension and attention concentration factors in traditional intelligence quotient (IQ) tests, an argument could be made against the contention that there is strong association between FDI and general intelligence. They maintained, "It is doubtful whether our understanding would be advanced by reducing the constructs of field independence and analytic functioning to an amorphous 'general intelligence' construct which bears no conceptual relationship to any major psychological theory" (Kagan & Kogan, 1970, p. 1326).

At the same time, the relationship between the FDI construct and personality has also been a perpetual focal point for scholarly debates. From the very start, Witkin and his colleagues (Witkin, 1959; Witkin, Karp, & Goodenough, 1959; Witkin, Lewis, Hertzman, Machover, Meissner, & Wapner, 1954) perceived the FDI construct to be closely related to personality. As a matter of fact, in their early publications, Witkin and his research team considered psychological differentiation to be a stable, structural aspect of personality. This interest in, and indeed the need to clarify the relationship between, styles and personality have since been echoed by many scholars who have held different views about the association (or distinction for that matter) between styles and personality.

Clearly, some scholars perceive styles as being embedded in the construct of personality. For example, Messick (1994) argued that styles should be organized within the broader personality system. Moreover, as far back as 1982, when reviewing Witkin's final book (Witkin & Goodenough, 1981), Korchin (1982) declared that "[f]ield dependence-independence theory has evolved into a major personality theory" (p. 602).

Other scholars believe that personality contributes to styles. For example, in reviewing the then-existing theories of intellectual styles, Cattell (1973) affirmed that "the inevitable conclusion is that the styles are the effect of the personality factors" (p. 396). Similarly, P. L. Myers (1988) proposed a hierarchy of styles of cognition (e.g., cognitive, perceptual, and verbal) and considered personality to be a source of individual differences within styles. Likewise, Furnham (1995) pointed out that the role of personality in styles appears to be "implicit in the writings of many educational and psychological researchers" (p. 398), despite the fact that this relationship is seldom articulated as such.

A third group of scholars consider the relationship between styles and personality to be bidirectional. For example, after an extensive discussion of the development of FDI from early childhood to adolescence in relation to aspects of personality and socialization, Kogan and Block (1991) concluded that the most credible view of the relationships between FDI, personality, and socialization is that "the three variables may be linked in a completely bidirectional, interactive manner" (p. 205).

Finally, still other scholars have been more cautious and have thus offered a more tentative view regarding the relationship of styles to personality and ability/intelligence. For instance, in reviewing work on Kagan's (1965) construct of reflectivity-impulsivity vis-á-vis Riding and Cheema's (1991) concept of holistic-analytic style dimension, Jones (1997a) noted that styles, "if not directly part of the personality, or intelligence, are at least intimately associated with various non-cognitive dimensions of personality, and cognitive dimensions of intelligence and academic performance" (p. 65).

Naturally, one would want to know the consequences of these diverse views with respect to the distinction (or association) between styles and both ability/intelligence and personality. Undoubtedly, confusion over the relationship of styles to ability/intelligence and personality slowed down research activities in the area of styles for some time, as noted by Sternberg (2001). At the same time, however, this confusion has also served as the catalyst for styles researchers' attempts to clarify these relationships. At the conceptual level, for example, Messick (1996) convincingly drew major distinctions between styles and abilities along several dimensions (see also Most & Zeidner, 1995). Jablokow and Kirton (2009) articulated the differences between styles and abilities by elucidating the relationships of creativity and problem solving to the level-style distinctions. Roodenburg, Roodenburg, and Rayner (2012) cogently elaborated how styles and personality, as two aspects of an individual, interact to influence an individual's behavior. Much earlier, Grigorenko and Sternberg (1995) asserted that styles are at the interface of ability/intelligence and personality. At the empirical level, the continuing debate over the distinction (or association) between styles and both abilities/intelligences and personality has also served as a strong impetus for researchers to conduct studies to clarify the issue (see Furnham, 2012; Roodenburg, Roodenburg, & Rayner, 2012; Zhang & Sternberg, 2006 for reviews).

Certainly, the aforementioned efforts at both the conceptual and empirical levels have been successful in highlighting the unique contributions of styles to human performance beyond ability/intelligence and personality. Nonetheless, these efforts continue to be sporadic because doubts about the uniqueness of the style construct persist (see Zhang, Sternberg, & Rayner, 2012b).

Searching for a Common Language and a Common Conceptual Framework

The fact that there was neither common language nor common conceptual framework within which work on styles could be understood was another reason why the field of styles lacked a clear identity for a long time. Some scholars (e.g., Evans & Waring, 2009; Messick, 1994; Miller, 1987; Vernon, 1963) attributed this identity issue to the immense number of style labels generated, compounded by a large number of style measures. Indeed, within the first few decades of research on styles, and especially during the "golden age" of the styles movement between the late 1950s and the early 1970s, the appearance of the large number of theories and models of styles gave rise to a correspondingly large number of labels (Messick, 1984; Riding & Cheema, 1991; Zhang & Sternberg, 2006), such as *brain dominance, cognitive style, conceptual tempo, defensive style, expressive style, responsive style, learning approach, learning style, learning pattern,* and *think style,* among others. As an indication of the large number of style labels, if one traces back some of the major reviews of the styles literature, one would realize that each time the work was reviewed, a different number of style labels would be mentioned, and that the number increased with the passage of time. As an illustration, when reviewing the then-existing work on styles, Hayes and Allinson (1994) noted that there were 22 different dimensions of "cognitive style" alone. Five years later, Armstrong (1999) identified 54 style dimensions. Finally, a review conducted by Coffield and his colleagues (Coffield, Moseley, & Ecclestone, 2004) showed, as Evans and Waring (2009) put it, a "bewildering library of style measures (over 71 theories of styles)" (p. 172). However, as Zhang and Sternberg (2006) pointed out, many of these styles had principally evolved from theories established on the basis of single studies with little subsequent empirical support. Moreover, different theorists emphasized different dimensions of styles in their conceptualizations, and they focused on different criterion features in their assessment of styles. Likewise, when new styles were proposed, adequate means were seldom built into the research to provide both convergent and discriminant validation, and the instruments assessing the style constructs were often introspective self-report measures.

In the history of the styles literature, this lack of a common language and of a common conceptual framework for understanding the styles literature ultimately held up progress in the field, particularly between the early 1970s and the mid-1980s (e.g., Jones, 1997a; Riding & Cheema, 1991). At the same time, however, this identity crisis arising from the absence of a common language and a common conceptual framework also motivated many scholars to endeavor to bring order to the body of styles literature. Between 1983 and 2009, six models were proposed that were aimed at systematically conceptualizing the various style concepts. These were: (1) Curry's (1983) "Onion" model; (2) Miller's (1987) model of cognitive processes and styles; (3) Riding and Cheema's (1991) model of cognitive styles; (4) Grigorenko and Sternberg's (1995) model of style traditions; (5) Zhang and Sternberg's (2005) threefold model of intellectual styles; and (6) Sadler-Smith's (2009) duplex model of cognitive styles (see Zhang, Sternberg, & Rayner, 2012b for a review; see also Chapter 2 in this volume for an introduction of three of these six models).

Linking the Field of Styles with Other Fields
Finally, the third factor that has contributed to the field's lack of identity is the limited contact that work on styles has had with the larger contexts of the business, education, and psychology literatures. For example, in the case of psychology, it is widely recognized (e.g., Kagan & Kogan, 1970; Messick, 1994; Morgan, 1997; Rayner & Riding, 1997; Vernon, 1973) that the field of intellectual styles has diverse philosophical and theoretical foundations, ranging from classical Greek literature, to the general literature on individual differences, to Jung's (1923) theory of personality styles. In the same way, work on styles has been informed by a variety of research traditions, most markedly by several branches of psychology (Messick, 1994). Despite this, there has been neither much articulation of exactly how styles are grounded in and associated

with constructs in the various domains of psychological inquiry that have supposedly been influential in research on styles, nor sufficient empirical evidence to support the claim for such a historical explanation.

Likewise, until about two decades ago, the majority of the styles work carried out in business contexts has been based almost exclusively on Jung's (1923) theory of personality styles and Kirton's (1961) theory of decision-making styles. Although research derived from these two style constructs was abundant, it was not clear whether or not the remaining massive number of style constructs would matter in business settings. Partially as a response to this circumstance, scholars have been making continuous efforts to build a bridge between the field of styles and the business world (e.g., Armstrong, van der Heijden, & Sadler-Smith, 2012; Cools, 2012).

Finally, although much of the styles literature has originated from research in education settings, until recently, it consisted mostly of studies that focused on the relationships between styles and students' academic performance. Understanding the impact of intellectual styles on students' academic achievement is certainly valuable to both styles researchers and educators. However, efforts to study styles in connection with other domains of education such as students' emotional development and career development, although equally important, are largely inadequate, as shown in several recent reviews (e.g., Gebbia & Honigsfeld, 2012; Zhang, 2011).

Controversial Issues Concerning the Nature of Intellectual Styles

Apart from having been faced with the identity issues discussed in the previous part, the field of styles has been challenged by three major controversial issues concerning the nature of intellectual styles: (1) styles as different constructs versus similar constructs with different labels (also known as the issue of style overlap); (2) styles as value-free versus value-laden (also known as the issue of style value); and (3) styles as traits versus states (also known as the issue of style malleability).

Style Overlap

As already discussed, the field's ambiguous identity has been partially attributable to the massive production of style labels. The existence of such a multitude of style labels has naturally made people wonder if there is any relationship among them. For example, if an individual had a strong preference for using the legislative style in studying biology, would this individual also be inclined to adopt the innovative decision-making style as an employee of Apple? What is the principal distinction between a learning style and, say, a cognitive style, a mind style, or a thinking style? Are styles different constructs or are they simply similar constructs but with different labels (Coan, 1974; Fowler, 1980; Miller, 1987; Riding, 1997)? Such questions have baffled not only laypeople who are interested in the notion of styles, but also scholars in the field of intellectual styles and beyond.

Style overlap (or style uniqueness for that matter) has always been a topic of intense discussion. Some scholars have indirectly participated in this deliberation by defining styles in such a way as to emphasize solely the unique characteristics of particular style labels and disregard other style labels. For instance, Anastasi (1988) defined *cognitive styles* as broad, systematic features that influence one's responses to a variety of situations. Likewise, Gregorc (1979) defined *learning* styles as the distinct behaviors that signify how individuals learn from and adapt to their environment.

By contrast, other scholars have focused on the commonalities among different style labels and have demonstrated more awareness of the relatedness of various style terms. In this regard, Tennant (1997) maintained: "'Cognitive style,' 'learning style,' and 'conceptual style' are related terms which refer to an individual's characteristic and consistent approach to organizing and processing information" (p. 80).

Still other scholars (e.g., Sternberg & Zhang, 2001) have embraced both the commonalities among all styles and the unique qualities possessed by each style. For example, while acknowledging that all styles are different from abilities, Sternberg and Zhang (2001) articulated the distinctions among learning styles, thinking styles, and cognitive styles by explaining how each of these styles could be used: "Learning styles might be used to characterize how one prefers to learn about (particular material/information); . . . Thinking styles might be used to characterize how one prefers to think about material as one is learning or after one already knows it; . . . Cognitive styles might be used to characterize ways of cognizing the information" (p. vii).

Over the years, these diverse views have engendered efforts to systematically examine the relationships among the massive style constructs. In this regard, the most explicit efforts have been manifested in the series of attempts to integrate the various style terms (e.g., the six integrative models mentioned earlier in this chapter; see Zhang, Sternberg, & Rayner, 2012b for details; see also Chapter 2 in this book).

Style Value

It was noted earlier that each of the many style models consists of at least two specific styles, and this has led to the existence of many different specific styles. In view of this, one might naturally ask: Are some styles more valued than others? Is it more worthwhile developing these styles than others? These questions pertain to the issue of style value.

Two scholars who stand out for their determined attempts to resolve the problem of style value are Nathan Kogan and Samuel Messick. Kogan (1973) proposed a threefold division among styles according to their value implications and their functional distance from the ability domain. Type I styles bear a strong resemblance to abilities, largely because they are measured by maximal-performance instruments that assess accuracy versus inaccuracy of response, and as such are uniformly valued. Type II styles, on the other hand, cannot be assessed in terms of accuracy of response, although some are more valued than others with regard to performance. Type III styles are characterized by their disconnection from response accuracy and from value judgment. Kogan and Saarni (1990) termed these styles "value-free, preference-oriented Type III cognitive styles" (p. 4).

Kogan's continuing concern with the issue of style value can be seen in at least another two of his publications. The first was his review of Witkin's 1977 Heinz Werner Lecture (Kogan, 1980). In tracing the development of Witkin's theory of psychological differentiation, Kogan (1980) analyzed Witkin's change of view regarding style value and asserted that "[p]ossibly the most fundamental difference between the 1962 position and the one presented in the Heinz Werner Lectures concerns the domain of value. The value-free aspect of the current position is addressed" (p. 597). Kogan (1980) commented that the FDI construct is not "quite as value free as Witkin would have liked it to be" (p. 597). He pointed out that while there were a good many findings showing that FI individuals perform better than do FD individuals on measures of FDI, evidence for the compensating strengths supposedly possessed by FD individuals in the interpersonal domain had yet to be found. In his second publication, nine years later, Kogan (1989) affirmed that styles were not and had never been value free, citing persuasive examples ranging from the realm of performance to the purposeful training of styles.

The issue of style value was also one of Messick's focal points in his elucidation of the nature of intellectual styles. For example, when Messick (1984) critiqued Kogan's (1973) threefold division of styles, especially concerning Type II styles, he contended that the styles that were typically not so highly valued might manifest strengths in special situations. In other words, styles can be value differentiated. A decade later, when delineating the differences between styles and abilities, Messick (1994) dealt with the issue of style value again. He stated that it is true that the most critical distinction between styles and abilities is that, unlike styles, abilities are unipolar and value directional, with high levels of abilities always preferable to lower levels. At the same time, however, he pointed out that some styles such as the FI-FD styles are also unipolar. Nevertheless, consistent with Kogan (1980), Messick (1994) asserted that despite the existence of ample evidence suggesting that FD individuals are more likely to be interpersonally oriented, there was no evidence to show that they possess superior interpersonal skills. Noticeably, in this publication, Messick (1994) shifted his position from believing that styles are mainly value differentiated to his conviction that styles are mainly value directional.

Finally, in one of his last publications (regretfully, Dr. Messick passed away in 1998), and while discussing the problems involved in the notion of style match, Messick (1996) once again persuasively expounded his view of style value. Referring to style match in a variety of educational contexts (e.g., instruction, vocational guidance, choice of academic major), Messick (1996) pointed out a number of difficulties in applying the notion of style match so as to optimize student learning and development. He asserted that of all the difficulties (e.g., problems with style measurement, problems in matching student stylistic characteristics with environmental demands, and so forth), the most challenging one was not that matching itself is technically intricate, but rather that it is profoundly value laden: "The question of what should be matched is the problem of prescription; the question of how to match is a problem of educational technology; the question of purpose and locus of choice are problems of social values and ethics" (Messick, 1996, p. 369).

In addition to Kogan and Messick, several other scholars have addressed the issue of style value. For instance, Shipman (1989) contended that the conceptual problems with styles (e.g., inconsistent definitions, relationships with other constructs, and so forth) have created at least four dilemmas for the educational use of styles, one being whether styles are value laden or value free. On this issue, Shipman held the view that despite the fact that one of the most appealing aspects of the style concept is its usefulness in characterizing the "how" as opposed to the "how much" of cognition, in the case of some styles, one pole *is* unambiguously more valued than the other, whereas in the case of others, no particular value preference is attached. Also, for instance, in delineating thinking styles, Sternberg (1996) stated: "A style of thought is a preference for using abilities in certain ways. It is not an ability itself, but rather a way in which one likes to utilize abilities. Thus, when we speak of individual differences in thinking styles, we are referring only to differences, not to 'better' or 'worse'" (p. 347). Even so, Sternberg's views on the style value issue have evolved over time. By the year 2005, Zhang and Sternberg (2005) argued that Type I intellectual styles – styles that are more creativity-generating and denote higher levels of cognitive complexity – are generally more adaptive than are Type II intellectual styles – styles that entail higher degrees of norm-conformity and are strongly indicative of cognitive simplicity.

To sum up, style value has been a thorny issue. It is a topic that has created obstacles to the field's advancement; at the same time, however, it has generated much empirical research and many conceptual arguments.

Style Malleability

As mentioned earlier, styles have sometimes been thought of as abilities and sometimes as personality traits. However, abilities and personality are known to differ with respect to their malleability. It is commonly accepted that individuals can improve their abilities in various ways, such as in the process of maturation, through being exposed to environments that are conducive to the development of their abilities, and by receiving purposeful training. In contrast, until a short time ago, personality was perceived as a set of innate traits that were difficult, if not impossible, to change (Caspi, Roberts, & Shiner, 2005; Helson, Kwan, John, & Jones, 2002). This distinction between abilities and personality traits raises the question: Where does the concept of style stand when it comes to the matter of malleability? Answers to this question relate to the third long-standing controversial issue in the field of intellectual styles: style malleability. There have been two contrasting views on this issue, with one in favor of styles being amenable to change and the other in favor of styles being stable. These competing views have been articulated in different contexts.

At the outset, scholars joined the dispute over style malleability in the context of defining various style constructs. Despite the fact that all these definitions recognize styles as people's preferred ways of processing information, they differ in one vital aspect. That is, some definitions depict styles as a "characteristic mode or way of manifesting cognitive and/or affective phenomena" (Royce, 1973, p. 178), suggesting that styles are stable traits, whereas others portray styles as being socialized and teachable (Sternberg, 1997).

Strongly believing that human beings have the capacity to change, Henson and Borthwick (1984) asserted: "Since it is readily recognized that the majority of humans are capable of changing, both teaching and learning styles can therefore be manipulated" (p. 6). That is to say, both teaching and learning styles can be modified. Sharma and Kolb (2011) alluded to the modifiability of intellectual styles in stating: "The learning style concept in the ELT (Experiential Learning Theory) is different in that learning style is not conceived as a fixed trait but a dynamic state" (p. 60). Fling, Thomas, and Gallaher (1981), in discussing the effects of meditation and quiet sitting on the development of personality styles as assessed by the *Myers-Briggs Type Indicator*, made a reference to Jung's (1946, 1969) work on meditation, and thus the malleability of personality styles. The researchers stated: "Jungian thought, on which this test is based, suggests that meditation seekers would be more introverted than extraverted, intuitive than sensing, feeling than thinking, and perceiving than judging on its four bipolar dimensions and/or might shift toward these poles with meditation practice" (Fling et al., 1981, p. 785).

The issue of style malleability has also been addressed in the context of focused discussion about specific style constructs, of which Witkin's FDI construct has always been the subject of much discussion. For example, some scholars (Bock & Kolakowski, 1973; Wertheimer, 1945) have argued, albeit with the support of minimal empirical evidence, that a high level of field independence in an individual is determined by a recessive gene on the X-chromosome. Other scholars (Connor, Schackman, & Serbin, 1978; Renner, 1970; Sherman, 1967), however, have underlined the modifiability of FDI by providing evidence that demonstrated the impact of socialization variables (e.g., age, sex-role patterns, child-rearing practices) on the development of styles beyond what could be explained by the X-linked hormonal factors. In fact, empirical evidence has led Witkin and his colleagues to change their views on the malleability of the FDI construct. In their earlier work (e.g., Witkin, 1959; Witkin, Karp, & Goodenough, 1959; Witkin et al., 1954), Witkin and his research team contended, based on empirical evidence, that the FDI cognitive styles were both pervasive (i.e., spanning diverse realms of functioning) and stable across time. In their later publications, however, Witkin and his associates (e.g., Witkin, 1978; Witkin, & Goodenough, 1977, 1981) reported studies of training effects and explicitly discussed the dynamic nature of FDI.

Apart from the FDI construct, Kirton's (1961) model of adaption-innovation decision-making and problem-solving styles (known as the A-I construct) has often been referred in discussions on the issue of style malleability. Kirton and his followers (e.g., Clapp & De Ciantis, 1989; Goldstein & Blackman, 1978; Kirton, 1976) have consistently held the view that the A-I styles cannot be modified. In 1993, Clapp declared: "With considerable evidence of both short- and long-term stability of cognitive preference, it is clear that any training intervention intended to change individual cognitive preference will fail" (Clapp, 1993, p. 1243). As another example, Tullett (1997) supported Kirton's assertion that the A-I styles are stable cognitive processes by both citing empirical findings and presenting conceptual arguments. Tullett argued that both the low corrections between age and A-I scores (normally ranging from 0 to −0.2) and the lack of systematic changes shown in test-retest coefficients could be used to support the stability of the A-I styles. Furthermore, Tullett believed that one of the reasons why some individuals leave their work environments must be that these individuals are unable to modify their intellectual styles consistently for long durations. In a relatively recent joint publication with Jablokow, Kirton once again maintained that the A-I styles cannot be modified (Jablokow & Kirton, 2009).

Over the years, these and similar arguments made by both sides in the debate over style malleability have resulted in confusion, which has certainly inhibited the field from advancing in many respects. At the same time, however, these debates have also stimulated researchers to seek a more balanced approach to the issue of style malleability. For instance, Vermunt (1992) argued that although learning styles[1] demonstrate a fairly high degree of stability, it does not mean that all learning components have to be considered as possessing stable characteristics. Similarly, in analyzing the literature on longitudinal studies of career personality types (a personality-centered style construct proposed by John Holland), Tracey and Robbins (2005) pointed out that scholars had adopted two fundamentally different views on the malleability of career personality types: the stability view and the developmental view. From the stability viewpoint, changes of career personality styles can be considered to be errors, while from the development viewpoint, they are seen as real change (see Chapter 8 in this book). In an edited book, *Perspectives on the Nature of Intellectual Styles* (Zhang & Sternberg, 2009), several scholars (e.g., Entwistle & McCune, 2009; Grigorenko, 2009; Rayner & Peterson, 2009) also alluded to the issue of style malleability. Once again, no consensus was reached.

Why This Book

As can be seen from the preceding discussion, a considerable amount of scholarship has been produced concerning the nature of intellectual styles. In particular, the past three decades have witnessed concerted efforts to invigorate the field (see also Zhang, Sternberg, & Rayner, 2012b). To varying degrees, these attempts have greatly advanced the field in that they are works that are better able to address the nature of intellectual styles as it concerns the identity of the field, especially with regard to the three controversial issues surrounding styles.

Nonetheless, two types of problems still remain. The first pertains to the skepticism of various critics regarding the existence and usefulness of the style construct. For instance, some serious doubts about styles were cast in a report

---

[1] Subsequently referred to as learning patterns within the context of research grounded in Vermunt's *Inventory of Learning Styles*.

led by Frank Coffield and colleagues (Coffield et al., 2004) at the University of London in the United Kingdom. This group of researchers declared that the notion of styles is largely irrelevant to further education in the United Kingdom. Likewise, the question of whether or not the notion of styles is useful remains debatable in the wider academic community and in society at large. For example, in an article entitled "Customized Teaching Fails a Test," published in the *Chronicle of Higher Education* (January 8, 2010, A6–A8), David Glenn analyzed at length the debate among psychologists over the issue of the so-called matching hypothesis (i.e., to match teaching styles to students' learning styles) and over the applicability of styles to the classroom. This analysis, as one would expect, did not lead to any conclusive statement about the utility of style match.

Although the attacks from critics are highly disputable, they could have detrimental effects. Practitioners in education and business alike who might have just begun to see the important roles that styles can play in human learning, performance, and development may now have doubts about whether or not their efforts to apply the notion of styles to their work are worthwhile. Similarly, although many pieces of the puzzle about styles have yet to be put in place, scholars in the field of styles and in its allied fields may lose their enthusiasm for doing research on styles because their work would largely appear as meaningless, at least to some people.

The second type of problems is that, despite its significance, the existing work relevant to the nature of intellectual styles, particularly with respect to the issue of style malleability, can only be said to have uncovered part of the whole picture. Currently, scholars' positions on this issue are based on conceptual arguments that are lacking in theoretical depth and on research findings that are largely anecdotal. For example, referring to his *Duplex Model of Cognitive Style*, Sadler-Smith (2009) asserted that unless an individual's neural circuitry infuses decision making as a result of particular damage to the brain, he/she has access to both the analytic mode and the intuitive mode. More importantly, both modes can be modified through learning and socialization. However, no research evidence was provided to substantiate this claim. From the perspective of etiology, Grigorenko (2009) argued that although they may have some partial genetic basis, styles are at least to some degree socialized. Unfortunately, research evidence supporting this argument was also lacking. In *The Nature of Intellectual Styles*, Zhang and Sternberg (2006) provided some empirical evidence to support their argument that styles are modifiable. However, the studies reviewed in Zhang and Sternberg's (2006) book were a small number of correlational ones that happened to involve testing the relationships of styles to several demographic variables such as age, gender, and birth order. As a result, Zhang and Sternberg's conclusion that styles can be modified needs to be further testified by a much fuller range of empirical findings that are examined more systematically and in greater depth.

A systematic and in-depth account of the malleability of styles is vital because if such an account cannot be offered, the confusion over whether or not styles can be developed will persist. Such confusion would not only further deter the advancement of the field, but also make practitioners, including educational and occupational psychologists as well as classroom teachers at schools and leaders in the business world, hesitant about using the concept of styles in their work. For example, if styles represent fixed traits, any attempt to teach or cultivate particular styles would very likely be to no avail. Moreover, research on styles would be equally pointless. On the other hand, if styles are fluid, attempts to teach and develop styles would be likely to succeed, and efforts invested in styles research would be more worthwhile. Therefore, a coherent account of style malleability has great potential not only for advancing the field of styles and its allied academic fields, but also for promoting the significance of applying the style concept in various domains of human life. Furthermore, because styles are at the interface between abilities and personality (Sternberg, 1997), and because styles have been proved to be central to many aspects of human learning and performance, progress in the field of styles should also enhance our understanding of the scientific inquiry into academic fields that are related to the field of styles.

About This Book

This book addresses the issue of style malleability in four parts. Part I consists of this general introductory chapter and Chapter 2. In particular, this chapter presents crucial general information about the field and provides the rationales for this book. In order to pave the way for presenting the evidence supporting the stance that styles are amendable, Chapter 2 introduces the specific style constructs/models and measures on which the empirical studies to be reviewed were based. Furthermore, Chapter 2 describes three integrative models of intellectual styles that serve as the conceptual frameworks for conceptualizing, analyzing, and presenting the research findings to be reviewed in Chapters 3 through 8. These models are Curry's (1983) "Onion" model, Grigorenko and Sternberg's (1995) model of style traditions, and Zhang and Sternberg's (2005) threefold model of intellectual styles.

Part II is composed of four chapters (Chapters 3, 4, 5, and 6). Each of these chapters critically reviews empirical work that deals with the notion of style malleability based on one particular socialization variable. Chapters 3 and 4 look at two socialization variables at the individual level – gender and culture – while Chapters 5 and 6 consider socialization variables at the institutional level – academic discipline and occupation. Empirical work examined in this part primarily adopted cross-sectional research designs and analyses.

Part III comprises two chapters (Chapters 7 and 8). Chapter 7 focuses on longitudinal studies with experiments, while Chapter 8 deals with longitudinal studies without experiments.

Finally, Part IV includes just a single chapter – Chapter 9. It evaluates the existing research on style malleability and makes recommendations for future research directions and for positive development of intellectual styles within the education arena and beyond.

2

Key Style Models and Measures

This chapter aims to set the scene for the review of the empirical findings in Chapters 3 through 8. It does so by introducing the theoretical foundations of the relevant literature. The chapter is composed of three parts. The first part describes three integrative models of intellectual styles. The second part illustrates the specific style models/constructs and instruments in which the empirical studies to be reviewed are rooted. The third part completes the chapter with some closing remarks.

Integrative Style Models

As mentioned in the previous chapter, the past two decades or so have witnessed the establishment of six integrative models that aimed at bringing order to the massive and disjointed body of literature on styles. Three of these integrative models are reviewed here because not only have these models addressed some of the controversial issues discussed in the previous chapter, but also they will serve as conceptual frameworks for making research hypotheses, or structuring research findings, or both, in the discussion of the existing literature surrounding the issue of style malleability in Chapters 3 through 8. The three integrative models are (1) Lynn Curry's (1983) "onion" model of learning styles; (2) Elena Grigorenko and Robert Sternberg's (1995) model of style traditions; and (3) the threefold model of intellectual styles that Zhang and Sternberg (2005) put forward.

Curry's "Onion" Model

Curry (1983) pioneered efforts to bring order to the diverse style labels in the field by classifying what she called *learning*-style measures into three layers resembling those of an onion. Initially including nine style measures, the three-layer onion model was subsequently expanded to contain 21 inventories

(Curry, 1987). The *innermost layer* of the onion is composed of style measures of personality dimensions. The *middle layer* comprises style measures that evaluate information processing. The *outermost layer* consists of style measures concerning individuals' instructional preferences.

Of all the existing integrative models, Curry's (1983, 1987) model stands out the most with regard to its concern with style malleability. Curry (1983) contended that learning behaviors are primarily governed by the styles rooted in the deep structure of personality (i.e., the innermost layer of the onion), translated through information-processing styles (i.e., the middle layer), and ultimately interact with instructional preferences (i.e., the outermost layer). Undoubtedly, such dynamic processes recognized in individuals' learning behaviors speak volumes about Curry's position on style malleability. Curry predicted that the styles in the outermost layer of the onion would show the greatest extent of modifiability, and that the styles in the innermost layer would be the least modifiable. Through providing test-retest reliability data, Curry (1983, 1987) substantiated her predictions.

Curry's model also deals explicitly with the issue of style overlap. In fact, Curry pointed out that the validity of the onion model could be confirmed by data that (1) show strong associations among measures in the same layer and (2) demonstrate that styles in the innermost layer are psychometrically crucial to those in the other two layers. In Chapter 8 of this book, the onion model is adopted in conceptualizing and presenting the existing findings of longitudinal studies without interventions.

Grigorenko and Sternberg's Model of Style Traditions

Grigorenko and Sternberg (1995) systematized the considerable number of style labels by identifying three traditions in the study of styles: cognition-centered, personality-centered, and activity-centered. Styles in the *cognition-centered tradition* most closely resemble abilities. Like abilities, styles in this tradition (e.g., reflective versus impulsive styles proposed by Kagan, 1965; field-dependent versus field-independent styles by Witkin, 1962) are evaluated by tests of maximal performance with "right" and "wrong" responses. The *personality-centered tradition* considers styles to be most similar to personality traits. Like personality traits, styles in this tradition (e.g., the career personality styles proposed by Holland, 1966; the personality styles by Jung, 1923) are assessed by tests of typical, rather than maximal, performance. The *activity-centered tradition* views styles as mediators of activities stemming from both cognition and personality (e.g., learning approaches proposed by Biggs, 1978; learning orientations by Entwistle, 1981).

Clearly, Grigorenko and Sternberg's classification of work on styles deals squarely with the long-standing issue of how styles relate to abilities and personality (see Chapter 1). Grigorenko and Sternberg (1995) asserted that styles are neither abilities nor personality; rather, some styles are more related to abilities and others more to personality. Zhang and Sternberg (2006) explicated Grigorenko and Sternberg's implied position on the three controversial issues concerning the nature of intellectual styles: style value, style overlap, and style malleability. However, within the context of elucidating their model, Grigorenko and Sternberg (1995) focused only on the issue of style malleability, maintaining that the activity-centered style tradition took little account of the development of styles and that the other two traditions did a better job in doing so. In Chapters 5 and 6 of this book, Grigorenko and Sternberg's (1995) model serves as the conceptual framework for organizing the research findings regarding the relationships of academic discipline and occupation, respectively, to intellectual styles. At the same time, the model provides a useful framework for the order in which the individual style models/constructs and their measures are presented later in this chapter.

Zhang and Sternberg's Threefold Model of Intellectual Styles
Based on empirical evidence and theoretical conceptualization, Zhang and Sternberg (2005) constructed the threefold model of intellectual styles. Zhang and Sternberg referred to their integrative model of styles as a *threefold* model for two reasons. To begin with, in this model, all existing intellectual styles are classified into *three* types: Type I, Type II, and Type III. *Type I styles* are more creativity-generating and denote higher levels of cognitive complexity. *Type II styles* suggest a norm-favoring tendency and denote lower levels of cognitive complexity. *Type III styles* may manifest the characteristics of either Type I or Type II styles, depending on the stylistic demands of specific situations or tasks. Second, this model deals with three long-standing controversial issues in the field of styles: style overlap, style value, and style malleability.

Compared with the other existing integrative style models, the threefold model is superior in at least three ways. First, it adopts the term "intellectual styles" to encompass all existing style labels, with or without the root word "style," whereas each of the other models uses a specific style label that precludes the existence of styles that do not use the same style label. For example, the use of "*learning* style" necessarily excludes styles that adopt the label "*cognitive* style." By using the umbrella term "intellectual styles," the threefold model recognizes the existence of all style models/constructs, irrespective of the "style" terms that they use. Thus, the threefold model can be considered the most inclusive integrative style model.

Second, the threefold model provides a common conceptual framework for styles. Unlike any of the other existing integrative style models, which pigeonhole an individual model into one particular group of style models, the threefold model has created the notion of style types, classifying all styles into three types by cutting across each of the individual style models. For example, the 13 styles in Sternberg's (1988) model are classified into three different style types, with five styles being classified as Type I styles, four styles as Type II styles, and another four as Type III styles (see the section under "Thinking Style and Its Assessment" in this chapter). Such a classification system enables individuals to understand their own and others' intellectual styles with respect to five easy-to-monitor dimensions of preferences: (1) high degrees of structure versus low degrees of structure; (2) cognitive simplicity versus cognitive complexity; (3) conformity versus nonconformity; (4) authority versus autonomy; and (5) collectivism versus individualism (see Zhang & Sternberg, 2005 for details). Each of these dimensions is a continuum.

The third noticeable strength of the threefold model is that it takes an explicit stance on each of the three long-standing controversial issues in the field. The model posits that most styles are value-laden rather than value-free; that all styles have both trait-like and state-like aspects, but for the most part are modifiable and hence more state-like; and that styles significantly overlap across theories, with each possessing its unique features. Specifically, Zhang and Sternberg (2005) observed that Type I styles tend to carry more adaptive values because they are often strongly related to desirable human attributes (e.g., openness, optimism, and a clear sense of identity; see also Zhang & Sternberg, 2009), and because almost without exception, all existing style training programs are aimed at developing Type I styles (see Chapter 7). Type II styles tend to carry less adaptive values because they are often strongly associated with undesirable attributes (e.g., neuroticism, pessimism, and a lack of sense of identity), and because almost all existing style training programs are targeted at reducing the use of Type II styles. Type III styles tend to be value-differentiated as they may show more or less adaptive values contingent on the stylistic requirements of the particular task or situation at hand. Zhang and Sternberg (2005) further contended that owing to their high level of dependency on situations and/or tasks, Type III styles are more dynamic than are Type I and Type II styles. Nevertheless, Zhang and Sternberg (2005) asserted that all styles can be modified. Finally, the threefold model posits that different style constructs share features in common, while maintaining their distinctive characteristics. In particular, Type I styles are often positively related to one another, and Type II styles are positively related with one another. It is important to keep in mind that although only 10 individual style models were included in the threefold model when it was initially proposed, it adopts an open system: any individual model can be incorporated into this threefold model once it meets the criteria of the threefold model.

The individual style models and their associated measures discussed in the threefold model of intellectual styles are the foundation for the scope of the literature review for each of the chapters in this book. Moreover, the three types of intellectual styles in the threefold model serve as the basis for the research hypotheses made in Chapters 3 and 4.

Individual Style Models/Constructs and Measures

As will be seen in Chapters 3 through 8, work that pertains to the issue of style malleability is primarily based on the 10 individual style models/constructs included in the threefold model of intellectual styles (Zhang & Sternberg, 2005). In addition, Kolb's (1976) model of learning styles has served as the theoretical foundation for many empirical studies of style malleability. In the remainder of this part of the book, each of the 11 style models and its associated constructs and assessment tools are introduced. The sequence of this introduction is guided by two frameworks. The first is Grigorenko and Sternberg's (1995) integrative model of three traditions in the study of styles. In accordance with their classification of style traditions, individual style models/constructs and their inventories are presented in the following order: cognition-centered tradition, personality-centered tradition, and activity-centered tradition. The second framework is that within each styles tradition, the sequence of the presentation follows the chronological order in which the style models/constructs have been established. As a model that takes into account all three traditions in the study of styles, and as the latest individual style model, Sternberg's theory of mental self-government, as well as its measures, is introduced last.

Based on these two guiding principles, the style models/constructs and their measures are presented in the following order: (1) Herman Witkin's (1948) construct of field dependence/independence; (2) Joy Paul Guilford's (1950) construct of divergent-convergent thinking; (3) Michael Kirton's (1961) model of decision-making and problem-solving styles; (4) Jerome Kagan's (1965) construct of reflectivity/impulsivity; (5) Ellis Torrance's (1988) model of modes of thinking; (6) Carl Jung's (1923) model of personality types; (7) John Holland's (1966, 1973) model of career personality types; (8) Anthony Gregorc's (1979) model of mind styles; (9) David Kolb's (1976) model of learning styles and its derivative – Peter Honey and Alan Mumford's (1982, 1992)

Learning Styles Questionnaire; (10) John Biggs's (1978) model of learning approaches and its associated constructs and research tools: learning orientation (Entwistle, 1981; Entwistle & Ramsden, 1983), learning preference (Rezler & French, 1975), and learning pattern (Vermunt, 1992, 1998); and (11) Robert Sternberg's (1988) model of thinking styles. With the exception of the specific styles in Kolb's (1976) model, the learning styles assessed by Honey and Mumford's inventory, and the styles associated with learning orientation, learning preference, and learning pattern, the styles in all aforementioned models were integrated into the threefold model of intellectual styles (Zhang & Sternberg, 2005). Table 2.1 presents the individual styles from each of the 10 models included in the threefold model, and these individual styles are classified into three types. In the following, each of the style models/constructs and its key assessment tool(s) are introduced.

At the same time, the Appendix provides additional information for each of the 10 principal inventories, each assessing one of the 10 style constructs included in the threefold model of intellectual styles. Furthermore, because the *Room-Adjustment Test* and the *Body-Adjustment Test* measuring field dependence/independence proposed by Witkin (1948) were used in a number of studies, further information on these inventories is also provided in the Appendix.

Field Dependence/Independence and Its Assessment
As the pioneering style construct in the field of intellectual styles, field dependence/independence (FDI), alternatively known as psychological differentiation, visual-spatial ability, and perceptual ability/style (Witkin, 1948; Witkin, Dyk, Faterson, Goodenough, & Karp, 1962), takes a cognition-centered approach to the study of styles. FDI refers to the extent to which people are dependent on – versus independent of – the organization of the surrounding perceptual field. *Field-independent* individuals prefer tasks that involve more cognitive restructuring because of their propensity to be free from external referents. *Field-dependent* individuals tend to be more socially oriented because of their higher levels of sensitivity to external referents.

The three most common research tools for assessing FDI are the *Rod-and-Frame Test* (Witkin et al., 1954; Oltman, 1968), the *Embedded Figures Test* (Witkin, 1971), and the *Group Embedded Figures Test* (Witkin, Oltman, Raskin, & Karp, 1971). Initially, Witkin et al. (1954) developed an apparatus known as the standard *Rod-and-Frame Test* (RFT). When taking the RFT, the test taker sits in a darkened room and is asked to watch a glowing rod surrounded by a shimmering square frame. The test administrator manipulates the rod, the frame, and the test taker's chair so that they are at different angles of tilts.

TABLE 2.1. *Intellectual Styles*

	Style Type	Type I	Type II	Type III
	[a]Learning approach	Deep	Surface	Achieving
	[b]Career personality type	Artistic	Conventional	Realistic, Investigative, Social, Enterprising
	[c]Mode of thinking	Holistic	Analytic	Integrative
	[d]Personality type	Intuitive, Perceiving	Sensing, Judging	Thinking, Feeling, Introversion, Extraversion
Style Construct	[e]Mind style	Concrete random	Concrete sequential	Abstract random, Abstract sequential
	[f]Decision-making style	Innovation	Adaptation	
	[g]Conceptual tempo	Reflectivity	Impulsivity	
	[h]Structure of intellect	Divergent thinking	Convergent thinking	
	[i]Perceptual style	Field independent	Field dependent	
	[j]Thinking style	Legislative, Judicial, Global, Hierarchical, Judicial	Executive, Local, Monarchic, Conservative	Oligarchic, Anarchic, Internal, External

Note: Theoretical foundations: [a]Biggs's theory of student learning, [b]Holland's theory of career personality types, [c]Torrance's construct of brain dominance, [d]Jung's theory of personality types, [e]Gregorc's model of mind styles, [f]Kirton's model of decision-making styles, [g]Kagan's model of reflectivity-impulsivity conceptual tempo, [h]Guilford's model of structure of intellect, [i]Witkin's construct of field dependence/independence, [j]Sternberg's theory of mental self-government.

The test taker is instructed to adjust the rod so that the rod is perfectly upright. To complete the task accurately, the test taker has to be able to ignore cues in the visual field. If the test taker adjusts the rod so that it is leaning in the direction of the tilted frame, he/she is considered to be dependent on the visual field and is categorized as field dependent. By contrast, individuals who disregard the external cues and use information from their bodies to adjust the rod to appear upright are categorized as field independent. Because it was difficult to find a darkroom in schools, psychiatric wards, and other locations, the standard RFT could not be conveniently administered. Therefore, a portable RFT apparatus (Oltman, 1968) was constructed.

Furthermore, owing to the fact that the administration of the RFT – be it the standard one or the portable one – is rather time consuming, Witkin (1971) constructed the *Embedded Figures Test* (EFT). This test also measures FDI, but without the disadvantages of the cumbersome RFT. The EFT is an individually administered, timed test that requires the participant to locate a simple figure incorporated within a complex figure. It consists of eight simple figures and 24 complex ones. In the test session, the test taker is given 24 trials, each using different complex figures and never using the same simple figure in two consecutive trials. During each trial, the figures are presented separately in the sequence of complex figure, simple figure, and complex figure again. The test administrator takes note of the time at which the test taker verbally indicates that he or she has identified the simple figure and keeps timing until the test taker successfully traces the simple figure within the complex one. The score is the time it takes for the test taker to indicate verbally that he or she has identified the simple figure, provided that it is done correctly. The total score is the total time taken to complete all 24 trials. Lower scores denote field independence, while higher scores suggest field dependence.

In addition, as documented in Witkin, Oltman, Raskin, and Karp's (1971) work, two versions of the *Embedded Figures Test* were developed for young children and one version for preschool children. Commonly known as the CHEF (*Children's Embedded Figures Test*), the first version of the EFT for children was developed by Goodenough and Eagle (1963). The CHEF was constructed to create an EFT-like situation especially appropriate for young children. Efforts have been made to provide children with interesting tasks and to avoid situations where children are required to pay attention for prolonged periods of time, in order to reduce frustration arising from failure and to ensure that children understand the tasks. For example, each of the complex figures represents a meaningful figure – unlike the adult version, in which complex figures are not representations of meaningful figures. However, the CHEF had the disadvantages of being bulky and expensive. A second version of the EFT for children – the *Children's Embedded Figures Test* (CEFT, Karp & Konstadt, 1963) – was therefore created to overcome the disadvantages of the CHEF.

The aforementioned two versions of the EFT for children are often used for children aged from 5 to 9 years. In 1972, Coates modified the CEFT for children aged between 3 and 5 years, resulting in the *Preschool Embedded Figures Test* (PEFT). The major modifications lie in the removal of the color in the figures and the reduction in the number of distracting simple forms in the complex figures. All three inventories (i.e., the CHEF, CEFT, and PEFT) have been reported to have good internal consistency reliability estimates, ranging from .70 to .90, with the majority being in the high .80s.

Finally, the *Group Embedded Figures Test* (GEFT, Witkin, Oltman, Raskin, & Karp, 1971) is a group-administered and timed paper-and-pencil performance test adapted from the individually administered EFT. The test takers are presented with eight simple figures and 25 complex figures (see Appendix for sample items). One of the eight simple figures is embedded within each of the 25 complex figures. The test takers' task is to locate and trace, within the context of the complex figures, as many of the simple figures as possible within three timed sections of 2, 5, and 5 minutes. The score on the GEFT is the number of items precisely traced. The higher an individual's score is, the more field independent he/she is; the lower an individual's score is, the more field dependent he/she is.

Good reliability data on the GEFT have been obtained in various forms, including test-retest, parallel forms, split-half, and scale internal consistencies (e.g., Lewin, 1983; Melancon & Thompson, 1989; Murphy, Casey, Day, & Young, 1997; Panek, Funk, & Nelson, 1980; Snyder, 1998). The validity of the inventory, however, although supported by most studies (e.g., Lewin, 1983; Melancon & Thompson, 1989; Murphy, Casey, Day, & Young, 1997; Zhang, 2004b), has occasionally been challenged (e.g., Cakan, 2003; Panek, Funk, & Nelson, 1980).

Despite the fact that it is often criticized for not being a style construct, but a perceptual ability (e.g., Dubois & Cohen, 1970; Jones, 1997; Richardson & Turner, 2000; Satterly, 1976; Spotts & Mackler, 1967; Stuart, 1967; Weisz, O'Neill, & O'Neill, 1975; see also Chapter 1 in this book), FDI can be said to be the most extensively researched style construct. As has been discussed in the previous chapter and as will be shown in the chapters to follow, scholars worldwide have demonstrated a substantial amount of research interest in their attempts to determine the malleability of FDI, both explicitly and implicitly, as they have in venturing into other areas of research concerning the FDI construct.

Divergent-Convergent Thinking and Its Assessment

A second cognition-centered style construct is divergent-convergent thinking. The notion of divergent-convergent thinking was initially introduced by Guilford (1950, 1967) when he put forward his model of the "structure of intellect." *Divergent* thinkers tend to solve problems and approach tasks in a flexible way, while *convergent* thinkers have a predilection for using their abilities in a rigid way. No single universally accepted test is associated with the assessment of divergent-convergent thinking, and the tendency toward divergent-convergent thinking is normally inferred from one's scores on various performance tests. In addition, the construct is also evaluated by measures – typically open-ended questions – that require respondents to generate multiple answers (Riding & Cheema, 1991). Interested readers are referred to the Appendix for sample inventories.

As a style construct, divergent-convergent thinking has not generated as many empirical studies as some of the other popular style constructs delineated in the threefold model of intellectual styles. Nevertheless, existing research suggests that findings bearing on divergent-convergent thinking have heuristic values for each of the three controversial issues concerning the nature of intellectual styles, and that the construct is well situated within the context of styles research (see Zhang & Sternberg, 2006 for a detailed discussion).

Decision-Making/Problem-Solving Style and the Kirton Adaption-Innovation Inventory

A third cognition-centered style model is Kirton's (1961) theory of styles for decision making, problem solving, and creativity. Kirton proposed that individuals can be placed on a continuum, with innovators at one extreme end and adaptors at the other. Individuals with an *innovative* style prefer to work in nontraditional ways and are not concerned about the social consequences of not producing acceptable solutions. Individuals with an *adaptive* style prefer to work within existing frameworks and tend to minimize risks and conflicts.

The innovative-adaptive style dimension is assessed by the *Kirton Adaption-Innovation Inventory* (KAI, Kirton, 1976, 1982). Comprising three scales (Originality, Efficiency, and Group Rule Conformity), the KAI is a 33-item self-report inventory. Respondents are required to indicate the difficulty (or ease) involved in maintaining a particular thought steadily for a relatively long time (e.g., as manifested in an individual's tendency to continue to pursue a creative idea). The items use a 5-point response scale to measure creativity from the viewpoint of style of creative behavior as opposed to the viewpoint of level of creativity. The inventory's theoretical response range is from 32 to 160, and its theoretical mean is 96. The scores suggest at what point along the continuum an individual falls. Individuals' responses are scored so that higher scores are indicative of an innovative style, and lower scores are suggestive of an adaptive style (see Appendix for further information).

Since its initial establishment in the United Kingdom, the KAI has been widely used in studying the styles of decision making, problem solving, and creativity among various occupational groups in a great number of cultural contexts. Cronbach's alpha coefficients normally range from the high .70s to the low .90s. Test-retest reliability coefficients are usually in the mid .80s. The internal structure of the inventory was assessed through factor analysis, and the external validity was examined by testing the KAI against measures of creativity. Results supported the independence of Kirton's decision-making style from creativity (e.g., Clapp, 1993; Joniak & Isaksen, 1988; Kirton, 1994a; Taylor, 1994).

Reflectivity-Impulsivity and the Matching Familiar Figures Tests

Reflectivity-impulsivity, also referred to as conceptual tempo, was originally introduced by Kagan and his colleagues (Kagan, 1965; Kagan, Rosman, Day, Albert, & Philips, 1964). *Reflectivity* is the tendency to consider carefully alternative possible solutions, while *impulsivity* is the tendency to respond hastily and without sufficient forethought.

The most widely used research tool for assessing the reflectivity-impulsivity construct is the *Matching Familiar Figures Test* (MFFT, Kagan et al., 1964). Different forms of the MFFT are available for preschoolers, school children, and adults. Typically, the MFFT is composed of two practice items and 12 test items. For each item, the test taker is presented with a standard stimulus (a picture) along with six[1] comparison stimuli, of which five vary slightly in detail from the standard one, and the remaining one is identical to the standard one (see Appendix for two sample items).

The test taker is instructed to select from the six stimuli the one that exactly matches the standard picture. The examiner measures the number of errors and the time taken to complete the test. The median point of each measure is normally used as the score for classifying the respondents. Respondents with shorter latencies and more errors are classified as impulsive, whereas those with longer latencies and fewer errors are categorized as reflective.

Over the years, the psychometric properties of the MFFT have been improved. Early studies revealed that the initial MFFT only yielded moderate reliability data. For example, Messer (1976) obtained internal consistency

---

[1] In the form for preschool children, the test contains one standard stimulus and four comparison stimuli.

coefficients of .76 for response time and .50 for errors. Messer also found test-retest coefficients to be .78 and .56 for response time and errors, respectively. Subsequent research (e.g., Becker, Bender, & Morrison, 1978; Cairns, 1977) also indicated that the MFFT's reliability, especially that for the error score, was not very satisfactory. Accordingly, attempts were made to revise the instrument, with the efforts of Cairns and Cammock (1978) and of Zelniker and Jeffrey (1976) particularly standing out, resulting in a 20-item *Matching Familiar Figures Test*, known as the *MFFT-20*. Cairns and Cammock (1978) reported split-half correlations of .91 for latency and .89 for errors. Other studies using the MFFT-20 show that the reliability of the MFFT has been improved (e.g., Buela-Casal, Carretero-Dios, De-los-Santos-Roig, & Bermudez, 2003; Kirchner-Nebot & Amador-Campos, 1998). For example, Kirchner-Nebot and Amador-Campos (1998) reported internal consistency of .94 for latencies and .77 for errors, while Buela-Casal et al. (2003) reported Spearman-Brown coefficients ranging from .92 to .98 for latencies for different age groups, and from .69 to .82 for errors for various age groups.

Mode of Thinking and Its Assessment
Mode of thinking has been conventionally known as brain dominance or hemispheric specificity. Research over the past three decades suggests that the two hemispheres of the human brain are more dynamic than static and are more interactive than was once believed. As a result, the terms "brain dominance" and "hemispheric specificity" have gradually been replaced by the terms "hemispheric style" and "hemispheric thinking style" (e.g., Albaili, 1996; Hassan & Abed, 1999). At the turn of the 21st century, Zhang (2002b, 2002c) referred to these terms as "mode of thinking" and considered three modes of thinking: *analytic* (originally left-brain dominance), *holistic* (originally right-brain dominance), and *integrative* (originally whole-brain).

The *Style of Learning and Thinking* (SOLAT, Torrance, McCarthy, & Kolesinski, 1988; Torrance & Reynolds, 1980; Torrance, Riegel, Reynolds, & Ball, 1976) was designed to measure the so-called brain dominance. It is a self-report inventory consisting of 28 items, with each item containing two statements, one of which is supposedly characterized by left-brain dominance (analytic mode of thinking), and the other by right-brain dominance (holistic mode of thinking). Respondents are required to choose one of the two statements or both. Choosing both statements is indicative of whole-brain dominance (integrative mode of thinking). Two sample items are included in the Appendix.

Reliability and validity data for the SOLAT (Youth Form) are reported in the *SOLAT Administrator's Manual* (Torrance, 1988). Cronbach's alphas are .77 for the analytic scale and .74 for the holistic scale. No reliability data are reported for the integrative scale in the *SOLAT Administrator's Manual.* In my study of Hong Kong university students, I (Zhang, 2002b) reported Cronbach's alphas of .75 for the analytic scale, .70 for the holistic scale, and .85 for the integrative scale. Similarly, my study of university students in the United States obtained Cronbach's alphas of .75 for the analytic scale, .73 for the holistic scale, and .83 for the integrative scale (Zhang, 2002c).

Although the *Manual* contains little information concerns the validity of the SOLAT (Youth Form), as Torrance (1988) pointed out, evidence accumulated for several earlier versions of the SOLAT (for details, see Torrance, 1988) supports its validity. It has been shown that in general, while creative problem solving and creative thinking require both the analytic and holistic modes of thinking, the essence of creative behaviors calls for a holistic mode of thinking. Furthermore, good internal construct validity was reported in my studies of American and Chinese university students (Zhang, 2002b, 2002c).

Some researchers (see Chapter 5) used the *Human Information Survey* (HIPS, Torrance, 1984) to assess brain dominance. The HIPS evaluates an individual's brain hemisphere processing preference. This paper-and-pencil test is composed of 40 items, each with three forced-choice options. The scale is structured in such a way so that two of the three choices are diametrically opposed to each other and are used to indicate left or right brain hemispheric preference, and the third choice is indicative of integrated brain functioning. Questions designed to tap left-brain functions suggest preferences for conformity, drawing conclusions, improving upon an intervention, recall of verbal material, sequential data, solving problems logically, specific facts, structured assignments, systematic discovery, and outlining. Questions constructed to measure right-brain functions indicate discovery through exploration, idea generation and invention, intuitive tactics nonconformity, relational thinking, spatial imagery, and summarization rather than specific details. The third choice is associated with integrated brain-hemisphere processing. The order of the three alternatives is randomized to minimize a pattern associated with A, B, C choices.

Internal scale reliability is reported to generally range from .82 to .86. Test-retest reliability data usually range from .55 to .86. Content and construct validity have also been demonstrated (see Szirony, Pearson, Burgin, Murray & Elrod, 2007).

Personality Type and the Meyers-Briggs Type Indicator
Jung (1923) asserted that individuals attend selectively to elements in their environments, seeking out the ones compatible with their supposed personality types (also known as personality styles) and avoiding or leaving

incompatible ones. These tendencies, according to Jung, fall along three dimensions: extroversion-introversion, sensing-intuitive, and thinking-feeling. Myers and McCaulley (1985) extended Jung's work by adding a fourth dimension – judging-perceiving. An *extraverted* (E) person leans toward the outer world of objects, people, and actions, whereas an *introverted* (I) person prefers the inner world of concepts and ideas. A *sensing* (S) person has a predilection for seeking the fullest possible experience of what is immediate and real, whereas an *intuitive* (N) person seeks the broadest view of what is possible and insightful. A *thinking* (T) person likes to make decisions based on rational and logical planning, whereas a *feeling* (F) person likes to make decisions based on harmony among subjective values. A *judging* (J) person tends to be concerned with seeking closure, sometimes without sufficient exploratory activities, whereas a *perceiving* (P) person tends to be attuned to incoming information and open to new events and changes.

The *Myers-Briggs Type Indicator* (MBTI), first published in 1943 and currently in its 19th print (Myers, McCaulley, Quenk, & Hammer, 1998), is the instrument commonly used to assess the four personality style dimensions. The MBTI is a self-administered inventory. The standard form of the MBTI is the 126-item Form G, with each item in the forced-choice format to permit choices between the desirable opposites in each of the four dimensions of preferences. Choices are always in the same dimension of preferences – E or I, S or N, but never E or N, T or P. There are two item types – word-pairs and phrase questions, with the former tending to reflect a truer preference and the latter being more reflective of everyday life and pressures (see Appendix for sample items).

The MBTI is scored for four indices: EI, SN, TF, and JP. Each response to each item is weighted 0, 1, or 2, with weights taking into account the popularity of the item, social desirability, omissions, and sex differences. The optical-scanning answer sheets of several Forms of the MBTI – including that of Form-G – can be scored by computer or using templates. Form-G can also be self-scored. Hand-scoring is accomplished with five hand-scoring templates, each for EI, SN, TF male, TF female, and JP.

The *MBTI Manual* for Form-G (Myers & McCaulley, 1993) reports good psychometric properties of the inventory. Internal consistency reliabilities based on split-half correlations of large samples from the MBTI data bank fall between .75 and .88 for EI; .73 and .91 for SN; .76 and .88 for TF; and .80 and .92 for JP. Median split-half correlations reported for smaller research samples from seventh-graders through adults are .82 for EI, .82 for SN, .77 for TF, and .84 for JP. Lower correlations generally come, as Myers and McCaulley (1993) anticipated, from younger or underachieving samples. Test-retest reliabilities reported in the manual for 28 groups with retest intervals ranging from one week to four years show median correlations of .84 for EI, .81 for SN, .72 for TF, and .81 for JP. Moreover, good concurrent validity is consistently reported for almost all occupations considered.

Jung (1958) argued that psychological functions apply not only to individuals, but also to civilizations, nationalities, and cultures. In other words, individual differences in personality styles can be used to characterize cultural differences. Indeed, the MBTI has been translated into many languages (e.g., Afrikanns, Arabic, Bahasa Malay, Chinese, Czechoslovakian, Danish, Dutch, Finnish, Flemish, French, German, Greek, Hungarian, Icelandic, Indonesia, Italian, Korean, Norwegian, Portuguese, Russian, Spanish, Thai, Vietnamese, and Zulu) and is widely used to assess the aforementioned four dimensions of preferences. These four underlying personality dimensions assessed by the MBTI have been found to be universal despite the fact that the external validity of the instrument is debatable (Sternberg, 1997). As McCaulley and Moody (2001) asserted, "Type cuts across ethnicity and culture" (p. 298). Nevertheless, there are also important differences in how personality styles are distributed within different cultural and ethnic groups.

Career Personality Type and Its Assessment
Based on empirical findings, Holland (1966, 1973) proposed that people can be classified into six types corresponding to six occupational environments: realistic, investigative, artistic, social, enterprising, and conventional (RIASEC). People of the *realistic* career personality type like to work on concrete tasks and enjoy outdoor activities. People with an *investigative* type of career interest like to be engaged in scientific work. People of the *artistic* personality type like to deal with tasks that provide them with the opportunities to use their imagination. *Social* people like to work in situations in which they can interact and cooperate with other people. People of the *enterprising* career personality type, like people of *social* career personality type, have a strong preference for working in groups, but prefer to take on leadership roles that require innovative thinking. Finally, *conventional* personality types like to work with data under well-structured situations.

Three inventories are commonly used to assess these career personality types: The *Self-Directed Search* (SDS, Holland, 1994), the *Vocational Preference Inventory* (VPI, Holland, 1975), and the *Strong Interest Inventories* (SII, Strong Jr., Donnay, Morris, Schaubhut, & Thompson, 2004). The SDS is a self-administered and self-scored inventory that assesses the six career interest types. Three principal forms of the SDS were created: Form-R, the original form, designed for use with high school students, college students, and adults;

Form E, developed for adults and high school students with limited education or reading skills; and Form CP, designed for professionals and adults in job transition.

In Form-R of the SDS, a total of 228 items are allocated in four parallel subtests, with each subtest respectively focusing on individuals' activities, competencies, occupational preferences, and self-estimates. The *activities* subtest measures individuals' career-relevant interests and contains 66 items in a like-dislike format. The *competencies* subtest assesses skills in performing specific tasks and consists of 66 items in a yes-no response format. The *occupational preferences* subtest assesses individuals' feelings of competence in different kinds of occupations and comprises 84 items in a like-dislike format. Finally, the *self-estimates* subtest requires individuals to rate their abilities and skills on a 7-point response scale, with "1" indicating low and "7" denoting high abilities/skills on each of the RIASEC scales. Upon completing the test, the test takers obtain a three-letter Holland code that indicates their three strongest areas of career personality styles. Sample items for each of the four subtests are provided in the Appendix.

First published in 1971, the SDS has been translated into more than 30 languages and has generated thousands of empirical studies all over the world (e.g., Bickham, Miller, O'Neal, & Clanton, 1998; Glidden & Greenwood, 1997; Swan, 2005). The great majority of these studies supported the reliability and validity of the SDS. The *SDS Manual* (Holland, 1994) reports good internal consistency (using KR-20) and test-retest reliability data as well as good concurrent and predictive validity data.

The VPI, like the SDS, is a self-administered and self-scored inventory. Initially published in 1953, the VPI has undergone eight revisions. The test takers mark their responses Y (Yes) or N (No) on a carbonless answer sheet to indicate which of the 160 occupations in the test they find interesting. The scoring page is revealed once the top page of the answer sheet is peeled away. Both raw scores and T scores are given. The *VPI Manual* (Holland, 1985b) provides evidence for the validity of the VPI as well as information on its internal consistency (KR-20) and the test-retest reliability of the VPI scales.

The development of the VPI, and particularly its rationale, was the foundation for Holland's (1973) theory of career personality styles, which in turn led to the establishment of the SDS. Holland (1985b) articulated several major similarities and differences between the two inventories, one of which was that the VPI is oriented more toward the needs of clinicians and career counselors engaged in individual counseling, whereas the SDS relies more on an individual's initiative and self-direction. Furthermore, the VPI measures four additional dimensions (i.e., self-control, masculinity, status, and infrequency) that are not evaluated in the SDS (see Holland, 1985b for details).

The SII is the third instrument that assesses the six career personality styles in Holland's (1973) theory and has generated research that has implications for the style malleability issue. The 2004 SII is the most recent version of a series of *Strong* interest inventories. The inventory was initially published in 1927 as the *Strong Vocational Interest Blank* (SVIB, Strong, Jr., 1927; see Hood & Johnson, 2002 for more details) and was designed for use with high school students, university students, and adults. The 2004 version contains 291 items that evaluate people's career-relevant interests in six areas: *Occupations, School Subjects, Work Activities* (e.g., making a speech and repairing a clock), *Leisure Activities, People* (day-to-day contact with various types of people), and *Your Characteristics*. In responding to the first 282 items (i.e., the first five parts of the inventory), respondents record their preferences by choosing from *strongly like, like, indifferent, dislike,* and *strongly dislike*. In responding to the nine items in the *Your Characteristics* part, respondents indicate how well each statement describes them by selecting from *strongly like me, like me, don't know, unlike me,* and *strongly unlike me*. Answers to the *Strong* inventory can only be scored by computer at scoring centers designated by the test Publisher.

The SII test profile provides five major types of information: (1) scores on six *general occupation themes* that reflect the test taker's overall orientation to work; (2) scores on 30 *basic interest scales* that indicate consistency of interests or disinterests in specific domains such as art and science; (3) scores on 122 *occupational scales* that represent various occupations and suggest the degree of congruence between the test taker's interests and the characteristics of people working in those occupations; (4) scores on five *personal style scales* that evaluate aspects of the style with which the test taker likes to learn, work, assume leadership, take risks, and deal with teamwork; and (5) scores on *administrative indices* that are designed to identify inconsistent or unusual profiles that call for special attention in interpreting the test results.

The SII's classification of career interest types is derived from Holland's (1966, 1985a) categorization of the six types of occupational environments. According to Case and Blackwell (2008), over the years, the psychometric properties of the series of *Strong* tests have been steadily improving. Reliability data have been chiefly obtained through internal scale reliability and test-rest reliability, while the validity of the inventory has been demonstrated through concurrent validity and external construct validity. Cronbach's alphas for all six general occupation themes rooted in Holland's (1966, 1985a) six career personality styles are above .90 for the 2004 version of the *Strong* (see Case & Blackwell, 2008 for more details).

Mind Style and the Gregorc Style Delineator

Gregorc (1979, 1984, 1985) proposed that individuals' tendency to use mediation channels or mind styles could be understood along two fundamental dimensions: use of space and use of time. Space refers to perceptual categories for acquiring and expressing information and is divided into concrete (or physical) and abstract (or metaphorical) space. Time is divided into two different ways of ordering facts and events: sequential (i.e., in a step-by-step or branchlike manner) and random ordering (i.e., in a web-like or spiral manner). These two poles of the two dimensions form four styles that Gregorc (1979) termed mind styles: *abstract-random*, *concrete-sequential*, *abstract-sequential*, and *concrete-random*. Individuals with the *abstract-random* mind style tend to approach learning holistically and prefer to learn in an unstructured way. Individuals with the *concrete-sequential* mind style tend to extract information through hands-on experiences and prefer well-structured work environments. Individuals with the *abstract-sequential* mind style have a propensity to adopt a logical approach to learning and prefer to deal with tasks that involve decoding written, verbal, and image symbols. Finally, individuals with the *concrete-random* mind style tend to take trial-and-error and intuitive approaches to learning and prefer to work independently.

The *Gregorc Style Delineator* (GSD, Gregorc, 1982) is a self-report inventory that comprises 40 self-descriptive adjectives structured into 10 columns, each consisting of four words. The respondents are required to rank the four words according to their preference for receiving and processing information (see Appendix for two sample items).

The technical manual for the inventory (Gregorc, 1984) reports alpha coefficients ranging from .89 to .93 and test-retest reliability coefficients ranging from .85 to .87. However, Gridley's (2006a) study of engineers resulted in scale alpha coefficients ranging from .67 to .79, while his (Gridley, 2006b) study of art collectors yielded scale alpha coefficients ranging from .53 to .79. Also, in his 1984 work, Gregorc reported good construct validity as evaluated by interviews and good predictive validity as shown by the correlations of GSD scores with attribute scores and by responses to descriptions resulting from the GSD. Employing confirmatory factor analysis, O'Brien (1990) examined the construct validity of the GSD, but found only minimal validity. However, submitting the items of the GSD to a factor analysis, Joniak and Isaksen (1988) obtained several orthogonal factors, largely supporting the internal structure of the GSD.

Kolb's Construct of Learning Style, Its Assessment, and Its Derivative

Based on such work as Kurt Lewin's (1936) model of person-environment interaction, Eric Erickson's (1950) theory of psychosocial development, and

Jean Piaget's (1952) model of cognitive development, Kolb (1976) proposed a stylistic model of experiential learning. Kolb (1976) described experiential learning as a process of transforming specific experiences into concepts that become guidelines for new experiences through reflection. Strongly believing in the dynamic nature of styles, Kolb (1976) proposed that individuals tend to go through a learning cycle of four basic modes: concrete experience (CE), reflective observation (RO), abstract conceptualization (AC), and active experimentation (AE). Specifically, according to Kolb, an individual initially focuses on the concrete and actual situation that he/she is in (CE), then reflects on the concrete experience from different perspectives (RO), generates logically sound conceptual insights into or explanations for what he or she has experienced through abstract conceptualization (AC), and finally tests and applies the newly developed insight or hypothesis in order to solve problems or make decisions through active experimentation (AE).

Kolb's (1976) *Learning Style Inventory* (LSI) is used to assess learning styles as manifested in individuals' levels of abstractness or concreteness and in their levels of activity or reflectivity in dealing with learning tasks. The inventory was designed for adults, and the time needed to complete the inventory is generally estimated to be 10 minutes. It has four words in each of nine sets. The words are associated with feeling, watching, thinking, or doing, thus corresponding to the four basic learning modes: CE, RO, AC, and AE. Scores on these four modes indicate the relative degree of abstractness versus concreteness and that of activity versus reflectivity, which, in turn, translate into four learning styles, each incorporating two characteristics. The four styles and their characteristics are (1) *accommodating*: concrete and active; (2) *diverging*: concrete and reflective; (3) *assimilating*: abstract and reflective; and (4) *converging*: abstract and active.

Since its creation in 1976, the LSI has been published in several versions (Kolb, 1985, 1993, 1995, 1999). The later versions were aimed either at addressing a major criticism that was directed toward the possible existence of a response-set bias caused by the one-style per column scoring format of the inventory or at increasing the ease of scoring. Both satisfactory Cronbach's alpha coefficients (ranging from the mid .70s to the high .80s) and split-half reliability coefficients (ranging from the mid .80s to the low .90s) have been reported for different versions of the inventory. The inventory has been translated into various languages and widely used across the globe.

Apart from the extensive research it has generated, Kolb's model of the learning cycle, along with its assessment tool (LSI), inspired Honey and Mumford to construct their style inventory: the *Learning Styles Questionnaire* (LSQ, Honey & Mumford, 1982, 1986, 1992). The LSQ, an 80-item forced choice (agree/disagree) questionnaire, was designed to elicit individuals' learning style preference by focusing on their behaviors. Four preferred learning styles corresponding to the four learning modes specified in Kolb's (1976) model of experiential learning cycle are assessed: activist, reflector, theorist, and pragmatist. Individuals identified as having the *activist* learning style prefer action-based learning. Individuals with the *reflector* style prefer work that involves data gathering and analyses. Individuals with the *theorist* style tend to focus on analyzing and integrating information. Finally, individuals with the *pragmatist* style prefer to work on tasks that are likely to generate practical solutions to problems.

Thus far, the LSQ has been used in both academic and nonacademic settings in a number of cultural contexts (e.g., Allinson & Hayes, 1988; Kelly, 1995; Seymour & West-Burnham, 1989; Wilson & Hill, 1994). Test-retest reliability data with Pearson product-moment correlation coefficients for the four styles have been found to range from .66 to .89 across a number of studies (e.g., Allinson & Hayes, 1988; Honey & Mumford, 1982, 1986; Sims, Veres, & Shake, 1989). With the exception of Fung, Ho, and Kwan's (1993) study, in which a 40-item version inventory was employed, all existing studies reported acceptable internal scale consistency estimates, with Cronbach's alpha coefficients ranging from the high .60s to the high .70s. However, the construct validity of the LSQ has sometimes been questioned (Duff, 1998).

Learning Approach, Its Assessment, and Its Derivatives
On the basis of quantitative data, Biggs (1978) concluded that there are three common approaches to learning: *surface, deep,* and *achieving* (see also Entwistle & Ramsden, 1983; Marton & Säljö, 1976). The *surface* approach to learning involves a reproduction of what is taught in order to meet the minimum requirements. The *deep* approach to learning involves a thorough understanding of what is learned. The *achieving* approach to learning focuses on maximizing one's grades. Each learning approach has two components: *motive*, which concerns why one learns; and *strategy*, which pertains to how one learns.

The two most commonly used research tools for assessing the three learning approaches are Biggs's (1987) *Learning Process Questionnaire* (LPQ) for school students and the *Study Process Questionnaire* (SPQ) for university students. These inventories were originally constructed to measure Australian and Canadian students' learning/study approaches. Subsequently, other versions of the LPQ and SPQ were constructed. For example, in 1992, the Hong Kong versions of the LPQ and the SPQ were established (Biggs, 1992). In 1994, when they studied Brunei university students, Watkins and Murphy came up with a simplified English as a Second Language (ESL) version and a Malay version. In 1995, Albaili established an Arabic version of the SPQ in his study of university students in the United Arab Emirates.

The LPQ has two forms. Form A was designed for middle and senior secondary school students, while Form B was designed for upper primary through junior secondary school students. Both forms of the LPQ contain 36 statements that contribute to six subscales: *deep-motive, deep-strategy, surface-motive, surface-strategy, achieving-motive,* and *achieving-strategy. Each* subscale has six statements. The SPQ has 42 statements grouped into the same six subscales. Each subscale has seven statements. All three inventories – the two forms of the LPQ and the SPQ – adopt a 5-point response scale, anchored by "1", indicating that the statement is *never or only rarely true* of the respondents and "5", indicating that the statement is *always or almost always true* of the respondents (see Appendix for sample items from the SPQ, Biggs, 1992).

All versions of the SPQ and the LPQ have proved to be fairly reliable and valid measures for assessing students' learning/study approaches. However, factor analyses have often found loadings for the two subscales in the achieving approach to be split between the deep and surface approach factors, resulting in two-factor solutions (see Albaili, 1995; Watkins, 1998; Zhang & Sternberg, 2000 for summaries).

In response to the repeated cross-loading of the achieving subscales, Biggs, Kember, and Leung (2001) refined Biggs's (1987) original SPQ to produce the *Revised Two-Factor Study Process Questionnaire* (R-SPQ-2F). The R-SPQ-2F is composed of 20 statements grouped into four subscales: *deep-motive, deep-strategy, surface-motive,* and *surface-strategy.* Each subscale has five statements. Test takers are required to respond on a 5-point Likert scale ("A through "E"), with "A" indicating that the statement is *never or only rarely true* of them, and "E" indicating that the statement is *always or almost always true* of them. Existing studies generally show Cronbach's alpha coefficients that are between the low .60s and the mid .80s. Furthermore, the 20 items usually load on two factors as expected, with one being dominated by items on the surface learning approach scale and the other by those on the deep learning approach scale.

In addition to the concept of learning approaches, three allied concepts that are roughly[2] in the same "family" of activity-centered styles have also played an important role in generating research on style malleability. These are: learning orientation, learning preference, and learning pattern. Entwistle and Ramsden

---

[2] "Roughly" because the styles of learning preference assessed in Rezler and French's (1975) Learning Preferences Inventory are more than just activity-based; they are also personality-based. See studies introduced in Chapter 5.

(1983) adopted the term "orientation" to refer to both consistency of approach and the existence of both learning approach and learning motivation. Drawing on the work of several researchers, including that of Biggs (1979), Marton and Säljö (1976), and Pask (1976), Entwistle and Ramsden (1983) constructed the *Approaches to Studying Inventory* (ASI) that assess the construct of learning orientation.

The ASI is composed of 64 items that contribute to 16 subscales, which in turn load on four major factors known as "orientations to study." The first factor, *meaning-orientation*, is dominated by high loadings of items denoting a deep approach to learning. The second factor, *reproduction-orientation*, is dominated by high loadings of items suggesting a surface approach to learning. The remaining two factors are relatively less prominent (Entwistle, 1988). The third factor, known as *achieving orientation*, is predominantly loaded by items that communicate a strategic approach to learning coupled with extrinsic and achievement motivations. The fourth and final factor is termed *nonacademic orientation*, suggesting chiefly disorganized study methods and negative attitudes towards learning.

Respondents are required to indicate the extent to which they agree or disagree with each of the 64 items on a 5-point Likert scale, with "0" indicating that they "*definitely disagree*" and "4" indicating that they "*definitely agree*." Subsequently, several versions of the ASI containing varying numbers of items were constructed. One of the latest versions is the *Approaches and Study Skills Inventory for Students* – short version (ASSIST; Tait, Entwistle, & McCune, 1998). The series of inventories constructed on the basis of the ASI, as well as the ASI itself, have been used in various cultural contexts and have generally been found to have acceptable reliability and good validity (e.g., Lonka & Lindblom-Ylänne, 1996; Reid, Duvall, & Evans, 2005; Richardson, 1990; Richardson & Cuffie, 1997; Watkins, Hattie, & Astilla, 1986).

The concept of learning preference, a second alternative term for the general notion of learning approach, has been chiefly operationalized through Rezler and French's (1975) *Learning Preferences Inventory* (LPI), which was initially designed for use with allied health students. It assesses six aspects of personality styles and learning preferences: the *abstract* style, a preference for learning theories and generating hypotheses, with a focus on general principles and concepts; the *concrete* style, a preference for learning specific and practical tasks, with a focus on skills; the *individual* style, a preference for working alone, with a strong emphasis on self-reliance; the *interpersonal* style, a preference for working with others, with a high value placed on harmonious relations; the *student-structured* style, a preference for learning through student-organized tasks, with an emphasis on autonomy and self-instruction;

and the *teacher-structured* style, a preference for working in a well-structured teacher-directed learning environment, with clearly identified expectations and tasks. The LPI is a self-administered test and is composed of nine test items, each containing six statements. Respondents are required to rank order the six statements within each item. The ranking is recorded on a 6-point Likert scale, with "1" indicating that the statement *promotes learning the least* for the respondents, and "6" denoting that the statement *promotes learning the most* for the respondents. While Rezler and French's (1975) initial study of the learning preferences of students in six allied health professions resulted in only moderate internal scale reliability estimates (ranging from .58 for the abstract style to .77 for the teacher-structured style), subsequent studies (e.g., Barris, Kielhofner, & Bauer, 1985; Rogers & Hill, 1980) yielded higher ones, ranging from the low .60s to the high .80s. In 1981, Rezler and Rezmovick reported internal consistency reliabilities for the six scales ranging from .72 to .88. The inventory has been reported to have good internal construct validity (Barris et al., 1985; Rezler & Rezmovick, 1981).

Finally, the term "learning pattern" was adopted by Vermunt (1998, 2011) to represent the more widely used term "learning style" or "learning approach." Based on interviews with Dutch university students about their learning experiences in higher educational institutions, Vermunt (1994, 1998) developed the *Inventory of Learning Styles* (ILS). The ILS distinguishes four learning patterns, each incorporating one or more of the following dimensions: cognitive processing strategies (e.g., relating, structuring, and memorizing), metacognitive regulation strategies (e.g., self-regulation and planning), learning orientations (i.e., learning motivation such as ego-orientation and task-orientation), and mental models of learning (i.e., conceptions of learning regarding the nature of learning, the student's role in learning, etc.; see Vermunt, 2011 for details). The four learning styles/patterns are: (1) meaning-directed, (2) reproduction-directed, (3) undirected, and (4) application-directed. Individuals with the *meaning-directed* style tend to adopt a deep processing learning strategy and to use self-regulated learning processes such as relating, structuring, and critical processing; they tend to perceive learning as individuals' construction of learning and to take responsibility for their learning. Individuals with the *reproduction-directed* learning pattern tend to rely on external regulation, memorizing, and analyzing; they tend to perceive learning as the intake of knowledge from information resources such as reading materials and teachers. Individuals with the *undirected* style tend not to rely on any regulation in learning; they are likely to be unsure about why they learn, relying on others (e.g., instructors and fellow students) to stimulate them in learning.

Finally, individuals with the *application-directed* style tend to adopt a concrete learning strategy, thinking of possible applications of what they learn to real life situations; they tend to be vocation-oriented in their learning motivation and to use both self and external regulation strategies, trying to apply the knowledge they acquire to practical matters.

Since its inception (Vermunt, 1992), the ILS has been tested in various studies with thousands of students in a number of cultural contexts, including Argentina, Belgium, Brazil, China, Finland, Indonesia, the Netherlands, Norway, Spain, Sri Lanka, Sweden, and the United States (see Vermunt & Vermentten, 2004 for a summary). The most recent version of the ILS (Vermunt, 1998) is composed of 120 statements concerning four learning components – cognitive processing strategies, metacognitive regulation strategies, conceptions of learning, and learning orientations – that evaluate the four learning patterns defined in the previous paragraph, namely meaning-directed, reproduction-directed, undirected, and application-directed. The inventory adopts a 5-point response scale on which the respondents indicate the degree to which the items describe their learning activities, their views and motives, their conceptions of learning, and their learning orientations. Internal scale reliability data as represented by Cronbach's alpha coefficients are reported to be generally good, ranging from .63 to .93, with the great majority of the alphas being .70 or higher (Marambe, Vermunt, & Boshuizen, 2012; Vermunt, 1998). Factor analysis of the items in the ILS has shown good internal construct validity (Vermunt & Vermetten, 2004).

Thinking Style and Its Assessment
Using "government" metaphorically, Sternberg (1988, 1997) contended that, just as there are many ways of governing a society, there are many ways in which people manage their activities. These ways of managing activities can be regarded as individuals' thinking styles. In managing their activities, people choose styles with which they feel comfortable. Moreover, Sternberg (1997) maintained that thinking styles are changeable in that individuals are at least somewhat flexible in their use of styles and try with varying degrees of success to adapt themselves to the stylistic demands of a given situation. For example, an individual who uses the legislative style when designing a research project may prefer to use the executive style when installing information into a new iPad according to written instructions. As a matter of fact, Sternberg (1997) discussed several factors that potentially affect the development of thinking styles, including culture, gender, birth order, and socioeconomic status.

The theory of mental self-government proposes 13 thinking styles that fall along five dimensions: functions, forms, levels, scopes, and leanings. On the basis of both theoretical conceptualization and empirical evidence, Zhang (2002a) classified the 13 thinking styles into three types. Type I styles include the *legislative* (preference for[3] doing things in one's own way), *judicial* (evaluating people or products), *liberal* (dealing with tasks in new ways), *global* (thinking with a holistic picture in mind), and *hierarchical* (distributing attention across multiple prioritized tasks) styles. Type II styles include the *executive* (implementing tasks with set guidelines), *conservative* (dealing with tasks in traditional ways), *local* (attending to concrete details), and *monarchic* (focusing on one thing at a time) styles. Type III styles include the *oligarchic* (distributing one's attention across multiple tasks without priorities), anarchic (turning one's attention to whatever task that comes along), *internal* (working independently), and *external* (working in groups) styles. Historically, the classification of these three types of thinking styles was the foundation for the construction of the three types of intellectual styles (Zhang & Sternberg, 2005). Thus, the characteristics of each of the three types of thinking styles match those of each of the corresponding three types of intellectual styles described earlier in this chapter.

The theory of mental self-government has been operationalized through several instruments, including the *Thinking Styles Inventory* (TSI, Sternberg & Wagner, 1992), the *Thinking Styles Inventory-Revised* (TSI-R, Sternberg, Wagner, & Zhang, 2003), and the *Thinking Styles Inventory-Revised II* (TSI-R2, Sternberg, Wagner, & Zhang, 2007). Each of the three versions of the inventory consists of 65 statements divided into groups of five, with each group assessing one of the 13 thinking styles in Sternberg's theory. Participants respond to each statement by rating themselves on a 7-point Likert scale, with "1" indicating that the statement does *not at all* represent the way they normally carry out their tasks, and "7" denoting that the statement does so *extremely well* (see Appendix for sample items).

Earlier studies using the original TSI (Sternberg & Wagner, 1992) consistently found unacceptably low internal scale reliabilities (the low .50s) in three of the 13 scales: local, monarchic, and anarchic. A close examination of the item-scale reliabilities from some of my previous data sets indicated that seven items needed to be revised: two in the local scale, three in the monarchic scale, and two in the anarchic scale. Subsequently, these items

---

[3] For brevity, the phrase "preference for" is omitted in the context of describing the remaining 12 thinking styles.

were rewritten, leading to the first revised version of the TSI – the TSI-R (Sternberg, Wagner, & Zhang, 2003). Results from the three revised scales indicated that the Cronbach's alphas for the local and the monarchic scales were considerably improved: the alpha coefficients increased from the low to mid .50s to nearly .70. The alpha coefficient for the anarchic scale, however, only showed slight improvement. Four years later, when it was clear that the anarchic scale continued to yield low internal scale reliability in various studies (e.g., Zhang, 2004a, 2004c), items in this scale were rewritten again. This endeavor led to the second revised version of the TSI – the TSI-R2 (Sternberg, Wagner, & Zhang, 2007). To date, the TSI-R2 has been tested in a number of studies (e.g., Zhang, 2009, 2010; Zhu & Zhang, 2011), all resulting in acceptable alpha coefficient (above .60) for the anarchic scale. Thus, all scales in the TSI-R2 possess satisfactory internal scale reliability. Two kinds of validity have been obtained: internal and external construct validity. Concerning internal construct validity, studies using all three versions of the inventory have consistently resulted in three-, four-, or five-factor solutions. These factors dovetail well with both the five dimensions of thinking styles originally proposed by Sternberg (1988) and the three types of thinking styles subsequently reconceptualized by Zhang (2002a). As for external construct validity, a wide range of studies (e.g., Chen & Zhang, 2010; Fjell & Walhovd, 2004; Murphy & Janeke, 2009; Shokri, Kadivar, Farzad, Sangari, & Ghana-ei, 2006) have demonstrated that the thinking style construct is associated with other constructs (e.g., emotional intelligence, personality traits, and mental health) in ways that are theoretically expected.

Up to now, the three versions of the Thinking Styles Inventory, along with the other three inventories[4] rooted in Sternberg's (1988) theory of thinking styles, have been validated in hundreds of studies carried out in different cultural contexts, including the United States (e.g., Bishop & Foster, 2011; Grigorenko & Sternberg, 1997), Spain (e.g., Cano-Garcia & Hughes, 2000), mainland China (Zhang & Sachs, 1997), Iran (e.g., Shokri et al., 2006), Korea (e.g., Park, Park, & Choe, 2005), Norway (e.g., Fjell & Walhovd, 2004), South Africa (e.g., Murphy & Janeke, 2009), Turkey (e.g., Fer, 2007), and the United Kingdom (Zhang & Higgins, 2008).

---

[4] Based on Sternberg's theory of mental self-government, three other inventories have been constructed and validated: (1) Thinking Styles in Teaching Inventory (Grigorenko & Sternberg, 1993); (2) Preferred Thinking Styles in Teaching Inventory (Zhang, 2003); and (3) Preferred Thinking Styles in Learning Inventory (Zhang, 2007). Because these three inventories are not relevant to the studies reviewed in this book, they are not detailed here.

Closing Remarks

In this chapter, I have provided a succinct account of the chief style models/constructs and their associated research tools that have played a pivotal role in generating the styles literature as a whole and in stimulating the research on style malleability in particular. I am now ready to turn to a critical review of the major empirical findings that address the issue of style malleability.

PART II

EMPIRICAL EVIDENCE: CROSS-SECTIONAL STUDIES

3

Gender and Intellectual Styles

Gender differences in intellectual functioning have long been a concern of many scholars (e.g., Burstyn, 1980; Friedman, 1963). However, it was the work of Maccoby and Jacklin (1974) that represented the first encyclopedic analysis of the literature on the psychology of gender differences. Maccoby and Jacklin (1974) concluded that three gender differences were well established: on average, girls had greater verbal ability than boys, and boys had better visual-spatial ability and better mathematical ability than girls.

In the field of intellectual styles, gender differences in field dependence/independence (FDI) – again, also known as psychological differentiation, visual-spatial ability, or perceptual ability/style (Witkin, 1948) – were already well acknowledged in the 1970s, with the most systematic reviews of research on gender differences in FDI being those of Witkin and Berry (1975) and van Leeuwen (1978). Based on evidence from numerous studies, both reviews concluded that there were consistent, although small, differences in psychological differentiation between males and females, with males tending to be more field independent than females. Three years later, however, Hyde (1981) questioned the attention given to gender differences in intellectual functioning, including gender differences in psychological differentiation, on the grounds that the differences found were small in magnitude.

The thrust of the argument in this chapter is that although the gender differences found are usually small in magnitude, and although it is undeniable that a small proportion of gender differences in styles are biologically determined (Dawson, 1972; Grigorenko, 2009; Grigorenko, LaBuda, & Carter, 1992; Salkind, 1979), the fact that these differences occur consistently merits further attention from both researchers and practitioners. The reason why researchers should be interested in this topic is that findings on the relationships between gender and styles can contribute to a better understanding of the nature of intellectual styles as it relates to style malleability. That is to say, if solid evidence for consistent gender differences in intellectual styles can be provided, one could argue that intellectual styles are dynamic partially as a function of different socialization processes that males and females tend to experience.

Practitioners in academic and nonacademic settings should be interested in achieving a better understanding of style malleability, particularly gender differences in intellectual styles, because such understanding has implications for educational practices and beyond. For example, if styles represent fixed traits, any attempt to encourage females or males to develop particular styles would probably be fruitless. If, in contrast, styles are modifiable, efforts to cultivate styles and to show sensitivity to gender differences in styles would be very beneficial to people's efforts to foster the desired styles.

The purpose of this chapter is to consider, in greater detail than was possible in the aforementioned reviews, the studies of FDI that bear on the issue of gender differences, and also to review studies of gender differences with respect to three other major style constructs: personality types/styles (Jung, 1923), learning approaches (Biggs, 1978), and thinking styles (Sternberg, 1988). It should be acknowledged that many other style constructs have also been tested in relation to gender. However, in order to restrict this review to a more manageable scope, only studies based on the aforementioned four style constructs were included for the present review. The selection of these constructs was based on two criteria. The first was that each of the first three style constructs (FDI, personality types, and learning approaches) was selected to represent, respectively, each of the three traditions in the study of styles: cognition-centered, personality-centered, and activity-centered (Grigorenko & Sternberg, 1995; see Chapter 2). The fourth style construct, thinking style, was selected because it is deemed to be the most general individual style construct, encompassing the styles of all three approaches in the study of styles (Sternberg, 1997). Furthermore, each of the three style constructs of FDI, personality types, and learning approaches had generated the most research on the topic of this chapter within its own style tradition.

The remainder of this chapter is divided into four parts. The first part introduces the major theoretical perspectives and existing research on gender-role socialization. The second part sets the parameters for the review. The third part introduces studies on gender differences in each of the selected style constructs and offers alternative explanations for the findings, all pointing to gender-role socialization as one likely cause of the largely systematic gender gaps in intellectual styles. The final part draws conclusions on the literature concerning the relationship between gender and styles, points out the limitations of the existing research, and discusses the implications of gender differences in intellectual styles for research and for education and beyond.

Gender-Role Socialization: Theoretical Perspectives and Research

This part sets the scene for the literature review of gender differences in styles. Because Chapter 2 has already provided a general introduction to the major theoretical approaches to the study of intellectual styles and has described the major models of intellectual styles, this part is devoted to describing the principal theoretical and research background to gender-role socialization, and also establishes the conceptual link between gender-role socialization and intellectual styles.

It is widely recognized in the literature that unclear terminology is one of the major obstacles to understanding gender-role research (Angrist, 1969; Unger & Denmark, 1975). In reviewing work on the effects of gender role on intellectual functioning, Nash (1979) broadly defined gender role as any attitudes, behaviors, expectations, or traits that are believed to characterize males and females. Gender-role socialization, according to Saucier, McCreary, and Saxberg (2002), "reflects the extent to which individuals internalize stereotypic notions about men's and women's personalities and act in gender stereotypic ways" (p. 1102). This definition is highly endorsed in this chapter.

Theoretical Perspectives

Over the years, alternative theories have been put forward to explain gender-role socialization. Broadly speaking, these theories fall into two categories: psychologically oriented theories (e.g., Bem, 1981; Freud, 1962; Kohlberg, 1966; Markus, Crane, Bernstein, & Siladi, 1982) and sociologically oriented theories (e.g., Bandura, 1986; Kagan, 1964; Lorber, 1994). Bussey and Bandura (1999) proposed that these two types of theories differ primarily along three dimensions. The first dimension pertains to the relative importance attached to psychological, biological, and socio-structural determinants. Psychologically oriented theories tend to emphasize intrapsychic processes that govern gender development, whereas socially oriented theories tend to focus on socio-structural determinants of gender-role socialization and functioning. The second dimension concerns the nature of the transmission models. Whereas psychologically oriented theories typically emphasize the cognitive construction of gender conceptions and behavioral styles within the familial transmission model, sociologically oriented theories stress the social construction of gender roles primarily at the institutional level. The third dimension concerns the temporal span of theoretical analyses. Psychologically oriented theories view gender identity as developing in early childhood rather than throughout one's life. Although the development of one's gender role is not always restricted to childhood, it happens at a much slower pace after childhood. According to these theories, the rules of gender-role behaviors vary to some extent – across social contexts and at different stages in one's life. Sociologically oriented theories, on the other hand, view gender development as occurring throughout the lifespan.

Although the two main approaches to studying gender-role socialization have significant differences, they share an important commonality, namely that an individual's gender role develops. A wide range of determinants shape an individual's gender-role orientations. These include cognitive, social, affective, and motivational processes. Interested readers are referred to Bussey and Bandura's (1999) work for a detailed discussion (see also Saucier et al., 2002).

At issue within the context of the present review are the consequences of gender-role socialization. Within the realm of gender-related constructs, one such consequence is gender-role stereotypes. Gender-role stereotypes are steadfastly held, well-defined concepts that prescribe how each gender ought to behave and/or perform. Early in 1964, Kagan suggested that culturally supported gender-role stereotypes were likely to generate gender-role standards – that is, expectations about how each gender should act (see also Nash, 1979).

Research Evidence
Since the publication of Terman and Miles's (1936) *Sex and Personality: Studies in Masculinity and Femininity*, there has been considerable research devoted to assessing and understanding gender-role-related individual differences. For example, studies have been conducted on gender-role socialization, gender-role stereotypes, and gender-role orientations. In the early 1970s, there was a growing awareness of the harmful effects of rigid conceptualizations of male and female gender roles, which resulted in a resurgence of interest in examining the factors that affect the development of gender-role attitudes in children (e.g., Maccoby & Jacklin, 1974; Huston, 1985), and attempts were made to eliminate the practice of assigning social roles to males and females. Nevertheless, research continued to show that young children (and adults) developed gender-role stereotypes (e.g., Halpern, 2000; Mason & Mudrack, 1996). At the same time, many other types of research efforts centered on gender-role socialization continued to flourish. Findings from two lines of investigation are of interest in this review. The first concerns the determinants of gender-role socialization for students, and the second pertains to the

impact of gender-role socialization on students' learning and developmental outcomes.

A great deal of research has indicated that young students are socialized into living up to the expectations of the so-called appropriate gender role. Many social-environmental factors contribute to young males' and females' socialization into gender roles, two of which have been found to be particularly influential: teachers' beliefs and parental influence. At school, teachers' beliefs and expectations about boys' and girls' competence and skills are the primary source of gender-role socialization (Halpern, 2000; Grossman & Grossman, 1994). Beyond school, one of the most powerful agents for gender-role socialization is parental influence (Eccles, Jacobs, & Harold, 1990; Kulik, 2005; McHale, Crouter, & Tucker, 1999). Furthermore, research has shown that teachers' and parents' beliefs and attitudes, which often favor boys (e.g., Sternberg & Zhang, 1995; Zhang & Sternberg, 1998; Zhang & Sternberg, 2011), not only perpetuate gender-role stereotypes among children, but also have a significant impact on their learning and developmental outcomes, such as their self-esteem, academic performance, and mental health (e.g., Eccles, Jacobs, & Harold, 1990; Kopper & Epperson, 1996; Kulik, 2005; McHale, Crouter, & Tucker, 1999).

Gender-Role Socialization and Intellectual Styles
The phenomenon of gender-role socialization has also been examined within the context of intellectual styles. Certainly, thus far, such research has primarily been limited to investigating the relationship between gender-role orientation and FDI (see section "Gender Differences in FDI Styles" under "Gender Differences in Intellectual Styles: Research Evidence" of this chapter). However, given the prevalent effects of gender-role socialization on cognitive functioning (e.g., Bem & Lenney, 1976; Jamison & Signorella, 2001), one could argue that the gender gaps in intellectual styles can be, at a minimum, explained in some measure the differential gender-role socialization processes experienced by males and females, as will be articulated in a later part of this review.

Setting Parameters: Literature Search Procedures and Results

General Search Procedures
In order to keep the literature review within a more manageable scope and to ensure a balanced review of work on the four selected models, in addition to the key words "gender and/or sex," key words for the research tools assessing each style construct were limited to one primary inventory for each style model. Therefore, for the field-dependent/independent style model, the

title "Embedded Figures Test" was keyed in. For personality types, the title "Myers-Briggs Type Indicator" was entered. For learning approaches, the titles "Learning Process Questionnaire" and "Study Process Questionnaire" were both entered because both assess students' learning approaches, with the former being used among school students and the latter among university students. Finally, for thinking styles, the title "Thinking Styles Inventory" was keyed into the search.

It was further specified that these key words be found in the abstracts. Finally, with the exception of the studies centered on thinking styles, only work published in peer-reviewed journals was selected. With regard to work on thinking styles, in addition to that published in peer-reviewed journals, some unpublished data sets were also examined. The reason for this was that of all four style models included in this review, the theory on thinking styles is the most recent. The inclusion of the unpublished data allowed for a more comprehensive review of the available data on gender differences in thinking styles.

Literature Search Results

The outcome of the literature search indicated that compared with the two constructs specified in the two more recent style models (i.e., learning approaches by Biggs and thinking styles by Sternberg), the two style constructs with longer histories (i.e., field dependence/independence by Witkin and personality types/styles by Jung) have been investigated much more extensively in relation to gender differences. It should be noted that although the literature search resulted in more or less the same number of articles for each of the four models, in the case of the two models with longer histories, review articles and/or meta-analysis studies were also located, with each review or meta-analysis study containing multiple studies. It should also be noted that although the literature search was limited to one style inventory for each theoretical model (with the exception of Biggs's learning approach model), abstracts of studies using an additional measure emerged in the case of FDI and in that of learning approaches because these two constructs have been operationalized through more than one inventory. For example, when the key words "Embedded Figures Test" were entered, abstracts of studies using the "Preschool Embedded Figures Test" appeared. Similarly, when the key words "Learning Process Questionnaire" were entered, abstracts of several studies using the *Approaches to Studying Inventory* (Entwistle, 1981) also came up. Because studies using the *Approaches to Studying Inventory* and those employing the *Learning Process Questionnaire* and the *Study Process Questionnaire* are considered to be studies generated by style constructs from the same

TABLE 3.1. *Studies of Gender Differences in Field-Dependence/Independence*

Sources	Sample Size	Sample Description	Number of Studies Presented
Allen & Cholet (1978)	2,088	Various	Meta-analysis of 25 studies
Alvi, Khan, & Vegeris (1986)	1,056	6th, 8th, 9th, 10th, and 12th graders	1
Bernardi (1993)	516	Practicing accountants	1
Busch, Watson, Brinkley, Howard, & Nelson (1993)	37	3- to 5-year-old children	1
Caño & Márquez (1995)	293	Athletes (aged 18 to 23 years)	1
Connor & Serbin (1977)	26	3- to 5-year-old children	1
Gilmore, Wenk, Naylor, & Stuve (1992)	100	Younger group: 17 to 23 years Older group: 63 to 91 years	2
Hite (2004)	90	College students	1
Jamison & Signorella (2001)	29	7th and 8th graders	1
La Torre, Gossmann, & Piper (1976)	34	12 males, 14 females, and 8 transsexuals (age not specified)	1
Massa, Mayer, & Bohon (2005)	237	Female college students	1
Massari & Massari (1973)	73	Preschool children (35 to 59 months)	1
Pearson & Ferguson (1989)	282	College students	1
Signorella & Jamison (1978)	93	8th graders	1
Stoesz, Jakobson, Kilgour, & Lewycky (2007)	38	College students	2
Van Leeuwen (1978)	Information not available	Various	A review of 33 studies
Witkin & Berry (1975)	Information not available	Various	A review of numerous studies

"family" of models in the styles literature (see Chapter 2), studies involving the Approaches to Studying Inventory were also included in this review.

Field dependence/independence. One hundred and eighty-eight abstracts were obtained. An initial reading of these abstracts indicated that 35 articles had to do with gender differences in FDI. Full texts of 34 articles were located, 17 of which directly addressed the issue of gender differences in FDI. Of these, two were review articles, one was a meta-analysis study, and the remaining ones were single studies. Details of these 17 articles are shown in Table 3.1.

Personality Types. Seventy abstracts were obtained. An initial reading of these abstracts indicated that 42 of the articles concerned gender differences in personality types. Full texts of 36 articles were located, and it was found that 27 of them directly dealt with the issue of gender differences in personality types, of which one reported meta-analysis research on 14 studies involving 19 samples. Details of these 27 articles can be found in Table 3.2.

Learning Approaches. Twenty-eight abstracts were obtained. An initial reading of these abstracts revealed that 20 of them appeared to be on gender differences in learning approaches. Full texts of these 20 articles were located, and 16 of which were found to have a strong focus on the issue of gender differences in learning approaches. Details of these 16 articles are presented in Table 3.3.

Thinking Styles. Fifty-one abstracts were obtained. An initial reading of these abstracts indicated that 23 of them appeared to have reported gender differences in thinking styles. Full texts of these 23 articles were located, of which 16 reported gender differences in thinking styles. Details of these 16 articles are provided in Table 3.4.

Furthermore, in order to portray a more accurate picture of findings on gender differences in thinking styles, I included some existing data sets. Out of 50 sets of data I collected between 1998 and 2012, the first 12 data files stored in my computer were examined. Two of the 12 data sets had already been used as the basis for published work on gender differences in thinking styles, so the remaining 10 data sets were analyzed for gender differences in thinking styles, the results of which are reported in this chapter. In addition, I requested information from nine researchers, of whom five were identified through their publications, and four were my doctoral students whose research was on thinking styles. Three researchers in the former group responded with their findings on gender and thinking styles, and the four doctoral students provided information on five independent data sets. Therefore, results for 18 unpublished data sets (10 from me and eight from other researchers) became available for the present review. Table 3.5 shows the details of these samples as well as essential findings from these samples.

Gender Differences in Intellectual Styles: Research Evidence

Although two conflicting patterns of gender differences in learning approaches were identified, clear patterns of gender gaps in FDI, personality types, and thinking styles were revealed. This part reviews the relevant studies centered on each of the four style constructs and offers alternative explanations for the findings. In particular, the discussion focuses on the effects of

TABLE 3.2. *Studies of Gender Differences in Personality Types*

Sources	Sample Size(s)	Sample Description	Number of Studies Presented
Baker (1985)	98	8th graders	1
Brooks & Johnson (1979)	209	Undergraduate and graduate students	1
Carlson (1963)	129	43 6th graders and both of their parents (86)	1
Carlson (1965)	49	6th graders and then as high-school seniors	1 (longitudinal)
Carlson & Levy (1968)	163	College and community adults	1
Cecil (2009)	299	Professors	1
Cross, Neumeister, & Cassady (2007)	931	Gifted adolescents	1
Fleenor & Taylor (1994)	12,115	Managers attending leadership development programs	1
Gillespie (1999)	246	12th graders	1
Gordy & Thorne (1994)	195	Undergraduate students	1
Hammer & Mitchell (1996)	1,267	Adults	1
Kaufman, McLean, & Lincoln (1996)	1,297	Adolescents and adults	1
Levy, Murphy, & Carlson (1972)	758	Undergraduate students	1
MacDonald, Anderson, Tsagarakis, & Holland (1994)	209	Undergraduate students	1
Mills (2003)	63 and 1,247	Teachers (63) and gifted students (1,247)	1
Nuby & Oxford (1998)	278	High school students	1
Romans (1996)	74	Trainee psychologists	1
Sak (2004)	5,723 (from 19 independent samples)	Various	A review of 14 studies
Salter (2003)	421	Community college students	1
Schurr, Ruble, & Henriksen (1988)	1,902	Undergraduate students	1
Seegmiller & Epperson (1987)	42	Undergraduate students	1
Shiflett (1989)	67	Undergraduate students	1
Spirrison & Gordy (1994)	174	Undergraduate students	1
Stalikas & Fitopoulos (1998)	946	Undergraduate students	1
Stever (1995)	97	*Star Trek* fans	1
Swiatek & Cross (2007)	339	11th graders	1
Zimmerman (2001)	1,712 and 575	Technical college students	1

TABLE 3.3. *Studies of Gender Differences in Learning Approaches*

Sources	Sample Size(s)	Sample Description	Number of Studies Presented
Burnett & Proctor (2002)	580	6th and 7th graders	1
Clarke (1986)	153	Undergraduate students	1
Dart, Burnett, Boulton-Lewis, Campbell, Smith, & McCrindle (1999)	484	2nd through 5th graders	1
Eklund-Myrskog & Wenestam (1999)	549	Upper secondary school students	1
Gledhill & Van Der Merwe (1989)	176	Final-year medical school students	1
Meyer, Dunne, & Richardson (1994)	410	Undergraduate students	1
Richardson & King (1991)	Information not available	Undergraduate students	A review of multiple studies
Rose, Hall, Bolen, & Webster (1996)	202	Undergraduate students	1
Sadler-Smith (1996)	245	Undergraduate students	1
Sadler-Smith & Tsang (1998)	183 and 225	Undergraduate students	1
Watkins (1996)	162	7th and 8th graders	1
Watkins & Hattie (1981)	518 and 249	Undergraduate students	2
Watkins & Hattie (1990)	1,274	7th, 8th, and 11th graders	1
Wilson, Smart, & Watson (1996)	165 and 118	Undergraduate students	1
Zeegers (2001)	200	Undergraduate students	1
Zhang (2000)	67 and 652	Undergraduate students	1

gender-role socialization on intellectual styles. It concludes with a synthesis of the findings grounded in all four style models, pointing out where these findings converge.

Gender Differences in FDI Styles

Scholars have long been engaged in the study of gender differences in FDI. Indeed, of all the four style constructs reviewed in this chapter, FDI has been the most frequently investigated in relation to gender differences. The great majority of the studies acquired in the literature search reported significant gender differences in FDI, with males scoring significantly higher on field independence than females. Furthermore, all these studies suggested that

TABLE 3.4. *Studies of Gender Differences in Thinking Styles*

Sources	Sample Size(s)	Sample Description	Number of Studies Presented
Balkis & Isiker (2005)	367	Undergraduate students	1
Chen (2001)	238	Undergraduate students	1
Fan (2008)	238	Undergraduate students	1
Fan & Ye (2007)	203	School teachers	1
Fer (2007)	402	Trainee teachers	1
Gridley (2007)	218	Professional fine artists and engineers	1
Grigorenko & Sternberg (1997)	199	Gifted school students	1
Ho & Maarof (2009)	509	Trainee teachers	1
Sternberg & Grigorenko (1995)	124	6th through 10th graders	1
Wu & Zhang (1999)	195	Undergraduate students	1
Verma (2001)	203	Undergraduate students	1
Zhang (1999)	151	Undergraduate students	1
Zhang (2002)	245	Undergraduate students	1
Zhang (2008a)	194	School teachers and university academics	1
Zhang (2008b)	99	Undergraduate students	1
Zhang (2009)	378	Undergraduate students	1

gender differences in FDI could be attributed to socialization effects in one form or another, all concerning gender-role socialization. In other words, this research showed that FDI is changeable as a function of gender.

The earliest review of research on gender differences in FDI was conducted by Witkin and Berry (1975) as part of their bibliographic review of work on psychological differentiation. In that review, Witkin and Berry mentioned that approximately 500 studies (out of 2,500) directly or indirectly concerned gender differences, and they conducted an in-depth analysis on 35 of the studies. The year 1978 saw the publication of van Leeuwen's review article that examined gender differences in psychological differentiation even more closely. Both reviews were conducted from a cross-cultural perspective and they collectively led to four conclusions. First, gender differences in psychological differentiation, although small, were largely consistent, with males tending to be more field independent than females. Second, gender differences in psychological differentiation were neither significant nor consistent until early adolescence. Third, the degree of gender difference varied across cultures, with gender gaps being wider in cultures in which social conformity is valued

TABLE 3.5. *Gender Differences in Thinking Styles: Unpublished Data Sets*

Data Set	Nature of Sample	Findings
1) Author*	Mainland Chinese undergraduate students (N=400)	Males > Females on the Legislative, Liberal, and Internal Styles
2) Author*	Mainland Chinese undergraduate students (N=270)	Males > Females on the Judicial, Global, and Liberal Styles
3) Author*	Filipino high school students (N=692)	Females > Males on the Hierarchical Style
4) Author*	American undergraduate students (N=121)	Males > Females on the Legislative and Liberal Styles
5) Author*	American undergraduate students (N=132)	Females > Males on the Local and Conservative Styles
6) Author*	British business personnel (N=152)	Females > Males on the Hierarchical Style
7) Chen[a]	Austrian high school students (N=189)	Males > Females on the Liberal Style
8) Yu[a]	MaCau Chinese high school students (N=183)	Males > Females on the Global, Liberal, and Internal Styles
9) Kyriakides[b]	Cypriot secondary school students (N=1721)	Females > Males on the Executive Styles; Females < Males on the Liberal and Anarchic Styles
10) Fan[a]	Mainland Chinese high school students (N=196)	Males > Females on the Legislative, Monarchic, and Internal Styles
11) Author*	Filipino undergraduate students (N=429)	Males > Females on the Legislative, Monarchic, and Internal Styles
12) Yong[a]	Mainland Chinese undergraduate students (N=304)	Males > Females on the Legislative, Global, Liberal, and Internal Styles
13) Yong[a]	Tibetan Chinese undergraduate students (N=651)	Males > Females on the legislative, Judicial, Global, Liberal, Internal, and Monarchic Styles
14) Kao[b]	Taiwan Chinese primary school students (N=369)	Males > Females on the Global Style; Females > Males on the Local Style
15) Author*	Mainland Chinese undergraduate students (N=424)	N.S.
16) Author*	Mainland Chinese academics (N=246)	N.S.
17) Author*	British business personnel (N=117)	N.S.
18) Yeh[b]	Taiwan Chinese pre-service teachers (N=178)	N.S.

Note: *Author = my own data set; [a]data from my doctoral students; [b]data from researchers identified through their publications.

more. Finally, gender-role orientation was significantly related to psychological differentiation: people scoring more stereotypically masculine were more field independent than those scoring more stereotypically feminine. Although the authors in both reviews acknowledged the possible roles played by biological factors in gender differences in psychological differentiation, they also cogently argued that sociocultural factors, particularly gender-role socialization, played an important part in the male-female gaps in psychological differentiation. Females' poorly developed psychological differentiation was attributed mainly to their authority-ridden, homebound existence at that time (see van Leeuwen, 1978; Witkin & Berry, 1975 for details).

One naturally wonders whether or not the conclusions made more than three decades ago in the two aforementioned reviews have stood the test of time. The answer to this question is affirmative. Studies published since the appearance of these two reviews have continued to demonstrate male-female differences in psychological differentiation. Moreover, all these studies point to the dynamic nature of intellectual styles, and they fall into one of three types: (1) those demonstrating age and gender interaction effects; (2) those suggesting the effects of boundary crossing; and (3) those revealing the association between better performance on tests of psychological differentiation (i.e., higher levels of field independence) and masculine gender-role socialization.

Age and Gender Interaction. While men have been reported to be relatively more field-independent than women, such a stable gender difference does not seem to exist among young children. On the contrary, young girls have been found to be more field independent than boys in a great number of studies. For example, Kloner and Britain (1984) found that 4- to 5-year-old girls scored significantly higher on the *Preschool Embedded Figures Test* (PEFT) than did boys of the same ages. In reviewing the styles literature for young children, Kogan (1983) asserted that it is possible that girls are initially more field independent than boys and that gender differences in FDI are reversed after about 5 to 6 years of age.

More recent studies have also shown the moderating role of age in the relationship between gender and FDI. For example, Busch, Watson, Brinkley, Howard, and Nelson (1993) examined the effects of age and gender on the performance of 37 3- to 5-year-old children on the PEFT and found that differences in the PEFT scores between boys and girls were not the same across the ages tested. For the 3-year-old group, boys were more field independent than girls, whereas for the 4-year-old group, the reverse pattern was found: girls scored higher on field independence than did boys. The same pattern was found in the 5-year-old group as that in the 4-year-old group.

The dynamic nature of FDI associated with age and gender has been further supported by studies conducted among older people. For instance, consistent with the general pattern of male-female differences in FDI, results from Gilmore, Wenk, Naylor, and Stuve's (1992) experimental study suggested that males were significantly more field independent than females. Moreover, in the older group, there was "a striking gender effect" (Gilmore et al., 1992, p. 659): the gender gap in FDI became even wider, with the highest levels of field dependence being found among elderly women.

Particularly when one considers that gender differences in FDI exist among young children, that these differences generally persist throughout people's lives after young adolescence, and that such differences become even more pronounced at older ages, one could be convinced that FDI can be developed. More importantly, the development of FDI differs for males and females – despite the fact that other variables (such as age and culture) also play an important role in this development. Previous reviews (e.g., van Leeuwen, 1978; Witkin & Berry, 1975) have argued that gender-role socialization is largely responsible for the gender gap in FDI. The following offers support for this argument by providing research evidence revealed in studies beyond previous reviews.

Boundary Crossing. That FDI can be developed has also been shown in studies indicating that the gender gap usually found between males and females could well disappear or even be reversed when there is boundary crossing. The phenomenon of boundary crossing (also known as "crossing borders") refers to individuals going into nontraditional fields, or taking on roles that are traditionally played by individuals of the opposite gender. Boundaries can be crossed at various levels, including cultural, social, functional, and professional (American Association of University Women, 2002; Tullett, 1997).

DeSanctis and Dunikoski (1983) speculated that gender differences may only occur in liberal arts groupings and that in male-oriented fields such as business, there may be no gender difference. This speculation has found support in studies of FDI. For instance, several studies found no difference in the *Group Embedded Figures Test* scores between male and female accountants (Bernardi, 1993; Pincus, 1985). Likewise, other studies found no significant difference in FDI between male and female students in business administration (DeSanctis & Dunikoski, 1983; Young, Kelleher, & McRae, 1989).

In accounting for this lack of significant gender difference in FDI with respect to boundary crossing, one cannot help but think that this lack of a gender gap could very well be attributed to women developing field independence as a result of being socialized in male-dominated fields. That is, by crossing the boundaries between female-oriented and male-oriented fields, women have equal opportunities (let's presume that women feel this way) with men to be challenged to do the same kind of work that men do. Thus, compared with women in traditional fields, women in nontraditional fields tend to be more field independent and more compatible with their male counterparts as far as the level of field independence goes.

A reversed gender gap and a reduced gender gap have also been found in the sports world. Female athletes have been found to be more field independent than male athletes (Pargman, 1977). Caño and Márquez (1995) found that female team-sport athletes scored significantly higher on field dependence than individual-sport athletes or nonathletes of both genders. In other words, the male-female gap in FDI is not static; rather, it is modifiable depending on the kinds of exposure that female athletes receive. Early in 1987, McLeod proposed that participation in structured sports, which require similar or identical skills, could reduce gender differences in FDI.

Gender difference (or lack of gender difference, or reversed gender difference) associated with boundary crossing is not unique to the literature on FDI. For example, all existing studies of adaptive and innovative styles using the *Kirton Adaption-Innovation Inventory* (Kirton, 1976) have revealed that among the general population, women are usually more adaptive and men are normally more innovative (e.g., Jacobson, 1993; Prato Previde, 1991). However, women in leadership positions are more innovative than their male counterparts (e.g., McCarthy, 1993; Tullett, 1995). Research has also lent support to Kirton's (1976) argument that the more boundaries people cross, the more innovative they are in their thinking. For example, female managers in engineering have crossed at least three boundaries: social, professional, and functional. First, these women have crossed the social boundary by going outside their homes into the workplace. Second, they have crossed the professional boundary of working in a field that is still dominated by men. Third, by taking up leadership positions, these women have also crossed the boundary of working within their internal organizational structures. Instead, they often work with people beyond their own organizations (see Tullett, 1995, 1997).

It should be noted, however, that the aforementioned explanations are merely speculative. In the absence of evidence from longitudinal studies, one cannot claim for certain that females' development of field independence is the result of boundary crossing. It is possible that females tend to venture beyond boundaries precisely because they have a higher level of field independence.

Gender-Role Orientation. The dynamic nature of FDI is also manifest in findings concerning the significant relationships between FDI and gender-role orientation. These findings indicate that better performance on psychological differentiation tasks (i.e., higher scores on field independence) is related to a masculine gender-role orientation, especially among females.

Signorella and Jamison (1978, 1986) conducted a series of studies among young adolescents of both genders. In one study (Signorella & Jamison, 1978), they tested eighth-grade boys and girls on the *Group Embedded Figures Test* and on the *Bem Sex-Role Inventory* (Bem, 1974). The *Bem Sex-Role Inventory* provides classifications of individuals as masculine, androgynous, or feminine on the basis of the difference between the average self-ratings on masculine and feminine adjectives. It was concluded that the best predictor of success on the GEFT among girls was a masculine gender-role orientation. However, for adolescent boys, no significant association was found between the two variables. After more than two decades, these results were replicated in studies with seventh- and eighth-grade adolescent boys and girls (Jamison & Signorella, 2001), confirming that better performance on the GEFT was "almost always" (p. 250) associated with higher masculine scores and lower feminine scores for girls.

Indeed, in their meta-analysis study of the association between gender-role orientation and cognitive performance, Signorella and Jamison (1986) concluded that for most types of spatial tasks, including the *Embedded Figures Test*, better performance is significantly related to higher masculine and/or lower feminine scores in both genders (especially for females) and at all ages. These results imply that when females perceive themselves as possessing more masculine characteristics (e.g., self-confidence, independence), they can achieve higher scores on field independence – or to be more precise, females can achieve the level of field independence usually achieved by males at the very least.

The question then is: How do girls acquire a masculine self-concept? Several scholars have argued that gender-role socialization is important in the development of field dependence/independence. Early in 1978, Signorella and Jamison alluded to the idea that the superior performance of girls with a masculine self-concept on psychological differentiation tasks is a result of socialization. They posited that if gender-role measures reflect past experiences, girls with a masculine self-concept should have had experiences like those of most boys that are conducive to better performance in psychological differentiation tasks and in other gender-typed activities (see also Bem & Lenney, 1976). In this respect, the success of girls with a masculine self-concept has been attributed to the masculine stereotyping of psychological differentiation tasks (Jamison & Signorella, 2001). That is to say, how psychological differentiation tasks are presented to individuals should make a difference in their task performance. People with a masculine self-concept, be they males or females, do better on FDI tests when the FDI tasks are described as masculine tasks as opposed to female tasks. If this argument stands, the same task presented in different ways should appeal differently to people with a masculine self-concept than to people with a feminine self-concept.

Experimental studies (Massa, Mayer, & Bohon, 2005) conducted among college students in the United States lent strong support to this argument insofar as the results obtained from female participants. In the first experiment, the researchers administered the *Group Embedded Figures Test* (GEFT) and the *Bem Sex-Role Inventory* (Bem, 1981) to 237 female students attending introductory psychology courses. Two different types of instructions concerning the GEFT were given, one emphasizing the empathetic nature of the task, and the other indicating that the GEFT is a test that requires spatial ability. The students were randomly assigned to the two instructional conditions. Results revealed that female students with a masculine gender-role orientation scored significantly higher on the GEFT (thus more field independent) when the test was described as measuring spatial ability, whereas female students with a feminine gender-role orientation scored significantly higher when the test was said to be measuring empathy. In the second experiment, however, when the same materials and procedure were used with 99 male students from introductory psychology courses, the GEFT scores of the participants who received the empathy instructions were not significantly different from the scores of those who received the spatial instruction.

Examining holistically the previously discussed studies involving the test of gender-role orientation, one will notice that gender-role orientation appears to have a stronger influence on the levels of FDI of females than on those of males. Females are also more sensitive to the "gender role" of the cognitive task (e.g., "this is a feminine task"). This general pattern of findings suggests that one should be more sensitive to females' higher levels of awareness of their gender-role orientation.

Gender Differences in Personality Types

As previously mentioned, research on gender differences in personality types using the *Myers-Briggs Type Indicator* (MBTI) has also been fruitful. While almost all existing studies investigated gender differences on the thinking/feeling (T/F) scale, some studies examined gender differences beyond the T/F scale, others studied the predominant personality types of gifted students, and still others investigated the relationships of MBTI scores to cognitive performance. Whereas the first two types of studies (i.e., studies focusing on the T/F scale and those going beyond the T/F scale) reported distinct differential personality types between males and females, the third type of studies (i.e., studies of gifted students) suggested that the personality profiles of gifted students tended to resemble those of males. At the same time, the fourth and final type of studies – that is, studies concerning the relationships between individuals' MBTI scores and their cognitive performance – indicated that male-oriented personality type people tended to perform better cognitively.

The remainder of this section first introduces these four types of studies and then puts forward possible explanations for the findings obtained from these studies. The discussion will, as in the context of studies centered on FDI introduced in the previous section, conclude with the notion that gender differences in personality types are largely attributable to gender-role socialization. That is to say, personality types can be developed as a function of gender.

Gender Difference on the T/F Scale. Of the four MBTI dimensions, the one that has received the most attention regarding gender differences is that of thinking/feeling (T/F scale). Early in 1985, on the basis of a data bank involving 250,000 people ranging from high school students to adults, Myers and McCaulley concluded that males tend to be thinking-oriented and that females tend to be feeling-oriented. Indeed, Myers and McCaulley (1985) found the gender gap in people's preference in thinking and feeling so pronounced that they provided separate norms for males and females in their MBTI test manual. Since then, the male-female gap on the T/F scale has been a topic of enduring research interest among scholars. All but one study (Schurr, Ruble, & Henriksen, 1988) in the current review reported that male and female type distribution comparisons yielded a thinking preference for males and a feeling preference for females (e.g., Gillespie, 1999; Stever, 1995; Swiatek & Cross, 2007). In the case of Schurr et al.'s (1988) study, one could argue that the researchers presumed that the gender difference was present because they had controlled for gender when examining the relationships between the MBTI scores and SAT scores. The populations investigated in these more recent studies were diverse, ranging from mainstream secondary school and university students to gifted students, and from mass media subcultures (e.g., Stever, 1995) to national samples (e.g., Hammer & Mitchell, 1996).

Gender Differences beyond the T/F Scale. Although the T/F scale is the one that has consistently shown a significant difference between males and females, a great deal of evidence indicates that there is also a general tendency for males and females to differ significantly along the other three MBTI personality dimensions. For example, among a nationwide sample of 1,297 adolescents and adults in the United States, Kaufman, McLean, and Lincoln (1996) found that a larger percentage of males were identified to have the personality styles of intuition, thinking, and perceiving, while sensing, feeling, and judging personality styles were more commonly found among females. Among 209 introductory psychology students in Canada, MacDonald, Anderson, Tsagarakis, and Holland (1994) identified the same gender differences in personality styles.

However, in studies of gifted students, gender differences have been much more regularly reported in two of the four MBTI dimensions: the introversion-extraversion and the thinking-feeling dimensions. In the three review articles (Cross, Neumeister, & Cassady, 2007; Sak, 2004; Swiatek & Cross, 2007) located in the current literature search, 33 studies (either cited or reviewed in the three articles) were reported to have found that gifted male students were more introverted and thinking-oriented, and that gifted female students were more extraverted and feeling-oriented, than would normally be found in the general population.

If one considers the gender differences in personality types across populations found in different studies, one must surely conclude that introversion, thinking, intuition, and perceiving types are more frequently found among males, whereas extraversion, feeling, sensing, and judging types are more commonly identified among females. The question then arises: Does the gender gap in personality types mean that males have an advantage over females? The answer seems to be affirmative, and such a claim can be substantiated by findings from two types of research. The first is research on the personality profiles of gifted adolescents, and the second concerns research on the relationship between personality types and cognitive performance. In the following, findings from these two types of research are highlighted.

Personality Profiles of Gifted Adolescents. The personality characteristics of highly able adolescents have been widely researched since the mid 1970s (e.g., Delbridge-Parker & Robinson, 1989; Hawkins, 1997; McCarthy, 1975; Swiatek & Cross, 2007). Although researchers have defined the concept of giftedness differently, ranging from high academic ability to special talents in such areas as music and sports, they have all come to one overriding conclusion: gifted adolescents tend to have different personality profiles from those of the general adolescent population, despite the fact that gender differences in personality types within the gifted population take on the same patterns as those within the general adolescent population (see earlier discussion).

For example, Sak (2004) analyzed the data from 14 studies that contained 19 samples involving 5,723 gifted adolescents and compared their scores on each of the eight personality type scales with those of the general adolescent population. Results revealed that compared with the general adolescent population, gifted adolescents scored higher on the introversion, intuition, thinking, and perceiving scales. Moreover, the most common personality types among the gifted adolescents were intuitive and perceiving. Finally, compared with male gifted adolescents, gifted females were significantly more extraverted and more feeling- and judging-oriented.

The aforementioned general findings on the personality profiles of gifted students have been supported by more recent studies. In one study, Cross, Neumeister, and Cassady (2007) examined the personality types of 931 gifted adolescents who were attending a public residential academy in the United States. The researchers concluded that in general, both genders in this gifted sample tended to show intuitive and perceiving styles. Furthermore, although no significant gender difference was found in the perceiving-judging dimension and the thinking-feeling dimension, gender difference was found in the introversion-extraversion dimension. As is the case in the general population, gifted males were oriented more toward introversion, and gifted females were oriented more toward extraversion. Finally, gender-specific comparisons between gifted and normative samples suggested that gifted females were oriented more toward introversion and thinking, and that gifted males were oriented more toward introversion, although no significant difference was found between gifted males and the males in the general population with respect to the thinking scale. Collectively, these gender-specific comparative analyses suggested that giftedness is associated with the thinking and introversion personality types.

In another study, Swiatek and Cross (2007) examined the personality style profiles of 339 gifted students who had just entered a state-funded residential academy for academically gifted adolescents in the United States. As in previous studies, as a whole group, these gifted adolescents were characterized by their high levels of orientation toward intuition and perception. Moreover, as in previous studies of both general populations and gifted adolescents, gifted males were found to have higher scores on introversion and thinking, whereas gifted females scored higher on the extraversion and feeling scales.

As a final example, Mills (2003) investigated the personality styles of gifted students as well as those of effective teachers of gifted students. Results indicated that both groups of participants showed a strong orientation toward thinking and intuition (see also Mills & Parker, 1998, a study of both Irish and U.S. gifted adolescents).

Observant readers would by now have come to the realization that the personality style profiles of males in the general population closely resemble those of the gifted population. In a previous section ("Gender Difference beyond the T/F Scale"), it was shown that in the general population, males are more commonly found to be introverted, intuitive, thinking, and perceiving (INTP) types and that females tend to be more extraverted, sensing, feeling, and judging types (ESFJ). Likewise, earlier discussion in this section suggested that the gifted population en bloc is oriented more toward introversion, intuition, thinking, and perceiving, which closely resembles the personality profiles of males in the general population. Moreover, the majority of the participants in the studies of the gifted were identified as academically gifted, which indicates that there is a strong association between INTP personality types and better academic performance. Putting all the aforementioned information together, one could argue that the match between males' personality style profiles and those of gifted adolescents implies that males are typically at an advantage, at least insofar as academic performance is concerned. On the basis of this line of reasoning, one could further contend that in general, males have an advantage over females. Such a logically derived claim has been substantiated by empirical findings as presented in the following section.

Personality Types and Cognitive Performance. Significant relationships have been found between the MBTI scales and cognitive performance, including academic achievement and performance on standardized tests. For example, higher academic achievement scores and higher grade point averages have been found with individuals oriented more toward the introverted and intuitive personality styles (Kalsbeek, 1989; Myers & McCaulley, 1985). Among the articles originally located for the present chapter, one study, by Kaufman, McLean, and Lincoln (1996), investigated the relationship between MBTI scores and scores on the *Kaufman Adolescent and Adult intelligence Test* (KAIT, Kaufman & Kaufman, 1993) among 1,297 adolescents and adults across the United States. It was hypothesized that introverted, intuitive, and thinking type individuals would obtain higher scores on different indices generated by the KAIT: Fluid, Crystallized, and Composite IQs. Results indicated that although not all hypotheses were supported, intuitive type individuals obtained significantly higher KAIT Composite IQs than did sensing type individuals.

In a second study, Schurr, Ruble, and Henriksen (1988) examined the relationships between *Scholastic Aptitude Test* (SAT) scores and personality variables, including scores on personality styles as assessed by the MBTI, among 1,902 students in a public university in the United States. After classroom achievement and gender were controlled for, personality variables explained a significant amount of variance in both verbal and mathematics scores. Results specific to the MBTI scores showed that students who were oriented more toward introversion, intuition, and perception achieved higher scores on verbal SAT scores than did students with other personality styles. Moreover, students with the intuitive and perceptive styles obtained significantly higher mathematics SAT scores than did students with other personality styles.

Similar findings have been obtained by other scholars such as Gillespie (1999) and Raiszadeh (1999).

Obviously, results based on this limited number of studies cannot tell us for certain whether or not males have an advantage over females with regard to cognitive performance because of their differences in personality styles. Moreover, as Myers, McCaulley, Quenk, and Hammer (1998) suggested, the advantage of a particular personality style is relative; it depends on such factors as the academic and social environment, the curriculum, and the academic field of study (see Chapter 5 on academic discipline and intellectual styles). However, existing studies do consistently indicate that the personality types more commonly found among males (INTP) are more strongly related to better cognitive performance than are the personality types more commonly found among females (ESFJ).

Accounting for Gender Differences in Personality Types/Styles. Unlike in the literature on gender differences in FDI, where there has been much discussion arguing for the socialization effects of gender, in the literature on gender and personality types, there has been little discussion about why males and females tend to differ in personality types. Nevertheless, results from a series of studies conducted by Carlson and his colleague in the United States in the 1960s (Carlson, 1963, 1965; Carlson & Levy, 1968) may shed light on the socialization effects of gender on the development of personality types. In one study, Carlson and Levy (1968) administered the *Carlson Adjective Checklist* (an inventory that measures social-personal orientation) and the MBTI to 133 middle-class college and community adults. As an aspect of self-concept, *social-personal orientation* refers to a tendency to define one's self-concept in terms of being either socially oriented or personally oriented. The researchers concluded that gender differences in social-personal orientation were clearly established, with males being more frequently personally oriented and females more frequently socially oriented. Furthermore, there was a clear association between social-personal orientation and the MBTI dimensions. Personally oriented participants tended to be intuitive and thinking types, whereas socially oriented participants tended to be sensing and feeling types. By implication, these two sets of results as a whole suggested that males were more commonly found to be intuitive and thinking types and females were more typically sensing and feeling types. In another study, a 6-year longitudinal investigation, Carlson (1965) found that girls showed a significant increase in social orientation and that boys demonstrated an increase in personal orientation.

The major contribution of the research of Carlson and Levy is that findings from this research could serve as a bridge between the literature on gender differences in personality types and the literature on the differential socialization processes between males and females. Carlson and Levy demonstrated in their research that males and females have different social-personal orientation self-concepts, and that these self-concepts are closely related to personality types. These findings direct one to seek explanations for gender differences in personality types from the evidence revealing the differential socialization processes between males and females.

It should be noted that when one postulates the possible effects of gender-role socialization on personality types, one presumes that personality types can be changed. Indeed, research has shown that personality types can be modified. For example, according to Caspi, Roberts, and Shiner's (2005) comprehensive review of research on personality development, one's personality, including one's personality styles, can develop well into one's 50s – as a result of not only maturational processes but also historical processes (Helson, Kwan, John, & Jones, 2002).

Returning to the differential personality style development of males and females, one can discuss the effects of gender-role socialization along two of the four MBTI dimensions with empirical support. These are the introversion-extraversion dimension and the thinking-feeling dimension – the two dimensions along which gender differences have been well established not only among the gifted population, but also among the general population, as previously discussed. Along the introversion-extraversion dimension, gender-role socialization effects are apparent. Hofstede (1980) contended that the stability of gender-role patterns is more socialized than it is biologically determined. For males, the predominant socialization pattern is to be more assertive, whereas for females, it is to be nurturing. Males are expected to be autonomous, decisive, and strong, and to be independent problem solvers. By contrast, females are expected to be caring, collaborative, and obedient, and to place a higher value on interpersonal relationships (Ferguson, 1992; Gilligan, 1982; Nash, 1979). Although many of the traditional views about males and females have largely been shown to be false, these gender-role stereotypical views persist within and beyond schools (see *The Jossey-Bass Reader on Gender in Education*, 2002). Given such gender-specific social expectations, males would be likely to become more introverted and independent, whereas females would be likely to become more extraverted and group-oriented. Therefore, it is not surprising that the literature has consistently shown males' preference for introversion and females' preference for extraversion.

As for the thinking-feeling dimension, girls' lower scores on the MBTI thinking scale could also be partially attributed to the ways in which they are socialized. For example, it has been widely acknowledged that mathematics requires high levels of analytical and logical thinking (Lawrence, 1993) – an attribute normally possessed by individuals high on the MBTI thinking scale. However, girls often do not receive encouragement to continue with their mathematics study when they need it. Betz (1992) pointed out that it is critical to remember that gender-role socialization shapes girls and boys differently, that girls are not encouraged to continue to take mathematics, and that girls may need more help in building confidence and reducing anxiety with respect to studying mathematics.

Although the grim picture of widespread gender inequality in the classroom portrayed by the research findings obtained by the "second-wave" feminists in the 1970s and early 1980s can be said to be virtually nonexistent today, girls are still often ignored in mathematics and science classes (e.g., Burton, 1996; Francis, 2000; Lee, 1996). For example, the report of the study on girls' educational experiences by the American Association of Women Education Foundation (1992) stated that in practically every mathematics class observed, select male students received attention to the exclusion of other students of both genders. That is to say, not a single girl received attention from teachers. The study also found that, beginning in middle school, females had less confidence in their mathematical ability than did males. This, again, indicates that girls' lower scores on mathematics and associated thinking skills and personality styles could be the result of the discouragement that girls have received over a long period of time. The confidence in learning mathematics that girls initially display at a younger age diminishes as a consequence of how they have been socialized into an environment in which they receive the subtle (or not so subtle) message that girls are not expected to do well in mathematics or any other subject matter that requires a thinking personality. This loss of confidence in mathematics (thus perhaps a preference for thinking) at a young age corroborates the finding that girls tend to become sturdily field dependent by early adolescence (Kogan, 1983).

Although the much-discussed gender gap regarding the average numbers of mathematics courses taken by boys and girls appears to be diminishing, gender differences remain in the kinds of courses taken by girls versus boys. According to a report by the American Association of University Women Educational Foundation in 2002, more girls were then enrolling in algebra, geometry, pre-calculus, trigonometry, and calculus than in 1990. However, girls were more likely than boys to end their high school mathematics studies with Algebra II.

Gender Differences in Learning Approaches
As in the case of the results generated from the FDI construct and the personality type construct, the results from existing studies on learning approaches

are very telling, and discussions on this research are vibrant. To begin with, the question of whether gender differences in learning approaches have received too much or too little attention from researchers is a controversial one (Meyer, Dunne, & Richardson, 1994; Richardson & King, 1991; Wilson, Smart, & Watson, 1996). As well, studies on gender differences in learning approaches have yielded largely inconsistent results; some have been statistically significant and others not. Furthermore, findings from studies that obtained significant gender differences in learning approaches are also inconsistent, with some indicating that males tended to use the deep learning approach more frequently than females, and others suggesting that females tended to use the deep learning approach more frequently than males. To account for these conflicting findings, some scholars have examined methodological issues surrounding this area of research, while others have looked into learning environments that may have elicited different learning approaches on the part of male and female students.

Too Much Attention or Not Enough Attention. As just mentioned, scholars disagree on the amount of attention that gender differences in learning approaches have been given. For example, based on both their own research and their review of the literature, Meyer and his colleagues (Meyer, Dunne, & Richardson, 1994; Richardson & King, 1991) concluded that gender was a very important factor in student learning, including learning approaches. Meyer, Dunne, and Richardson (1994) argued that "gender differences constitute a potentially important and neglected source of variation in student learning which, when detected in context, can and should be explicitly managed by academic practitioners" (p. 469). On the other hand, two years after Meyer and his colleagues advanced their argument, Wilson, Smart, and Watson (1996), in discussing the results of their study, expressed their confidence in asserting that there was no gender difference in approaches to learning with the students in their study. Wilson and her colleagues' confidence came from three sources: (1) the results of their own research on first-year psychology students, showing no gender difference in learning approaches; (2) the fact that only two of the nine previous studies they had reviewed identified significant gender differences; and (3) their argument that even Richardson and King (1991), advocates of research on gender differences in learning approaches, had indicated that the magnitudes of the statistically significant differences were small.

Contradictory Findings. With respect to the findings identified in the present literature review, some revealed gender differences, while others did not (e.g., Wilson et al., 1996; Zeegers, 2001). Of the studies revealing significant gender differences in learning approaches, some (e.g., Meyer et al., 1994; Sadler-Smith, 1996; Zhang, 2000) generally indicated that males scored higher on the deep learning approach and that females reportedly used the surface approach and (to a lesser extent) the achieving learning approach more frequently. However, other studies (e.g., Burnett & Proctor, 2002; Dart, Burnett, Boulton-Lewis, Campbell, Smith, & McCrindle, 1999; Gledhill & van Der Merwe, 1989) obtained the opposite findings, that is, that males tended to score higher on the surface approach and (to a lesser extent) on the achieving approach, whereas females tended to score higher on the deep learning approach.

In the case of males scoring higher on the deep learning approach and females scoring higher on the surface approach and somewhat higher on the achieving approach, Meyer et al. (1994) systematically analyzed the responses to a modified and expanded version of the *Approaches to Studying Inventory* (Entwistle, 1981) of 410 students in a higher educational institution in South Africa. The researchers concluded that male students distinctively manifested a deep approach to learning and that female students clearly showed an achieving learning approach. In another study, based on the responses to the *Revised Approaches to Studying Inventory* (Entwistle & Tait, 1994) of 245 business studies students in the United Kingdom, Sadler-Smith (1996) concluded that males reported adopting a deep approach to learning and that females reported using a more surface-orientated learning approach. As a final example, results from my study of learning approaches (as assessed by the *Study Process Questionnaire*, Biggs, 1987) among university students in Hong Kong and mainland China are also generally supportive of findings showing that females tend to use the surface and achieving approaches to learning and that males tend to report a deep approach to learning (Zhang, 2000).

The opposite findings, that males tended to report using the surface approach to learning and (to a lesser degree) the achieving approach, whereas females tended to report using a deep approach to learning have been obtained among students of elementary schools, secondary schools, universities in several parts of the world, including Australia, Finland, the Philippines, and South Africa. For example, using the deep and the surface scales of the *Learning Process Questionnaire* (Biggs, 1987), Burnett and Proctor (2002) investigated the learning approaches adopted by 580 elementary school students in Australia. Girls reported adopting the deep learning approach more frequently than did boys, whereas boys scored significantly higher on the surface learning approach than did girls. Similarly, in studying the learning approaches of 549 upper secondary school students in Finland, Eklund-Myrskog and Wenestam (1999) found that boys scored significantly higher on the surface learning approach, although gender difference in the use of the deep approach to learning did not reach a statistically significant level (see also Dart, Burnett, Boulton-Lewis, Campbell, Smith, & McCrindle, 1999; Watkins & Hattie, 1981).

As a final example, Gledhill and van Der Merwe (1989) examined the learning approaches of final-year medical school students in South Africa. Males tended to report using the surface and achieving learning approaches more often, whereas females reported using the deep learning approach more often.

Accounting for the Contradictory Findings. Wilson et al. (1996) identified several methodological issues that could have contributed to the fact that some studies found no significant gender difference and others did. These methodological issues include the lack of reporting effect sizes, the use of data sets with less than satisfactory response rates, differential representation of male and female participants in research samples, and the employment of inappropriate statistical procedures. All of these issues are, no doubt, important ones. However, considering that the statistically significant results in the current review generally fall into two categories of findings that tell opposite stories about the specific ways in which males and females differ in their learning approaches, one needs to go beyond considering methodological issues in interpreting the literature.

In addition to gender, there are many other factors, both personal and environmental, that can influence people's learning approaches (see Figure 5.1 "Model of Student Learning" in Chapter 5). Consider the effects of age and school level. Age has often been found to interact with gender to make a significant difference in students' learning approaches (Sadler-Smith & Tsang, 1998). In explaining the gender differences they found among Finnish upper secondary school students, Eklund-Myrskog and Wenestam (1999) contended that the gender gap in learning approaches might be specific to the age/grade level at which students were confronted with the matriculation examination. Boys and girls use different learning approaches to meet the special educational demands of the matriculation examination. Indeed, how students are assessed determines the way students learn (Biggs, 2010). The nature of the subject matter learned also requires different learning approaches (again, see Figure 5.1 "Model of Student Learning" in Chapter 5). As a final example, people from different cultures might be influenced by social desirability to varying degrees, which could lead individuals to score differently on the various learning approaches (Hui & Triandis, 1989; Watkins, 1996).

However, regardless of the methodological issues and despite the other factors that possibly confounded the findings concerning gender differences in learning approaches, there appears to be a great deal of evidence for the differential learning approaches reported by males and females. These systematic gender differences in learning approaches do not appear at random; rather, they are likely to be the outcome of the differential socialization processes that males and females experience within and beyond school contexts. Early in 1976, Marton pointed out that students' approaches to learning depend on their perceptions of the content, the context, and the demands of the learning tasks. Meyer et al. (1994) argued that all environmental factors in learning are open to being presented in a manner that differentiates between males and females. For example, there is evidence suggesting that university science departments tend to challenge the personal identity and confidence of female students, especially of those who have received their secondary school education in single-sex schools (Thomas, 1988). Unfortunately, such destruction of self-confidence is not conducive to a learning attitude that would translate into a deep learning approach. Researchers have found that self-confidence is critically related to a deep approach to learning (Burnett & Proctor, 2002). Clarke's (1986) study of medical school students in Australia dovetailed with such a finding, revealing that women reported a surface approach to learning, lower levels of academic self-confidence, and higher levels of fear of failure. Such evidence implies that females tend to adopt a surface approach to learning at least partially because of their lack of confidence and their fear of failure. In explaining their finding that a much larger percentage of male psychology major students were classified as having a constructive (deep) conception of learning (in contrast to female students), van Rossum and Schenk (1984) asserted that the different conceptions of learning were "largely formed in the upbringing and all the educational situations a person participates in" (p. 82). Richardson and King (1991) commented that van Rossum and Schenk's explanation signified that female students were less likely than male students to be exposed to the cultural influences that promote a deep approach to learning. That is to say, gender-role socialization might have contributed to the gender gap in learning approaches.

Gender Differences in Thinking Styles
Gender differences also exist in thinking styles. In fact, noticeable patterns of gender differences have been identified. Among the published studies, the predominant pattern is for males to score higher than females on four of the five Type I thinking styles (legislative, judicial, global, and liberal styles; the exception being the hierarchical style) and the internal style. By contrast, females tend to score higher than males on three of the four Type II styles (executive, conservative, and local styles; the exception being the monarchic style). These general patterns have been identified among school students, school teachers, university students, and academics in several cultural contexts, including Hong Kong, mainland China, Turkey,[1] and the United States

---

[1] It should be noted, however, that in the particular sample of Turkish university students being referred to in this context, males scored higher on the external style rather than the internal style.

(e.g., Balkis & Isiker, 2005; Tucker, 1999; Zhang, 2008). This general finding revealed in the published work is supported by 10 of the 17 unpublished data sets obtained from Austria, Cyprus, mainland China, Macau, and the United States (see also Table 3.5).

Most likely owing to the fact that examining gender differences in thinking styles was not among the major aims of the above studies, only one of them (Balkis & Isiker, 2005) discussed the possible factors that might have contributed to gender differences in thinking styles. In explaining their finding that males scored higher on Type I styles and the external style, Balkis and Isiker (2005) alluded to the effects of gender-role socialization, stating that: "The findings can be interpreted through the different roles which are attributed to the members of each gender in Turkish society. While girls are brought up under social pressure and are expected to be conventional and obedient, boys are brought up to be extroverted individuals and are expected to preserve the customs in Turkish society" (p. 291).

Indeed, Zhang and Sternberg (2006) made similar remarks. In observing the general pattern in our study that males tended to score higher on the global style and that females tended to score higher on the local style, we commented that this general finding seemed to confirm the stereotypical view that men are expected to focus on the bigger picture and to make "major" decisions, whereas women are expected to make "minor" decisions and to be more careful so as to get the details correct. Regarding the general finding in our study that males tended to score higher on the legislative and liberal styles than did females, we argued that this gender gap also has much to do with gender-role socialization. Traditionally, the legislative and liberal styles have been more acceptable in men than in women. Most societies expect men to set the rules and women to follow them. This tradition is changing, yet it would probably be fair to say that many of the disadvantages women have experienced in sciences, business, and elsewhere have stemmed from the fact that it is considered stylistically inappropriate for women to give orders rather than to follow them. Even today, young girls are socialized into stylistic roles in a way that is to their disadvantage if they later try to succeed in a variety of life pursuits.

However, the one exception to the pattern of males scoring higher on Type I styles and females scoring higher on Type II styles is worth noting. That is, males have consistently been found to score higher on the monarchic style, a Type II style, whereas females have consistently been found to score higher on the hierarchical style, a Type I style. Although this finding seems to be at odds with the general finding that males tend to score higher on Type I styles and females score higher on Type II styles, it should not be surprising whatsoever if one considers the different gender role expectations. Traditionally, men are generally perceived to be successful if they simply do well in one thing: playing the role of the breadwinner of the family. Similarly, in modern society, men are often regarded as being successful as long as they do well in their careers. However, women have always been expected to play multiple roles. Traditionally, women are expected to take care of everything that has to do with the family, including farming, cooking, and taking care of not only their children, but also their husbands, their parents, and their in-laws. In modern times, women continue to play multiple roles, not only within their families, but also at work. To be successful, women have to be able to set priorities for the various functions they are expected to serve (Pinker, 1997). Again, it would not be surprising if such social expectations affected the ways young boys and girls are socialized in today's world. Such socialization would contribute to the development of the differences in thinking styles between men and women.

As in the literature generated by the previous three style models (FDI, personality types, and learning approaches), the literature on thinking styles contains studies that revealed no gender difference (e.g., Gridley, 2006b; Grigorenko & Sternberg, 1997; Zhang, 2008). This is also the case with four of the 17 unpublished data sets previously mentioned. However, the lack of significant findings in these studies does not mean that gender differences in thinking styles do not exist. As previously discussed, the great majority of studies have not only revealed gender differences, but also shown particular patterns of gender differences in thinking styles, patterns that can be explained largely by gender-role socialization and that are also in concert with findings based on other models (see the following section, "Summary").

Moreover, there could be various reasons why some studies did not identify gender differences. For example, it is possible that other relevant factors were not taken into account when the relationship between gender and thinking styles was examined. One such factor is age. When Fan and Ye (2007) investigated the thinking styles of Shanghai primary and secondary school teachers, although they did not identify any gender difference among the younger groups of participants, they found that among the participants aged between 41 and 50 years, female teachers scored significantly higher on the local style than did male teachers. Occupation is another obvious factor. Gridley (2007), for example, found that among artists, there was no significant gender difference in thinking styles. However, in the same study, Gridley found that among engineers, males scored higher than did females on the internal style. In other words, when potential confounding factors in the relationship between gender and thinking styles were controlled for, significant gender gaps in thinking styles emerged. Moreover, the ways in which males and females differed in thinking styles in Gridley's study were consistent with those revealed in the general trends – males score higher on the internal style, and females score higher on the local style.

Summary: General Findings across the Four Models

Having been introduced to the findings based on each of the four style models, one might naturally be wondering whether or not a coherent story can be told when findings across the four models are examined collectively. The answer is affirmative. This assertion can be substantiated through highlighting the main findings based on each model and by showing where these findings converge.

Although, to varying degrees, there are exceptions to the general findings on gender differences in styles based on all four models, a principal finding stands out in studies grounded in three of the four models. That is, in general (with the exception of findings centered on learning approaches), males tend to employ Type I intellectual styles and styles that are more personally oriented, whereas females tend to employ Type II intellectual styles and styles that are more socially oriented. Specifically, with regard to Witkin's concept of psychological differentiation, males are generally more field independent than are females. Concerning Jung's construct of personality type, males generally tend to be oriented more toward introversion, thinking, intuition, and perceiving, whereas females generally tend to be oriented more toward extraversion, feeling, sensing, and judging. Finally, in relation to Sternberg's construct of thinking styles, males generally score higher on Type I thinking styles and the internal style, whereas females normally score higher on Type II thinking styles and the external style (see Table 2.1 in Chapter 2 for classification of style types).

With respect to the concept of learning approaches, however, two conflicting, but equally predominant, trends can be discerned in the findings. One general trend suggests that males tend to adopt the deep approach to learning and females tend to adopt the surface approach to learning, whereas the other trend suggests the opposite. One factor possibly responsible for such conflicting results is the higher degree of modifiability of learning approaches compared with the other three style constructs. If one looks at Curry's (1987) onion model of styles, one will notice that the learning approach construct lies much closer to the outermost layer of the "onion." Being closer to the outermost layer of the Curry's onion, learning approaches are expected to be more amenable to change as a function of one's learning environment than are the other three style constructs.

At this point, observant readers might be wondering about an apparent inconsistency in the classification of styles. In accordance with our threefold model of intellectual styles (Zhang & Sternberg, 2006), this review has classified four personality types (i.e., thinking, feeling, introversion, and extraversion) and four thinking styles (i.e., oligarchic, anarchic, internal, and external) into the Type III style category. However, results from the present review of gender differences in intellectual styles appear to suggest that the internal thinking style and the introversion and thinking personality types possess strong characteristics of Type I styles (i.e., they seem to have more adaptive value) and that the external thinking style and the extraversion and feeling personality types possess strong characteristics of Type II styles (i.e., they seem to have more maladaptive value). It might then be asked: Should the internal thinking style and the introverted and thinking personality types be re-classified as Type I intellectual styles, and the external thinking style and the extraverted and feeling personality types be reclassified as Type II styles? I would argue that such a proposed reclassification would be premature. Our original classification of the three types of styles was based on a much broader review of the literature on intellectual styles, whereas findings in this chapter are restricted to those concerning gender differences in four style constructs. Any attempt to reclassify the aforementioned styles should await further research evidence supporting what has been revealed in the present findings regarding gender differences in styles.

Conclusions, Limitations, and Implications

Conclusions

As pointed out at the beginning of this chapter, early researchers (e.g., Van Leeuwen, 1978; Witkin & Berry, 1975) reviewed work on gender differences in FDI, only one of the many style constructs in the field of intellectual styles. The present review has gone far beyond examining work that was merely rooted in FDI. Obviously, the present review is also significant because the previous reviews on gender differences in styles were all done more than three decades ago. Results of this review fundamentally support those of the two previous systematic reviews (van Leeuwen, 1978; Witkin & Berry, 1975). That is, by and large, there are consistent gender gaps in intellectual styles. In the context of the present review, this is particularly true with regard to the findings based on investigations of FDI, personality types, and thinking styles. The findings on the relationship between styles and gender should lead one to draw the conclusion that styles can be developed partially on the basis of the different socialization patterns of men and women. Nevertheless, it must be remembered that this conclusion should be drawn with one's consideration of the limitations of the existing research on gender and styles.

Limitations

It should be noted once again that findings centered on learning approaches are essentially equivocal. In addition, there are at least three general limitations with the existing body of literature on gender differences in intellectual styles.

First, as has been demonstrated, there is a general lack of research on style differences based on gender. As a matter of fact, obtainable research is confined to studies based on only several models despite the existence of the massive number of style constructs. Second, as is the case in other research topics dealt with in this book, studies on gender and styles also seldom report effect sizes.

The third and final limitation of the existing literature on gender and styles is that there has been virtually no research on gender differences in styles that takes an experimental approach or a qualitative approach, nor has there been any research that is longitudinal in nature. Such limitations await future researchers to be overcome. Unlike correlational studies, experimental, qualitative, and longitudinal studies are more rigorous in the sense that findings from such studies would be more informative with regard to addressing such questions as exactly how and why males and females tend to differ in their intellectual styles.

Three questions arise from the inconsistent findings on learning approaches and the general limitations in existing research on gender differences in styles. First, what can researchers do to understand better some of the conflicting results documented in this review, especially in relation to gender differences in learning approaches? Second, what can researchers do to overcome the more general limitations of existing work? Third, despite the limitations of the studies reviewed here, what are the practical implications of the findings for education and beyond? The remainder of this chapter answers these questions.

Implications for Research

To understand the conflicting findings centered on learning approaches, researchers must design and execute investigations that have a clear and rigorous research agenda. Most noticeably, researchers must deal with some of the methodological issues raised by Wilson et al. (1996). These include, but are not limited to, obtaining satisfactory response rates, ensuring roughly equal representation of male and female participants in research samples, and employing appropriate statistical procedures in data analyses.

More generally, in order for the claim that the gender gaps in intellectual styles can be at least partially attributable to gender-role socialization to be substantiated, much more research needs to be conducted, and researchers are strongly encouraged to make every effort to address the aforementioned limitations in the research on gender and styles. Furthermore, researchers must be aware that there are other factors that potentially confound the relationship between gender and intellectual styles. Such factors must be taken into account when investigating gender differences in styles.

Finally and more broadly speaking, the overall finding that styles can differ on the basis of gender has an important implication for conducting research on styles in general. At present, only a small proportion of the existing literature on styles takes the gender variable into account when examining the relationships between styles and other constructs. With the importance of the role of gender in intellectual styles having been reinforced by the present review, and given that the styles of males and females may develop differently, researchers should make a special effort to distinguish the potential confounding effects of gender on the relationship between styles and other constructs under investigation. That is to say, taking gender into account will enable researchers to obtain research findings that will portray more accurately the relationships between styles and the other constructs.

Implications for Education and Beyond

As mentioned in Chapter 1 and illustrated in Chapter 2, Zhang and Sternberg (2006, 2009b) have argued that compared with Type II styles (typified by a tendency toward nonconformity), Type I intellectual styles (characterized by a creativity-generating tendency) are more adaptive and should be encouraged. Other scholars (e.g., Kaufman & Baer, 2009; Sadler-Smith, 2009) have endorsed this argument with their own empirical data and conceptual arguments. At the same time, the current review has demonstrated that males generally score higher on Type I styles and styles that tend to be more personally oriented, whereas females generally score higher on Type II styles and styles that tend to be more socially oriented.

Collectively, what do these findings say about males and females? They suggest that males are generally encouraged to develop creativity-generating intellectual styles and to be autonomous, whereas females are typically expected to think more traditionally, to conform to existing rules and procedures, and to be group oriented. Such a general message from these findings, however, presents a challenge to the education arena. That is, Type I styles have been empirically shown to be more adaptive than Type II styles (see Chapter 2). Furthermore, in at least the school context, styles that are more personally oriented (e.g., the introversion personality type and the internal thinking style) are often associated with better school performance. Results in the current review encompassing studies spanning several decades and studies based on four carefully selected style models indicate that gender differences in intellectual styles are generally consistent and widespread. As discussed earlier, although much more needs to be done to understand further the origins of these gender differences, it does seem that differential socialization patterns associated with gender-relevant concepts such as gender-role beliefs, gender-role expectations, and gender stereotyping are partially responsible for these differences. In the education arena, it appears that learning environments have yet to be designed to be more female-friendly. The issue of gender differences in intellectual styles has to be acknowledged by various parties in educational institutions (e.g., teachers, student development educators, senior managers), particularly by classroom teachers because they have the most direct contact with students and thus exert the strongest impact on students, both males and females.

The question then is: What can teachers do to create a learning environment that provides males and females with equal opportunities for excellence in achievement and that encourages female students to use more Type I intellectual styles that are often associated more closely with future success?

Consider the following suggestions. Teachers could open up discussions with students on gender differences in intellectual styles. As illustrated earlier, the gender gaps in intellectual styles are largely created by environments, and in particular, by the ways in which males and females are differentially socialized. Traditional stereotypical views of males and females still sturdily affect teachers' teaching and students' learning and development in modern educational settings. Therefore, these traditional values must be put forward for open discussions. Ultimately, the aim of such discussions is to build up female students' confidence and to assist them in overcoming their fear of failure (or fear of success) as a result of gender stereotyping. Misconceptions associated with gender stereotyping must be corrected.

One way in which teachers could help their female students overcome their fear of failure/success and develop their Type I intellectual styles is by providing them with more opportunities to expand their repertoires of learning experiences. A great deal of research evidence has indicated that boundary crossing is conducive to the development of intelligence, creativity, and Type I intellectual styles (Nash, 1979; Tullet, 1997; Zhang & Sternberg, 2006). By encouraging female students to venture into territories that they never thought they, as females, would enter, and guiding them in the process, teachers could help female students conquer their fear of failure/success in areas that are perceived as male "territories." This can be done, for example, through implementing nontraditional role assignments within and beyond the classroom. It is common to observe that males tend to be assigned to leadership roles in student associations and organizations. Indeed, it is often the case that females look to males for leadership. Teachers could help change such common practice by directly assigning female students to leadership roles, expressing higher expectations for female students, and encouraging students to be involved in peer activities that are gender integrated, as opposed to gender segregated. Moreover, teachers could take a step further by educating parents and society to change their attitudes toward and expectations for female students. For example, parents can be educated to avoid involving their children in activities in a gender-typed way. Instead, parents should engage their children in a wide range of activities, be they traditionally feminine or masculine ones.

For certain, teachers could also do a great deal to create a classroom climate that would accommodate female students' preferred way of learning (e.g., a so-called feeling classroom that is warm and involving). However, as a follow-up step to these proposed strategies, teachers could also deliberately challenge female students to develop ways of learning and thinking that they may not be comfortable with initially, but that ultimately could well be beneficial to their positive development. This is especially true for students in higher educational institutions. As pointed out by Sadler-Smith (1996), all students in higher education, regardless of age and gender, are required to use their initiative in learning.

As another example, in the era of information technology, in which computerized instruction (and, at times, assessment) is becoming increasingly more popular across different levels of educational institutions worldwide, it is more important than ever before to be sensitive to gender differences in intellectual styles. A great deal of research has suggested that the outcomes of using computerized instruction and assessment can vary dramatically depending on many factors, including individual-difference variables such as gender and intellectual styles. In this respect, female students and students with an inclination to use Type II styles and socially oriented styles are generally disadvantaged (Canino & Cicchelli, 1988; Yelland & Lloyd, 2001; Zhang & He, 2003). Therefore, in designing and implementing computerized instruction and assessment, teachers should take steps to ensure that female students have equal opportunities to demonstrate their success in learning. At the same time, more support should be provided for female students to acquire the skills necessary to do well in learning through using computing and information technology.

Perceptive readers might, by now, be wondering: What about the fact that males perform more poorly in verbal skill areas? Shouldn't this be considered as well? They might further ask: What are the broader educational implications of the general finding that males and females differ in their intellectual styles?

For example, what is the role of teacher education in this? How can curriculum and assessment perpetuate or help eliminate unfair gender treatment in the classroom?

So far, much of the discussion has been focused on how teachers should encourage female students to develop Type I styles because this review suggests that females tend to score lower on Type I styles – styles that seem to be more conducive to better learning and development. However, encouraging female students to develop Type I styles does not mean that teachers should pay less attention to male students, and in particular to the areas in which male students tend to be weak, such as in performance related to verbal skills. Therefore, it is clear that teachers need to strike a balance between encouraging female students to develop Type I styles using the aforementioned strategies on the one hand, and addressing male students' needs such as in the area of verbal skills on the other. More specifically, there is a need to create curriculum and assessment that would help reduce unfair gender treatment. There are many ways to achieve this balance so as to promote gender fairness. Researchers and practitioners in the field of intellectual styles would recommend that teachers design a curriculum that would allow diverse intellectual styles. Such a curriculum should concern not only the contents of teaching and learning, but also instructional methods and assessment formats. Teachers could be engaged in many activities to allow for diverse intellectual styles among students. For example, teachers could facilitate students' use of different intellectual styles by diversifying their instructional methods and assessment schemes. This diversification is necessary because whereas some students may learn better when teachers' instructions leave plenty of room for imagination, others may learn more effectively when teachers provide more detailed guidelines. Ultimately, a learning environment that allows for diverse styles and that encourages the use of Type I styles would lead to positive learning and developmental outcomes.

It is true that teachers are in the best position to adopt strategies to narrow the gender gap in intellectual styles (or more broadly, gender gaps in intellectual functioning) among students because teachers interact with students for a significant amount of time, regardless of the levels of schooling at which students study. However, it should be realized that the differences in intellectual styles associated with gender are the outcomes of the interaction among many factors that are intricately intertwined. It should be further recognized that the gender gap (and gaps based on many other factors) in intellectual styles has existed throughout human history and in all cultures. It has been deeply embedded in student learning and development, and it has been the concern of many scholars for at least the past half-century (Friedman, 1963).

For such a gender gap (or any other gap) to be narrowed, concerted and long-term efforts are required not only from teachers, but also from other parties in educational institutions and in society at large.

For example, within an educational institution, student development educators can do much to cultivate diverse intellectual styles among both male and female students. For example, they could design and implement programs aimed at cultivating students' tendency to appreciate and openly discuss different values and traditions, in particular those that entail gender-stereotypical views.

Outside educational institutions, society – particularly parents – could contribute to the reduction of gender gaps in intellectual styles (again, more broadly, intellectual functioning). As evidenced from research findings, children's intellectual function and behaviors have much to do with parental gender-stereotyped beliefs, values, achievement expectations, and parent-child interactions (Eccles, Jacobs, & Harold, 1990; Huston, 1983; Katz, 1987; Kulik, 2005; McHale, Crouter, & Tucker, 1999). Given such research evidence, parents must be aware of the important role they play in their children's intellectual and behavioral development. Such awareness can be raised through, among other channels, the close collaboration of schools with parents. In this respect, one example of educating parents about the critical role they can play in their children's intellectual development, including the development of intellectual styles, would be conducting workshops for parents in which gender-related issues, among other topics, could be addressed.

Finally, it should be noted that the implications of the general finding that the intellectual styles of males and females develop differently have been discussed solely within the academic context. Nonetheless, this does not mean that the implications of the different intellectual styles associated with different socialization patterns of men and women are less important in nonacademic settings. On the contrary, much can be done and should be done to show sensitivity to gender differences in intellectual styles generally. At the very least, men and women should be given equal opportunities for challenging tasks, for when women are challenged to go beyond borders, their Type I intellectual styles will be developed.

4

Culture and Intellectual Styles*

Are intellectual styles universal, or are they culture-specific? How would the answer to this question address the issue of style malleability? Answers to these questions are important not only because they can inform future research in the field, but also because they have implications for education and for the general public.

This chapter takes the argument that intellectual styles are adaptable a step further by integrating some of the major conceptualizations and empirical investigations of the relationships between culture and styles. The chapter is divided into five parts. The first part introduces the concept of culture and the theoretical models of culture. In particular, it describes one of the most prominent theoretical models of culture: Geert Hofstede's (1980) four-cultural systems. The second part discusses the conceptual link between culture and intellectual styles and proposes a guiding hypothesis concerning the relationships between culture and intellectual styles. The third part describes the literature search procedures and results. The fourth part reviews studies that are relevant to the hypothesis. Finally, the chapter closes with a discussion on the limitations of making and testing the aforementioned hypothesis and the implications of the reviewed findings for research in the field and for education and beyond.

Culture and Theoretical Models of Culture

Culture

There have been many insightful definitions of culture (e.g., Adler, 2001; Brislin, Bochner, & Lonner, 1975; Tylor, 1958). In this book, I use Hofstede's

---

* The present chapter draws heavily on the work by Sternberg and myself, titled "Culture and Intellectual Styles," published in *Handbook of Intellectual Styles* (Zhang, Sternberg, & Rayner, 2012).

(1990) definition of culture: "the collective programming of the mind that distinguishes the members of one category of people from another" (p. 4). This chapter restricts its survey of cross-cultural studies of intellectual styles to cultural distinctions based on countries and regions or ethnic groups within countries (see also Chapter 9 where the discussion is broadened to include other socialization variables).

Theories of Culture
In the broad cross-cultural literature, theoretical models of culture have been constructed by scholars in different academic fields. For example, in anthropology, Edward Hall (1976) proposed a cultural classification of high-context culture and low-context culture. In psychology, based on their study of the self-construct of different people across cultures, Hazel Markus and Shinobu Kitayama (1991) divided cultures into interdependent self-construal ones and independent self-construal ones. In sociology, John Berry (1991) articulated an ecocultural model with the aim of comprehending the systematic relationships among ecological, cultural, and behavioral variables. All these models could be used effectively to argue that culture influences intellectual styles. However, the cultural dimensions described in Hofstede's (1980, 1997) theoretical model in the field of management are selected to guide this chapter because the conceptual links between these cultural dimensions and the intellectual styles under discussion are the most obvious. Moreover, Hofstede's model distinguishes itself from the other models by its concern with multiple dimensions of culture.

Hofstede's Cultural Dimensions and Their Conceptual Link to Intellectual Styles
Hofstede's cultural dimensions are the result of his analysis of a database (containing data from two successive survey rounds, four years apart) established by a multinational corporation (IBM). Of the 71 countries for which survey data were available, 40 countries had sample sizes that were considered to be large enough to allow for reliable comparison. The survey was designed to identify employees' basic cultural values. Four basic dimensions emerged from the surveys: power distance, uncertainty avoidance, individualism (versus collectivism), and masculinity (versus femininity).

Power Distance. The basic issue involved in power distance is human inequality, which refers to the extent to which the less powerful members of a society accept the unequal distribution of power and expect this to be the case. The level of power distance is socially determined and is endorsed by the followers as much as by the leaders. Jones and Herbert (2000) suggested that a low power-distance society is conducive to creativity because it allows individuals more freedom. In contrast, in a high power-distance society, creativity tends to be stifled because much greater emphasis is placed on hierarchies, rules, and conformance. In cognitive terms, this means that in societies of higher power distance, people with less power tend to accept the ideas of the more powerful players without questioning, and rely, to some extent, on the ones with more power to think and make decisions for them. The opposite of all of this is true in societies of low power distance.

Uncertainty Avoidance. Uncertainty avoidance pertains to a society's tolerance for ambiguity, that is, the levels of comfort (or discomfort) that members of a society feel in unstructured situations. People in low uncertainty-avoidance cultures tend to be more tolerant of new ideas and less rule-oriented. By contrast, people in high uncertainty-avoidance cultures tend to be less tolerant of new ideas and to have a propensity to seek clarity through rules and regulations. In cognitive terms, this might suggest that people from higher uncertainty-avoidance cultures may sometimes reduce uncertainty by relying on the help and guidance of other people rather than thinking for themselves. It also suggests that people from low uncertainty-avoidance cultures tend to be more reflective and to think in more relativistic terms. They are able to tolerate ambiguity better.

Individualism versus Collectivism. This dimension concerns the relationship between the individual and the collectivity in a given society. Not only does this relationship refer to people's ways of living together (e.g., in families), but also, "it is intimately linked with societal norms (in the sense of value systems of major groups of the population" (Hofstede, 1980, p. 214). This means that it affects people's "mental programming" (Hofstede, 1980, p. 214). Individualist societies are more tolerant of individual thoughts and behaviors. Thus, individuals in such societies are less concerned with doing "safe" things and are more willing to take risks. On the other hand, collectivist societies are less tolerant of distinctively individual thoughts and behaviors. It follows that people in such societies are more concerned about doing things in ways that are approved of by other members of the society, and such approval is often achieved by avoiding risk-taking. In cognitive terms, people in individualist societies tend to think in ways that defy the crowd, whereas people in collectivist societies tend to think in ways that communicate conformity.

Masculinity versus Femininity. This dimension refers to the distribution of emotional roles between males and females. The predominant socialization patterns are for males to be more assertive and for females to be more nurturing. As has already been noted in the preceding chapter, Hofstede (1980) maintained that the stability of gender-role patterns has more to do with socialization than with biological factors. In masculine societies, assertiveness and decisiveness are more valued. By contrast, rule-following and obedience are much more appreciated in feminine societies. In cognitive terms, people from masculine cultures tend to be engaged in new ways of thinking, whereas people from feminine cultures tend to be engaged in more conventional thinking.[1]

By the year 2001, Hofstede had constructed an index for each of the four cultural dimensions for 66 countries. Although there were some exceptions, a general trend was identified. Broadly speaking, the economically more developed countries usually fall on one end of each of the four continua: low power distance (L_{PD}), low uncertainty avoidance (L_{UA}), individualism (I), and masculinity (M) – referred to as "$L_{PD}L_{UA}IM$" for the sake of brevity; while the economically less developed countries normally fall on the other end of each of the four continua: high power distance (H_{PD}), high uncertainty avoidance (H_{UA}), collectivism (C), and femininity (F) – referred to as "$H_{PD}H_{UA}CF$."

The Conceptual Links between Culture and Intellectual Styles: A Hypothesis

If one compares the characteristics of Type I intellectual styles, as described in Chapter 2, with the characteristics of Hofstede's $L_{PD}L_{UA}IM$ societies, one will observe a resemblance between the two, although the former represent individual characteristics and the latter societal ones. By the same token, one could easily detect a correspondence between the characteristics of Type II intellectual styles and those of $H_{PD}H_{UA}CF$ societies.

Thus, based on the conceptual similarities between intellectual styles and Hofstede's cultural dimensions, one might expect that people in Hofstede's $L_{PD}L_{UA}IM$ countries (which are usually economically more advanced and with higher levels of what most societies term "modernity") tend to employ Type I intellectual styles, and that people in Hofstede's $H_{PD}H_{UA}CF$ countries (often, economically less developed and with lower levels of modernity) tend to employ Type II intellectual styles (see Figure 4.1).

This hypothesis can be extended to ethnic groups within countries. That is, people in Hofstede's $L_{PD}L_{UA}IM$ groups, typically the predominant ethnic group of a country, tend to employ Type I styles, and people in Hofstede's $H_{PD}H_{UA}CF$ groups, typically the ethnic minority groups of a country, tend to employ Type II styles.

---

[1] These conceptions of masculine and feminine can be viewed as stereotypical. I wish to make clear that I refer here to Hofstede's use of the terms, not my own.

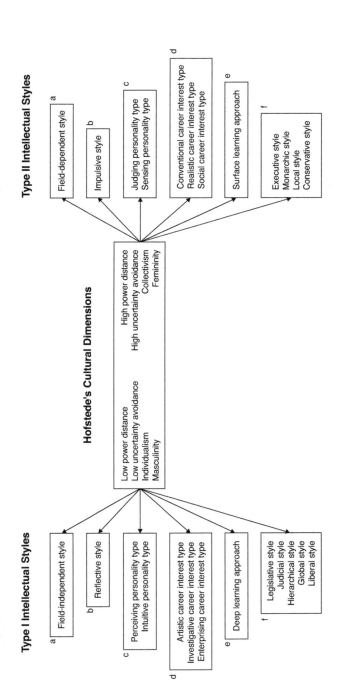

FIGURE 4.1. Hypothesis on Culture and Intellectual Styles

Footnotes:
[a] Witkin's construct of field dependence/independence
[b] Kagan's model of reflectivity-impulsivity conceptual tempo
[c] Jung's theory of personality types
[d] Holland's theory of career interest types
[e] Biggs' theory of student learning
[f] Sternberg's theory of mental self-government

However, this hypothesis may not be always true, and there are at least four reasons for this. First, country/region/ethnic group is not the only dimension along which each of the cultural-dimension indices differs. The indices also differ according to other major socialization variables, most notably age, gender, occupation, and educational level (Hofstede, 1980). Second, within each country/region/ethnic group, people of different social classes and, of course, individuals of the same social class may fall on different points on each of the four continua. Third, with the increasing speed of modernization (as typified by rapid economic growth), those cultures that once tended toward, say, collectivism might begin to manifest more individualism (Matsumoto, 2002). According to Hofstede (1980), a society's economic evolution or modernity is a major determinant of social norms. Finally, people of the same culture may exhibit quite different characteristics on Hofstede's cultural dimensions. For example, generally speaking, Japanese culture is characterized by its avoidance of conflict and overt criticism at the individual level. However, at the group or organizational level, uncertainty is often acknowledged (Pascale & Athos, 1981; Westwood & Low, 2003). It is with these caveats that the general hypothesis regarding the relationship between culture and intellectual styles was made, which, of course, does not apply to each and every individual case, be that cross-cultural or within a culture.

Literature Search Procedures and Results

Because the research hypothesis was made within the context the threefold model of intellectual styles (Zhang & Sternberg, 2005), the literature search was confined to the 10 style constructs included in the threefold model (see Chapter 2 in this book). A separate literature search was carried out for each of the 10 style constructs, and each complete search was conducted using a combination of two sets of key words. The first set of key words constituted the label(s) commonly used for the particular style construct of interest. For example, the term "field dependence/independence" and "psychological differentiation" were entered for Witkin's (1962) model, while "personality type" and "personality style" were entered for Jung's (1923) model. The second set of key words included the most commonly used measures of the particular style construct under consideration. For example, for Witkin's model, the phrases "Embedded Figures Test" and "Group Embedded Figures Test" were entered, and for Jung's model, the phrase "Myers-Briggs Type Indicator" was keyed in.

As a result of this search, more than 10,000 abstracts appeared. An initial reading of these abstracts suggested that 105 of them might be relevant to the topic of this chapter. Full texts of 101 of the 105 abstracts were located and read, of which 76 were thought to address the relationship between culture and intellectual styles. These publications converged on six style constructs: (1) field dependence/independence (Witkin, 1948; 21 publications), (2) reflectivity-impulsivity (Kagan, 1965; 13 publications), (3) personality types/styles (Jung, 1923; 13 publications), (4) career interest/personality types/styles (Holland, 1973; 10 publications), (5) learning approaches (Biggs, 1978; 13 publications), and (6) thinking styles (Sternberg, 1988; six publications). Findings of the majority of the publications are discussed in the next part, and key information on all these publications is listed in Table 4.1.

Culture and Intellectual Styles: Empirical Evidence

Although it is likely that culture influences intellectual styles, investigators have made very little concerted effort to systematically investigate cross-cultural differences (or similarities) in intellectual styles. The reason for this is that direct comparisons are often associated with several major problems, such as a lack of common understanding of the construct under investigation and incompatibility of the samples involved. Nonetheless, existing studies can very well be informative regarding the malleability of intellectual styles as a function of culture. To what degree is the prediction concerning the relationships between intellectual styles and Hofstede's cultural dimensions supported by existing research? What are some of the challenges to this prediction? This part addresses these questions by presenting empirical findings based on the aforementioned six style constructs.

Field Dependence/Independence and Culture

On the basis of the definitions of field dependence and field independence (Witkin, 1948; see Chapter 2) and on the definition of each of Hofstede's cultural dimensions, one would expect people in societies (be they at the national level or at the within-culture level) that fall on the $L_{PD}L_{UA}IM$ ends of Hofstede's cultural continua to be more field independent. By contrast, people in societies that fall on the $H_{PD}H_{UA}CF$ ends would be expected to be more field dependent (also see Figure 4.1).

Clearly, among all the existing style constructs, Witkin's field-dependence/independence (FDI) construct is the one that has been the most intensively studied in cross-cultural settings, both at the national level and at the within-culture level. Findings from earlier studies (those conducted in the 1960s and 1970s) generally support the present hypothesis. However, empirical findings since the 1980s tend to be at odds with this hypothesis.

TABLE 4.1. *Studies of Styles in Cross-Cultural Settings*

Sources	Sample Size	Sample Description	Number of Studies Presented
Studies on Field Dependence/Independence			
Bagley & Mallick (1998)	Not specified	9- to 11-year-olds in Jamaica, India, Japan, and China; 9- to 11-year-old Anglo-Celtic children born in England, children of the Blackfoot Nation of Montana and Alberta, Italian and Anglo-Celtic children in Canada	A review of 10 studies
Berry (1966)	n1=90; n2=30	The Temne group in Sierra Leone and the Eskimo of Baffin Island as the primary sample; a Western group as the secondary sample	1
Buriel (1975)	80	First-, second-, and third-generation Mexican-American children; Anglo-American children as a comparison group in the United States	1
Buriel (1978)	80	Mexican-American (first-, second-, and third-generation) and Anglo-American first through fourth graders in the United States	1
Dawson (1966)	159	Apprentices working at the Marampa iron ore mine in Sierra Leone	1
Dawson (1967)	78	Children from two tribes (Temne and Mende) in Sierra Leone	1
Dershowitz (1971)	n1=50; n2=68; n3=30	n1: 10-year-old Jewish boys attending an all-male Hebrew school; n2: 10-year-old Jewish children who served as the original Witkin et al. (1962) sample; n3: White Anglo-Saxon Protestant boys (U.S.)	1
Engelbrecht & Natzel (1997)	200	African-American and Black South African fourth and fifth graders (United States and South Africa)	1
Gonzales & Roll (1985)	197	Mexican-American and European-American fourth, fifth, eighth, and 12th graders and first-year university students in the United States	1

Gruenfeld & MacEachron (1975)	329	Managers and technicians in 22 non-Western countries	1
Hite (2004)	90	University juniors and seniors in a large public university in the southeastern United States	1
Nedd & Gruenfeld (1976)	1,419	Grade 9 students from six cultural groups in Trinidad	1
Ramirez, Castaneda, & Herold (1974)	541 + 541	541 Mexican-American school children and their mothers from three communities in southern California, United States	1
Rovai, Gallien, Jr., & Wighting (2005)	Not specified	African-American students	A review of 4 studies
Sanders, Scholz, & Kagan (1976)	184	Fifth and sixth grade Anglo-American and Mexican-American children	1
Siann (1970)	64	Zambian and non-Zambian school children in Lusaka, Zambia	1
Sinha & Shrestha (1992)	240	Nepalese children between 6 and 8 years of age, Nepal	1
Vigeland (1973)	200	10- or 13-year-olds raised in two rural communities in Norway	1
William, Anshel, & Quek (1997)	973	Young athletes in Australia, New Zealand, and Singapore	1
Witkin (1967)	Not specified	Adult males in Sierra Leone; Tenne and Eskimo children; 10-year-old Jewish boys in comparison with white Protestant boys of Anglo-Saxon derivation in the U.S.	A review of 4 studies
Wober (1966)	173	Workers of all levels (from laborers to trained mechanics) employed in a large Nigerian industry	
Studies on Reflectivity-Impulsivity			
Adejumo (1979)	200	7- and 9-year-old boys from four public schools in Nigeria	1
Ausburn & Ausburn (1983)	6	Boys aged between 10 and 15 years from a small village in Papua New Guinea	1
Engle, Klein, Kagan, & Yarbrough (1977)	160	Rural children aged 5, 7, 9, and 11 years in Guatemala	1
Heckel, Allen, Andrews, Roeder, Ryba, & Zook (1989)	200	Adult male incarcerates (108 Black and 92 White) in a state correctional system, United States	1

(continued)

TABLE 4.1 (*continued*)

Sources	Sample Size	Sample Description	Number of Studies Presented
Huang & Chao (1998)	150	American and Chinese graduate students at a state university in the United States	1
Juliano (1977)	120	Disadvantaged and middle-class boys aged between 8 and 11 years in the United States	1
Mumbauer & Miller (1970)	64	4-year-old preschool children – half from culturally disadvantaged (Black) families and half from middle- and upper-class families in the United States	1
Resendiz & Fox (1983)	24	6- to 10-year-old Mexican-American children in a rural town in the United States with predominantly Mexican population – half the participants retarded and half non-retarded	1
Resendiz & Fox (1985)	110	Urban Mexican children aged 5 and 9.	1
Salkind, Kojima, & Zelniker (1978)	5,055	5- to 12-year-old American, Japanese, and Israeli children	1
Smith & Caplan (1988)	100	Chinese-American children aged 6 to 10 years	1
Smith & Ribordy (1980)	72	5- and 6-year-old boys in seven urban kindergartens in Chicago, United States; racial background – white, black, and Hispanic	1
Zucker & Stricker (1968)	30	5-year-old black children in the Amityville Headstart Center, United States	1
Studies on Personality Types			
Bents & Wierschke (1996)	52	Students, librarians, staff, and professors from a university in Austria (aged 18 to 94 years)	1
Broer & McCarley (1999)	119	Mainland Chinese nationals who held managerial or professional positions in a Chinese joint venture company in the People's Republic of China	1

Hammer & Mitchell (1996)	1,267	A U.S. national sample stratified by gender, ethnicity, and geographic location	1
Hedegard & Brown (1969)	320	Black and white university freshmen in the United States	1
Huang & Huang (1991)	1059	Chinese university students in Taiwan	1
Levy, Murphy, & Carlson (1972)	758	Black university students in the United States	1
Osterlind, Miao, Sheng, & Chia (2004)	1,111	University medical students (aged 19 to 24 years) in mainland China	1
Shade (1983)	n1=52; n2=75; n3= 180	African-American and European-American school and university students	3
Shade (1985)	178	Ninth grade students (92 African-Americans and 86 European-Americans) in the United States	1
Stalikas, Casas, & Carson (1996)	249	Anglophone university students in Quebec, Canada	1
Tobacyk & Cieslicka (2000)	182	University students (average age 21) in Poland	1
Uhl & Day (1993)	n1=1,198; n2=314; n3=287	n1: University students in the United States; n2: first-year university students in Canada; n3: grade 12 students in Canada	1
Yao (1993)	293	Female school administrators in mainland China	1
Studies on Career Interest/Personality Types/Styles			
Einarsdóttir, Rounds, Agisòttir, & Gerstein (2002)	n1=449; n2=438	n1: clients (average age: 23.5 years) at a university counseling center in Iceland; n2: university students (average age: 24 years) in Iceland	1
Fouad & Dancer (1992)	557	Male engineering students and professionals in Mexico or the United States	1
Gade, Fuqua, & Hurlburt (1984)	n1=48; n2=56	Two samples of grades 10 to 12 students from two Indian tribes, Canada	1
Glidden-Tracey & Greenwood (1997)	145	University students in the United States	1
Khan, Alvi, Shaukat, Hussain, & Baig, (1990)	376	University students, Pakistan	1

(*continued*)

TABLE 4.1 (*continued*)

Sources	Sample Size	Sample Description	Number of Studies Presented
Lonner, W. J. (1968)	n1=452; n2=327	n1: psychologists; n2: accountants (Austria, Germany, and Switzerland)	1
Payne & Sabaroche (1985)	101	14- to 16-year-olds in their final year of schooling in Dominica	1
Rounds & Tracey (1996)	41,234	various	A meta-analysis study of 96 RIASEC correlation matrices from five U.S. ethnic minority groups and 18 countries
Swanson (1992)	357	African-American college students	1
Yang, Stokes, & Hui (2005)	811	Adults in Hong Kong and mainland China	1
Studies on Learning Approaches			
Bernardo (2003)	404	University freshmen (16 to 21 years) in the Philippines	1
Brand (2001)	335	University music majors in mainland China and the United States	1
Gow & Kember (1990)	1043	University students in Hong Kong	1
Gow, Balla, Kember, Stokes, et al. (1989)	514	University freshmen and seniors in Hong Kong	1
Hui & Triandis (1989)	119	Hispanic and non-Hispanic U.S. Navy recruits	1
Mpofu & Oakland (2001)	376	Black and white school students (average age: 12 years) in Zimbabwe	1
Niles (1995)	208	Australian-born and overseas university students in Australia	1
Samuelowicz (1987)	145 + 136	Faculty members and overseas students in Australia	1

Volet, Renshaw, & Tietzel (1994)	554	Local and Southeast Asian university students in Australia	1
Watkins & Mboya (1997)	327	15-year-old black South African secondary school students	1
Watkins, Reghi, & Astilla (1991)	n1=509; n2=386	14- to 16-year-old Filipino and Nepalese school students	2
Watkins & Sethi (1999)	694	Mexican-American and European-American secondary school students	1
Wong & Lin (1996)	2,123	Primary and secondary school students in Canada, Hong Kong, Malaysia, mainland China, Nigeria, and Zimbabwe	1
Studies on Thinking Styles			
Bernardo, Zhang, & Callueng (2002)	429	University students in the Philippines	1
Cano-Garcia & Hughes (2000)	210	University students (aged 18–24 years) in Spain	1
Nachmias & Shany (2002)	110	Eighth and ninth graders in Israel	
Zhang (2001)	209 + 215	University students in Hong Kong and mainland China	1
Zhang (2002b)	212	University students in the United States	1
Zhang & Sternberg (1998)	646	University students (aged 19–24 years) in Hong Kong	1

The earliest study was conducted by Witkin, Dyke, and Faterson (1962). The researchers provided extensive empirical evidence indicating that, compared with children in other societies, children in the United States were generally more field independent. Subsequent investigations among other cultural groups within the United States (i.e., African Americans, American Indians) found that children from minority groups tended to be more field dependent than Caucasian children. Also, during the 1960s and 1970s, a number of studies were conducted among children from economically less developed countries in Africa. For example, Berry (1966) and Dawson (1966, 1967) studied the FDI levels of children of tribal groups in Sierra Leone; Okonji (1969) and Wober (1966) studied tribal groups in Nigeria; and MacArthur (1970) and Siann (1970) carried out empirical research among Zambian boys and girls. Consistently, these groups fell within the more field-dependent range across several measures of FDI (e.g., *Rod and Frame, Block Design Tests*, and the *Embedded Figures Tests*).

In another study, Gruenfeld and MacEachron (1975) investigated the FDI differences among 329 managers and technicians in 22 non-Western countries that were at various stages of modernization and development: seven in South America, another seven in Sub-Saharan Africa, three in Central America, two in North Africa, another two in South Asia, and one country in the Middle East. For each country, statistics of economic development were selected from Harbison, Maruhnic, and Resnick's (1970) quantitative analysis of modernization and development and constructed into six indices for the study: economic development, cultural development, health care services, educational achievement, nutrition, and morality. Results strongly supported the researchers' hypothesis that the levels of field independence would be systematically associated with the levels of economic development of the respective countries: the higher the levels of economic development of a country, the more field independent the individuals of that country would be.

Some of the earlier studies of people's FDI not only demonstrated that people from more economically deprived countries tend to be less field independent than people from economically more advanced countries, but also revealed subcultural differences in cognitive styles. For example, when Dawson (1966) studied two of the tribal groups in Sierra Leone, the Mende and the Temne, he found that the Mende children were more field independent than the Temne children. Apparently, the levels of power in the two groups were very different. This could have been because the Mende children lived in a culture in which great emphasis was placed on giving children responsibilities at a very young age (which was thus a manifestation of a low power distance), whereas the Temne children were brought up in a culture in which strong emphasis was placed on conformity to adult authority and in which extreme forms of physical punishment were commonly used to enforce conformity (an apparent indicator of a high power distance). That is to say, children's levels of FDI can develop differently depending on the culture in which they grow up.

Support for the present hypothesis regarding the relationship between FDI and Hofstede's cultural dimensions can also be found in some of the more recent studies, although to a much lesser extent. At the national level, Engelbrecht and Natzel (1997) found that African-American 4th and 5th graders were significantly more field independent than South African 4th and 5th graders. At the within-culture level, results from several more recent studies (e.g., Bennett, 2002; Shade, 1997) also pointed to the field-dependent tendency of African-American students and the field-independent propensity of their Caucasian peers. Again, these are trends that may or may not apply in individual cases.

However, many more recent studies do not support the present hypothesis. For example, in a review of a series of studies conducted between the mid-1980s and the mid-1990s, Bagley and Mallick (1998) reached the conclusion that students who were from, in Hofstede's terms, cultures known for their high individualism and lower power distances (in this case, students from Canada, the United Kingdom, and the United States) were more field dependent, whereas students from cultures that have been generally agreed by anthropologists to be collectivist cultures that value conformity (in this case, Chinese and Japanese cultures) were more field independent. In searching for explanations for these unexpected findings, Bagley and Mallick made two convincing points, both communicating the dynamic nature of intellectual styles. First, because cognitive abilities have increased significantly every decade in American children (and in Chinese and Japanese children; Flynn, 1984, 2007), the use of American norms for the late 1960s and early 1970s (Witkin, Oltman, Raskin, & Karp, 1971) for Chinese and Japanese children in the 1990s may not accurately reflect the degree of difference between the two groups on the FDI measures. Underlying this explanation is the assumption that children's intellectual styles change as their cognitive abilities change. Second, people can become more field independent as a result of their exposure to new cultural and educational experiences. Indeed, the second explanation finds empirical support in many acculturation studies (e.g., Dershowitz, 1971; Ramirez, Castaneda, & Herold, 1974). For example, in Buriel's (1978) study, using three different measures of FDI, no evidence was found to support the assumption that Mexican-American children would be more field dependent than Anglo Americans, as had been found in previous studies (e.g., Buriel,

1975; Sanders, Scholz, & Kagan, 1976). However, given that the large majority of the Mexican-American participants in Buriel's study were from a pool of second- and third-generation students, it is possible that these children had been acculturated into the mainstream American culture in general, and into school culture in particular, which explains why they did not differ in their levels of FDI from their European-American peers. In other words, the Mexican-American children might have developed a tendency to be field independent in their way of processing information at least partially as a result of their having been socialized in the mainstream American culture.

Finally, existing research has pointed to the complex relationship between FDI and culture. For example, in studying two cultural groups of Gurungs and Brahmins residing in contrasting ecologies of the hills and plains, respectively, of Nepal, Sinha and Shrestha (1992) concluded that although the effect of culture was not significant, it played a critical role jointly with ecology. Similarly, Vigeland (1973) did not find the hypothesized significant difference between two communities with different cultural values in Norway. However, a closer examination of the data revealed that there was an interactive effect based on gender. Within the group (i.e., Community East) that was expected to score higher on field independence, girls had deranged such a tendency to be field independent.

Reflectivity-Impulsivity and Culture

On the basis of the definition of reflectivity and impulsivity (Kagan, 1965; see Chapter 2) and the present hypothesis concerning the relationship between styles and Hofstede's cultural dimensions, one would expect people from societies that fall on the $L_{PD}L_{UA}IM$ ends of Hofstede's cultural continua to be generally more reflective, and people from societies that fall on the $H_{PD}H_{UA}CF$ ends to be generally more impulsive (also see Figure 4.1). Like the construct of FDI, reflectivity-impulsivity has also been widely investigated in a great number of countries (e.g., China, Guatemala, Japan, Jerusalem, Poland, Northern Ireland, and many others). However, unlike studies of FDI, which have had a strong focus on comparing different cultural groups, studies of reflectivity-impulsivity have been more focused on validating the inventory for assessing reflectivity-impulsivity (i.e., the *Matching Familiar Figures Test*) with respect to its use in the relevant cultures in which the studies were conducted. Of the studies that have taken a comparative approach, some support the hypothesis that people from economically less developed cultural settings tend to be more impulsive, whereas others do not. Either way, findings from these studies have revealed the dynamic nature of reflectivity-impulsivity.

Studies supporting the hypothesis have been conducted at both the national level and the within-culture level. On the national level, for example, Solis-Cámara and Fox (1985) concluded that compared with American, Japanese, and Israeli children, Mexican children were, on average, more impulsive. Similarly, after their investigation among children in a small village (known as Wiava) in the Eastern Highlands Province of Papua New Guinea (PNG), Ausburn and Ausburn (1983) asserted that the PNG students' performance level on the *Matching Familiar Figures Test* was significantly below that expected for peers of their age and educational level in developed countries. Ausburn and Ausburn contended that this low-level performance could be mainly attributed to the PNG students' lack of exposure to tasks that require visual analysis, as required by the *Matching Familiar Figures Test*. That is to say, students' reflectivity can be enhanced through exposure to visual tasks.

Within the United States, several studies have compared the levels of reflectivity-impulsivity between African-American and European-American research participants and found that African Americans are, on average, significantly more impulsive than Americans of European origin. For example, early in 1968, Zucker and Stircker found that lower socioeconomic-class African-American preschool children were more impulsive than their middle-class white peers. Mumbauer and Miller (1970) reached the same conclusion – that disadvantaged preschool children (with one half of this group being black) were more impulsive than were culturally advantaged children from middle-class families (see also Juliano, 1977).[2] Zucker and Stircker (1968) offered an explanation for such a finding. They started from a cultural perspective consistent with Hofstede's dimension of power distance, and arrived at an explanation from a psychological perspective. They argued that because children from disadvantaged families are more likely to be required to be obedient (Bernstein, 1965), they tend to be more externally oriented in terms of learning motivation. Furthermore, compared with internally motivated students, externally motivated students are less persistent in tasks (Crandall, Katkovsky, & Preston, 1962; Rotter, 1966). In other words, children from disadvantaged families might have developed higher levels of impulsivity as a result of growing up in a family environment that demands higher levels of obedience. This explanation is highly plausible because exhibiting obedience – a typical form of conformity – is in line with the use of what Zhang and Sternberg (2005) called Type II intellectual styles, of which the impulsive style is one.

---

[2] Note that these studies are rather old and the pattern of results may well have changed in the present day.

Among the existing comparative studies, findings that present challenges to the hypothesis regarding the relationship between impulsivity-reflectivity and culture are abundant. For example, Adejumo (1979) found a lack of evidence to support the commonly held assumption that African Americans are generally more impulsive. Among 72 kindergarten boys, Smith and Ribordy (1980) did not find any significant difference in impulsivity-reflectivity based on either race or socioeconomic status. Nonetheless, a closer examination of the conditions under which these findings were obtained would lead one to be in favor of the argument that reflectivity-impulsivity is dynamic. Several studies have suggested that culture may affect the development of this style dimension indirectly, through interacting with other variables.

One such variable is educational level. For example, when studying a group of 200 adult male offenders (108 African Americans and 92 European Americans) in a state correctional system in the United States, Heckel, Allen, Andrews, Roeder, Ryba, and Zook (1989) found that African-American offenders were significantly more impulsive, on average, than their European-American counterparts were. However, such a racial difference was not found in a comparative group of college students. In general, differences tend to disappear, or at least to be reduced, among people of higher educational levels.

The effect of educational level on reflectivity-impulsivity can be further illustrated by a more recent study conducted by Huang and Chao (1998). In investigating the levels of reflectivity-impulsivity among 75 Chinese and 75 American graduate students enrolled at a state university in the United States, Huang and Chao found that the Chinese students were significantly more reflective than their American peers. Of course, there could be many possible explanations for this finding. However, one most likely factor that enhanced their level of reflectivity was the unique educational background of these Chinese students. By traveling to the United States to pursue their postgraduate education, the foreign Chinese students had crossed a cultural boundary. Tullett (1997) argued that boundary crossing is conducive to creative thinking and that the more boundaries people cross, the more creative thinking they tend to use (see also Hill, Puurula, Sitko-Lutek, & Rakowska, 2000; see Chapter 3 for more details). In addition, it should be noted that the Chinese participants in Huang and Chao's study were composed of a highly selective group of students, given the high levels of academic ability required to become an overseas graduate student in the United States in the 1990s. In other words, the Chinese students' levels of reflectivity might have been boosted by their educational and other kinds of experiences.

Personality Type and Culture

The personality types based on Jung's (1923) theory have also been investigated in relation to culture. As mentioned in Chapter 2, Jung (1958) had long pointed out that psychological functions are applicable not only to individuals (types), but also to civilizations, nationalities, and cultures. That is to say, individual differences in personality styles can be used to portray cultural differences.

In the threefold model of intellectual styles, the intuitive and perceiving personality styles are classified as Type I styles, the sensing and judging personality styles as Type II ones, and the remaining ones as Type III styles. Together with the specifications of Hofstede's cultural dimensions, this classification of the MBTI personality types was the basis for my prediction that individuals from societies that fall on the $L_{PD}L_{UA}IM$ ends of Hofstede's cultural continua would be more intuitive and perceiving, whereas people from societies that fall on the $H_{PD}H_{UA}CF$ ends would be more sensing and judging (also see Figure 4.1). This prediction is confirmed by findings in the majority of empirical studies (e.g., Broer & McCarley, 1999; Hedegard & Brown, 1969; Hammer & Mitchell, 1996; Levy, Murphy, & Carlson, 1972), although it is challenged by findings of some other studies (e.g., Shade, 1983, 1986; Tobacyk & Cieslicka, 2000).

Nearly all the studies supporting this hypothesis have been conducted at the within-culture level. Researchers of these studies primarily aimed to identify the predominant MBTI types of their research participants from different ethnic groups. As early as 1969, Hedegard and Brown reported that, compared with their Caucasian counterparts, students of African descent tended to use more concrete and tangible ways (i.e., more sensing) than abstract and intellectual ways (i.e., less intuitive) in dealing with their environments. By the same token, Levy, Murphy, and Carlson (1972) investigated the MBTI types of university students of African descent and identified significantly higher proportions of judging and sensing types compared with their findings among students of European descent. Hammer and Mitchell (1996) examined the MBTI types of a national sample (1,267 adults aged 18 to 94 years) ethnically matched according to the 1990 census in the United States. The researchers found that there was a significantly higher proportion of sensing types among African Americans when compared with the overall sample, which was highly dominated by European Americans.

In one of his earliest publications, Jung (1958) turned his attention to the possible personality style differences between Eastern and Western civilizations and suggested that people in the former were predominantly introverts and people in the latter were predominantly extraverts. This has been empirically supported by some studies showing that among Chinese nationals, sensing and judging types tend to be overrepresented. For example, studies of MBTI types among mainland Chinese business administrators and professionals (e.g., Broer & McCarley, 1999; Yao, 1993) revealed that there was a preponderance of sensing and judging types. Similarly, among Taiwanese university students, Huang and Huang (1991) also found an overrepresentation of sensing and judging types.

However, the hypothesis with respect to the differences in the MBTI types based on cultural groups has also been challenged. A case in point concerns the research findings on the differences between African Americans and European Americans. Given the social and economic disadvantages that African Americans have generally experienced when compared with their European-American counterparts in the United States, one would expect African Americans to be more sensing and judging and European Americans to be more intuitive and perceiving, on average. However, according to Shade's (1986) review of the literature, no significant difference was found in the MBTI types of individuals of African descent versus those of European descent prior to school grade 3 or after the first year of college. Moreover, contrary to the present hypothesis, Shade's own research on ninth-grade students has repeatedly found that students of African descent are, on the whole, more perceiving, whereas European Americans are more judging (Shade, 1983, 1986). These non-significant results and results that challenged the present hypothesis, however, do not mean that personality styles are static. Quite the contrary, these results suggest that students of African descent might have developed their perceiving and intuitive personality styles, for being in the United States can be perceived as more of a culture-boundary-crossing phenomenon for families with an African origin than for families with a European origin. From a cognitive-developmental perspective, boundary crossing is closely associated with the development of Type I intellectual styles (Tullett, 1995).

Career Personality Type and Culture

Cross-cultural studies of career interests based on Holland's (1973) model typically have one of the following three objectives: (1) to test the criterion-related validity of the *Self-Directed Search* (SDS); (2) to examine the structure underlying the career interest/personality styles/types of racial-ethnic groups within the United States or of other national groups; or (3) to identify differential patterns of career personality types. This research has, in general, lent great support to Holland's model, although the model has not gone unchallenged.

In the threefold model of intellectual styles, the artistic career personality type is classified as a Type I style, the conventional career personality type as a Type II style, and the remaining ones as Type III styles. In this chapter, on the basis of Hofstede's cultural dimensions and the definition of each of the six types of career interests, I anticipated that individuals from societies that fall on the $L_{PD}L_{UA}IM$ ends of Hofstede's cultural continua would tend to express a stronger interest in artistic, investigative, and enterprising careers, whereas people from societies that fall on the $H_{PD}H_{UA}CF$ ends would tend to be more interested in the conventional, realistic, and social types of careers (also see Figure 4.1).

Regarding both the criterion-related validity of the SDS and the degree to which data from various cultures fit Holland's circular order model, it was anticipated that data sets from $L_{PD}L_{UA}IM$ cultures would be better predictors of people's career personality styles and show a better model fit than those from $H_{PD}H_{UA}CF$ cultures. Hofstede's cultural dimensions (and their often associated factors – economic development and level of modernization) are related to a nation's (or ethnic group's) occupational structure, particularly to its distribution of career personality styles (Hall, 1975; Rounds & Tracey, 1996). According to Hofstede's model, cultures falling on the $H_{PD}H_{UA}CF$ ends of Hofstede's dimensions would necessarily place constraints on individuals' career interest styles, such as depriving individuals of the opportunities to be exposed to certain types of occupations and to develop the career interest styles they might have developed had they been socialized in a society that falls on the $L_{PD}L_{UA}IM$ ends of Hofstede's cultural system. Following this logic, one would have solid grounds for predicting that such restrictions would lead to poorer prediction of people's career interest styles and poorer model fits for $H_{PD}H_{UA}CF$ cultures. Likewise, one would predict that data from $L_{PD}L_{UA}IM$ cultures would demonstrate stronger construct validity of Holland's model than would those from $H_{PD}H_{UA}CF$ cultures.

These hypotheses, although not without their challenges (e.g., Fouad & Dancer, 1992; Swanson, 1992), are empirically supported by the findings of many studies (e.g., Einarsdòttir, Rounds, Agisòttir, & Gerstein, 2002; Gade, Fuqua, & Hurlburt, 1984; Khan, Alvi, Shaukat, Hussain, & Baig, 1990; Leung & Hou, 2001; Payne & Sabaroche, 1985; Rounds & Tracey, 1996). Again, however, these mixed findings collectively support the argument that intellectual styles are dynamic.

Support for the hypothesis regarding the relationships between culture and Holland's career interest styles can be found in studies aimed at achieving all three objectives mentioned earlier. First, criterion-related studies support the hypothesis by showing that the SDS's predictive validity is relatively lower for samples from Hofstede's $H_{PD}H_{UA}CF$ cultures. For example, among a sample of 376 university students in Pakistan, Khan, Alvi, Shaukat, Hussain, and Baig (1990) found that students' SDS codes were not good predictors for career readiness. Similarly, in Hong Kong, Leung and Hou (2001) found that among 777 Chinese high school students, the correspondence between the students' SDS high-point career interest codes and their tentative choices of university majors and careers – known as "hit rates" – was generally lower than that obtained in previous studies in the United States. These lower predictive validities could have been attributable to educational systems (educational systems being part of cultural practices) that tend to exercise more power and control, placing constraints on students' development of career interests. For example, in Hong Kong, students are required to choose either a science stream or an arts stream at the end of junior high school (i.e., 9th grade in the United States). Such early commitment might have prevented students from developing career interest styles that they would have developed otherwise. Consequently, the results of their SDS test might not have corresponded very well with their choices of university majors or of actual career interest styles. Thus, examining this inhibition of development from a different perspective, one could argue that intellectual styles, as represented by career personality types in this context, can be changed.

Second, it was predicted that data from $L_{PD}L_{UA}IM$ cultures would have a better structural fit with Holland's model than those from $H_{PD}H_{UA}CF$ cultures. Support for this hypothesis is strong, although somewhat mixed. For example, a research team led by Einarsdòttir (Einarsdòttir et al., 2002) found that the underlying structure of vocational/career interests of a sample of 438 university students in Iceland (a country that falls on the $L_{PD}L_{UA}IM$ ends of Hofstede's cultural continua) resembles that of U.S. benchmark samples. The researchers attributed this similarity mainly to the fact that the Icelandic culture has similar rankings to those of the United States on Hofstede's dimensions and that both countries are characterized by a high level of economic prosperity.

Incorporating the notion of economic development, as assessed by gross domestic product per capita (GDPPC), and two of the four Hofstede's value systems (masculinity-femininity and individualism-collectivism), Rounds and Tracey (1996) conducted a meta-analysis of data sets from 20 ethnic samples in the United States, 76 international samples (representing 18 countries), and 73 benchmark samples in the United States. Although the degree of fit of data with Holland's model was not significantly related to GDPPC and masculinity-femininity, countries with more individualistic values fit the model better than did countries with more collective values. Nonetheless, the present hypothesis concerning the relationships between career interest styles and culture also failed to receive support from data of some countries. For example, contrary to my prediction (and indeed, the prediction of Rounds and Tracey made in 1996 as well), data from Australia and Canada showed a significantly poorer model fit when compared with the U.S. benchmark data sets.

Further challenges to the present hypothesis were found in other studies. For example, Swanson (1992) concluded that the structure of career interest types among African-American university students was similar to that of European-American university students. Cross-nationally, holding gender and occupation constant, Fouad and Daucer (1992) found strikingly similar structures of career interest styles among engineers in Mexico and in the United States. Similar research findings were obtained as early as the 1960s. For example, Lonner (1968) concluded that American, German, Swiss, and Austrian psychologists were more similar to one another than to accountants within their respective countries. Given such evidence, one could argue that it is not ethnic or national cultures that shape people's career personality styles, but rather occupations (see Chapter 6). However, such an argument would be ill-grounded in the absence of solid empirical support because there is also substantial evidence revealing differences that ethnic and national cultures have made in people's career interest styles. Furthermore, going back to the nature of intellectual styles with regard to style malleability, one could argue that regardless of whether it is occupation or ethnic and national cultures that matter more in people's intellectual styles, intellectual styles are dynamic.

Finally, the hypothesis regarding the patterns of career interests expressed by people of different cultural groups also finds support in studies conducted in the mid-1980s. In a first study, Payne and Sabaroche (1985) administered the *Self-Directed Search* and the *Vocational Preference Inventory* to 101 14- to 16-year-old school children in Dominica, a Caribbean nation with a relatively underdeveloped economy. Although data suggested that the Dominican adolescents could be fairly reliably classified into Holland's six career interest types, the significantly positive relationship found between the social and realistic types in their study was not consistent with Holland's theory. According to Holland's model, the social and realistic types should be opposite to each other, with the former being "people-oriented" and the latter being "things-oriented." Such a finding, albeit contrary to the prediction of Holland's model, makes good sense in the context of Dominica. Payne and Sabaroche (1985) cogently argued that "many Realistic or 'things-oriented' occupations in a country such as Dominica involve a significant 'Social' component. Auto mechanics, for example, would not normally work mostly out of sight of the public, but be self-employed and rely for custom on their ability to have good interpersonal rapport with clients" (p. 154).

Similarly, the hypothesis concerning patterns of career interest styles also finds support in Gade, Fuqua, and Hurlburt's (1984) study of Native American high school students. The researchers first compared Holland's SDS scores between students in two Indian tribes – Swampy Cree students, who were boarding students in an all-white community school district, and Peguis students, who were enrolled in a local reserve school district. The Swampy Cree female students scored significantly higher on the investigative scale, whereas the Peguis males scored significantly higher on the social and conventional scales. Despite the failure to find differences across boys and girls between the two tribal groups, this finding revealed that, in general, there was an acculturation effect of students' being exposed to the culture in the all-white community on their career personality styles. That is, the Swampy Cree students displayed more of the characteristics of the investigative career personality style, partially as a result of their interaction with white students.

Learning Approach and Culture

As introduced in Chapter 2, the threefold model of intellectual styles (Zhang & Sternberg, 2005) classified each of the three learning approaches specified in Biggs's (1978) model into one of the three types of intellectual styles. The deep learning approach is categorized as a Type I style, the surface approach as a Type II style, and the achieving approach as a Type III style. In the present context, two related hypotheses were made. First, it was predicted that individuals in societies that normally fall on the $L_{PD}L_{UA}IM$ ends of Hofstede's cultural continua would tend to adopt the deep approach to learning, whereas people in societies that usually fall on the $H_{PD}H_{UA}CF$ ends would tend to use the surface approach to learning (also see Figure 4.1). Second, individuals in $L_{PD}L_{UA}IM$ societies would tend to be rewarded for using the deep approach to learning in that they would perform better academically than learners using the surface learning approach, whereas in $H_{PD}H_{UA}CF$ societies, surface learners would tend to be rewarded in that they would obtain significantly better academic achievement than learners using the deep approach.

However, the question is: To what extent are these predictions supported or disconfirmed by the literature? The answer is: of the hypotheses concerning the relationships of cultural dimensions to all the style constructs discussed in this chapter, those relating to learning approaches are the ones most seriously challenged by empirical data.

In line with the first hypothesis concerning the relationship between culture and learning approaches, two popular claims are often made in cross-cultural studies of learning approaches: (1) that students of African descent and of Hispanic descent have a greater preference for the surface approach to learning than do students of European descent (see Watkins & Mboya, 1997); and (2) that students of Asian descent tend to be rote learners, adopting the surface approach to learning (see Brand, 2001; Watkins, Reghi, & Astilla, 1991). Although some earlier works support these assertions (e.g., Bradley & Bradley, 1984; Samuelowicz, 1987), some of the more recent findings contradict both notions.

For example, comparative studies on the learning approaches of students of African descent (and Hispanic descent) and students of European descent in several cultures (e.g., Mpofu & Oakland, 2001; Watkins & Mboya, 1997) failed to reveal a significant difference between the learning approaches adopted by the compared groups. Similarly, some research comparing the learning approaches of Asian students with those of Caucasian students also disagrees with the stereotypical view that students of Asian descent are rote learners (e.g., Brand, 2001). Traditionally, the higher academic achievement of Asian students compared with that of their Western counterparts has been attributed to the value they place on hard work that is mainly characterized by rote learning, among other factors (see Li, 2002). However, such a view has also been challenged (e.g., Watkins, Reghi, & Astilla, 1991). Moreover, there is evidence indicating that American and Australian students of European descent show a greater tendency to rely on the surface approach to learning than do their Asian peers, including students from Hong Kong, the Philippines, and Nepal (e.g., Brand, 2001; Gow & Kember, 1990).

Nonetheless, since the stereotypical view of Asian students' as rote learners was first challenged, some scholars have argued that there are caveats to this challenge. For example, Niles (1995) argued that as there is also some evidence indicating that Asian students are examination-oriented (Gow et al., 1989), stronger evidence is needed to refute such a long-held view about Asian students. Furthermore, Watkins, a strong opponent of the stereotypical view of Asian learners, found that learning approaches were significantly affected by social desirability (Watkins, 1996). Watkins concluded that such a relationship cast doubt on some of the previous findings suggesting that Asian students were more likely to use the deep approach to learning than were Australian students (see also Hui & Triandis, 1989).

One can also see the dynamic nature of learning approaches as they relate to culture from yet another perspective. For example, Volet, Renshaw, and Tietzel (1994) examined the changes in students' learning approaches between the beginning and the end of a semester. Research participants were a group of local Australian students and a group of Southeast Asian students enrolled in an Australian university. Results indicated that by the end of the semester, the differences in learning approaches between the two cultural groups found at the beginning of the semester had disappeared. The researchers concluded that the similarity in learning approaches between the two groups found at the end of the semester was attributable to the Southeast Asian students adapting to the demands of the academic course and the learning environments. That is to say, the Southeast Asian students had developed learning approaches that were more in tune with the local academic culture.

Finally, the second hypothesis, regarding the relationship between learning approaches and academic achievement, is supported by results from several cultural contexts in Watkins's (2001) review of relevant studies. Most noticeably, consistent with the hypothesis, using the deep approach to learning was not associated with better academic achievement in India, Fiji, and Japan – countries that fall on the $H_{PD}H_{UA}CF$ ends of Hofstede's continua. Also in line with the hypothesis, the surface approach to learning was encouraged in such $H_{PD}H_{UA}CF$ cultures as Hong Kong, Nepal, Nigeria, and South Africa. A more recent study conducted in Zimbabwe (Mpofu & Oakland, 2001) also indicated that although deep learners of European descent performed better academically than surface learners of the same descent, students of African descent who reportedly adopted the deep approach to learning did not perform better academically than surface learners of the same descent. Evidently, the anticipated positive relationship between good academic achievement and the surface learning approach as well as the anticipated negative relationship between poor academic performance and the deep learning approach have both been found among students in cultures that tend to be on the $H_{PD}H_{UA}CF$ ends of Hofstede's continua, and in some cultures with lower levels of modernity. It is possible that the learning approaches of these students were affected by the general cultural ethos that called for conformity in the cultural contexts.

Thinking Style and Culture

Finally, thinking styles as proposed in Sternberg's (1988) theory of mental self-government have also been examined in relation to culture. Based on the definition of Hofstede's cultural systems and that of the three types of thinking styles (Zhang, 2002a), it was first predicted that individuals from societies that fall on the $L_{PD}L_{UA}IM$ ends of Hofstede's cultural continua would tend to use Type I thinking styles and the internal style, whereas people from societies that usually fall on the $H_{PD}H_{UA}CF$ ends would tend to use Type II thinking styles and the external style (also see Figure 4.1). Secondly, it was predicted that in $L_{PD}L_{UA}IM$ societies, Type I and internal thinking styles would be rewarded, and thus these styles would have a positive relationship with better academic performance, whereas in $H_{PD}H_{UA}CF$ societies, Type II and external thinking styles would be rewarded, and thus these styles would be significantly related to better academic achievement.

With respect to the first hypothesis, concerning the relationship between culture and thinking styles, although a great number of empirical investigations have been conducted into the thinking styles of people in different cultures, to date, only two studies (Zhang, Fu, & Jiao, 2008; Zhang, Postiglione, & Jiao, 2012) have directly tested this relationship. Both studies were conducted at the within-nation level and compared the thinking styles of ethnic-minority Tibetans with those of the majority Han people.

If China as a whole nation is classified as an $H_{PD}H_{UA}CF$ society, the Tibetans could be said to carry more characteristics of people from an $H_{PD}H_{UA}CF$ society than do the Han people. In other words, Tibetan people's thinking styles are expected to be more conservative than are those of the Han people. There are many possible reasons why the Tibetans use Type II styles more frequently than do their Han counterparts. The most obvious reasons are Tibet's secluded geographical location, its disadvantaged economy, an education system that is deeply rooted in monastery education (distinguished by its emphasis on reciting the scriptures), its traditional values such as modesty and respect, as well as Tibetan people's strong sense of culture preservation.

In one study, Zhang, Postiglione, and Jiao (2012)[3] compared the thinking styles of Tibetan university students with those of Han Chinese university students. The *Thinking Styles Inventory* (Sternberg & Wagner, 1992) was administered to 408 Tibetan students from the Tibetan Autonomous Region and Gansu Province and to 920 Han Chinese students from three major cities in China: Beijing, Nanjing, and Shanghai. Furthermore, two focus group interviews were conducted, one involving two Tibetan scholars and the other involving 11 Tibetan students from Tibet University. Apart from showing that the theory of mental self-government is valid for Tibetan students, results indicated that compared with the Han students, Tibetan students scored significantly higher on Type II thinking style scales but significantly lower on Type I thinking style scales. In addition, compared with their Han counterparts, Tibetan students indicated a stronger preference for working with others as opposed to working independently. These results have lent complete

---

[3] This work was first presented at an international conference on higher education in Kunming, mainland China, in November 2004.

support to the first hypothesis surrounding the relationship between thinking styles and culture.

In another attempt to understand Tibetan people' styles of thinking as compared with those of the Han majority group in mainland China, Zhang, Fu, and Jiao (2008) investigated Tibetan university teachers' teaching styles and their preferences for students' learning styles. This objective was achieved by analyzing the interview data from a group of Tibetan university teachers and the comparative survey data gathered from university teachers in Nanjing and Tibet. Quantitative data lent complete support to our prediction that Tibetan teachers were significantly more conservative in their teaching than their Nanjing counterparts. However, the data only partially confirmed our prediction that Tibetan teachers would teach less creatively. Interview data suggested that to deal with the rapidly changing world, university teachers in Tibet are becoming more creative in their teaching. That is to say, although for the aforementioned reasons, Tibetans teachers' intellectual styles are still relatively more norm-favoring when compared with those of the mainland Chinese teachers, Tibetan teachers' intellectual styles are changing in the direction of being more creative – most likely, as a response to the changing environment.

The second hypothesis is largely supported by results from studies of the contributions of thinking styles to academic achievement. For example, generally as expected, in secondary school settings in Hong Kong and Israel and in university settings in Hong Kong, the Philippines, and Spain, students with Type II thinking styles tend to be higher academic achievers, whereas those who score higher on Type I thinking styles tend to be lower academic achievers (Bernardo, Zhang, & Callueng, 2002; Cano-Garcia & Hughes, 2000; Nachmias & Shany, 2002; Zhang & Sternberg, 1998). Also, as expected, university students in the United States tend to be rewarded academically for their Type I thinking styles (Zhang, 2002b). However, contrary to the conventional view that mainland Chinese students are conservative in their thinking styles, there is research evidence indicating that Type II thinking styles are penalized with regard to university students' academic achievement. That is to say, Chinese university students who reported using Type II thinking styles tend not to perform well academically (Zhang, 2001).

Certainly, one should always keep in mind the many caveats involved in drawing any conclusion about any research finding. For example, apart from the widely acknowledged possibility that the same assessment tool used in different cultures may very well result in scores that are not comparable, the relationships between thinking styles and achievement may also differ, based on such variables as school grade level and subject matter (Zhang, 2004c,

2007). Nonetheless, existing research on thinking styles in different cultural contexts suggests that culture does play a role in people's thinking styles. The previously mentioned varying relationships between thinking styles and academic achievement in different cultural contexts are not surprising. In order to maximize their academic achievement levels, it may have been necessary for students to adapt their thinking styles to the demands of the cultural contexts in which they learned. To this end, I would argue, once again, that intellectual styles are more dynamic than static.

Summary: General Findings Across the Six Models

Although very few existing studies have made direct comparisons of intellectual styles among people from different cultural settings, the literature anchored in the six style constructs (i.e., field dependence/independence, reflectivity-impulsivity, personality type, career personality type, learning approach, and thinking style) reviewed here points to the significant impact of culture on intellectual styles. It was predicted that people from Hofstede's low power distance, low uncertainty avoidance, individualism, and masculinity cultures would tend to use intellectual styles that are more creativity-generating (i.e., Type I styles), and that people from Hofstede's high power distance, high uncertainty avoidance, collectivism, and femininity cultures would tend to use styles that are more norm-conforming (i.e., Type II styles).

Clearly, the literature contains some findings, particularly those generated by some studies rooted in the reflectivity-impulsivity and learning approach constructs, that do not lend support to the research hypothesis. Even so, collectively, the findings founded on the six style constructs strongly support the research hypothesis. In the preceding sections, it has been argued that those research findings supporting the hypothesis explicitly demonstrate that intellectual styles can be changed. Moreover, explanations have been made as to why, even when the research hypothesis is not confirmed, the dynamic nature of intellectual styles is still indisputable. The explanations put forward are plausible because several challenges (or, more accurately, threats) inherently increase the likelihood of failure in the research hypothesis to be confirmed. Broadly speaking, these challenges/threats to the confirmation of the hypothesis can be classified into three types.

The first concerns the measures adopted in the studies. For one thing, the use of style measures with norms from decades ago for people in the contemporary era may not always be appropriate as results from these measures may not consistently and truly reflect the style differences among various cultural groups today. For another, results obtained with the same measure in different cultures may not be comparable all the time. The second type of challenges/threats to the confirmation of the research hypothesis centers on the phenomena of acculturation and adaptation. In a number of studies reviewed in this chapter, the lack of support for the research hypothesis can be attributed to the possibility that the cultural groups under investigation had already been acculturated into or had already adapted to their "new" environments by the time when their intellectual styles were examined (e.g., Buriel, 1978; Volet et al., 1994). Finally, the third type of innate threats to the studies' bearing out the research hypothesis pertains to the fact that the impact of culture on intellectual styles is at times indirect. That is, other socialization variables such as gender, educational level, and academic subject matter could moderate the relationships between culture and intellectual styles. Based on these and other reasons previously elaborated, one could conclude with confidence that people's styles develop differently as a function of their socialization in varied cultural contexts.

Limitations and Implications

In this chapter, I have discussed the roles that culture may play in the development of intellectual styles. I have made and tested a hypothesis based on the nature of intellectual styles as well as on one of the most prominent theories of culture – that of Hofstede's cultural dimensions. Furthermore, based on research evidence, I have concluded that although the research hypothesis is not always supported, the dynamic nature of intellectual styles is clearly manifested. Nevertheless, it should be acknowledged that making and testing such a hypothesis have several limitations. To begin with, one may argue that making and testing such a hypothesis could be flawed because Hofstede's model has been criticized for using a dichotomized method of showing cultural differences, resulting in such related problems as unjustifiable generalizations and the ignoring of subtleties (Clark, 2003). Second, making and testing such a hypothesis tend to promote stereotypical views of the intellectual styles of people from different cultures. Third, as has been repeatedly pointed out, there are many caveats that have to be kept in mind when considering the findings obtained in cross-cultural studies of intellectual styles, including macro-issues such as the measurement tools used, the meaning of a particular style construct, the comparability of samples, the dynamic nature of culture, and the process of modernization, as well as micro-issues such as research participants' age, educational level, gender, motivation, occupation, and socioeconomic status.

Despite these and other potential limitations, the existing research suggests that the importance of culture in people's intellectual styles is undeniable. The culture in which individuals are socialized may well help shape their intellectual styles. Likewise, none of the limitations just mentioned should prevent scholars from inquiring into the general role of culture (and its strong correlate, the economy) in the development of intellectual styles. On the contrary, these limitations point to future directions for this area of research. This review shows clearly that although scholars' research interest in identifying the role of culture in intellectual styles can be traced back almost half a century, existing research in this area can be said to have only uncovered a small part of the whole picture. Most noticeably, serious cross-cultural research has been conducted on the basis of only one style construct – that of FDI. More vigorous cross-cultural studies of intellectual styles need to be designed and carried out. These studies should be systematic ones, characterized by using sound research tools, taking into a fuller account of variables that may moderate or mediate the relationships between styles and culture, integrating multiple research methodologies, and involving research participants from as many cultural settings as possible. In particular, researchers should be engaged in experimental studies that delve into the process of people's development of styles that can be claimed to be largely the consequences of culture. However, research on such a scale cannot be carried out by any one researcher alone. Concerted efforts from researchers across the globe are needed to enrich this field of investigation.

Naturally, one would want to know the practical significance of the findings from a review such as this. Because of the lack of statistics necessary for conducting a meta-analysis research and for reporting the effect sizes of the results in the studies reviewed here, only a general review of the literature has been conducted. Nonetheless, because of the strong and consistent evidence presented here, some implications of the present findings for education and for the general public may be proposed.

To begin with, an awareness of the relationship between culture and styles could be beneficial to all parties in educational institutions. For example, teachers could benefit from such an awareness. Increasingly, teachers teaching at various levels – from kindergartens to universities – deal with students from diverse cultures. An understanding of the possible impact of culture on styles may raise teachers' levels of cultural sensitivity in dealing with students with diverse cultural backgrounds. The impact of culture on intellectual styles requires that teachers attend to differences in intellectual styles based on not only the more commonly recognized variables such as age and gender, but also the often neglected variable of culture. Teachers' sensitivity to students' diverse intellectual styles associated with culture can be manifested in a wide variety of teaching practices, ranging from teachers' expectations toward students to their interpersonal interactions with students, and from teaching styles to assessment methods.

Likewise, students today find themselves interacting with peers from diverse cultures more than ever before. If students have an understanding of the present findings, they may become more respectful for, and tolerant of, different cultural values and traditions. Such knowledge could be particularly beneficial to students working effectively in group contexts. The present findings could stimulate students to become more open-minded to different ways of processing information and to different approaches of solving problems.

School and university counselors could also benefit from an appreciation of the present findings. It is true that any professionally trained counselor would already have learned about the importance of taking students' cultural values into account when working with students. It is also likely that these counselors are well aware of the notion of styles. However, evidence revealed from this systematic review of work on the intricate relationships between culture and styles should make counselors feel more confident in applying their knowledge about culture and styles to their professional practice.

A good understanding of the present findings should also be of assistance to senior managers of educational institutions who are perhaps in the best position to make policies that affect the degree to which the relationship between culture and intellectual styles is taken into account in the learning environment. In contemporary educational institutions, senior managers deal not only with an increasingly diverse student population, but also with a progressively more diverse staff population. Such diversification of student and staff populations calls urgently for educational environments – including environments for administration as well as teaching and learning environments – that allow for multiple intellectual styles, particularly creativity-generating styles. It calls for educational environments that accommodate cultural diversity. One way of creating such educational environments is to take into consideration the complex relationships between culture and styles when making and implementing educational policies.

By the same token, the present findings have implications for the general public. For example, instead of holding on to stereotypical views about the intellectual styles of different cultural groups, one should realize that styles are not static. People who experience culture shock should be confident that it is only a matter of time before they adapt to the new cultural setting they are in. With an understanding of what has been discussed in this chapter, people may develop more effective styles as the length of their stay in (or their exposure to) the new cultural environment increases. The same applies to those who believe in their own cultural superiority. People in Hofstede's $L_{PD}L_{UA}IM$ cultural systems (often, economically advantaged societies) should realize that their counterparts on the other ends of Hofstede's continua might be just as creative in their thinking if they were in environments that encourage creativity-generating intellectual styles. Every individual should realize that different cultural settings require different intellectual styles and that intellectual styles can be developed as a response to the challenges presented by new cultural environments.

5

Academic Discipline and Intellectual Styles

As early as 1928, J. Bateman Young and Edwin Shoemaker found in their study that chemistry majors tended to be extroverted and literature majors tended to be introverted. More recently, Entwistle and McCune (2009) argued that the development of intellectual styles ("the disposition to understand," to use Entwistle and McCune's term) must be understood in relation to the "cultures of disciplines" (p. 51). "These cultures have distinctive ways of thinking and practicing which shape what will be seen as ability and what students must attend to show effective sensitivity to context" (Entwistle & McCune, 2009, p. 51; see also McCune & Hounsell, 2005).

Chapters 3 and 4 have demonstrated the modifiability of intellectual styles by providing research evidence indicating that people's styles change largely as a function of gender-role socialization and culture. This chapter and Chapter 6 investigate if individuals exposed to specific learning and work environments can be socialized into developing similar intellectual styles, with this chapter focusing on style variations in different academic settings and the next one on style differences in different nonacademic occupational settings.

Specifically, this chapter critically examines studies that investigated the intellectual styles of students in different academic disciplines. It demonstrates that students' intellectual styles generally vary as a function of academic disciplines/majors (or specific areas of study within disciplines). Such empirical evidence supports the argument that intellectual styles are adaptable. The chapter posits that it is possible that the reason why different academic disciplines are dominated by students with different intellectual styles is that students are attracted to particular disciplines/majors/areas (for brevity, these three terms will be used interchangeably hereafter, depending on the specific contexts of discussion) that suit their predisposed intellectual styles. At the same time, however, the chapter contends that the aforesaid phenomenon – that different academic disciplines are dominated by different intellectual styles – can also be attributable to students adapting their styles to the academic environment in which they learn.

The remainder of this chapter is composed of three parts. The first part describes the method of this review. The second part discusses the studies conducted based on each of the style models involved in this literature. In the final part, some conclusions are drawn and the implications of the findings for educational practice are discussed.

Literature Search Procedures and Results

General Search Procedures

Literature search for this chapter was conducted independently by myself and one of my doctoral students whose research is on intellectual styles. Each complete search was carried out using three sets of style-relevant key terms in tandem with such words or phrases as "major," "academic major," "discipline," and "academic discipline"; with terms that indicate broad academic disciplines such as "arts" and "science"; with terms that suggest more specific disciplines such as "nursing," "architecture," and "accounting"; and with terms referring to specific learning contexts such as "course," "program," and "subject." The first set of style-relevant terms was a series of commonly used style labels such as cognitive style, learning style, and learning approach. The second was a set of style terms that are specific to the most commonly studied style models introduced in Chapter 2. For example, the term "perceptual style" was entered for Witkin's (1962) model, "mind style" for Gregorc's (1979) model, "decision-making style" for Kirton's (1976) model, "personality type" or "personality style" for Jung's (1923) model, and so forth. The third set of style-relevant terms constituted the specific name(s) of the inventory(or inventories) based on each of the style models (also see Chapter 2).

The search started with the 10 style models delineated in the threefold model of intellectual styles (Zhang & Sternberg, 2005), followed by other style models/constructs such as Kolb's (1976) learning style construct and Riding and Cheema's (1991) construct of cognitive style as assessed by the *Cognitive Styles Analysis*. It was specified that all the aforementioned key words, in any combination, were to be found in the abstracts. This search resulted in about 2,000 abstracts. A preliminary reading of these abstracts showed that 57 of them appeared to describe studies of style differences based on academic disciplines. Full texts of 55 of the 57 abstracts were found, and a careful reading of these 55 publications suggested that 39 of them reported empirical studies on the topic of this chapter. A subsequent search mainly involved locating publications in a snowballing fashion, starting with the aforementioned

39 publications. Eventually, it was determined that 53 publications – one a review chapter and the remaining ones research articles – were suitable for inclusion in the current review.

A Brief History Revealed
Results of the literature search described in the preceding section suggested that there had long been attempts by styles researchers to understand the differences in intellectual styles among students studying in different academic disciplines. As noted at the beginning of this chapter, the earliest effort to study this phenomenon can be traced back to Young and Shoemaker's (1928) study of the differences between the personality styles of chemistry students and literature students in the United States. Early research on field dependence/independence (FDI) among students at different educational levels engaged in different academic activities (e.g., physical and biological sciences, mathematics, engineering, social sciences, elementary school teaching, and social science teaching) in the 1950s and 1960s (e.g., Linton, 1952; Pierson, 1965; Zytowski, Mills, & Paepe, 1969) also has heuristic value for researchers investigating style differences among students across different academic disciplines in the higher education setting.

Formal study of style differences across academic disciplines began in the early 1970s. Of the 53 studies to be reviewed in this chapter, eight studies were conducted in the 1970s, the majority (six) of which focused on studying the differences in the levels of FDI among university students across various disciplines. This is not surprising given that Witkin's FDI construct was the pioneering one in the field of styles. In the 1980s, empirical studies concerning the topic of this chapter showed a moderate increase (in all, 12 studies were located). Moreover, the style constructs examined became more diverse. The number of studies based on styles more directly related to students' learning (e.g., the notion of study approaches/learning preferences, hemispheric style, and Kolb's notion of experiential learning) was clearly the largest among the available studies. At the same time, Witkin's FDI construct continued to guide research in this area. The 1990s continued to witness a moderate rise in the number of studies on the topic of this chapter (a total of 20 studies were located), with studies rooted in style constructs more relevant to teaching and learning dominating the body of literature (e.g., four studies concerned the notion of study process/learning preferences and four concerned the notion of hemispheric style). Other style constructs that served as the theoretical foundations of these studies were Jung's (1923) concept of personality types/styles, Kolb's (1976) notion of learning styles, Gregorc's (1979) concept of mind styles, and Witkin's (1948) FDI construct. Finally, the first decade of the 21st century saw a reduction in the productivity of this research. In all, 13 studies emerged from the literature during this time. Two theoretical constructs – Jung's personality styles and the notion of learning approaches and learning/teaching preferences (as discussed by Biggs, 1978; Entwistle, 1981; Rezler & French, 1975) – continued to play a major role in generating these studies, whereas Witkin's FDI construct was no longer influencing research in this area. At the same time, several studies based on Sternberg's (1988, 1997) construct of thinking styles reported findings relevant to the topic of this chapter. All but three studies (Kim, 2010; Leo-Rhynie, 1985; Leung & Zhou, 2001) were conducted in higher education institutions.

Research Findings

What motivated these investigations into style differences among students from different disciplines? At what levels were students' style differences examined? What research methods were employed in these studies? What did these studies show? Before giving a detailed account of these studies, I shall provide a general response to these questions.

The motivation behind these studies varied: in some cases, it was the wish to enhance the quality of teaching and learning; in others, it was the desire to improve the quality of academic and career advising; in still others, it was the wish to assist students in selecting their major and ultimately to increase students' chances of being successful and satisfied in their careers; finally, for some studies, the driving force was the desire to improve guidance and vocational decision making.

Based on the levels of comparisons, these studies can be broadly classified into seven types. Level I studies compared the styles of students in the generally categorized disciplines of science, social science, and arts and humanities. Level II studies compared the styles of students in more specific disciplines/majors (e.g., mathematics, physics, and music). Level III studies compared the styles of students in different fields/areas/programs within the same discipline (e.g., elementary education, secondary education, rehabilitation and special education, and adult education in the discipline of education). Level IV studies compared the styles of students in different courses in the same program/major/area of concentration. Level V studies examined the different learning styles used by the same students when studying different courses. Level VI studies investigated the style differences between practitioners and students in the same academic discipline (e.g., accountants versus accounting students). Level VII studies looked at the differences in the styles of students in the same major/program but studying at different university class/educational levels (e.g., undergraduate versus graduate students in teacher education).

All these studies adopted questionnaire surveys as the method of data collection, and with the exception of two studies, they all obtained statistically significant findings. Further questions arise with respect to these studies: Do the statistically significant findings make sense? How could results from these studies be explained in relation to the notion of style malleability? How could one explain the findings that were not statistically significant? The remainder of this part addresses these questions by reviewing the previously mentioned 53 publications.

The sequence of this review follows two guiding frameworks. The first is Grigorenko and Sternberg's (1995) classification of the three traditions in the study of styles (see Chapter 2). Accordingly, studies grounded in style models from the cognition-centered tradition will be reviewed first. These will be followed by studies grounded in style models from the personality-centered tradition, which in turn will be followed by those from the activity-centered tradition. Finally, studies based on a style model that encompasses all three traditions in the study of styles – Sternberg's (1988) theory of mental self-government – will be reviewed. The second guiding framework is that the studies would be presented according to the chronological order in which the style models were proposed, with studies rooted in the earliest style model being reviewed first. Based on these two guiding frameworks, the studies are presented in the following order in which the style models are listed: (1) Witkin's (1948) construct of FDI, (2) Kirton's (1961) model of decision-making and problem-solving styles, (3) Torrance's (1988) model of modes of thinking, (4) Jung's (1923) model of personality types/styles, (5) Holland's (1973) model of career personality types, (6) Gregorc's (1979) model of mind styles, (7) Kolb's (1976) model of learning styles, (8) Biggs's (1978) model of learning approaches and its associated constructs on learning orientations (Entwistle, 1981) and learning preferences (Rezler & French, 1975), and (9) Sternberg's (1988) model of thinking styles.

FDI and Academic Discipline

Largely owing to the fact that Witkin's (1948, 1962) notion of FDI is the ultimate classic style construct, research on style differences among students from different academic disciplines began, like many other types of research efforts involving the notion of intellectual styles, with investigations using the FDI construct in the 1950s. Indeed, in 1976, in discussing the role of FDI styles in academic performance and in teacher-student relations, Witkin pointed out that the link between FDI and academic choice(s) is based on the degree to which a particular academic field calls for the particular cognitive skills associated with either a more field-dependent style or a more field-independent style. In other words, Witkin believed that students are attracted to a given academic discipline because they may see themselves as possessing cognitive skills that are demanded by that particular discipline, whether that involves more field dependence or more field independence.

However, this "theory of attraction," according to Witkin (1976), only partly explains why students from some disciplines (e.g., physical and biological sciences, mathematics, and engineering) are more field independent, and students from other disciplines (e.g., social sciences, counseling, and elementary education) are more field dependent. Indeed, in the same publication, Witkin made clear his view that FDI is changeable. He asserted: "[I]t seems fair to say from the evidence now on hand that socialization factors are undoubtedly of overwhelming importance in the development of individual differences in field dependence versus field independence. At the same time, it may be that genetic factors are implicated as well, although probably to a much smaller degree" (Witkin, 1976, p. 47). With academic discipline as one of the major socialization variables, and citing a number of studies conducted among students of different educational levels, Witkin (1976) declared: "Not surprisingly, a consistent finding of most of these studies is that more field independent students favor domains in which analytical skills are called for, whereas more field dependent students avoid such domains" (p. 50).

To Witkin, the similarity in the levels of FDI among students in the same discipline is the product of both self-selection by the students (i.e., students are attracted to the program) and selection by the discipline. There are at least two ways in which a discipline can select students. One relates to the kind of skills (cognitive and noncognitive) that a discipline requires from the students; the other relates to the academic achievement of students in that particular academic discipline. Those students who make an effort and succeed in adapting their cognitive styles to the demands of the discipline and perform well academically tend to stay in the discipline they initially selected. However, those who either do not make an effort to adapt or make an effort but do not succeed tend to leave the discipline. Consequently, students in a given academic discipline tend to display similar levels of FDI.

The preceding arguments centered on the socialization of academic discipline prevail in the studies involving the FDI construct, as they do in many studies based on other style constructs reviewed in this chapter. The 11 individual empirical studies involving the FDI construct examined students' levels of FDI at four different comparative levels: Levels I (four studies), II (three studies), III (three studies), and VI (one study).

The first of the four Level I comparative studies based on Witkin's concept of FDI was conducted by DeRussy and Futch (1971). The researchers compared the levels of FDI of 16 students majoring in chemistry, physics, or mathematics with those of 16 liberal arts students. Their prediction that students majoring in liberal arts would be more field dependent than those majoring in the three natural science subjects (deemed more technical by the researchers) was supported. As it involved only 32 research participants, the results from DeRussy and Futch's (1971) study are certainly not to be generalized. Nevertheless, historically, this study inspired many other studies of style differences across disciplines – those grounded in Witkin's FDI construct and beyond.

The second Level I comparative study was carried out by Witkin and his research team (Witkin et al., 1977). In order to test the utility of the FD-FI cognitive styles in predicting students' stability and change in academic majors and to provide guidance counselors with useful information about students, Witkin and his colleagues followed a large group of students (n=1,422) from university entry to final college majors, and through graduate/professional school specialties. Based on the characteristics of FD-FI styles and on the nature (and, by implication, the requirements) of the academic fields, the researchers predicted that relatively field-independent students would be likely to enter science majors and relatively field-dependent students would be likely to enter majors in education. The researchers did not make any prediction for students in the more broadly gauged[1] majors (e.g., sociology and psychology), which do not communicate in any discernible way specific requirements regarding either FD or FI styles. The results of the study suggested that students' choice of major was associated with FD-FI styles in ways predicted by Witkin's theory. At the final-year university level and at the graduate level, students' FD-FI styles made a significant contribution to their choice of educational-vocational specialties beyond what was predicted by *Scholastic Aptitude Test-Verbal* and *Scholastic Aptitude Test-Mathematical* scores. Moreover, students whose preliminarily selected majors were compatible with their FD-FI styles were more likely to remain in those majors through undergraduate education and into graduate school.

One could say that the aforementioned phenomenon manifests a tendency for students to gravitate naturally toward educational domains that suit their FD-FI styles. This conjecture cannot be denied. However, the stylistic characteristics of an academic field can also be partially attributable to the

---

[1] Broad-gauged disciplines refer to those that may offer opportunities for both field-dependent and field-independent individuals.

accentuation of particular styles after students have been attracted to that field, for one simple line of reasoning: one may choose to enter a major that is generally compatible with one's styles. To be successful in any particular field, however, individuals have to continue to understand the nature of the field and to develop the styles required by that particular field. To borrow the major tenet shared by all theories of person-environment interaction (e.g., Barker, 1968; Stern, 1970), human beings create the environment, and the environment in return exerts a coercive force on human behavior. To apply this belief to the current topic, students choose to enter a particular academic discipline, and the academic discipline in turn influences the development of students' styles by "demanding" that students meet its requirements.

The third Level I comparative study grounded in Witkin's FDI construct was carried out among 203 pre-university students in Jamaica (Leo-Rhynie, 1985). The research participants were broadly classified as an arts-emphasis group and a science-emphasis group. The results of this study suggested that the *Group Embedded Figures Test* (GEFT) significantly discriminated between the two groups of students, with the science students scoring significantly higher on the GEFT than the arts students. The researcher expressed her belief in style change by stating that the study's results should be made known to educators so that they could build into their courses strategies that would assist students in the development of more adaptive cognitive skills, including cognitive styles. The researcher asserted: "[T]he acquisition of these skills should not be left to chance – they have to be deliberately fostered" (Leo-Rhynie, 1985, p. 26).

The final Level I comparative study based on the FDI construct was conducted among 75 overseas Chinese and 75 American graduate students in the United States (Huang & Chao, 1995). The students were studying in three broadly classified disciplines: (1) social science and humanities, (2) natural science, and (3) engineering. Research participants' GEFT scores did not reveal any significant difference based on academic discipline (or on culture and gender). Nonetheless, the researchers explained that the similarity in styles among the research participants from the three broad disciplines might have been attributable to the fact that this group was rather homogenous in the sense that they had all received significantly more education than the general population.

The socialization of FDI happens not only at the level of broad academic fields, but also at the more specific level of academic majors. Results from the three Level II comparative studies – studies comparing FDI differences of students from specific majors – indicated that although students from the same broad academic discipline (e.g., arts or science) may have shared similar cognitive styles, when their levels of FDI were compared according to their specific academic majors, significant differences were revealed.

The first study (Peterson & Sweitzer, 1973) focused on investigating the levels of FDI of architecture students. The primary research participants were 20 architecture majors from each of the first three university class levels: freshman, sophomore, and pre-junior. To clearly identify the FDI levels of the architecture students, the researchers also recruited 20 students studying in other fields (but excluding students from the College of Design, Architecture, and Art[2]) across the university to serve as the comparison group. Significant findings were obtained that revealed the socialization effects of academic majors at two different levels. To begin with, as expected, compared with students from the other majors, the architecture students were significantly more field independent. Furthermore, also in line with the researchers' prediction, the variability in the levels of FDI among the architecture majors decreased over the years, with the variability being the largest among freshmen and the smallest among pre-juniors. The first finding is consistent with the argument that the nature of architecture is such that architecture students tended to be socialized into using the FI style more than did students in the other academic majors. At the same time, the finding regarding the decreasing variability of FDI among architectural students signifies that as students went through their undergraduate education, their intellectual styles became increasingly more alike – most probably owing to the fact that they were socialized more and more in the same academic environment.

The second Level II comparative study (Morris & Bergum, 1978) also involved students from architecture. This time, undergraduate architecture students (n=25) were compared with students majoring in business (n=13). Despite the small sample sizes, statistically significant findings were obtained. Consistent with what Peterson and Sweitzer (1973) found, results of this study showed that architecture students demonstrated higher levels of field independence than did the students in the comparison group.

The third Level II comparative study (Kelleher, 1997) differed from the previous two studies in that the research participants from four majors were all drawn from the same broad discipline – all were studying for a Bachelor's degree in commerce in a business school. The research participants were 61 Canadian undergraduate students majoring in accounting, finance, management, and marketing. Results indicated that although the commerce students

---

[2] Students in this college were excluded from the study because their levels of field independence presumably tend to be high because of the nature of the disciplines in which they were studying. This exclusion should have helped reduce the sampling bias associated with the nature of the academic disciplines under consideration.

as a group generally scored higher on the *Group Embedded Figures Test* (GEFT) when compared with the general population, students majoring in accounting, finance, and marketing demonstrated higher levels of field independence than did the management students. It is possible that compared with the other three majors, management tends to attract students with a lower level of field independence. However, it is also possible that the management students became less field independent than did students in the other three majors as they went through college. Complementarily, it is possible that the nature of studies in accounting, finance, and marketing is more conducive to the development of field independence than is that of studies in management. Furthermore, there could be several reasons for the GEFT's failure to separate the levels of FDI among the other three groups (i.e., accounting, finance, and marketing students), the small sample size of the study being one of them.

While results obtained from various levels of comparative studies are discussed more generally later in this chapter, it should be noted here that the levels of FDI are all relative, depending on the particular groups that are being compared. Take the case of the results from the latter two of the three Level I comparative studies just described. When compared with architecture students, business students showed significantly lower levels of field independence. However, when compared with the general population, the undergraduate business majors, as a group, demonstrated a higher level of field independence. Moreover, in the same business program, different undergraduate majors also tended to show varying levels of field independence. Such style differences in relative terms exist at yet a more specific level: Level III comparative studies, which are described in the following.

Three Level III comparative studies – studies that examined FDI variations among students of the same major but in different areas of specialization – were identified in the literature. All three studies involved participants majoring in teacher education. The first study (Petrakis, 1981) can be said to be a pseudo-comparative study because the actual participants were only 73 students majoring in physical education. Even so, Petrakis (1981) made his research hypothesis on the basis of what is known about the teaching profession. The researcher pointed out that in the teaching profession, field-independent individuals tend to choose to teach mathematics and science, whereas field-dependent individuals are more likely to be interested in teaching social sciences and elementary education. Petrakis hypothesized that because careers in physical education entail a scientific background, the physical education majors would tend to be more field independent. Results of the study were somewhat supportive of the researcher's prediction in that the physical education undergraduate majors were moderately more field independent when compared with the general population.

With the aim of exploring the potential role of cognitive style in academic counseling, the second Level III comparative study (Frank, 1986) examined the differences in FDI among 427 female teacher education majors. The research participants were enrolled in eight areas of specializations: natural sciences, mathematics, business, humanities, family and child development, home economics, special education, and speech pathology. Frank's (1986) belief in the socialization effects of academic settings on intellectual styles was obvious because he made his research hypothesis based on Witkin's idea that underlying the relationship between FDI and academic interests is the degree to which a particular area of training emphasizes cognitive skills and personality attributes associated with either an FI style or an FD style. As a result of such training, at least most of the students who had studied for some time in an academic discipline should have either adapted their styles to suit the learning environment or intensified the particular styles required by that discipline. Results of the study showed that even after students' ACT (*American College Testing*, both verbal and mathematical) scores were adjusted, statistically significant differences were found. Students in specialization areas that emphasize abilities in structuring and analysis, and are characterized by an atmosphere that requires a minimal amount of interpersonal contact (in this case, natural sciences, mathematics, and business), were more field independent than students specializing in areas that underscore interpersonal interactions (in this case, humanities, family and child development, home economics, special education, and speech pathology).

The third and most recent Level III comparative study (Collins, White, & O'Brien, 1992) was carried out among 303 pre-service and in-service vocational education teachers. The research participants, all training to be vocational teachers for either secondary or post-secondary education, were from nine categories of occupational teaching specialties. Very much in line with what was found in Frank's (1984) study of education teachers, the GEFT scores obtained in Collins et al.'s (1992) study suggested that research participants of technical, business, and electrical specialties were significantly more field independent than those of academic support, drafting/construction, general industrial, cosmetology, and health specialties.

Finally, the socialization effects of academic discipline on students' levels of FDI have also been manifested in a fourth type of comparative studies – studies that tested FDI differences between practitioners in a given domain and students studying in the very same domain. As previously noted, this type of studies is classified as Level VI comparative studies in this chapter. One such study that was rooted in the FDI construct was located in the current literature search.

In an attempt to understand if individuals' intellectual styles can be developed as a result of being socialized in particular academic disciplines, Sofman, Hajosy, and Vojtisek (1976) studied the levels of FDI among 24 male undergraduate students and 24 male faculty members. Half of the participants were science students and faculty members, and half were non-science students and faculty members. A shortened form of Witkin's *Embedded Figures Test* (EFT) developed by Jackson (1956) was administered to all research participants. It was predicted that both students and faculty members specializing in sciences would display greater field independence than would those in the non-science groups. It was further predicted that this difference would be more pronounced between the science and non-science faculty members than between the science and non-science students. The logic behind Sofman et al.'s (1976) second hypothesis was straightforward: if different academic disciplines require different intellectual styles, and if a screening-out process does occur in areas of study, those who remain in a particular discipline after their student years should more clearly possess the particular style(s) demanded by that discipline.

Results indicated that there was no significant difference in the levels of FDI between science and non-science students. However, the predicted significant difference between science and non-science faculty members did occur, supporting the idea that their intellectual styles were typical of those demanded by their particular disciplines. There could be a number of possible reasons why the anticipated difference was not found in the student group. One such reason might be the fact that the research sample was too small. One could argue, however, that the small sample size was not the likely cause of a non-significant finding in the student group because the same number of faculty members participated in the study. Although this argument may seem reasonable at first, one should bear in mind that investigating the difference in intellectual styles between science and non-science faculty members may not require a larger group for the simple reason that faculty members have undergone the selective filtering process imposed by the nature of their disciplines. Consequently, their style differences can be more easily detected. As will be seen later in this chapter, several studies based on other style models have also shown that style differences are better defined among people already in different professions than are those among students who are acquiring knowledge in the same domains.

Decision-Making and Problem-Solving Style and Academic Discipline
Since its inception, Kirton's (1961) model of decision-making and problem-solving styles (typically assessed by the *Kirton Adaption-Innovation Inventory*, or KAI; Kirton, 1976) has guided a great deal of research on style differences among people who work in different settings (see Chapter 6 in this volume). At the same time, it has also led to a small number of studies examining style differences among students studying in different academic disciplines. Three such studies were found in this current literature search.

All three studies were conducted at the Level II comparative analysis – investigating the levels of adaptation-innovation of students from specific academic majors – and all three were carried out in the United States. The first study (Elder, 1989) was conducted among 104 undergraduate students from various majors enrolled in general psychology classes at a medium-sized midwestern university. An analysis of variance for the KAI scores by university major did not yield a statistically significant difference. Elder (1989) offered several possible explanations for this lack of significant relationship between adaptation-innovation scores and university majors, all reflecting his belief that students' intellectual styles can be socialized into ones that are more in tune with what is required in particular academic majors. For example, he postulated that the lack of significant findings might have been attributable to the fact that the research participants were still at an early stage in their university program – most being freshmen and sophomores taking a general psychology course. He also thought that the way in which the participating university had categorized its majors might have been one factor responsible for the findings.

The second study (Pettigrew & King, 1993) focused on understanding the levels of adaption-innovation among nursing students compared with those of the general population in the United States. Participants were 60 first-year nursing students and 73 non-nursing students. Based on findings obtained from studying professionals in nursing, the researchers anticipated that nursing students would be more adaptive and less innovative than non-nursing students. This hypothesis was confirmed. In addition, the study found that within the group of nursing students, traditional age (18 to 22 years) students tended to be more innovative in style than nontraditional age students. The researchers did not comment on these findings. Nevertheless, both findings make good sense. As just noted, the researchers made their research hypothesis on the basis of findings from studies of nursing professionals: nursing students were expected to be generally tending toward being adaptive. If nursing professionals are more adaptive in their problem-solving style, it should be no surprise that nursing students become more adaptive as they progress in their university education. Furthermore, because nontraditional-age students are usually ones whose career aspirations tend to be more crystallized as a result of career exploration, they tend to be more motivated to learn and dedicated to learning. For this reason, the predominant intellectual style of one particular discipline should manifest itself even more among nontraditional-age students than among traditional-age students. That is to say, the difference based on age within the nursing group in Pettigrew and King's (1993) study might suggest that although students with the adaptive style tended to be attracted to the nursing program, nontraditional-age students tended to be socialized into being even more adaptive in their problem-solving style by virtue of their being in the nursing learning environment.

Finally, the dynamic nature of adaptive-innovative styles is vividly shown in Mitchell and Cahill's (2005) study of the plebe turnover at the U.S. Naval Academy. The primary research participants were 1,134 students entering the U.S. Naval Academy class of 2000. Students were administered the KAI on the first day of a summer program, known as the Plebe Summer – a seven-week nonacademic training program required to be completed by all entering students in the summer prior to the freshman year. Ninety-eight plebes voluntarily withdrew before completing the program. Data were compared with those obtained from five other samples in nonmilitary universities. Results indicated that compared with the five samples of nonmilitary university students, the plebes were significantly less innovative in their problem-solving style. Furthermore, compared with the 98 dropouts from the summer program, the ones who stayed were less innovative. Both results reflect the regimentation-style climate of the military academy. In other words, in terms of person-environment fit, plebes with a more adaptive style may be more compatible with the cognitive style required in the military than those with an innovative style. As argued by the researchers, there was clearly a preselection based on intellectual style, either through the admissions process or though self-selection, or both. Despite this preselection into the military program, students who chose to stay in the program must have, to varying degrees, adapted themselves to the military environment, which strongly favors an adaptor-oriented style. As suggested by the researchers, military doctrine and bureaucracy tend to wear down innovative thinkers. Such wearing-down might have resulted in some students' withdrawing from the program and other students' adapting to the new environment in which they found themselves.

Mode of Thinking and Academic Discipline
As a style model that focuses on examining how people learn and think, Torrance's (1988) model of brain dominance (again, more recently termed as

mode of thinking) was the basis for a number of studies concerning the topic of this chapter. These studies mainly involved Level I and Level II comparative analyses and were carried out in Canada, India, the United Arab Emirates, and the United States in the 1980s and 1990s. In order to assess students' modes of thinking, the studies employed either one of the two versions of *Your Style of Learning and Thinking* (SOLAT, Torrance & Reynolds, 1980; Torrance, Reynolds, Ball, & Riegel, 1978) or the *Human Information Processing Survey* (HIPS, Torrance, 1984).

Four of these studies were Level I comparative analyses. The very first study (Raina & Vats, 1983) was carried out in India with 166 undergraduate students in the science and arts faculties of a higher education institution. The participants took the SOLAT (Torrance et al., 1978). It was found that science students scored significantly higher on the left-hemispheric style of thinking and learning and arts students obtained higher scores on the right-hemispheric style of thinking and learning, as expected in accordance with the nature of sciences and that of arts.

Similar findings were obtained when Monfort, Martin, and Frederickson (1990) and Lavach (1991) examined the hemispheric preferences of undergraduate students in the United States. Both studies employed the HIPS (Torrance, 1984). Monfort et al. (1990) tested the HIPS on 1,023 students in liberal arts, business, and education. Students in liberal arts were shown to be right-brained in information processing, whereas students in business were found to be left-brain thinkers. At the same time, students in the colleges of education, special arts, and sciences were shown to use their left and right hemispheres equally frequently in processing information.

Lavach (1991) administered the HIPS to 275 students majoring in the humanities (including English, fine arts, modern language, music, philosophy, and religion), natural sciences (including biology, chemistry, computer science, mathematics, and physics), and social sciences (including anthropology, economics, elementary education, government, history, psychology, and sociology). Results from the HIPS scores discriminated the hemispheric preferences of the students from the three broadly categorized disciplines. Students from the humanities tended to be more holistic in their mode of thinking, students from the social sciences tended to be more analytic in their mode of thinking, and students in the natural sciences indicated a strong preference for a more integrated mode of thinking.

The final Level I comparative study of hemispheric preferences was carried out among undergraduate students in the United Arab Emirates (Albaili, 1993). The research participants were 190 students in the social sciences (including education, history, psychology, and sociology) and applied sciences (including biology, chemistry, computer science, and physics). Results showed no significant difference with regard to the left-hemispheric style and the integrated style. However, on the right-hemispheric scale, students in the applied sciences scored significantly higher than did those in the social sciences.

The researchers of all the four studies mentioned were clearly in favor of the argument that styles can be changed, and all from the perspective of the task demands arising from the nature of the academic disciplines in which students are studying. For example, Raina and Vats (1983) contended that although studying a particular academic subject may require bi-hemispheric information processing to some extent, the relative participation of the two hemispheres could vary considerably. Such variations exist because some academic areas lend themselves more easily to analysis and tend to "draw the mind in that direction" (Raina and Vats, 1983, p. 88), whereas others tend to place a premium on symbolic and intuitive processes. Similar reasoning was given by the researchers of the other three studies presented earlier. Arguably, prolonged socialization in a given academic domain would be likely to develop students' information-processing styles, no matter in which direction their minds are drawn.

Apart from being shown in the aforementioned studies, the socialization effects of academic disciplines on students' brain hemispheric preferences have also been demonstrated in studies that tested their hemispheric styles at Level II comparison. Two such studies were located. One study (Kienholz & Hritzuk, 1986) involved 59 graduate architecture students and 50 medical students (university levels unspecified) in Canada. Architecture and medical students were selected because they were deemed to be typified by possessing academic backgrounds in arts and sciences, respectively. The SOLAT (Torrance & Reynolds, 1980) was used to measure hemispheric preferences. As expected, results indicated that the architecture students scored higher in the right-hemispheric style and that the medical students showed a stronger preference for processing information using the left hemisphere.

The other study (Mishra, 1998) was conducted in India with 434 postgraduate students majoring in commerce, fine arts, management, and science. The research tool employed was once again the SOLAT (Torrance & Reynolds, 1980). The study found that the commerce, fine arts, and management students tended to use the right hemisphere in information processing. At the same time, the science students displayed a tendency to use the left and right hemispheres of the brain fairly equally in a synchronized manner.

It was previously mentioned that the current review is confined to introducing studies that were presented in the 53 publications located. However, it is worth noting research findings reported in three doctoral dissertations (all produced in the United States in the early 1980s) that were reviewed in Monfort et al.'s (1990) work. All three dissertations reported Level II comparative studies of students' hemispheric preferences, and their findings lent support to the studies reported earlier in this section. Specifically, Silbey (1980) found that compared with the general population in the United States, graduate and undergraduate students in a business school scored significantly higher on the left-hemisphere scale but lower on the right-hemisphere scale. Ghosh (1980) compared the differences in hemispheric preferences of artistically, mathematically, and musically talented adolescents and concluded that the artistically gifted showed a distinct preference for information processing that primarily relied on the right hemisphere, the mathematically talented students preferred the left and integrated functions, and the musically talented indicated a preference for a combination of the right and integrated functions of the brain. Finally, Losh (1983) compared the hemispheric preference scores of undergraduate students majoring in computer programming with those of the general population in the United States. Results suggested that the computer programming students had a stronger preference for the analytic mode of thinking, which is expected based on the nature of computer science.

Personality Type and Academic Discipline
In view of the long-term interest of styles researchers in the Jungian types, the productivity of research on personality type differences based on academic disciplines can only be said to be modest. Six such studies were identified: one Level II, three Level III, and two Level VII comparative studies. It should be noted that although this line of research was pioneered by Rezler and French in 1975, it was not until 1997 that scholars continued with this research interest. Personality types/styles of participants were assessed by various versions of the *Myers-Briggs Type Indicator.*

At the Level II comparison, Boreham and Watts (1998) examined the differences in personality types between 130 first-year education students and 30 applied physics students in Australia. The average age of the education students was 20 years, and although the university class level of the physics students was not specified, their average age was 22 years. It was found that the students from the two majors were clearly differentiated by the T-F (Thinking-Feeling) dimension. In general, the feeling type was dominant among education majors, and the thinking type was more prominent among physics majors. In explaining the findings, the researchers clearly utilized the theory of attraction, stating that education is an area of study that tends to attract students oriented toward people and values (characteristics of the feeling type), and that physics is a course of study that is more likely to attract individuals oriented toward ideas and principles (features of the thinking type). Nonetheless, the researchers communicated their belief in style changes by noting the different learning cultures created by the two different majors: education encourages a culture built on action, cooperation, sympathy, and sociability, whereas physics promotes a culture built on logic, objectivity, and reasoning. I would take an additional step in arguing that it is possible that the students' personality styles were further strengthened by their learning environment.

Among the three Level III comparative studies, the first was the classic[3] study carried out by Rezler and French (1975) in the United States. The research participants were 139 female students from six allied health sciences: medical art, medical dietetics, medical technology, medical record administration, occupational therapy, and physical therapy. Results indicated that students from each of the six areas of studies scored higher on items contributing to a particular personality type than did students in at least one other area of studies. However, distinct personality types were shown most clearly for medical technology and occupational therapy students because each of these two groups had a personality type that was largely absent in the other groups. The ISTJ (introverted-sensing-thinking-judging) personality type exhibited by the medical technology majors was absent among students of medical art, medical dietetics, occupational therapy, and physical therapy. Similarly, there was a common personality type in the occupational therapy group (i.e., EN/SFP extraverted-intuitive/sensing-feeling-perceiving) that was absent in all other groups. Of course, these distinct patterns of personality styles could be explained, once again, by both the theory of attraction and the theory of accentuation.

The second Level III comparative study (Stilwell, Wallick, Thal, & Burleson, 2000) was also carried out among students of medical sciences in the United States. This study involved a sample that was in transition from university to the world of work. Data were collected from 3,987 student graduates from 12 medical schools between 1983 and 1995. The aim of the study was to explore the associations between personality styles and career choices. It was found that medical graduates who were introverted and feeling personality types tended to choose primary care specialties, whereas those who were extraverted and thinking types tended to choose surgical specialties. At the same time,

---

[3] Classic in the sense that it was the very first study to examine personality type/style differences among students of different academic disciplines and it is one of the most widely cited studies in this area of research.

the researchers compared the differences between the personality types of graduates in the 1980s and the 1990s and those of physicians in the 1950s, and concluded that the personality types of doctors had generally changed from perceiving to judging. The researchers pointed out that such a general change might be partly associated with the increases in technology and information in all medical fields.

The most recent Level III comparative research was conducted among students studying music in the United States (Steele & Young, 2008). The research participants were 382 music education and music therapy majors. What is unique about this publication is that both similarities and differences in the personality styles of students in the two areas of study were reported. Both groups were dominated by the ENFP (Extraverted-Intuitive-Feeling-Perceiving) and ENFJ (Extraverted-Intuitive-Feeling-Judging) types. At the same time, although both majors demonstrated a stronger preference for extraversion, the music therapy students expressed a stronger preference for introversion than did the music education majors. That is to say, while the common factor of music may have been the reason why students in the two majors shared similarities in personality styles, as suggested by Steele and Young (2008), the different professional objectives of the two majors may have contributed to the development of some of their personality styles differently.

The dynamic nature of styles has also manifested itself in the study of the differences in personality styles between students in the same academic discipline but for different durations – that is, Level VII comparative studies. Two studies based on Jung's model of personality styles were identified, with the first one being centered on engineering students (Rosati, 1997) and the second one on Master in Teaching (MiT) students (Willing, Guest, & Morford, 2001).

In Rosati's (1997) study, data were collected from 1,913 engineering students in Canada from 1987 through 1993. Based on the nature of engineering science, Rosati anticipated that success in the engineering program would be more related to the INTJ (introverted-intuitive-thinking-judging) personality styles. Results largely confirmed this prediction, indicating that, compared with entry students, students (especially male students) who had successfully completed the first-year engineering program scored significantly higher on three of the four personality styles that were theoretically predicted: the I (introverted), T (thinking), and J (judging) types. This suggests that the personality styles of students who had been in the program for a year were socialized into the engineering culture, while the personality styles of the entry students were yet to do so.

Willing et al.'s (2001) study was slightly different from Rosati's (1997) in that it explored research participants' style differences not only with a Level VII comparison, but also with a Level III comparison. Moreover, the socialization effects of academic culture on personality styles were even more pronounced in Willing et al.'s study. Specifically, Willing, Guest, and Morford (2001) administered the MBTI to a group of 525 Master's in Teaching (MiT) students. At Level VII comparison, the researchers compared the MBTI scores of the MiT students with those of previous samples of pre- and in-service teachers and with those of the general population. At the same time, they compared the personality styles of students who had entered the MiT program immediately following the completion of their bachelors' degrees with the personality styles of students who had delayed their entry into the MiT program for one or more years. It was found that the MiT students differed significantly from both the pre-service and in-service teacher education students and the general population on the SN (sensing-intuitive) dimension, with the MiT students being significantly more intuitive. In other words, more teacher education and training were associated with the intuitive personality style. This finding is in line with Myers and McCaulley's (1989) conclusion that people with more advanced degrees tend to be more intuitive than the general population.

The dynamic nature of personality styles is further shown by more in-depth analysis revealing that the differences between the MiT students and the undergraduate students were concentrated almost entirely among the students who had delayed their entry into the MiT program. In other words, students who had gained other types of experiences (after receiving their Bachelor's degrees) before entering the MiT program were even more intuitive than the remainder of the participants. This finding is not surprising, bearing in mind how Piaget (1952) elucidated the occurrence of cognitive development: one's cognitive development occurs when one overcomes cognitive dissonance that often entails difficulties. It is inevitable that the MiT students who had delayed their entry into the program would have encountered and overcome more difficulties than those who had entered the MiT immediately after they obtained their Bachelor's degrees. The additional experiences that the delayed-entry MiT students had gained might have challenged them to develop the more creativity-generating, Type I (intuitive) style. Indeed, this finding dovetailed well with the finding that teachers who reported more experiences beyond school teaching scored significantly higher on Type I thinking styles than did their counterparts (Zhang & Sternberg, 2002).

Finally, Willing et al. (2001) also conducted a Level III comparison. That is, within the MiT sample, the personality styles of students specializing in elementary education were compared with those of students specializing in secondary education. The result was that the TF (thinking-feeling) and SN (sensing-intuitive) dimensions clearly distinguished the students majoring in elementary education from those majoring in secondary education: the elementary education majors tended to show sensing and feeling styles, whereas the secondary education majors tended to report intuitive and thinking styles. This difference could well have resulted from the differences in the objectives and the structures of the two study programs.

Career Personality Type and Academic Discipline
Since its inception, Holland's career personality type model has become one of the prominent paradigms in guiding educational research and practice. The importance of the correspondence between people's career personality types and the environment in which people learn and work has been very well documented (Borchers, 2007; Holland, 1973, 1994). However, the current literature search yielded only four studies that were especially designed to investigate the differences in career personality types among students in different academic disciplines. These studies were conducted in three cultures – Belgium, Hong Kong, and the United States – and they all yielded statistically significant results. All findings were obtained from participants' responses to the *Self-Directed Search* (Holland, 1973, 1994).

The earliest research (Utz & Hartman, 1978) was a Level III comparative study conducted among business school graduating seniors majoring in three different specialties (accounting, behavioral studies, and marketing) in the United States. Data were gathered from two samples – one in 1976 (n=92) and the other in 1977 (n=104). Based on the nature of each of the areas of concentration, the researchers predicted that the accounting group would have a Holland summary code of CIS (conventional-investigative-social), the behavioral studies group an ESC (enterprising-social-conventional) code, and the marketing group an EIS (enterprising-investigative-social) code. Results indicated that the hypothesized summary codes were generally able to differentiate the students from the different concentration areas, particularly with regard to two of the three concentration areas. The CIS (conventional-investigative-social) code distinguished the accounting students from students in behavioral studies and marketing. By the same token, the ESC (enterprising-social-conventional) code drew a clear line between the behavioral studies students and the students in the other two areas of study (i.e., accounting and marketing). However, nothing could be stated about the special characteristics of the marketing students vis-à-vis those of the other two groups of students. There could be a number of reasons why the marketing students' characteristics were not clearly distinguished by their SDS code, one of which is that the formation and strengthening of the career personality styles among marketing students may need more time, beyond their senior year.

The second study (Batesky, Malacos, & Purcell, 1980), a Level II comparative investigation, was also carried out in the United States. Research participants were 49 physical education and recreation majors. Results suggested that the Holland summary code of SER (social-enterprising-realistic) was dominant among the physical education students, and that the summary code of SAE (social-artistic-enterprising) prevailed among the recreation majors. Noticeably, both groups had a strong social orientation. Nonetheless, as the researchers pointed out, the significant differences found in the two groups at the secondary-code level may have contributed to the selection of a specialization area. I would take it step further and contend that it could also have been the case that after students had studied in different areas of specialization, their characteristics, as denoted by their secondary Holland codes, became more prominent.

The third study, a mixture of Levels I, II, and III comparative analyses, was carried out at a university in Belgium (De Fruyt & Mervielde, 1996). Nine hundred and thirty-four final-year students who were enrolled in different majors participated in the study. A number of statistically significant findings were obtained. First, compared with students from the behavioral and social sciences and the humanities, students in industrial, bio-, agricultural, and applied engineering scored higher on the realistic scale. Second, science and bioengineering majors shared the common characteristics of the investigative career personality style, whereas students from languages, history, law, economics, and political and social sciences scored the lowest on the investigative scale. Third, students in arts, language, and history obtained the highest scores on the artistic scale. Fourth, compared with students in other faculties, students in psychology and educational sciences faculties scored higher on the social scale.

Apart from the aforementioned findings, the study revealed differences in career personality types in even more specific areas of study. For example, within the faculty of applied sciences, students studying in the engineering-architecture program had high scores on the artistic scale but low scores on the conventional scale, whereas the opposite was the case among students in the mechanical-electronic program.

Finally, the latest study (Leung & Zhou, 2001) on this topic was carried out in Hong Kong to examine the concurrent validity of the SDS for measuring the career interest styles of Hong Kong Chinese upper secondary school students. The research participants were 777 students studying in either the science stream or the arts stream. The results indicated that the science students had higher scores on the realistic and investigative scales, whereas the arts students had higher scores on the artistic, social, and enterprising scales. Such differences, based on the two broad categories of science versus arts, are reasonable in view of the nature of the two different academic disciplines.

Mind Style and Academic Discipline
As the final personality-centered style model examined in this chapter, Gregorc's (1979) notion of mind style, like that of Holland's career personality type, has not been very productive in generating studies of intellectual styles in different academic disciplines. Again, only four studies were found. Carried out either in Canada or in the United States, these studies involved Level I and Level II comparative analyses.

Largely as a Level II comparative analysis, the first study (Stewart & Felicetti, 1992) was aimed at understanding if marketing majors shared a preferred learning style. To achieve this objective, the researchers administered the *Gregorc Style Delineator* (GSD, Gregorc, 1982) to 101 marketing majors, 65 students majoring in other areas of study, and 99 students whose majors were undecided. Results indicated that the dominant learning styles of students majoring in marketing were concrete-sequential and abstract-random. Furthermore, differences at a more specific level were also found. Among the marketing majors, students who indicated career interests in either sales or advertising were more likely to be random learners, whereas students who expressed interest in a career in marketing management showed a strong propensity for sequential learning.

The second study (Seidel & England, 1999), a Level I comparative investigation, was conducted among 100 undergraduate students in the United States. Among the research participants, 35 were majoring in natural sciences, 35 in social sciences, and 30 in humanities. Results suggested that the GSD was able to distinguish the students majoring in the three broad areas of studies, particularly the students from natural sciences and humanities. Of the natural science majors, 86 percent scored high on the sequential direction. Of the humanities majors, 85 percent scored high on the random direction, whereas the scores of the students majoring in social sciences were distributed fairly evenly across the GSD styles. These findings concerning the natural science and humanities students are consistent with what would be expected considering the nature of the two broad areas of studies and the definitions of the relevant learning styles. Sequential learners prefer to work on tasks that entail order and logical sequence, as is the case with natural science students. Random learners, on the other hand, tend to pay close attention to human behaviors and to be attuned to their environment, as do humanities students.

O'Brien (1992) investigated style differences among 263 students enrolled in foundations of education classes. The students were pursuing their studies in eight different majors: adult education, arts, business, early childhood or elementary education, rehabilitation and special education, sciences, secondary education, and vocational teacher education (thus a Level II comparative study). It was found that students majoring in early childhood or elementary education and in rehabilitation and special education scored significantly lower on the AS (abstract-sequential) style, whereas students majoring in business scored the lowest on the AS style. This finding is congruent with the nature of learning involved in the relevant majors. Furthermore, students majoring in rehabilitation and special education scored higher on the AR (abstract-random) style. People with a preference for the AR style tend to place more emphasis on emotional attachments and relationships than on analytic deduction and material reality. Thus, it was not surprising that the rehabilitation and special education students scored higher on the AR style, nor should it be unexpected that business students showed the least concern with feelings.

The final investigation (Drysdale, Ross, & Schulz, 2001) differed from the three aforementioned studies in that it explored style differences across academic disciplines by examining the relationship between students' mind styles and their academic achievement in different courses. Data were collected from 4,546 students taking 19 courses in various disciplines, with many students taking more than one of the courses. Data analyses and discussion were conducted at the first level of comparative analysis. In science and math-related courses, higher achievers tended to be sequential learners, whereas in fine arts courses, higher achievers tended to be random learners. One could argue that those students who achieved higher scores in particular courses already had the intellectual styles required by the nature of the courses. However, it is equally plausible that in the process of pursuing their learning in different environments, students either acquired the styles needed to succeed in the learning environments or strengthened their existing styles that were already congruent with the learning environments.

Kolb's Construct of Learning Style and Academic Discipline
As mentioned in Chapter 2, Kolb (1984) believed strongly in style change. He conjectured that while people's learning styles may affect their choice of academic disciplines and professional areas, their existing styles can be accentuated through being socialized by the learning norms within an academic

discipline or a profession. Six studies conducted at different comparative levels (Levels II, III, V, and VI) were located in the current literature review. The studies employed one of the three versions of the *Learning Style Inventory* (LSI, Kolb, 1976, 1984, 1995). All except one study obtained significant results.

In the first study (a Level II comparative study), Zakrajsek, Johnson, and Walker (1984) attempted to find out the differences in learning styles between 96 students in physical education and 89 students majoring in dance in the United States. However, no significant difference was found between the two groups of students – both groups indicated a strong preference for concrete experiences. The researchers postulated that the lack of a significant difference was probably attributable to the concrete experiences involved in studying in both academic majors. It can be argued that the exposure of students from both majors to learning environments that were characterized by concrete, hands-on learning experiences either elicited or strengthened students' concrete learning style.

Also focusing on a Level II comparison, Biberman and Buchanan (1986) investigated the learning style differences among students majoring in accounting, economics/finance, management, marketing, social sciences, natural sciences, humanities, and applied sciences. The 300 participants were studying in either the School of Management or the College of Arts and Sciences at a university in the United States. Results indicated that students from different majors preferred different learning styles: accounting and science majors scored as convergers; management, marketing, and humanities majors scored as divergers, with the former two groups scoring higher than the latter; economics/finance majors scored as accommodators; and students majoring in social sciences scored as assimilators.

A final Level II comparative study was conducted by Mishra (1998) in India. Four hundred and thirty-four postgraduate students in the departments of commerce, fine arts, humanities, management, and science at Delhi University responded to the *Learning Style Inventory* (Kolb, 1985). Results suggested that students from different departments tended to use different styles of learning: arts students preferred the concrete learning style, fine arts students showed a preference for reflective observation, management students had a strong tendency to learn through active experimentation, and science students tended to learn through abstract conceptualization. The learning style preference dominant in each of the four departments is congruent with the nature of the respective academic discipline. Thus, it is possible that students were partially socialized into using the styles required in the academic areas in which they pursued their learning.

A Level V comparative study was carried out by Jones, Reichard, and Mokhtari (2003) who examined the relationships between learning styles and academic disciplines from a different perspective. The researchers aimed to see if the same students would use different learning styles when they studied different subject matters. Participants were 105 community college students in the United States. The *Learning Style Inventory* was slightly modified so that the questions in the inventory elicited students' learning styles used in different subject matters. Four subject matters were incorporated in the questions of the inventory: English, mathematics, science, and social sciences. Results demonstrated that students tended to "style flex" (i.e., temporarily use styles not typical of their dominant styles) when they studied different subjects. One could argue, as did Jones et al. (2003), that the fact that students "flexed" their styles when studying different subjects can be interpreted as students' adopting different learning strategies. However, one could also interpret this phenomenon from a different perspective: the students did perceive the different requirements for completing tasks in different disciplines, and they "style flexed" because they perceived the need to adapt to the different learning environments presented by different courses. If they remained in a particular learning environment long enough, the "learning strategy" they used would develop into a learning style. This transformation from learning strategy to learning style is strongly indicative that styles can be cultivated.

The final two studies (Brown & Burke, 1987; Katz & Heimann, 1991) based on Kolb's construct of learning style are similar in the sense that both studies examined the relationships between learning styles and academic disciplines at two comparative levels simultaneously. That is, both studies compared the learning styles of students and practitioners in the same disciplines – Level VI comparisons. In addition, one of the studies (Katz & Heimann, 1991) also looked into style differences at Level II comparative analysis, and the other one (Brown & Burke, 1987) examined differences at Level III analysis.

Katz and Heimann (1991) investigated the learning styles of students and practitioners in five health professions: clinical psychology, nursing, occupational therapy, physical therapy, and social work. Six hundred and twenty-nine first-year students and practitioners with at least two years of professional experience participated in the study. Significant results were obtained for both Level II and Level VI comparative analyses. Results of the Level II comparative analysis showed that in comparison with the students and practitioners in the other four health professions, those in occupational therapy were more likely to be accommodators. Furthermore, occupational therapy students were the least abstract among all groups. Concerning the results from the Level VI comparative analysis, occupational therapy practitioners were found to be more abstract in their learning styles than occupational therapy students. In other words, there was a trend for individuals to become more abstract in their learning style as their engagement in the field of occupational therapy became longer and more intense. Moreover, greater variance in styles was found among students than among practitioners. It makes good sense that students varied more in their learning styles than did the practitioners because students had been socialized into the relevant disciplines for a shorter duration than had been the practitioners. Indeed, such a finding is strongly supportive of the argument that styles can be socialized: the longer different people are socialized in the same environment, the more alike people's intellectual styles become.

Brown and Burke (1987) compared learning style differences among business students majoring in three different areas of studies: accounting, finance, and marketing. At the same time, they examined the learning styles of accounting students and accounting practitioners. Student participants were 674 undergraduates from the aforementioned three majors and one undecided group. Practitioner participants were 359 alumni, all in accounting. Results were significant at both levels of comparison.

The Level III comparative analysis revealed significant differences in learning styles among the student groups with declared majors and the undecided group. The accounting students showed a balanced profile with no marked preference for either the abstract style over the concrete style or the active style over the reflective style. Like the accounting group, the finance and marketing groups had a balanced preference on the active-reflective dimension. However, whereas the finance students showed a strong preference for the abstract style, the marketing students showed a strong preference for the concrete style. In the case of the undecided group, a moderate-to-strong preference was shown for the divergent learning style. It was concluded that this set of findings lent support to the expectation that students from different academic disciplines would be distinguished by their preferences for different intellectual styles.

The Level VI comparative analysis of the learning styles of four aggregated accounting groups revealed a trend toward the convergent learning style. The four groups (from the least convergent to the most convergent) included: (1) first- and second-year accounting students, (2) third- and fourth-year accounting students, (3) 1984 and 1983 graduates who were working toward fulfilling the requirements for the professional designation of Chartered Accountants (CA), and (4) 1982 and 1981 graduates who had already achieved their CA designation. This trend toward the convergent style suggests that the more education and practical experiences the students and practitioners gained in the field of accounting, the more convergent their learning style became. As argued by Brown and Burke (1987), this trend is in tune with Kolb's conjecture concerning accentuation and development of style preferences through specialized and professional education and practice.

Learning Approach and Academic Discipline

Being an activity-centered style construct and perhaps because of its close connection with students' learning processes and learning outcomes, Biggs's (1978) construct of learning approach and its allied concepts (see Chapter 2), such as learning orientation (Entwistle, 1981), learning preference (e.g., Rezler & French, 1975), and learning pattern (Vermunt, 1992, 1998), have been some of the most fruitful concepts in generating styles research, including research under consideration in this chapter. Eight studies that clearly focused on investigating style variations in different academic disciplines were identified in the current literature search. The earliest study was conducted in the United States (Rogers & Hill, 1980), and the most recent one was carried out in Australia (Smith & Miller, 2005). In the following, the eight studies are reviewed based on the levels of comparison classified earlier in this chapter.

Among the eight studies, four were conducted at Level II comparative analysis. In the first Level II comparative study, Richardson and Cuffie (1997) examined the differences in the learning orientations of university students in Barbados, using Entwistle and Ramsden's (1983) *Approaches to Studying Inventory*. The research participants were 508 students from four faculties – arts, law, natural sciences, and social sciences – at the University of West Indies, Cave Hill Campus. Compared with their peers in the faculty of arts, students in law and social sciences were found to report a significantly more reproduction-oriented/surface learning approach. Although the researchers did not explain the research findings, their belief in style change was clearly demonstrated by their advocating that students should be helped develop more effective approaches to studying, particularly the meaning-oriented/deep learning approach. The researchers stated that "such an intervention should see the implementation of a study skills program designed to encourage students to employ metacognitive strategies in their learning. The intervention should also require an examination of the course structure, the teaching and assessment methodology and the teaching/learning environment as it is possible that the learning approach or style choice of students is influenced by these variables" (Richardson & Cuffie 1997, p. 73).

The second Level II comparative study was carried out by Booth, Luckett, and Mladenovic (1999) in two universities in Sydney, Australia. Aiming to understand the learning approaches of accounting students, the researchers compared the data gathered from 374 accounting students studying at the two universities with previously reported norms for arts, education, and science students in Australia. Results obtained from students' responses to the *Study Process Questionnaire* (Biggs, 1987) suggested that compared with the arts, education, and science students, the accounting students tended to be more surface, but less deep in their learning approaches. The researchers commented that the accounting students' generally surface approach to learning might have reflected their appropriate response to a learning environment that favored the surface learning approach in its design, content, and assessment structure. Such a learning environment may have to do with the nature of the accounting science. Indeed, the researchers cited two studies in Hong Kong (Chan, Leung, Gow, & Hu, 1989; Gow, Kember, & Cooper, 1994), which also found that accounting students were strongly inclined to focus merely on the fundamentals and on reproducing them through rote learning.

The third Level II comparative investigation (Skogsberg & Chump, 2003) was undertaken among university students in the United States. The researchers administered Biggs, Kember, and Leung's (2001) *Two-Factor Revised Study Process Questionnaire* to 87 psychology majors and 92 biology majors. Although no significant difference with respect to the surface approach to learning was found between the two groups of students, a significant difference was found concerning the deep approach to learning. Compared with their peers in biology, the psychology students scored significantly higher on the deep approach to learning scale. The researchers attributed the tendency for psychology students to use the deep learning approach to the nature of psychological science – learning the psychological science requires students to focus more on understanding feelings and emotions and to retain course information through integrating knowledge and expressing how they feel about a topic. Indeed, the finding that psychology majors tended to adopt the deep learning approach was consistent with what was obtained in the study to be introduced next.

The final Level II comparative study (Smith & Miller, 2005) was also conducted among university students in Australia. Two hundred and forty-eight students majoring in business and psychology responded to the *Study Process Questionnaire* (Biggs, 1987). Results indicated that compared with their peers in business studies, the psychology students scored significantly higher on the deep learning approach, but lower on the surface learning approach. The researchers noted the strong support that their findings lent to Becher's (1994) characterization of "soft pure" and "hard applied" disciplines. As maintained by Becher (1994), in a "soft pure" discipline (e.g., psychology), the emphasis is on a learning process that primarily involves such intellectual activities as understanding and interpreting ideas, critically evaluating the given information, and establishing coherence in an argument. By contrast, students studying in "hard applied" disciplines (e.g., business) tend to be preoccupied with the outcome of being able to master their physical environments and to develop relevant products and techniques. Obviously, Becher's portrayal of the way in which students pursue knowledge in the "soft pure" disciplines is similar to what is entailed in the deep approach to learning, while his depiction of the manner in which students study in the "hard applied" disciplines is suggestive of the surface approach to learning. Smith and Miller (2005) postulated that the differences in learning approaches between psychology and business students could be either attributable to students' adapting their learning approach to their academic environment or indicative of a tendency for students to pursue a degree in a particular discipline that suits their predisposed intellectual styles. That is to say, students in psychology and business might have developed different approaches to learning at least partially as a result of having been socialized in different academic environments.

In studying students' style differences across academic disciplines, Eley (1992) took a relatively novel approach in that he investigated if the same students would use different learning approaches in different courses (classified as a Level V comparative analysis in this chapter). The research sample was drawn from Monash University in Australia. Each of the participants was taking two courses simultaneously. Specifically, 74 students were enrolled in both biochemistry and microbiology courses, 152 in both financial accounting and business law, 54 in both chemistry and mathematics/or statistics courses, and 40 in both English literature and politics/or philosophy. The participants responded to an adapted version of the *Study Process Questionnaire* (Biggs, 1987) and a questionnaire that assessed students' perceptions of the courses. It was concluded that the same students did adopt different learning approaches in the respective two courses that they took, depending on their perceptions of the courses. In other words, the learning environment – or more precisely, the students' perceptions of their learning environment – might have led the students to modify the styles that they used in learning. Certainly, as I mentioned earlier in the context of discussing the findings of Jones et al. (2003) based on Kolb's concept of learning styles, some people may argue that adopting different learning approaches in two different courses can be considered as students' changing their learning strategies. My response remains the same: any learning strategy that is repeatedly used over an extended period of time can be developed into an intellectual style. Furthermore, it should be remembered that changes in intellectual styles may take time, but the potentially slow rate of style change does not mean that styles cannot be changed.

Finally, the discussion on investigating students' learning approaches in different academic disciplines turns to three studies that share one similarity: they all involved a Level VII comparative analysis – a comparison of style differences of students studying in the same discipline but at different educational levels.

The study by Rogers and Hill (1980) was carried out purely at the Level VII comparative analysis. The researchers administered the *Learning Preferences Inventory* (Rezler & French, 1975) to two samples of students pursuing their degrees in occupational therapy at the University of Southern California in the United States. The first sample comprised 24 students at the Bachelor's degree level and 16 students at the Master's degree level, while the second sample was composed of 35 students in the Bachelor's degree program and 14 students in the Master's degree program. Results did not reveal any significant difference in the learning preferences between the occupational therapy students studying at the two different educational levels. Instead, it was found that both Bachelor's and Master's students preferred learning experiences that were concrete, interpersonal, and teacher-structured. That is to say, the study revealed the unique learning preferences of occupational therapy students.

Compared with Rogers and Hill's (1980) study, Lonka and Lindblom-Ylänne's (1996) study can be said to be more complex in the sense that it not only examined style differences between students studying in the same discipline at different educational levels (thus a Level VII comparison), but also looked into the style differences across two academic disciplines (hence a Level II comparison). Using an adapted version of Entwistle and Ramsden's (1983) *Approaches to Studying Inventory*, Lonka and Lindblom-Ylänne (1996) investigated the learning approaches of university students in Finland. Research participants were 59 students in psychology and 116 students in medicine. For both academic disciplines, the participants were studying either in their first year (referred to as novice students by the researchers) or in their fifth year (referred to as advanced students). Significant findings were obtained at both comparative levels. The psychology students, especially the advanced students, tended to report a preference for a meaning-directed learning orientation, whereas the medical students reported a preference for a reproduction-directed learning orientation. This finding should not come as a surprise given the differential features of the two academic disciplines. The study of psychology more often requires students to think critically about the phenomena involved, which is conducive to the development of a deep approach to learning, whereas the study of medicine is more likely to require students to appreciate directly applicable information, which tends to encourage the surface approach to learning. Readers may recall that the finding in this study that psychology students tended to adopt the deep learning approach corroborates the findings obtained in two of the previously discussed studies (Jones et al., 2003; Smith & Miller, 2005).

Similarly, Barris, Kielhofner, and Bauer's (1985) study conducted in the United States went beyond the Level VII comparative analysis as it also included a Level III analysis. Like Rogers and Hill (1980), Barris and her colleagues administered Rezler and French' (1975) *Learning Preference Inventory* to their research participants. The research sample was composed of 29 Bachelor's degree students in physical therapy, 23 Bachelor's degree students in occupational therapy, and 17 Master's degree students in occupational therapy. Results did not reveal any difference in style preferences between physical therapy and occupational therapy Bachelor's degree students. Students from both areas of studies displayed a strong preference for learning that is teacher-structured and concrete and that allows for high levels of interpersonal interaction. Nonetheless, a significant difference was identified between students studying at the two different educational levels: the Master's degree occupational therapy students expressed a significantly stronger preference for abstract learning than did both groups of undergraduate students. It is possible that as students progressed in their occupational therapy studies, their preferred learning style changed from more concrete to more abstract. There are several possible explanations for the lack of a significant difference between the two groups of undergraduate students. For example, it might have been because of the small sample size. It is also possible that the undergraduate students had not been socialized in their respective areas of focus long enough to develop significantly different intellectual styles.

Thinking Style and Academic Discipline
To date, virtually no study has focused solely on students' thinking style differences across academic disciplines. This is perhaps partially attributable to the fact that Sternberg's (1988, 1997) theory of thinking styles is the most recent individual style model, and partially because there exists sufficient research evidence regarding the topic of this chapter based on other style models. Nonetheless, several studies reported findings concerning style differences based on academic disciplines. A brief review of the reported findings on thinking style differences across disciplines should assist our understanding of the literature on style malleability.

Four sets of findings in four different studies were identified. In a study of 255 university students in Hong Kong, Zhang (2004c) reported that students majoring in social sciences and humanities used the executive and external styles more often than did students studying in the natural science disciplines.

Balkis and Isiker's (2005) study of 367 Turkish university students showed that students in the social sciences tended to use the conservative thinking style more often than did the students who majored in the natural sciences, fine arts, and foreign languages. Moreover, students who studied in the fine arts were more likely to employ the oligarchic style than were students majoring in the social sciences, natural sciences, and foreign languages. Fer's (2007) study of 402 university students in teacher education programs revealed that students whose specialized areas of study were language, science, and mathematics scored significantly higher on the executive style than did those who were specializing in administration, architecture, business, economics, engineering, and the social sciences. Finally, Kim's (2010) study of 209 high school students also suggested a significant relationship between thinking styles and their intended academic disciplines as represented by students' expression of their choices of future careers. Students with a preference for the liberal or external thinking styles tended to choose social sciences as their future careers, whereas students who scored lower on the external thinking style were more likely to choose the fields of computing or mathematics as their future careers. Clearly, all these aforementioned findings were within expectations, given the features of each of the thinking styles and the nature of the academic disciplines involved.

Summary and Further Discussion

As shown in the preceding discussion of the existing empirical work, all but three studies on the relationship between intellectual styles and academic disciplines obtained significant findings, indicating that students studying in different disciplines tend to use specific intellectual styles. In general, it is well recognized that this phenomenon might be indicative of students choosing academic disciplines that would accommodate their intellectual styles. Equally emphasized is the possibility that the different learning environments created by different academic disciplines both challenge students to develop new intellectual styles and help strengthen students' styles that are congruent with the nature of particular disciplines. Therefore, one must inevitably conclude that intellectual styles are modifiable and that academic disciplines can greatly influence the development of students' intellectual styles.

Apart from the explanations given thus far, there is a general point worth making in supporting the argument that students' intellectual styles change as a function of the academic disciplines in which they pursue their studies and that is: the nature of an academic discipline may affect students' intellectual styles through interacting with many other factors/variables. This may be best illustrated by Figure 5.1.

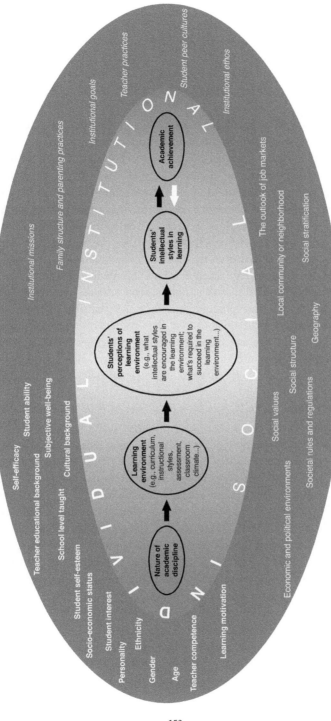

FIGURE 5.1. Model of Student Learning

Students' intellectual styles are the outcome of interactions among many variables, of which the nature of an academic discipline can be a critical one. The nature of an academic discipline shapes the learning environment in terms of curriculum, instructional styles, assessment, classroom climate, and so on.

The learning environment in turn influences how students perceive it. For example, the various components in the learning environment may help students form their views about such matters as what kind of intellectual styles a learning environment encourages (e.g., rule following, creative thinking, memorization, deep understanding, individual learning, interpersonal skills, etc.) and what they possibly need to do to succeed in that particular learning environment. These perceptions in turn may help students either develop or strengthen the kind of intellectual styles that they believe the learning environment requires. In this way, the use of intellectual styles that match the demands of the learning environment may facilitate better academic achievement. It should be noted that the double arrows drawn between intellectual styles and academic achievement signify not only that intellectual styles can affect academic achievement, but also that students' levels of achievement (or more precisely, evaluation of their levels of achievement) are likely to provide feedback to students concerning whether or not (perhaps even to what degree) they need to modify their intellectual styles for future academic success.

Moreover, the relationships among the variables in the five ovals in the inner part of Figure 5.1 are not always straightforward; they can be influenced by many socialization factors at the individual, institutional, and social levels. For example, these factors may include (1) at the individual level: students' and teachers' gender, age, cultural background, ethnicity, personality, socioeconomic status, subjective well-being, students' ability, interest, self-esteem, and learning motivation, and teachers' competence, educational background, and the school level at which they teach; (2) at the institutional level: educational institutions' goals, missions, and ethos, family structure and parenting practices, teachers' practices, and student peer cultures; and (3) at the social level: geography, local community or neighborhood, social rules and regulations, social stratification, social structure, social values, economic and political environments, and the outlook of job markets. Of course, by no means is this list of the socialization factors inclusive.

Substantial empirical evidence can be found for the relationships between variables in any two adjacent ovals and indeed, for the relationships between variables in any two of the five ovals in Figure 5.1 – alone or in combination with one or more of the socialization factors outside of the five small ovals. For example, the influence of students' perceptions of their learning environment on their intellectual styles has been well documented (e.g., Kember, Leung, & McNaught, 2008; Laschinger, 1992; Nijhuis, Segers, & Gijselaers, 2005). As another example, intellectual styles have been shown to influence students' academic achievement (Cano-Garcia & Hughes, 2000; Jones, 2001; Tinajero & Páramo, 1997). At the same time, there is abundant research evidence concerning the influence of the socialization factors on the variables in any one of the five centrally located ovals. For instance, in this book, Chapter 3 illustrated why intellectual styles can be partially the product of gender-role socialization, while Chapter 4 documented the impact of culture on the development of intellectual styles.

The aforementioned observation about the interplay between intellectual styles and other factors/variables does not contradict the view that students tend to be attracted to particular academic disciplines. The point being made here is that intellectual styles can change as a result of interacting, directly and indirectly, with many variables and a whole constellation of socialization factors. Among these, the nature of the academic discipline could be a critical socialization variable in students' development of intellectual styles.

Conclusions and Implications

Certainly, research on the relationship between academic disciplines and intellectual styles, like any other area of research reviewed in this book, has great room for improvement. For example, all the studies reviewed in this chapter were cross-sectional studies. Findings from longitudinal research on this topic would be much more informative than those generated by the studies reviewed in this chapter because the results of longitudinal research can facilitate a better understanding of how exactly students' intellectual styles are developed through their socialization in different academic disciplines. Despite this and other possible limitations, the literature reviewed in this chapter is quite telling: intellectual styles can change as a function of academic discipline. There are at least four reasons for making such an assertion. First, as pointed out earlier, all except three studies reported statistically significant findings. Nevertheless, when discussing their non-significant findings, the authors of these studies made it explicit that students' intellectual styles can change partially as a function of the academic disciplines in which students pursue their learning (Elder, 1989; Huang & Chao, 1995; Zakrajsek et al., 1984; see earlier discussion). Second, the studies reviewed here were based on nine different style models that are widely used in other lines of investigation in the field of intellectual styles. Third, across the studies, the research findings were derived from seven different levels of comparative analyses. Finally, the research findings were obtained from a wide range of cultures – beyond those cultures in which theories of intellectual styles usually originated, and where studies of styles concerning most topics were typically conducted (e.g., the United States, the United Kingdom, Australia, and Canada). For example, in quite a number of the studies reviewed, the data sources were from such cultures as Barbados, Belgium, Finland, Hong Kong, India, Indonesia, Jamaica, mainland China, Turkey, and the United Arab Emirates.

As with any other research topic on intellectual styles, one would naturally wonder about the practical implications of the topic reviewed here for education, especially for higher education, given that all but three studies were carried out in higher educational institutions. That is, what does the general finding that academic disciplines can shape students' intellectual styles mean for different parties in the education sector? One could argue that the findings reported here should communicate practical meanings to students, teachers, counselors, and senior managers.

An understanding of the findings discussed here can assist students in selecting a major or, for some, in switching to a different academic major. It may help students anticipate their own levels of academic success in a particular field of study. Such an understanding may also encourage students, especially those who desire to pursue their learning in an academic discipline but do not possess precisely the kind of intellectual styles required by the nature of that discipline, to make efforts to acquire or strengthen the styles needed.

The findings introduced in this chapter should raise teachers' awareness of the impact of learning environments on students' development of intellectual styles and, subsequently, on students' levels of success in specific fields of inquiry. Teachers are the most powerful agents in shaping students' learning environment. Therefore, teachers should try all means to create effective learning opportunities for students with various styles. In particular, they should endeavor to challenge and support students whose predominant intellectual styles may not be a good match with the nature of their learning environment.

Academic advisors and career counselors also need to learn about how academic disciplines influence students' ways of thinking and learning. Such knowledge may assist advisors and counselors in better predicting students' choices of academic majors upon entering higher educational institutions and in providing students with more sensible advice regarding selecting or switching majors.

Finally, school and university senior managers should be informed of the impact of different academic disciplines on the development of students' intellectual styles. Such an understanding should assist senior managers in making policies that better meet the teaching and learning needs inherent in different academic disciplines.

6

Occupation and Intellectual Styles

"It is a truism within the profession of architecture that it takes 'something' special to be an architect."
– Peterson and Sweitzer, 1973, p. 195

One could argue that a large portion of that "something" that all architects share consists of intellectual styles. Like academic discipline, occupation is a socialization factor that transcends culture and promotes intellectual styles unique to a particular occupation or professional group. In other words, people in each occupation tend to have a particular personality profile, or rather, in the context of this book, a particular profile of intellectual styles. In fact, more than two decades ago, Gottfredson and Holland (1989) assigned three-letter Holland Occupational Codes to 12,860 occupations.

This chapter addresses the malleability of intellectual styles through systematically reviewing empirical findings indicating that people in the same nonacademic occupation/profession are likely to have similar intellectual styles. The remainder of this chapter is organized into three parts. The first part sets the parameters for this review. The second part presents the studies anchored in each of the style models used to examine the issue under consideration. In the final part, some conclusions are drawn and the implications of the findings for organizational development are noted.

Literature Search Procedures and Results

General Search Procedures
The search for the materials for this chapter followed all but one of the procedures described in the previous chapter. That is, the key words, such as "major," "discipline," "course," "program," and "subject," which were relevant to academic settings, were replaced with such terms as "managers,"

"employees," "executives," "staff," "organization," "organizational," and "work environment." As in the previous chapter, the search resulted in about 2,000 abstracts. A preliminary screening of these abstracts indicated that 60 concerned studies of styles based on occupational/professional groups. Full texts of 49 of the 60 abstracts were located. A careful reading of these 49 publications suggested that 26 publications reported empirical findings on the relationships between occupations and intellectual styles. As was the case with the literature search for all the other chapters in this book, the snowballing technique was adopted. Ultimately, it was determined that 52 publications – all being journal articles – were appropriate for inclusion in the current review.

Results of the Literature Search

Results of the literature search indicated that although as early as 1943, Strong had elaborated the differences in the preferred ways of processing information among various occupations, it was not until the late 1960s that styles researchers formally launched their investigations into intellectual styles among different occupational groups. The earliest study (Barrett & Thornton, 1967) was, unsurprisingly, again inspired by Witkin's concept of field dependence/independence (FDI). The most fruitful research on the relationship between styles and occupations, however, was generated by Kirton's (1961) model of decision-making and problem-solving styles and Jung's (1923) model of personality types. While studies based on Kirton's model were mostly conducted in the 1980s and 1990s, those rooted in Jung's personality types span the past four decades (i.e., the 1980s, 1990s, 2000s, and 2010s). Several studies were anchored in each of another four style constructs specified in the threefold model of intellectual styles (Zhang & Sternberg, 2005): Holland's (1973) model of career personality types, Gregorc's (1979) mind styles, Kolb's (1976) concept of learning styles, and Sternberg's (1988) model of thinking styles. However, no study was found to be based on the remaining three style constructs in the threefold model of intellectual styles: Kagan's (1965) construct of reflectivity-impulsivity, Biggs's (1978) concept of learning approaches, and Torrance's (1988) model of modes of thinking.

Research Findings

As in the previous chapter, a general picture of the findings is painted at first, followed by a detailed description of the findings from the individual studies based on each of the seven style models. This general picture relates to the levels of comparison at which the style differences of various occupational groups have been examined, the research methods adopted, and the general research findings obtained.

With respect to the levels of comparison, the studies fall into six types. The first type of studies, to which the majority of the studies belong, compared the styles of a particular occupational group with those of the general population[1] or of the student population studying in the same field as the occupation being investigated. The second type of studies compared the styles of employees/personnel in different professions/occupational groups (e.g., artists versus engineers). The third type of studies compared the styles of employees/personnel specializing in different areas of a professional or occupational group (e.g., nurses working in different departments of the medical field such as critical care, maternity, and post-anesthesia care). The fourth type of studies compared the styles of employees/personnel within the same occupation but with different ranks (e.g., managers, senior managers, and partners in accounting). The fifth type of studies compared the styles of employees within the same profession but with different job functions (i.e., internally oriented and externally oriented). Finally, the sixth type of studies compared the styles of employees in the same profession but with different racial backgrounds.

All the studies used questionnaire surveys as the method of data collection, with the exception of Higgins and Zhang's (2009) study, which used focus group interviews in addition to a questionnaire survey. Furthermore, all the studies yielded statistically significant findings. Two questions arise with respect to these findings: Do the findings make substantive sense? To what extent did they address the issue of style malleability? The rest of this part answers these questions by reviewing the aforesaid 52 research articles.

As in the previous chapter, the sequence of presenting these studies is guided by two general frameworks: Grigorenko and Sternberg's (1995; see also Chapter 2) categorization of the three approaches to the study of styles and, within each approach, the chronological order in which a particular style model was published. Thus, the studies are discussed in the following order in which the style models are listed: (1) Witkin's (1948) model of FDI styles, (2) Kirton's (1961) model of decision-making and problem-solving styles, (3) Jung's (1923) model of personality types, (4) Holland's (1973) model of career personality types, (5) Gregorc's (1979) model of mind styles, (6) Kolb's (1976) model of learning styles, and (7) Sternberg's (1988) model of thinking styles.

---

[1] Unless specified otherwise, "general population" refers to the national population of the particular country in which the study being reviewed was conducted.

Field Dependence/Independence and Occupation

As indicated earlier, the pioneering research into the relationship between styles and occupation, like research concerning almost every single topic in the field of styles, was based on Witkin's notion of FDI, which was measured by either the *(Group) Embedded Figures Test* (Witkin, 1971; Witkin, Oltman, Raskin, & Karp, 1971) or the *Rod-and-Frame Test* (Oltman, 1968; Witkin et al., 1954). Nevertheless, research on the topic of this chapter has not been as fruitful as that in many other research areas grounded in FDI – only nine studies were found – and such investigations have been only undertaken with three groups: engineers/technicians, sports personnel/professional dancers, and accountants.

The earliest study (Barrett & Thornton, 1967) was conducted in the United States among 46 engineers and technicians and 11 male college students who served as a comparison sample. Based on the close resemblance between the characteristics of field-independent (FI) people and the description of engineering job functions, the researchers predicted that their engineer and technician participants would be significantly more field independent than both the male college students and the general population. FDI was measured by the *Rod-and-Frame Test*, and the results fully supported the prediction. Moreover, when the FI scores of the engineers and technicians were compared with those of the general population of the same age group, the difference became even greater, pointing to the engineers' and technicians' higher levels of field independence. Although the researchers attributed their main research target group's higher levels of field independence to "certain unique perceptual capabilities" (Barrett & Thornton, 1967, p. 793) that the group possessed, it is also possible that the engineers and technicians had increased their tendency to be field independent as a result of working in an environment that demanded frequent use of the field-independent style. After all, as stated by Barrett and Thornton (1967), the description of engineering job functions bears striking similarities to that of the FI style.

Eight years after leading the aforementioned study, Barrett led a second study (Barrett & Trippe, 1975). This time, the research was conducted among sports personnel and professional dancers in the United Kingdom. Data were gathered from a group of professional dancers and from highly skilled and medium-ability level athletes in four sports (tennis, soccer, cricket, and track and field, N=153). The results indicated that while the athletes' levels of FDI did not differ by ability level in three (soccer, cricket, and track and field) of the four sports groups, highly skilled tennis players were significantly more field dependent than medium-ability tennis players. Furthermore, although there was no significant difference between the professional dancers and the highly skilled athletes in the four sports, the highly skilled tennis players were significantly more field dependent than the highly skilled track and field athletes. Together, the two sets of results suggest that FDI can differ according to both the type of sports that athletes play and the ability level at which athletes play. One could argue that given there were so many groups to compare, the significant findings could have been statistically attributable to chance. However, it could also be argued that the significant findings reflect true differences in styles between the relevant groups because these findings make substantive sense. Tennis is an open-skill sport and requires a high level of field dependence, whereas track and field is a closed-skill sport, which requires a higher level of field independence. Furthermore, high-ability athletes engaged in the two types of sports would tend to have higher levels of either field independence or field dependence than medium-ability athletes. This might have been the reason why the top-class track and field athletes obtained higher FI scores than did the highly skilled tennis players.

The finding that the type of sports can make a difference in athletes' levels of FDI was confirmed by two studies conducted in Spain in the 1990s. In the first study, Caño and Màrquez (1995) administered the Spanish translation of the *Group Embedded Figures Test* to 102 athletes who were engaged in individual sports, 98 athletes who were playing team sports, and 93 non-athletes. Results indicated that for both males and females, those who were in team sports were more field dependent than were the non-athletes. Moreover, the female team sports players were more field dependent than the females in individual sports or non-athletes of both genders (see also Chapter 3). The researchers argued that the differences might be associated with the participants' choice of sports: individual or team sports (or no sports). However, it is also likely that the higher levels of field dependence found among the team-sport players were partially the result of socialization by the nature of team sports. The fact that the female team-sports players had a higher level of field dependence than all the other participants in the study is particularly noteworthy. As elaborated in Chapter 3, females are more likely to be socialized into using the field-dependent style. In addition, team sports demand high levels of collaboration – a strong feature inherent in field dependence. Both these factors could increase the likelihood of female team-sports athletes using the field-dependent style.

In the second study of Spanish sports personnel, Tabernero and Màrquez (1999) compared the levels of FDI among 53 individual-sports athletes, 52 team-sports athletes, 46 basketball referees, and 54 non-athletes. Results were largely within expectations in that the individual-sport players were more field independent than the team-sport players, and the team-sport players were more field dependent than the non-athletes. Unexpectedly, however, the basketball referees were found to be more field dependent compared with the other groups of research participants. Although they did not specifically explain their unexpected result, in discussing the findings of their study more generally, the researchers firmly maintained the view that FDI is dynamic by postulating that it can be acquired over years of being engaged in sports.

Finally, a series of five studies were carried out among accountants in the United States and Canada. The initial research was undertaken by Pincus (1985) in the United States and involved 124 practicing accountants. Additionally, to obtain a better understanding of the level of FDI of this group of accountants, Pincus compared the FDI of her sample with the FDI of three student samples from previous studies (DeSanctis and Dunikoski, 1983; Lusk & Wright, 1981a, 1981b). Based on the nature of accounting work, Pincus (1985) anticipated that practicing accountants would be more field independent than accounting students. However, contrary to expectations, the practicing accountants in Pincus's study were significantly less field independent than those in two of the three aforesaid student samples. One reason why Pincus's (1985) findings were largely contradictory to her research hypothesis might be that the study did not take into account such possible moderating factors as the length of working experience, the level of seniority, and the functional areas (e.g., tax, auditing, and consulting) of the accountants. This explanation makes good sense because the other four studies, which did take at least one of these and other factors into consideration, unanimously concluded that practicing accountants tended to develop their levels of field independence as a result of socialization in the accounting work environment.

In one of these studies, Bernardi (1993) considered the seniority of practicing accountants. Research participants were 170 managers who were higher in rank and 346 senior accountants who were lower in rank. Results indicated that as a group, the practicing accountants in Bernardi's study were more field independent than both the normative samples in the published test and the 124 accountants in Pincus's (1985) study. When taking seniority into account, Bernardi found that the senior accountants were more field independent than the managers. This finding makes practical sense in that senior accountants tend to be much more involved in specific tasks that demand higher levels of field independence, whereas managers tend to be more involved with people, which requires more field dependence. In other words, it is possible that the different styles reported by the senior accountants and the managers were attributable to the socialization effects of the different work environments.

Mills (1995) extended the previous two studies (Bernardi, 1993; Pincus, 1985) by not only examining accountants' levels of FDI, but also assessing the mobility-fixity of her research participants with respect to FDI. Mobility refers to the ability of individuals to change their intellectual styles or mental processing to accommodate the demands of a specific situation or task. Mills's (1995) study involved 49 accountants in the United States. In addition to finding that the accountants as a group tended to be more field independent than field dependent, Mills discovered that a good proportion (15 out of 49) of the research participants demonstrated high levels of style mobility. Moreover, senior managers were significantly more likely to show style mobility than were participants in the other three groups. The findings concerning style mobility in Mills's study relate well to the issue of style malleability: people do change their styles as a function of situational demands.

A good understanding of the FDI levels of accountants has also been facilitated by another study conducted by Mills (1997). In this study, Mills (1997) considered the accountants' level of seniority in their organizations. The research participants were 127 accountants, including 20 junior accountants and 70 senior accountants, 15 managers, 13 senior managers, and 9 partners. It was found that more senior accountants (i.e., partners and senior managers) scored significantly lower on field independence than did the other three groups of accountants, which concurred with the findings obtained in Bernardi's (1993) study. In explaining the findings, like Bernardi (1993), Mills (1997) turned to the different types of tasks in which accountants of different levels are routinely engaged. To be precise, Mills (1997) attributed the differential levels of field independence among accountants of different ranks to the differences in the levels of intensity of computer use between frontline accountants and those who hold senior positions in an organization. The work of frontline accountants involves more use of computers than does the work of senior managers and partners. It has long been argued that computer use necessitates the use and development of the field-independent style (Canino & Cicchelli, 1988; Mills, 1995).

The last of the five studies of accountants was conducted by Hicks, Bagg, Doyle, and Young (2007) among 113 practicing accountants in Nova Scotia, Canada. The research participants were across three ranks, including trainees, managers, and partners, and were working in the functional areas of tax, auditing, estate planning, consulting, and valuation. Possibly because of the small sample size in each of the functional areas and the undocumented data on the specific nature of the tasks carried out by accountants in each of the three different ranks, no statistically significant difference was found based on rank and functional area. Nonetheless, it was concluded that as a group, accountants were more field independent than field dependent.

As mentioned earlier, the existing research on FDI style differences based on occupations is relatively limited. Even so, the studies reviewed here are rather telling: people's levels of FDI can be developed through being socialized in their work settings. Not only do people in the same occupation tend to have the same predominant intellectual style, but also the FDI levels of people in the same occupation can differ depending on their seniority within their organizations, the nature of their routine tasks, and their specialty areas. This applies to both occupations that have been investigated: sports and accounting.

Decision-Making and Problem-Solving Style and Occupation
As mentioned earlier, in their book entitled *The Nature of Intellectual Styles*, Zhang and Sternberg (2006) devoted a whole chapter to focusing almost solely on the discussion of research based on Kirton's adaption-innovation (KAI) style construct. Within this discussion, Zhang and Sternberg argued for the dynamic nature of styles by reviewing the empirical work revealing close relationships between adaptive-innovative styles and occupations. The current literature search resulted in 15 studies, of which 10 were detailed in Zhang and Sternberg's (2006) book. Therefore, in this section, these 10 studies are only briefly mentioned, while the five newly identified studies are presented more fully.

Broadly categorized, the 15 studies fall into four types that addressed the malleability of the adaptive-innovative styles as assessed by the KAI (Kirton, 1976). These include studies that examined (1) the relative positions of the KAI means of particular occupational groups in relation to the KAI mean of the general population; (2) the subfunctions within an occupation; (3) the nature of the tasks; and (4) the nature of the tasks along with the length of service in an occupation.

Relative Positions of KAI Means. Jacobson (1993) administered the KAI to 54 top-level managers and executives employed in various service-sector occupations in the United States, and found that the research participants' KAI mean was statistically higher than that of the general population. Although the researcher pointed out that the finding might have reflected the relatively higher levels of education of the research sample compared with the general population, it can be argued that the research sample's higher KAI mean score could be at least partially attributable to the participants' engagement in management work that had encouraged their use of the innovative style.

Indeed, several other similar studies (e.g., Foxall, 1986; Foxall & Payne, 1989; Keller & Holland, 1978; Lowe & Taylor, 1986; Thomson, 1980; see Zhang & Sternberg, 2006 for details), which were conducted by various scholars in different cultures such as Malaysia, Singapore, the United Kingdom, and the United States, reached the same conclusion: organizations that operate in relatively more stable and predictable environments and are more mechanistically structured and strongly emphasize continuity and efficiency (e.g., accounting firms, banks, nursing, and occupational groups involved in various forms of production) tend to fall on the adaptive end of the KAI continuum. By contrast, organizations that operate in relatively more dynamic and unpredictable environments, that are more organically structured, and that have a strong need to adapt to constant change in the outside world tend to fall on the innovative end of the KAI continuum. It could be argued that people with an innovative style, as opposed to an adaptive style, tend to be drawn to different occupations. However, even if this were the case, the different work environments associated with different occupations would be likely to promote different levels of innovative style or adaptive style.

Subfunctions within an Occupation. Not only does an occupation as a whole tend to encourage a particular level of innovative or adaptive style, but also different departments within the same occupation tend to cultivate different levels of adaption/innovation. In this regard, based on his research among engineers in a company in the United Kingdom, Kirton (1980) concluded that, no matter what an organization's overall orientation is, the tasks of specific departments can be broadly classified into two principal types of subfunctions: internally oriented and externally oriented. Moreover, managers working in internally oriented departments are more likely to be adaptive, whereas managers working for externally oriented departments are more likely to be innovative. Kirton's (1980) assertion has subsequently been confirmed by research carried out not only among managers but also among nurses.

For example, Foxall and Payne (1989) administered the KAI to 115 mid-career managers enrolled in an MBA program in the United Kingdom and to a similar group of 123 managers enrolled in three Australian business schools. The internally oriented group included cost accountants, technical engineers, general managers (administrative), and personnel in operation production, whereas the externally oriented group was composed of financial accountants, management engineers, general managers (directive), and personnel in marketing. Results suggested that the KAI means of members of the externally oriented subgroups tended to be higher (i.e., more innovative) than those of the internally oriented subgroups.

The aforementioned findings obtained in Foxall and Payne's (1989) study were replicated in three other studies of managers (Foxall, 1990; Foxall, Payne, & Walters, 1992; Kirton & Pender, 1982) in Australia, the United Kingdom, and the United States (see Zhang & Sternberg, 2006 for details). In explaining their findings, the researchers showed a shift from using the theory of attraction to using the theory of accentuation over the years. In their earlier work, Foxall and Payne (1989) noted that managers' employment experience made managers gravitate toward organizational climates most suited to their preferred styles of cognitive functioning. In a later publication, Fox et al. (1992) pointed out that the task orientations of mature organizations typically require either predominantly adaptive or predominantly innovative intellectual styles. Certainly, these researchers did not explicitly endorse the idea that those who are attracted to a particular occupation because their initial styles are suitable to the demands of the occupation may further develop those styles as a result of working in that job setting. However, one cannot rule this out because individuals have to develop or strengthen either a more innovative or a more adaptive style in order to function well in line with what is required by the nature of the tasks in which they were engaged.

Nature of Tasks. In fact, several researchers (e.g., Engle, Mah, & Sadri, 1997; Pettigrew & King, 1997; Rosenfeld, Winger-Bearskin, Marcic, & Braun, 1993; Tullett, 1995) alluded to the strong possibility that the nature of the tasks inherent in an occupation had encouraged their research participants to develop their intellectual styles. For example, Rosenfeld et al. (1993) compared the adaptive-innovative styles of 44 successful entrepreneurs with those of technology managers in one company (n=189) and those of Kirton's (1987) original sample (n=516). The successful entrepreneurs consisted of three types of individuals: (1) individuals who had founded a business, (2) individuals whose business had a positive cash flow after two years, and (3) individuals for whom the business was their primary means of financial support. It was found that the group of entrepreneurs was the most innovative, with Kirton's original sample being the least innovative and the technology managers being in the middle. Rosenfeld et al. (1993) contended that the entrepreneurs' higher innovative score could be attributed to the need for successful entrepreneurs to generate a large number of new ideas to tackle the problems of a new business and to be free from established rules during the initial launch. In other words, individuals who were engaged in tasks that allowed greater degrees of autonomy tended to score higher on the innovative style. However, it should be noted that according to the definition of successful entrepreneurs used in Rosenfeld et al.'s (1993) study, this group of participants must have been running their respective business organizations for some time. Therefore, it is possible that the innovative style of these entrepreneurs had also been accentuated partially as a result of leading their business to continuing success in the competitive business world.

A second study was conducted by Engle et al. (1997) in the United States. The researchers compared the KAI scores of two independent groups. The first group was composed of 54 entrepreneurs who were all small-business owners, and the second group included 79 employees working for four different companies representing a wide range of service, manufacturing, and sales sectors. The study confirmed Rosenfeld et al.'s (1993) findings, concluding that the small-business owners were significantly more innovative and less adaptive than the group of employees.

In Belgium, Tullett (1995) investigated the KAI mean score of 133 project managers who were in charge of projects that involved the implementation of significant initiatives in their organizations. Compared with the KAI mean score reported for managers in general (Kirton, 1994b), the KAI mean score for the project managers was significantly higher. Tullett asserted that this finding was not surprising because project managers often work across functional boundaries. The nature of the tasks involved in change projects is such that managers of such projects are often confronted with new situations. They thus may have become more innovative in the process of meeting the challenges presented by new situations.

A final study that supports the modifiability of innovative-adaptive styles as a function of the nature of tasks undertaken was carried out by Pettigrew and King (1997) among nurses in the United States. Participants were 266 staff nurses working in 13 regional acute-care hospitals. It was found that nurses who were working in different settings (and thus performing different types of tasks) tended to exhibit different levels of innovation/adaption. Nurses in pediatric, psychiatric, critical care, and medical-surgical settings obtained significantly higher innovative mean scores, whereas nurses working in maternity, ambulatory, operating room, and post-anesthesia settings obtained significantly higher adaptive mean scores. It seems that nurses who work for a long time in a setting (such as any one in the former group) that requires them to develop innovative ways of dealing with unpredictable situations and that allows them the flexibility to try different nursing interventions to meet individual patients' specific needs develop a more innovative style. On the other hand, nurses who frequently undertake tasks in a relatively more predictable hospital setting (such as any one in the latter group) that requires more routine work and that does not provide them with the opportunity to try new nursing methods tend to develop an adaptive style over time.

Nature of Tasks along with Length of Service. Finally, the dynamic nature of adaptive/innovative styles was also manifested in two studies that took into consideration not only the nature of tasks intrinsic to an occupation, but also the length of service of the research participants. The first study was conducted by Hayward and Everett (1983). Research participants were 67 professional staff within a local government in the United Kingdom. According to the length of service, the participants were grouped into junior-, intermediate-, and senior-level employees. Based on the nature of tasks performed by local government employees, which is characterized by abiding by rules and procedures, the researchers anticipated that the local government employees would be significantly more adaptive than would be the general population. It was further anticipated that the KAI mean of the senior staff would be located toward the adaptive pole of the KAI continuum and that the KAI mean of the newly recruited junior group would be located toward the innovative pole. All predictions were confirmed.

In the second study, P. A. Holland (1987) administered the KAI to 91 employees working in branches of clearing banks in the United Kingdom. Among the 91 participants, 40 were classified as trainees and 51 as established managers. Based on the nature of the tasks involved in branch banking – essentially observing set procedures and working toward short-term goals – Holland (1987) predicted that the KAI mean of the established managers would be significantly lower (i.e., more adaptive) than that of the general population and that the KAI mean of the trainees would reflect that of the general population. Results fully confirmed the researcher's predictions and lent support to Hayward and Everett's (1983) study findings.

The results of the aforementioned two studies are particularly relevant in arguing for the accentuation theory over the attraction theory, because the KAI mean of new recruits reflected that of the general population. That is to say, new recruits usually begin their training with a much more innovative style, and after they work for a significant amount of time in an occupation that demands respect for established rules and procedures, their problem-solving style would become more adaptive.

Personality Type and Occupation
Relative to the amount of research on style differences across occupational groups based on other style constructs, research concerning personality types is considerably more substantial. Early in 1985, Myers and McCaulley reviewed a number of studies demonstrating the significant differences among various occupations in a number of countries, including Canada, Hong Kong, Italy, mainland China, South Africa, the United Kingdom, and the United States. The current literature search identified 15 studies independent of those that had been documented by Myers and McCaulley (1985). Of these, four studies were conducted in the 1980s and the remaining 11 were carried out between the mid-1990s and 2010. The studies involved several occupational groups,

including medical personnel, organizational coaches and decision makers, engineers (computer programmers, computer software engineers, and managers), real estate agents, and accountants. As in studies of the KAI means in various occupations where the scores of the research participants were compared with the KAI mean of the general population, the majority of the studies of different occupational groups' personality types compared research participants' MBTI types with those of the general population. Except for one study (Passmore, Holloway, & Rawle-Cope, 2010), all the studies used the full version of the *Myers-Briggs Type Indicators* (Myers & McCaulley, 1989, 1993).

Medical Personnel. Several studies have examined the personality types of medical personnel with different job functions, including nursing assistants, nurses, doctors, health care executives, and senior medical staff. In one study, Daub, Friedman, Cresci, and Keyser (2000) investigated the personality styles of 316 nursing assistants in the United States. Research participants consisted of 213 nursing assistants working in traditional (i.e., institutional) nursing homes and 103 nursing assistants from the Program of All-Inclusive Care for the Elderly (PACE), which is community-based. The nursing assistants as a whole, regardless of their work setting, tended to score higher on sensing and judging (SJ; 74%) compared with the general population (46.6%).

The prevalence of SJ types among nursing assistants found by Daub et al. (2000) was also identified in Jain and Lall's (1996) study of 34 nurses with different ethnic backgrounds (Caucasian, Asian, African-American, and others) in the United States. Of the 34 nurses in the study, 15 had a combined dominant personality type of sensing, feeling, and judging (SFJ). Jain and Lall (1996) commented that the personality types found among the nurses seemed to be consistent with the requirements of the nursing profession. That is, nurses need to be practical, realistic, conservative, and respectful of rules and hierarchy; they also need to be effective problem solvers and caregivers.

While the two studies, taken together, indicated that an effective nurse needs to have an SJ personality style, other studies have found that medical personnel working at higher levels (doctors, health care executives, and senior managers) need to have a TJ personality style. For example, as part of a larger survey aimed at investigating the relationship between specialty choice and job satisfaction, Clack, Allen, Cooper, and Head (2004) studied the personality styles of doctors in the United Kingdom. The researchers administered the MBTI to 464 medical graduates who had qualified from the School of Medicine and Dentistry at King's College between 1985/86 and 1989/90. It was concluded that compared with the UK general population, the doctors were more introverted, intuitive, thinking, and judging (INTJ).

The predominance of TJ personality types identified by Clack et al. (2004) was also found in two studies involving two other types of medical personnel: health care executives and senior medical staff working in emergency departments. Shewchuk and O'Connor (1995) investigated the personality types of a nationwide sample of 522 health care executives in the United States. Based on the nature of work involved in health care management, the researchers hypothesized that the personality types of their participants would be predominantly TJ types. This hypothesis was confirmed, with 63 percent of their research participants falling into one of the four TJ cells: ESTJ, ISTJ, ENTJ, and INTJ.

Similarly, when Boyd and Brown (2005) studied the personality types of 68 senior medical staff working in emergency departments in two different parts of Australia, they found the most common personality types to be ENTJ. The researchers noted that while 17 percent of their research participants were classified as ENTJ types, only 3 percent of the general population exhibited this combination of personality types.

The common thread linking the aforementioned three studies is the prevalence of thinking and judging (TJ) types among senior medical personnel. The combination of the TJ personality style dimensions suggests a way of dealing with situations through objective decision making within a rigid timescale. Of course, one could argue that people with these personality characteristics are more likely to be drawn into these occupational groups. However, these personality stylistic features could also have been acquired and enhanced on the job. The prevalence of TJ personality types found in the three studies did not exist by chance. Indeed, the researchers of all of the aforementioned three studies alluded to the socialization of styles. Boyd and Brown (2005) commented that the personality characteristics exhibited by their participants were consistent with what was demanded by the tasks they performed in the emergency departments of the hospitals. Shewchuk and O'Connor (1995) contended that individuals tended to stay in a work environment that allowed them to adapt to work processes and conditions. Similarly, Clack et al. (2004) pointed out the need for doctors to modify their styles to enhance their communication with their patients.

Finally, it should be noted that across the latter two groups of research on medical personnel (nurses and doctors/senior managers), there is an overlap in personality style at a higher level. That is, the judging personality style is shared by nurses who are predominantly SJ types and doctors/senior managers who are principally TJ types. The judging personality style may be a reflection of the general work environment in hospitals, where decision making within strict time constraints is constantly required.

Organizational Adviser and Decision Makers. Two studies pertained to different levels of advice giving and decision making in organizations. Together, the two studies showed that making "bigger" decisions was strongly associated with the intuitive (N) and the thinking (T) personality types. In the first study, Roach (1996) examined the personality types of 298 organizational decision makers in the United States. The research participants were classified into three levels of decision makers in various organizations: supervisors, managers, and executives. It was found that although TJ types were predominant in the entire research sample, the three levels of decision makers differed along the introversion versus extraversion (I/E) dimension and the sensing versus intuitive (S/N) dimension. Introversion-sensing types were prevalent among supervisors – the lowest level of decision makers of the three, whereas extraversion-intuitive types were widespread among the executives – the highest of the three levels of decision makers. Among the managers (the middle-level decision makers), the preference for extraversion versus introversion was roughly evenly distributed, as was that for sensing versus intuitive. In explaining the varying personality styles of the three different levels of decision makers, Roach (1996) took a dynamic view of styles, attributing the different personality styles to the different nature of the tasks performed by decision makers of different levels. For example, the researcher noted that ISTJ types were common among the supervisors because the primary function of the supervisors was to maintain the status quo through an established routine. On the other hand, ENTJ types were most prevalent among the executives because the work of this group consisted primarily of formulating the strategies that provided overall guidance to an organization. In other words, these decision makers' personality styles could have been at least partially shaped by their work experience.

The study conducted by Passmore, Holloway, and Rawle-Cope (2010) is related to Roach's (1996) study in the sense that it also investigated the personality types of decision makers – although a very different kind of decision makers. The research participants in Passmore et al.'s (2010) study were 261 British and Irish executive coaches. Executive coaches have backgrounds in personnel or general management, and their major job function is to give advice either to individual colleagues within their organizations or to other organizations. Their principal mission is to promote performance. They can be perceived to be decision makers because they decide on and give advice to individuals and organizations concerning where and how they should develop. The research participants were asked whether or not they were aware of their MBTI types, and those who responded positively were instructed to select one from each of the four personality type dimensions: extraverted versus introverted, intuitive versus sensing, thinking versus feeling, and judging versus perceiving. Results indicated that the most striking personality style reported among the executive coaches was intuitive (N). Furthermore, compared with counselors and the general population, the executive coaches reported a stronger preference for thinking (T). The researchers commented that the strong preference for intuition and thinking may have reflected the nature of the coaching role. In other words, working as executive coaches may have played an important part in their acquisition of the NT personality styles.

Computer Professionals. Between the mid-1980s and the beginning of the 21st century, four publications involving the study of computer professionals and engineers appeared. These studies consistently suggested that the ISTJ personality type was prevalent among these personnel. A first study was conducted by Bush and Schkade (1985) in the United States. The research participants were 40 programmer analysts from within computer organizations per se and 18 systems analysts from user organizations. Results indicated that the single largest personality type among these computer professionals was ISTJ, with 25 percent falling into this category compared with 6 percent in the general population.

Three years later, Buie's (1988) study of 47 computer professionals employed by a private firm in the United States reached the same conclusion. That is, the most common personality type among computer professionals was ISTJ. Similarly, when Capretz (2003) examined the personality styles of 100 software engineers in Canada, he also obtained the same result. The research participants were studying in private or public universities, working for the government, or working for software companies. Finally, employing a shorter version of the MBTI, Smith's (1989) study of 54 systems analysts in South Africa again obtained precisely the same findings.

The consistent findings across these four studies, carried out in three different countries, cannot be considered coincidental. It is certainly possible that people of ISTJ personality styles tend to enter (or to be selected for) computer-related occupations. However, the nature of computer professionals' work might also necessitate the strengthening of their ISTJ personality styles. For example, computer professionals often deal with concrete problems alone, and working alone is more suited to people with introverted and sensing personality styles. Computer professionals also frequently engage in conceptual thinking and making judgments of the problems at hand, which requires the thinking and judging aspects of their personality styles.

Real Estate Agents. In the literature on the differences in people's personality styles, two studies concerned real estate agents. The first one was conducted by Waldo and Reschetz (1988) in the United States. Data were collected from 85 sales employees working for three large real estate firms in Illinois. Results indicated that the number of extraverted (E) individuals, as anticipated, was more than that of introverted (I) individuals. However, this tendency for real estate agents to be extraverted was not statistically different from that among the general population. Likewise, as predicted, among the study sample, there were more judging (J) individuals than perceiving (P) individuals. However, once again, compared with the data for the general population, the data for the real estate agents were not statistically different. Nevertheless, it was found that those participants who scored as ESJ (extraversion-sensing-judging) types were especially overrepresented among the sales winners. Waldo and Reschetz (1988) argued that preferences for extraversion, sensing, and judging – or at least the effective use of those attitudes and functions – may be conducive to better sales performance. However, one cannot rule out the possibility that successful sales experiences reinforced or even encouraged the development of the extraverted, sensing, and judging style preferences.

Almost three decades later, Cahill (2007) conducted a study among real estate agents, again in the United States. The research participants for this study were 301 real estate advertisers from four states. This sample of research participants, according to Cahill (2007), was primarily composed of real estate agents with longer tenure and ones who were more successful compared with the total population of real estate agents. Cahill's (2007) findings were consistent with those of Waldo and Reschetz (1988) in that the E and J types outnumbered the I and P types, respectively. However, the extent to which the EJ types were the dominant styles among the personality styles of Cahill's (2007) research participants was much greater than that among Waldo and Reschetz's (1988) participants. Cahill (2007) found that among his research participants, 75.6 percent scored as EJ types. This is three times higher than that of the general population.

Although only two studies of real estate agents' personality styles were identified, and although the lack of nonstatistical significance in Waldo and Reschetz's (1988) study might have been attributable to its small sample size, the similar findings of the two studies as well as the more prominent findings in the more recent study (Cahill, 2007) signify the dynamic nature of personality styles. To begin with, it should be kept in mind that compared with the general population of real estate agents, the research participants in Cahill's (2007) study had longer tenure and were more successful. Therefore, it is possible that they had acquired the EJ personality styles to a much greater extent than had the participants in Waldo and Reschetz's (1988) study. The differing degrees of EJ types shown in the two studies could also be indicative of generational effects. It should be borne in mind that the two studies were conducted almost three decades apart. That is to say, the real estate agents in the more recent study could have been required by the nature of their job to be more extraverted and judging than those in the 1980s had been. Finally, regardless of the differential findings across the two studies, it is clear that real estate agents, at least those in the United States, tend to be more extraverted and judging in their personality styles.

Accountants. The final occupational group involved in the study of personality styles was accountants. Two such studies were identified, both having been carried out in the United States in the first decade of the 21st century. The first study (Abdolmohammadi, Read, & Scarbrough, 2003) was conducted among 90 auditors working for five international firms located in the northeast of the United States. Based on findings among accounting students (Fisher & Ott, 1996), the researchers predicted that the practicing accountants' predominant personality type would be sensing and thinking (ST). As predicted, the percentage of research participants with the ST personality type in Abdolmohammadi et al.'s (2003) study was 46 – the highest among all combinations of personality types.

Stetson (2007) administered the MBTI online to 65 members of a state Certified Public Accounting Society in Oklahoma. Two major findings emerged. First, the thinking (T) personality style among accountants was predominant, with 70.5 percent of the research sample being T types, whereas 40.2 percent of the general U.S. population scored higher on the thinking personality dimension (versus feeling). Secondly, the most common personality style combination for this sample was STJ (39.1%) – nearly twice as common as in the general U.S. population (20.3%).

Thus, collectively, the aforementioned two studies suggest that the ST personality style is important for being an accountant – at least in the United States. Although the researchers of these studies did not attribute their findings to any specific factor, Abdolmohammadi et al. (2003) appeared to have acknowledged the malleability of personality styles by including "socialization" as well as "selection" in the title of their publication.

Career Personality Type and Occupation

As was noted at the beginning of this chapter, many occupations were assigned Holland Occupational Codes (Gottfredson & Holland, 1989) rooted in Holland's (1966, 1973) theory of career personality types. Thus, it is not an overstatement to say that of the research on the relationship between occupations and styles, research on the career personality types of different occupations has been the most fruitful. Within the context of the present chapter, only the five studies identified in the aforementioned literature search process are reviewed here. All five studies were carried out in the United States. Among these studies, three were conducted by Walsh and his colleagues between the late 1970s and early 1980s, and the remaining two appeared in 2005.

In their first study, Walsh, Horton, and Gaffey (1977) examined the career personality types of 165 male and female college-degreed workers in three traditionally male-dominated occupations (engineering, medicine, and ministry), corresponding to three of Holland's environmental categories respectively – realistic (R), investigative (I), and social (S). The research participants (66 males and 99 females) were administered both the *Self-Directed Search* (SDS, Holland, 1972) and the *Vocational Preference Inventory* (VPI, Holland, 1975). Results obtained from the two inventories consistently suggested that men in the traditionally male-dominated occupations, when compared with women in those same occupations, tended not to report higher mean raw scale scores. The major message of these findings is that the participants differed in career personality types based on the occupational groups they were in – irrespective of gender.

Walsh, Bingham, Horton, and Spokane (1979) further studied career personality type differences across occupations by focusing on a group of 155 female college-degreed workers. Moreover, the researchers built the variable "race" into their study. Data were gathered from 44 black female professional workers and 111 white ones. Again, both the SDS and the VPI were administered. The participants were employed in three traditionally male-dominated occupations – engineering, medicine, and law – corresponding, respectively, to the realistic (R), investigative (I), and enterprising (E) career personality types in Holland's occupational/environmental categories. Walsh et al. (1979) concluded that none of the three scales respectively from SDS and VPI significantly differentiated between the black and white women working in the same occupations. In other words, the career personality types of the participants varied as a function of their occupations – irrespective of race.

Finally, Walsh, Hildebrand, Ward, and Matthews (1983) conducted another study on black and white female workers, once again using both the SDS and VPI. This sample was different from the one used in Walsh et al.'s (1979) study in that it was composed of black and white female non-college-degreed workers. The 110 research participants were three groups of workers – laboratory technicians, sales clerks, and clerk-typists – who fall, respectively, into Holland's categorization of people with investigative (I), enterprising (E), and conventional (C) career personality styles. Results indicated that although black and white women in the same occupation tended to be more different than similar on the VPI scales, they scored similarly on the SDS scales.

In other words, race mattered in the female workers' career personality types when assessed by the VPI, but not when measured by the SDS. Undoubtedly, as illustrated in Chapter 4, it makes good sense that racial backgrounds matter in people's intellectual styles. At the same time, however, Walsh et al.'s (1983) study, like the two studies introduced before it (i.e., Walsh et al., 1977; Walsh et al., 1979), supported the notion that occupations make a significant difference in people's career personality styles.

In explaining the relationship between career personality styles and occupations, Walsh and his colleagues (Walsh et al., 1977; Walsh et al., 1979) used Barker's (1968) theory of behavior settings. They postulated that when women work in traditionally male-dominated occupations, they tend to be busier, more involved, more versatile, and more committed to their profession and to their professional environment. As a result, they develop career personality styles that are demanded by their job. In other words, people's career personality styles can be developed through their efforts to meet the challenges in their work environments.

In this connection, two studies published in 2005 lent strong support to the argument that people's career personality styles can be socialized on the job. A first study was conducted by LaBarbera (2005) using the SDS. The research participants were 144 family/general practice physician assistants (FP PAs) and 76 surgical PAs. In general, the Holland profile of this group of physician assistants was found to be SIREAC (social, investigative, realistic, enterprising, artistic, and conventional). However, when comparing the FP PAs with the surgical PAs, LaBarbera found that the former scored significantly higher on the social (S) scale, whereas the latter scored significantly higher on the realistic (R) scale of the SDS. LaBarbera (2005) proposed that this fine-grained difference might have been attributable to the fact that there were more women among the FP PAs and more men among the surgical PAs. This could be partially true because Holland's theory of career personality type has long been criticized for being gender-biased, with the S scale in favor of women and the R scale in favor of men. However, one cannot exclude the possibility that the differential nature of FP PAs' tasks and of surgical PAs' tasks might also have contributed to the finding. FP PAs usually need to communicate with doctors and patients when performing their duties at work, whereas surgical PAs do not normally need to do so. One of the outcomes of working in family/general practice versus surgical work environments could be that the two types of PAs develop different career personality styles.

Indeed, results from Swan's (2005) study of female carpenters in comparison with male carpenters and with normative samples of men and women supported the aforementioned argument. Research participants were a national sample of 411 female carpenters and a sample of 137 male carpenters from 19 states in the United States. Results generated from the research participants' responses to the SDS showed that the average realistic (R) score for female carpenters was more than two standard deviations higher than that for the normative adult females and three-quarters of a standard deviation higher than that for the normative adult males. The profiles for both male and female carpenters were dominated by higher R scores. The difference in the R scores between male and female carpenters was slightly more than one half of a standard deviation. As a matter of fact, the mean differences of the male and female carpenters were less than one standard deviation in all six Holland codes. In other words, the comparisons made from various perspectives suggested that both the female carpenters and the male carpenters scored high on the R scale and that in general, their career personality styles were quite similar. Swan (2005) remarked that "[t]he women's Realistic scores in this study appear extremely high relative to the rest of their profile" (p. 657). It is possible that the female carpenters had been attracted to the occupation because their career personality style was dominated by the R type. Equally possible, the female carpenters further developed the realistic career personality style as a result of having been socialized on the job.

Mind Style and Occupation
Considering the popularity of Gregorc's (1979) model of mind styles among styles researchers, one should say that the number of studies on different mind styles by occupations is small: only two studies were located. The first was conducted by Wenham and Alie (1992) in the United States. The researchers investigated the mind styles of 140 people in seven occupational groups from a support component of a Fortune 500 firm. The seven occupational groups were composed of technicians, mechanical engineers, drafters/designers, model makers, systems analysts, electrical engineers, and secretaries. As anticipated, the mind styles of the participants varied by occupations. For example, in the concrete-sequential style, technicians differed from mechanical engineers, model makers, and secretaries. As another example, the abstract-sequential style distinguished between electrical engineers and secretaries. It was concluded that, as an entire sample, the research participants exhibited a strong preference for sequential ordering. At the same time, the different groups were distinguished from one another by some dominance of concrete space factors. This set of findings is reminiscent of findings based on other style constructs (e.g., Kirton's innovative-adaptive styles and Jung's personality styles) in that it showed that particular style characteristics both permeate different occupations because the occupations share similarities, and separate these

occupational groups because the nature of work involved in each occupation is not exactly the same.

The second study was carried out by Gridley (2006a), also in the United States. The research participants were 26 female engineers solicited at receptions for such organizations as the Society of Industrial Engineers and the Society of Materials Engineers. Based on previous findings showing that engineers' personality style was often sensing-thinking-judging (STJ), Gridley (2006a) predicted that the female engineers' mind styles would be predominantly concrete-sequential on the *Gregorc Style Delineator* (GSD, Gregorc, 1982). This prediction was fully supported, with 98 percent of the female engineers reporting a stronger preference for the concrete-sequential style than for the other GSD styles.

It is certain that one cannot draw a definitive conclusion based on the results of merely two studies. Notwithstanding this, both studies reviewed here happened to involve the investigation of engineers' mind styles, and both suggested a prevalence of the concrete-sequential style. Moreover, researchers of both studies pointed out the consistency between their findings obtained on the basis of Gregorc's concept of mind styles and findings anchored in the Jungian personality types. Given this, one could argue that these consistent findings across studies and across style models have practical significance. From the perspective of the theme of this chapter, one could say that their mind styles might have predisposed the engineers to choose to enter the engineering profession. Equally, one could contend that it is likely that these engineers had become even more concrete-consequential in their intellectual styles as they progressed in the engineering profession.

Kolb's Construct of Learning Style and Occupation

Similar to the amount of research on mind styles among different occupations, the quantity of research based on Kolb's learning style construct as it pertains to different occupational groups is small. In fact, the current literature search only resulted in one relevant study. Collins and Milliron (1987) investigated a group of professional accountants' learning styles from three distinct geographical areas in the United States: the midwest, central, and eastern regions. Kolb's (1976) *Learning Style Inventory* was administered to 334 accountants working for nine accounting firms, including four Big Eight CPA (Certified Public Accounting) firms, four local CPA firms, and one large industrial firm. Two major findings stood out. First, as a group, the accountants distinguished themselves as convergers: fifty-three percent of the research participants scored as convergers, while the remaining 47 percent were roughly evenly distributed among the other three style categories

(17 percent being assimilators, 17 percent being accommodators, and 13 percent being divergers). Second, the accountants in management positions were more convergent than were accountants in staff positions. With respect to the second finding, Collins and Milliron (1987) offered two contrasting explanations. On the one hand, individuals with a predominantly convergent style might have been more likely to remain in the profession and be promoted to managerial positions. On the other hand, the accountant managers might have shifted toward the convergent style as they advanced in their careers. While the former explanation is consistent with the theory of attraction, the latter is in tune with that of accentuation.

Given that only one study relevant to the topic of this chapter was rooted in Kolb's construct of learning styles, one would naturally wonder if the findings are of any practical significance. This is a legitimate concern. However, if one examines the findings concerning accountants across the studies based on the various stylistic models introduced in this chapter, one will notice that Collins and Milliron's (1987) findings are in concert with findings from some of the other studies. For example, sensing-thinking (ST) attitudes emerged as the most common personality style combination for accountants in Abdolmohammadi et al.'s (2003) and Stetson's (2007) studies. People with the ST personality style combination are noted for their preference for dealing with concrete tasks and for their tendency to be less expressive of their emotions. The same stylistic characteristics are found in people with the convergent style. Indeed, as claimed by Collins and Milliron (1987), Kolb's (1976) construct of learning style is deeply rooted in Jungian personality types (Jung, 1923).

Thinking Style and Occupation
As the latest individual model of styles, Sternberg's (1988) theory of mental self-government has generated at least five studies that pertain to the association between styles and occupation. Research participants in these studies were assessed by either the *Thinking Styles Inventory* (Sternberg & Wagner, 1992) or the *Thinking Styles Inventory – Revised II* (Sternberg, Wagner, & Zhang, 2007).

The earliest study was conducted by Sternberg and Grigorenko (1995). The research participants were 30 humanities teachers and 33 science teachers teaching in four schools in the United States. It was found that the humanities teachers tended to use Type I thinking styles in their teaching and that the science teachers preferred to use Type II thinking styles. In explaining their findings, Sternberg and Grigorenko (1995) argued that although the results were not necessarily consistent with anything intrinsic to the disciplines themselves, they were consistent with the ways in which the subject matters in the two disciplines were taught in schools in the United States. Teaching humanities in schools requires that teachers allow students more freedom to express their ideas through discussing various issues, whereas teaching sciences requires teachers to be more facts-oriented. In other words, the way that teachers were required by their work environments to be engaged in their teaching tasks might have contributed to the development of their teaching styles.

The second study (Gridley, 2006b) was conducted among 128 professional fine artists in the United States, including professional painters, college artists, and printmakers. Results suggested that the research participants significantly preferred thinking that involves inventing and using new ideas (legislative style – a Type I style) to carrying out instructions (executive style – a Type II style). These professional fine artists also indicated their preference for change (liberal style – a Type I style) over the status quo (conservative style – a Type II style). Of the four forms of styles (hierarchical, oligarchic, monarchic, and anarchic) described in the theory of mental self-government, the artists showed the strongest preference for the Type I hierarchical style. In other words, the fine artists scored higher on Type I (creativity-generating) styles than they did on Type II (norm-favoring) styles. Again, one could argue that the fine artists were attracted to professions that allow more creativity. Even if this were the case, one could also say that the fine artists' creativity-generating thinking styles were acquired or strengthened through working in the field of fine arts.

In another study, Gridley (2007) compared the thinking styles of 71 professional fine artists with those of 147 engineers in the United States. Based on the nature of work inherent in the two different professions, Gridley (2007) predicted that compared with the artists, the engineers would be more inclined to execute the plans of others (executive style) and would prefer to perform more highly prioritized tasks (hierarchical style). In contrast, the artists would be more prone to devising their own plans (legislative style) and would be more likely to prefer to work independently (internal style). These predictions were fully supported by the data. Although the researcher did not discuss specifically the issue of style malleability, the reasons he gave for the significant differences found between the two groups of professionals revealed his belief in the change of styles. For example, regarding the engineers' preference for using the executive style, Gridley (2007) pointed out that "engineers usually work for clients whom they must please by implementing plans endorsed by the clients" (p. 179). Concerning the artists' inclination to use the internal style, Gridley noted that creating art is "almost exclusively a solitary activity" (p. 179). That is to say, the different nature of work intrinsic to the two different professions calls for the deployment of different thinking styles.

The fourth study (Higgins & Zhang, 2009) differed from the previous three in that it took into account research participants' rank and length of service at work and it used a qualitative research procedure apart from a self-report questionnaire. The research participants were 152 human resource (HR) practitioners who were pursuing membership of the Chartered Institute of Personnel Development in the United Kingdom. Quantitative analyses of the data indicated that in general, the thinking styles of the HR practitioners tended to be creativity-generating, in line with the nature of HR work. However, more detailed analyses showed that creativity-generating styles were preferred predominantly by practitioners with higher ranks and/or who had served longer in their organizations. This finding was confirmed by the data gathered from six focus group interview sessions with roughly one-third of the participants who had responded to the *Thinking Styles Inventory – Revised II* (Sternberg et al., 2007). The interviewees stated that although working at the highest level of HR departments may require higher levels of creative thinking such as in decision-making and delegating tasks, lower-level staff working in HR departments are more often engaged in executing tasks rather than in making strategic decisions. This finding is consistent with that in the previously reviewed studies (e.g., Foxall & Payne, 1989; Kirton & Pender, 1982) based on Kirton's adaption-innovation style construct.

Finally, the results from Verbeke, Belschak, Bakker and Dietz's (2008) research on the relationships among sales performance, social competence, thinking styles, and general mental ability (GMA) can perhaps be used to discuss the dynamic nature of styles from a different perspective. In their initial study, Verbeke et al. (2008) tested these relationships among 171 salespeople of a Dutch company selling print advertising materials. Only three thinking styles (legislative, judicial, and executive) were included in the study. It was found that the salespeople performed well when high GMA was combined with the use of the judicial style and a high score on social competence. However, when individuals with high GMA lacked the judicial style and social competence, they became the company's worst performers.

To verify the findings, the researchers (Verbeke et al., 2008) replicated the study with 107 salespeople from 31 companies. The sample covered diverse industries, including banking, consultancy, pharmaceuticals, human resource management services, and information technology. Sales tasks involved selling complex business solutions – both products and services. Findings in the replication study were strikingly similar to those obtained in the initial study of

171 salespeople from one single company. That is to say, among the salespeople, the tendency to use the judicial style was strongly associated with good sales performance. Once again, the question arises: Were individuals with the judicial style attracted to sales tasks, or had their experience in the sales business made them more judicial in their thinking? Once more, in both cases, the answer can be affirmative.

Summary and Further Discussion

As revealed in the preceding discussion of the existing literature, statistically significant findings were obtained in all studies. These studies consistently suggest that not only can people of different occupational groups have different intellectual styles, but also people in the same occupation can have different intellectual styles depending on a wide range of factors, including job functions, specialty areas, the nature of routine tasks undertaken, and level of seniority in one's organization. Although very few researchers (e.g., Clack et al., 2004; Tabernero & Màrquez, 1999) have explicitly discussed the development of styles as a result of people's socialization in different occupations, many (e.g., Abdolmohammadi et al., 2003; Jain & Lall, 1996; Rosenfeld et al., 1993; Tullett, 1995) have alluded to the dynamic nature of intellectual styles.

In reviewing the aforementioned studies, I have already made it clear that I believe that intellectual styles can be developed in consequence of being socialized in particular occupational settings and being recurrently engaged in specific tasks. In addition to the specific comments made in the context of each of the individual studies, I would like to complete this line of argument by introducing relevant considerations advanced by other scholars.

Early in 1988, Kirton put forward the concept of "cognitive climate." A cognitive climate represents the aggregate of the individual group members' intellectual styles. It reflects the dominant or preferred mode of problem solving and decision making of the group as an entire entity (Kirton & McCarthy, 1988). Kirton (1988) stated that "every organization has its own particular 'cognitive climate', and at any given time most of its key individuals reflect the particular mode" (p. 76). Nevertheless, Kirton (1988; Kirton & McCarthy, 1988) did not explain how a cognitive climate is formed.

It was Hayes and Allinson (1998) who took an unambiguous stance on the power of organizations in shaping individuals' intellectual styles, through illustrating various "mental models" (p. 855). A mental model provides the context in which information is viewed and interpreted. For example, Hayes and Allinson (1998) endorsed Kim's (1993) argument that organizations are capable of developing supra-individual or collective mental models.

According to Kim (1993), the individual learning cycle is a process that involves modifying beliefs and encoding the resultant changes into the individual's mental model. At the same time, organizational learning is dependent on individuals improving their mental models, resulting in explicit and shared mental models.

Also, for instance, Hayes and Allinson (1998) argued for the dynamic nature of intellectual styles by elaborating the concept of "collective memory" proposed in Doyle Conner, Kinicki, and Keats's (1994) model of mental process. The mental activities in each of the four stages – attention, encoding or interpretation, storage and retrieval from memory, choice and outcome – in Doyle Conner et al.'s (1994) model lend support to the notion that individuals' intellectual styles can be socialized in the workplace. For example, in the attention stage, individuals achieve a common understanding of the key information that should be attended to. In the encoding stage, individual thoughts are woven into a collectively shared framework used for absorbing the information. In the storage stage, organizational members are socialized into adhering to established routines, and they are programmed to learn and preserve accepted knowledge and behavior and filter out any information that contradicts the accepted knowledge and behaviors. This model presumes that any organization has a collective memory, a memory that persists over time regardless of changes in organizational membership. Although the concept of collective memory can be easily perceived as an overstatement because organizational membership should have a significant impact on work settings (Barker, 1968), Doyle Conner et al.'s (1994) four-stage mental model vividly portrays how individuals' ways of information processing can be shaped by their work environments.

Conclusions and Implications

Without a doubt, evidence from longitudinal research on this topic could be much more enlightening than what has been learned from the studies discussed here. Results from longitudinal investigations could better inform us about how people of different occupational groups acquire and strengthen particular intellectual styles by virtue of being in their professions. However, as in the case described in the previous chapter, and indeed other chapters of this book, the lack of longitudinal research and other possible limitations of the existing work cannot discredit what the literature reveals: people's intellectual styles can change as a result of their working in different occupations. The reasons for making such a claim are in line with the reasons for asserting that students' intellectual styles change as a function of their academic disciplines.

These are as follows: (1) all studies yielded significant findings; (2) the studies were rooted in a number of influential style models; (3) the investigations were conducted at various comparative levels; and (4) the data were from a fairly good number of countries/regions. These reasons have been discussed in the previous chapter, so they are not elaborated here.

What requires elaboration, however, are the practical implications of the general finding that people's intellectual styles can change at least partially as a result of their socialization in their professions or the workplace. One could argue that there are a minimum of three ways in which an understanding of the unique stylistic characteristics of different occupational groups could be beneficial, both at the organizational level and at the individual level.

First, such an understanding could help an organization deal with the rapidly changing world. The world is changing and so are the demands of different occupations. Keeping abreast of the development of the nature of an occupation may assist an organization in attracting and retaining employees whose styles are more suitable for the organization. Second, it could enhance the effectiveness and efficiency of staff training. When staff-training programs take into account the notion of intellectual styles, especially how styles develop, they are more likely to be successful, resulting in members' personal growth and the organizations' development. Finally, an understanding of the differences between the intellectual styles of a particular occupational group and those of its clients could enhance the communication between the two parties and increase the level of success of an organization, hence cultivating the highest possible levels of professional standards.

PART III

EMPIRICAL EVIDENCE: LONGITUDINAL STUDIES

7

Longitudinal Studies with Interventions

Previous chapters argued for the position that styles can be changed primarily through reviewing work that focused on the relationships between styles and socialization variables (i.e., culture, gender, academic discipline, and occupation). The underlying assumption was that styles can be said to be modifiable if they differ significantly along socialization dimensions. Reasons were provided as to why and how the various socialization variables should have contributed to changes in people's intellectual styles. However, the studies reviewed in previous chapters are mainly cross-sectional ones. To make a more convincing argument for the assertion that styles are adaptable, one has to show that styles do change over time.

This chapter and Chapter 8 review longitudinal studies of styles, with this chapter documenting studies that involved interventions and Chapter 8 describing nonintervention studies. This chapter consists of three parts. The first part describes the method of this review. The second part presents, for each of the style models included, the major intervention methods used to induce style changes and the key findings obtained. In the final part, some limitations of the current literature are noted and my contention that intellectual styles can be changed is reaffirmed.

Literature Search Procedures and Results

General Search Procedures
In view of the lack of longitudinal studies, with or without interventions, great care was taken to identify any study that was longitudinal, regardless of the style model on which the study was based. In order to locate the maximum number of studies, three doctoral students who were doing their dissertations on intellectual styles were recruited to assist in the literature

search. The students were instructed to search for longitudinal studies using three sets of style-relevant key words in combination with such key words as "longitudinal," "intervention," "experimental," "experiment," "change," "malleable," "malleability," "modifiable," and "modifiability." The first set of style-relevant key words was a series of commonly used style labels such as cognitive style, learning style, thinking style, teaching style, learning approach, study approach, learning pattern, and learning preference. The second was a series of style terms that are specific to some style models. For example, for Witkin's (1962) model, the term "perceptual style" was used; for Kagan's (1965), "conceptual tempo"; for Kirton's (1976), "decision-making style"; for Gregorc's (1979), "mind style"; for Jung's (1923), "personality type" or "personality style"; and so forth. The third set of style-relevant key words included the specific name(s) of the inventory (or inventories) based on each of the style models/constructs.

The search started with the 10 style models specified in the threefold model of intellectual styles (Zhang & Sternberg, 2005), but was subsequently expanded to other style inventories such as Riding and Cheema's (1991) *Cognitive Styles Analysis*, Kolb's (1976) *Learning Style Inventory*, Honey and Mumford's (1982, 1992) *Learning Styles Questionnaire*, and Vermunt's (1992, 1998) *Inventory of Learning Styles*. It was specified that all the aforementioned key words, in any combination, be found in the abstracts. This search resulted in 81 abstracts that appeared to describe longitudinal studies of style changes. To make sure that all relevant studies were located, one of the three doctoral students and I continued the search. In this follow-up search, only the three sets of style-relevant words were keyed in, without their combination with the terms that convey the notion of malleability. During this follow-up search process, roughly 3,800 abstracts were read. An initial reading of these abstracts led to our belief that another 60 abstracts could concern longitudinal investigations of styles. Subsequently, an attempt was made to locate the full text for each of the 141 (the initial 81 plus the 60 follow-up) abstracts. All were located and read. It appeared from these full texts, however, that only 101 publications (including journal articles, book chapters, and dissertations) pertained to longitudinal studies of styles. Subsequent search efforts mainly involved identifying potential relevant works in the list of references provided in each of the 101 publications. Ultimately, 129 publications were determined to be suitable for inclusion in the review of longitudinal investigations of intellectual styles. Among these, 90 publications concerned longitudinal studies with interventions and 39 dealt with longitudinal studies without interventions. In addition, three doctoral students (distinct from the aforementioned three students who helped in the literature search) agreed to have their experimental findings presented in this book. This chapter describes the 90 publications concerning interventional studies (84 being reports of individual studies and 6 being review articles) and the three sets of experimental data from my students, while the next chapter discusses the results suggested by the 39 publications on longitudinal studies without interventions.

Literature Search Results: Longitudinal Studies with Interventions
Results from the previously described literature search suggest that attempts to modify people's styles have long been an interest of styles researchers. However, given the long history of the field and the massive number of style constructs and style measures available to investigate these constructs, the productivity of this research is very low. The earliest attempt was made by Kagan, Pearson, and Welch (1966) and was aimed at reducing impulsivity and improving reflectivity. This was paralleled by investigations into the modifiability of field dependence as defined by Witkin (1948; see also Witkin, Goodenough, & Karp, 1967). In all, the literature search yielded 39 studies that concerned the conceptual tempo construct and 20 studies that dealt with perceptual styles. Moreover, seven publications that reviewed work on these two classic style constructs were located. Indeed, throughout the 1970s and 1980s, the style models adopted in research on modifying styles were almost exclusively those of Kagan's and that of Witkin's. Furthermore, this research took place largely in laboratory settings. Since the late 1980s, however, research on conceptual tempo has practically come to a standstill, and there has also been a significant reduction in the number of studies on perceptual styles.

By contrast, longitudinal studies aimed at enhancing students' deep approach to learning (also known as the meaning-oriented learning approach) based on several alternative models (e.g., Biggs, 1978; Entwistle, 1981; Vermunt, 1992) have been on the increase. In all, 12 studies based on the general notion of learning approaches were identified. The first study appeared in 1997 (Kember, Charlesworth, Davies, McKay, & Scott, 1997), and the remaining ones have been published since 2002.

Excluding the aforementioned studies, research based on other style models is either nonexistent or anecdotal. The current literature search resulted in five studies of divergent-convergent styles, three studies of brain dominance (again, also known as mode of thinking), and one each on Kolb's (1976) *Learning Style Inventory,* Honey and Mumford's (1982) *Learning Styles Questionnaire,* Myers's (1962) *Myers-Briggs Type Indicator,* and the *Kirton*

Adaption-Innovation Inventory (Kirton, 1976). Finally, Sternberg's (1988) model of thinking styles is beginning to generate some longitudinal experimental studies, four of which are reported in this chapter.

Research Findings

What is the overall picture painted by the 90 publications and three sets of unpublished data on the training of styles? What were the main research methods (e.g., populations studied, intervention methods, and lengths of treatment) adopted by studies based on each model? What were the main purposes of these studies (e.g., to develop particular styles, to examine generalization effects, and/or to identify parallel gains)? Was there a general direction toward which the training programs were designed to change the participants' intellectual styles? How long did the training effects last? What are some of the major factors that played important roles in the processes and outcomes of styles training? The remainder of this part is devoted to answering these questions by reviewing findings based on each of the aforementioned models. First, the studies based on the two classic models (Kagan's and Witkin's) are discussed, followed by those based on the general notion of learning approaches. The discussion then turns to a review of the studies based on six other models: Guilford's, Torrance's, Kolb's, Honey and Mumford's, Jung's, and Kirton's. Finally, three sets of data and one published study are presented, all of which are based on Sternberg's model of thinking styles.

Modifying Conceptual Tempo

The fact that impulsive conceptual tempo is inferior to reflective tempo with respect to cognitive performance has long been known (see Readence & Bean, 1978 for a summary). For this reason, researchers have attempted to modify impulsivity through various programs. As mentioned earlier, the earliest attempt was made in 1966, and throughout the 1970s and 1980s, many scholars were engaged in this endeavor. Indeed, the year 1975 saw the first publication in which several studies aimed at modifying conceptual tempo were reviewed (Epstein, Hallahan, & Kauffman, 1975) within the context of a discussion on the implications of the reflectivity-impulsivity construct for special education. Three years later, a more comprehensive review appeared (Readence & Bean, 1978). This review was devoted solely to the modification of the impulsive style. In 1979, a third review (Abikoff, 1979) came out. This review also considered the modifiability of conceptual tempo within a larger context. Although occasionally the same study was discussed in more than one of the three reviews, for the most part, each of the three reviews covered a different series of studies, respectively. Apart from these three reviews, 39 individual studies were located. In what follows, findings from the three reviews are analyzed first. Then, the findings of the 39 individual studies are synthesized.

Epstein et al. (1975) reviewed six studies that were of two types. The first type consisted of studies aimed at increasing latency of response and the second at reducing errors in response. Different training methods (e.g., forced delay, self-instructed delay, direct modeling, strategy instruction, increasing motivation, film-mediated modeling) led to varying degrees of effectiveness in modifying conceptual tempo. Moreover, findings differed as a function of such factors as the objectives of the studies (increasing latency or reducing errors), gender (Debus, 1970), and school class level (Heider, 1971) of the research participants. Despite the variations, the general conclusion of this review was clear: "External forces can modify a disposition toward conceptual tempo" (Epstein et al., 1975, p. 20).

The second review, indeed the first and only review whose sole objective was to evaluate experimental studies on modifying impulsive tempo, was conducted by Readence and Bean (1978). The authors reviewed 18 studies that adopted one of the four broad types of interventions: (1) using reinforcers, (2) using modeling, (3) using instructions in efficient scanning strategies, and (4) using distinctive feature training. While readers are referred to the original publications of this review article for details, the conclusions drawn by the authors are summarized here.

It was concluded that in general, research that aimed at reducing impulsivity had achieved "a modicum of preliminary success" (Readence & Bean, 1978), p. 334). All four broad types of interventions were regarded as holding promise for improving impulsive students' learning performance. However, there was no clear indication as to which type of intervention was the most effective and could have long-term effects. More specifically, four conclusions were reached. First, reinforcement interventions reduced impulsivity on a short-term basis. Second, reflective modeling in combination with self-guidance appeared to be the most effective intervention in modifying impulsive behaviors on matching tasks. Third, direct instruction in reflective scanning strategies met with success in changing impulsive search behaviors on matching tasks. Finally, training impulsive children to seek relevant distinctive features in tasks was effective in improving their problem-solving skills.

The third and most recent review of the effects of training programs on modifying impulsivity was conducted by Abikoff (1979). Like Epstein et al. (1975), Abikoff evaluated the intervention studies on modifying conceptual tempo within a larger context, in this case in the context of reviewing the effects of cognitive training interventions on several areas of cognitive functioning, including cognitive impulsivity. Abikoff (1979) reviewed 13 studies that involved the use of a variety of cognitive measures, of which 10 studies were concerned with measuring reflectivity-impulsivity. The most valuable information presented in this review was that cognitive training was more effective in modifying impulsivity than in improving any other area of cognitive functioning. In summarizing the results of the studies, Abikoff affirmed that cognitive training appears to be most effective in modifying impulsivity and that evidence for improving other areas of cognitive functioning is equivocal. Further information about the studies discussed in these three review articles is shown in Table 7.1.

Certainly, the reviews mentioned earlier consistently suggest that impulsivity can be reduced through interventions, and concomitantly, that reflectivity can be improved. However, all the studies included in the reviews were reported before 1979, that being the year when the most recent review was published. Since then, what has the literature been saying about the effects of intervention programs in modifying impulsivity and further, their generalizations to other cognitive or behavioral functions? The following provides a synthesis of the studies published since 1979 and those that were published before 1979, but were not included in the previously discussed three reviews. As noted earlier, there are 39 such studies: 30 that were published in or after 1979 and nine published in or before 1978.

Broadly speaking, these 39 studies can be discussed along four dimensions. The first relates to the research populations. With very few exceptions (e.g., Brown, Meyers, & Cohen, 1984; Mcmillan & Janzen, 1984; Schleser, Meyers, & Cohen, 1981; Schleser, Cohen, Meyers, & Rodick, 1984), the majority of the studies were conducted among special populations: clinical or nonclinical. Clinical populations solely involved young children, including hyperactive children, children with Attention Deficit Disorder, non-self-controlled children, juvenile delinquents, mildly retarded children, incarcerated juveniles, children with learning difficulties, institutionalized psychiatric adolescents, children with anger and aggressive behaviors, and conduct-disordered institutionalized boys. Nonclinical populations included such groups as the elderly, children from socially and economically disadvantaged backgrounds, and children who were classified as being impulsive through various screening procedures. This tendency to focus on special populations was in line with the trend shown in the studies included in the three previously mentioned reviews. As such, the objective of the interventions in the existing research

TABLE 7.1. *Reducing Impulsivity/Enhancing Reflectivity: Studies Included in Three Review Articles (Abikoff, 1979; Epstein et al., 1975; Readence & Bean, 1978)*

Authors	Country	Sample Size@	Age (years)	Nature of Sample	Type of Training	Intensity of Training	Time for Post Test	Outcome Variables	Significant Improvement	Follow Up	Significant Improvement at Follow-Up
Camp et al. (1977)	US*	(22+12)/832	second grade boys	22 screened aggressive boys and 12 normal boys	1. cognitive-behavioral treatment	daily 30-min sessions over 6 weeks	within 3 weeks after the training	MFFT	yes (L)	no	
					2. aggressive control group			WISC-R	yes (only in mazes subscale)		
								WRAT-RT	no		
								ITRA-AR	no		
					3. normal control group			TR-LNA&A	yes (only in TR-A)		
Cohen & Przybycien (1974)	US*	50/98	9–12	screened impulsive children	1. peer modeling	one session#	immediate	MFFT	yes (L&E)	no	
					2. control group						
Cullinan et al. (1977)	US*	33/40	9–12	impulsive learning-disabled males	1. modeling	one 6-min session	immediate	MFFT	yes (E-1,2)	3 weeks	no (L&E)
					2. modeling and self-verbalization						
					3. control group						
Debus (1970)	Australia	100/320	8–10	screened impulsive children	1. reflective model	one session #	immediate	MFFT	yes (L) (only yes in L showed yes in E)	2.5 weeks (MFFT)	yes (L-3) (only for girls)
					2. impulsive model						
					3. change model			DRT	no (L & E)		
					4. dual model						
					5. control group						

(*continued*)

TABLE 7.1 (*continued*)

Authors	Country	Sample Size@	Age (years)	Nature of Sample	Type of Training	Intensity of Training	Time for Post Test	Outcome Variables	Significant Improvement	Follow Up	Significant Improvement at Follow-Up
Denney (1972)	US*	72/231	second grade boys	screened rational and analytic children (according to their conceptual style)	1. analytic-reflective model	one session#	immediate	MFFT	yes (L)	10-14 days (CST)	
					2. analytic-impulsive model						
					3. relational-reflective model			CST	yes		yes
					*2 (analytic and relational children)						
					4. relational-impulsive model			PST	yes		
					5. control group						
Douglas et al. (1976)	Canada	29	6–10	aggressive boys	1. training (including modeling, self-verbalization, and strategy training)	24 1-hour sessions over 3 months for children; 6 consultation sessions for teachers; 12 sessions for parents	immediate	MFFT	yes (L&E)	3 months	yes (L&E)
								SCT	yes (in aggression & realistic subscales)		yes (in withdrawal & realistic subscales)
								PMT	no		no
					2. control group			BVMGT	yes (L)		no
								DTLA-MT	no		no
								DARD	yes (only in listening comprehension)		yes (in oral reading and oral comprehension)
								WRAT	no		no
								CRS-P&T	no		no

Egeland (1974)	Italy*	66/260	6–8	screened impulsive children	1. delaying response 2. scanning 3. control group	eight 30-min sessions over 4 weeks	immediate	MFFT	yes (L&E)	2 months (MFFT)	yes (L&E)
								SAT	no	at the end of the school year (GMRT)	yes
Erickson, Wyne, & Routh (1973)	US*	30	11–16	educable mentally retarded children	1. response-cost condition (withdrawal of tokens as punishment) 2. standard condition	directly compare the performance under these two conditions		MFFT	yes (L&E)	no	
Finch et al. (1975)	US*	15/45	11.3	impulsive emotionally disturbed boys	1. verbal self-instruction 2. delaying response 3. control group	six 30-min sessions over three weeks	the day after the training	MFFT	yes (L-1,2 & E-1)	no	
Heider (1971) – experiment 1	US*	80	7	middle-class and low-class boys	1. forced delay 2. increased motivation (reward to less mistakes) 3. strategy instructions 4. control group	one session #	immediate	MFFT	Only low-class boys: yes (L – 2&3) & (E – 3)	no	

(*continued*)

TABLE 7.1 (*continued*)

Authors	Country	Sample Size[@]	Age (years)	Nature of Sample	Type of Training	Intensity of Training	Time for Post Test	Outcome Variables	Significant Improvement	Follow Up	Significant Improvement at Follow-Up
Heider (1971) – experiment 2	US*	80	9	middle-class and low-class boys	1. forced delay 2. increased motivation (reward to less mistakes) 3. strategy instructions 4. control group	one session #	immediate	LT-FS	Only low-class boys: yes (L – 3) & (E – 1&3)	no	
Kagan, et al. (1966)	US*	80/155	first graders	screened impulsive children	1. delaying response instruction & similarity with the trainer 2. delaying response instruction 3. control impulsive group 4. control reflective group	three 30–40-min sessions over 2 or 3 days	6–8 weeks after training	MFFT IRT	yes (L-1&2) no	no	
Kendall & Finch (1978)	US	20/51	10–11	screened impulsive children	1. cognitive-behavioral treatment 2. control group	six 20-min sessions over 4 weeks	immediate	MFFT SR-IS SR-ICCI OR-ICBC OR-LCS	yes (L&E) no no yes no	3 months	yes (L&E) no no yes no
Massari & Schack (1972)	US	28	6.5	lower-class black male first graders	1. positive reinforcement 2. negative reinforcement	*2 (impulsive and reflective children)	one session #	immediate	TCDLT	yes (E-2<1)	no	

Meichenbaum & Goodman (1971)-Study 1	US*	15	7-9	students of a opportunity remedial class in school	1. cognitive self-guidance treatment group	two 20 min sessions over 1 week	immediate	MFFT	yes (L-1)	4 weeks	yes (L-1)
					2. attention control group			PMT	yes (E-1&2)		yes (E-1&2)
					3. assessment control group			WISC	yes (1)		yes (1)
Meichenbaum & Goodman (1971)-Study 2	US*	15/60	kindergarteners and first graders	screened impulsive children	1. cognitive modeling group	two 20 min sessions over 1 week	immediate	MFFT	yes (L-1&2) (E-2)	no	
					2. cognitive modeling plus self-instructional training group						
					3. attention control groups (a minimal modeling condition)						
Moore & Cole (1978)	US*	14	8-12	hyperkinetic children	1. cognitive self-instructional training	six 30-min sessions#	immediate	MFFT	yes (L)	no	no
					2. matched placebo control group			TR-CCB	no		
					3. time control group			CEFT	yes		
								WISC	yes (in coding subtest and prorated IQ)		
Orbach (1977)	US	55/140	8-11	screened impulsive children	1. similarity with the trainer & delaying response	one 15-20-minute session	one day after the training	MFFT	yes (L-1,2,3 & E-2,3)	no	
					2. detailed scanning						
					3. visual discrimination						

(*continued*)

199

TABLE 7.1 (continued)

Authors	Country	Sample Size	Age (years)	Nature of Sample	Type of Training	Intensity of Training	Time for Post Test	Outcome Variables	Significant Improvement	Follow Up	Significant Improvement at Follow-Up
Ridberg, et al. (1971)	US*	100/185	fourth-grade boys	screened reflective and impulsive children	1. model without verbalization and scanning 2. model with verbalization but no scanning *2 (reflective model and impulsive model) 3. model with scanning but no verbalization 4. model with verbalization and scanning 5. control group	one session #	immediate	MFFT	yes (L&E) (reflective model for impulsive children)	1 week	yes (L&E) (reflective model for impulsive children)
Yando & Kagan (1968)	US	160	first graders	normal students	1. with reflective teachers 2. with impulsive teachers	7–8 months	immediate	MFFT	yes (L)	no	
Zelniker & Oppenheimer (1973)	Israel*	60/200	5–6	screened impulsive children	1. matching to sample test training 2. differentiation test training	one session #	immediate	TT-DF, P&C	yes (E-2 in TT-DF)	no	

Zelniker & Oppenheimer (1976)	Israel*	135/450	5–6	screened impulsive children	1. multiple transformation differentiation training 2. multiple transformation differentiation training with novel transformations 3. single transformation differentiation training with novel transformations 4. matching training 5. control group	one session #	PLT: MASP & TT-DF, P&C	yes (E-1,2,3,4) & (E-1,2,3<4 in TT-DF)	no
Zelniker, et al. (1972)	US	40	8–9	normal students	1. matching to sample test training 2. discriminating familiar figures test training	one session #	immediate MFFT	yes (L&E)	no

Notes:

IRT: inductive reasoning test
PMT: Porteus Maze test
WISC: Wechsler Intelligence Scale for Children
DRT: Design Recall Test
LT-FS: A Language Task: Forming a Sentence
TT-DF; P&C: transfer tests (distinctive features and prototype and control)
TCDLT: Two-Choice Discrimination Learning Task
CST: Conceptual Style Test
PST: Picture Sorting Test
PLT: Perceptual Learning Test
MASP: Match-to-a-Standard Problems
SAT: Stanford Achievement Test
GMRT: Gates-Macginitie Reading Test
SR-IS: Self Report: Impulsive Scale
SR-ICCI: Self Report: Impulse Control Categorization Instrument

* inferred from authors' affiliations
\# training duration not reported
L: latency
E: error
Immediate: immediately after training
@ Sample size: x/y stands for x selected from y

OR-ICBC: others-rating: Impulsive Classroom Behavior Scale
OR-LCS: others-rating: Locus of Conflict Scale
WISC-R: Wechsler Intelligence Scale for Children- Revised
WRAT-RT: Reading Test from the Wide Range Achievement Test
ITRA-AR: Auditory Reception from the Illinois Test of Psycholinguistic Abilities
TR-LNA&A: Teacher-Rating: Low Need Achievement and Aggression
SCT: Story Completion Test
BVMGT: Bender Visual-Motor Gestalt Test
DTLA-MT: Memory Tests from the Detroit Tests of Learning Aptitude
DARD: Durell Analysis of Reading Difficulty
CRS-P&T: Conners Rating Scales for Parents and Teachers
WRAT: Wide Range Achievement Test
TR-CCB: Teacher-Rating Scale of the Children's Classroom Behaviors
CEFT: Children's Embedded Figures Test

can be said to be much more remedial than developmental (see Table 7.2 for details).

The second dimension concerns the aims of the studies. Although the principal objective of all studies was to examine the effects of the interventions in modifying conceptual tempo, the majority of the studies also looked into research participants' performance either on parallel gains or on generalization tasks in such domains as general intelligence, specific aspects of intelligence, academic achievement, affective development such as locus of control and self-concept, as well as in-classroom behavior and social skills. Examining these parallel gains or performance on generalization tasks is important because the research findings obtained can be used to enhance our understanding of the critical functions of conceptual tempo in other domains of human performance.

The third dimension is the nature of the interventions administered in these studies, which can be analyzed in at least four ways: types of interventions, directorship, intensity of training (including length and frequency), and participant involvement. Broadly speaking, interventions can be of five types: (1) cognitive-oriented, (2) behavioral-oriented, (3) physical exercises, (4) drug administration, and (5) any combination of the aforementioned four types. The most common of these is cognitive-behavioral. Directorship refers to how the research participants receive training instructions. Whereas research participants in some experimental studies received instructions directly from the experimenters, those in other studies were taught how to use self-instructions. Concerning intensity of training, 22 of the 39 studies involved a one-off training session (in some cases, one training session could contain several procedures), and the remaining 17 contained multiple training sessions lasting from one week to one year, with the typical length of experiment being several weeks. Finally, regarding participant involvement, the majority of the studies simply involved the target participants, while several studies rendered training to parents and/or teachers of the target groups in addition to the target groups (i.e., children).

The final dimension concerns the nature of the data as it relates to the timing of data collection. Data of some studies came from immediate post-tests, be the interventions one-off training sessions or multiple-session training over several weeks. The majority (27) of the 39 studies provided this type of data. The data of other studies were obtained through either a delayed post-test (six studies took this approach) or an immediate post-test accompanied by a follow-up test (six studies took this approach). One study (Kendall & Braswell, 1982) recorded data from an ongoing assessment, a post-treatment assessment, a 10-week follow-up assessment, and a 1-year follow-up assessment.

TABLE 7.2. Experimental Studies (Modifying Impulsivity/Enhancing Reflectivity): Individual Studies

Authors	Country	Sample Size[@]	Age (years)	Nature of Sample	Type of Training	Intensity of Training	Time for Post Test	Selected Outcome Variables	Significant Improvement	Follow Up	Significant Improvement at Follow-Up
Barrickman et al. (1995)	US	18	7–17	patients with ADHD	1. bupropion medication 2. methylphenidate medication	daily	10 weeks	MFFT CDI CMAS	yes (E) yes yes	no	
Bell et al. (1983)	US*	45	10–16	institutionalized aggressive, impulsive males	1. cognitive tasks 2. control group	14 sessions (2 per week)	2 weeks after training	MFFT PMT	yes (L&E) for both C & E groups (more for E)	no	
Bender (1976)	US	70/122	first graders	screened impulsive children	1. verbal self-instruction strategy training 2. tutor verbalized strategy training 3. verbal self-instruction without explicit strategy training 4. attentional materials control 5. in-class control	10–25 minutes for 4 consecutive days	immediately after every training session	MFFT	yes for training groups (especially for verbal self-instructions)	no	
Briggs & Weinberg (1973)	US	99/145	fourth grade boys	screened impulsive and reflective children	1. "fast" treatment (instructions and feedback) 2. "slow" treatment (instructions and feedback) 3. Control	20 minutes to 1.5 hrs	3 minutes after training	MFFT WISC Draw-a-line	yes for all	A new study	yes

(continued)

TABLE 7.2 (continued)

Authors	Country	Sample Size	Age (years)	Nature of Sample	Type of Training	Intensity of Training	Time for Post Test	Selected Outcome Variables	Significant Improvement	Follow Up	Significant Improvement at Follow-Up
Brown et al. (1984)	US*	27	4–5	preschool children	1. self-instruction	13 consecutive weekly session (30 min. per session)	after 5 and 9 weeks of training	MFFT	yes (L) for self-instruction group	no	
					2. skills training			5 other tasks	mixed		
					3. control						
Brown (1980)	US*	116	8 and 13	hyperactive children	1. modeling	two 7-min videotapes for modeling group; specific instruction for specific task group; no treatment for C group	1 week after training	MFFT	yes (children receiving no drug therapy improved more than those who did)	no	
								Coding subtest on the WISC-R	yes (only those receiving both drug therapy and psychoeducational treatment)		
					2. specific-task instruction			School related copying task	no		
Brown et al. (1986)	US*	33	6–13	ADD children	1. drug/attention control	twice weekly 1-hour session (22 sessions over 3 months) Attention control also 22 one-hour sessions over 3 months	immediate	MFFT	yes (cognitive therapy only)	3 months after termination of all treatment	yes (cognitive therapy only)
					2. cognitive therapy/placebo			CCT	no	3 months after termination of all treatment	no
					3. drug/cognitive therapy			WISC-R	no		no

204

Butter (1979)	US*	30/98	Third and fourth grade boys	screened impulsive boys	1. visual	one 20-minute session	immediate	MFFT	visual group: yes (E); Haptic group: yes (both L & E)	no
					2. haptic	one 10-minute session		HMT	both groups: yes (both L & E)	
Cohen et al. (1981)	US*	60	second graders	children of preoperational and concrete operational (Piagetian) stages	1. self-instruction		Immediate	MFFT	yes: Self-instruction more effective; Concrete operational children improved more	no
					2. content only	#				
					3. control group					
Cole & Hartley (1978)	US	36/120	second graders	screened impulsive children	1. strategy training	one 25-minute session	Immediate	MFFT	yes, all three training groups, with primary reinforcement being the most effective	no
					2. strategy training with primary reinforcement					
					3. strategy training with secondary reinforcement					
					4. control group					
Copeland & Hammel (1981)	US	30	6–11	school children	1. cognitive self-instruction	two 20-minute sessions within	6 days after training	MFFT	both groups improved	no
								BVRT	both groups improved	
					2. attention control			OR-T	both groups improved	
								PMT	CSI more conducive to higher scores	

(*continued*)

TABLE 7.2 (*continued*)

Authors	Country	Sample Size	Age (years)	Nature of Sample	Type of Training	Intensity of Training	Time for Post Test	Selected Outcome Variables	Significant Improvement	Follow Up	Significant Improvement at Follow-Up
Denney (1981–82) – Experiment 1	US	42	65–75	middle-class elderly adults	1. instructing slow (instructed to take time to respond to MFFT items) 2. instructing fast 3. instructing standard	brief training in two practice items	immediate	MFFT	no	no	
Denney (1981–82) – Experiment 2	US	48	65–75	middle-class elderly adults	1. modeling average 2. modeling faster than average 3. modeling slower than average	brief training via modeling 5 items	immediate	MFFT	no	no	
Denney (1981–82) – Experiment 3	US	156	65–75	middle-class elderly adults	1. fast (with strategy training–ST) 2. standard (with ST) 3. slow (with ST) 4. fast (no ST) 5. standard (no ST) 6. slow (no ST)	brief training on 6 items	immediate	MFFT	yes (L for the fast group only)	no	
Egeland (1974)	US*	72/260	second graders	screened impulsive children	1. search strategy training 2. delay responses 3. control	eight 30-minute sessions over 4 weeks	immediately and 2 months after training	MFFT	yes (for training groups on immediate post-test)	2 months	yes (strategy training only)
								Vocabulary test	yes (both training groups)		
								Comprehension test	yes (only search strategy group)		

Feindler et al. (1986)	US*	21	13–18	institutionalized psychiatric male adolescents	1. treatment (relaxation, self-instructions, use of coping statements, assertive social interactions, evaluation of one's behavior, etc.)	12 sessions (#) over 8 weeks	immediate	MFFT	yes (for the treatment group)	Yes (#)	yes
					2. control group 1			Behavioral Rating Scale for Children	yes		yes
					3. control group 2						
Feindler et al. (1980)	US*	36/100	12–15	multi-suspended delinquents	1. three groups receiving the same treatment separately (e.g., self-instructions, thinking ahead skills, assertion without aggression, alternative responses to provoking stimuli	ten 50-minute sessions over 7 weeks	immediate	MFFT	yes (L)	no	
								Self-control Rating Scale (teacher rating)	yes		
					2. control group			Problem Solving Inventory	yes		
Genshaft & Hirt (1979)	US	60/333	7–8	screened black and white impulsive children	1. model with self-instruction	1 hour daily for 2 weeks	immediate	MFFT	yes (both black and white children when trained by models of their own race	no	
					2. children received 2 trials with model's instructions			Picture arrangement sub-test of WISC and WISC-R			
					3. children received 2 trials while self-instructing						
					4. children received 2 trials while self-instructing covertly						
					5. control						

(*continued*)

TABLE 7.2 (continued)

Authors	Country	Sample Size	Age (years)	Nature of Sample	Type of Training	Intensity of Training	Time for Post Test	Selected Outcome Variables	Significant Improvement	Follow Up	Significant Improvement at Follow-Up
Glenwick & Barocas (1979)	US*	32/150	fifth and sixth graders	screened impulsive children with classroom behavior difficulties	1. children's parents and teachers trained to instruct children (PT group)	two 50-minute session weekly for 4 weeks	immediate	MFFT	yes (for all groups)	5 weeks	yes (E) (for PT, P, and Control groups)
					2. children's teachers trained to instruct (T group)			WRAT	yes (for PT group)		
					3. children's parents trained to instruct (P group)			PMT	yes (for T group)		
					4. children trained by experimenter (CH group)			WISC	yes (for T group)		
								Teacher Rating (classroom behaviors)	yes (for PT group)		
					5. assessed but not trained (Control)			Parent rating (home behaviors)	yes (for P and control groups)		
Gow & Ward (1980)	Australia	30/41	15–20	mildly retarded adolescents receiving training at a work preparation center	1. training (collating a 24-page booklet, accompanied by self-verbalization of strategies	one session #	delayed #	MFFT	yes (for both groups)	no	
					2. normal training of the center			PMT			
Hartley (1986) – Experiment 1	UK	7	7–8	working-class children	1. role enactment (act clever)	one session #	immediate	MFFT	yes (role enactment superior)	no	
					2. control			Speech reflexivity	no		

Hartley (1986) – Experiment 2	UK	6/34	10	working-class children	1. role enactment (act clever)	one session #	immediate	MFFT	yes (role enactment superior)	no
					2. control			Speech reflexivity	no	
Hartley (1986) – Experiment 3	UK	12/21	7	working-class children	1. role enactment (act clever)	one session #	immediate	MFFT	yes (role enactment superior)	no
					2. control			Speech reflexivity	no	
Hartley (1986)- Experiment 4	UK	8/28	6	working class children	1. role enactment (act clever)	one session #	immediate	MFFT	yes (role enactment superior)	no
					2. control			Speech reflexivity	no	
Holmes (1981)	US	30	11–14 13–18	mildly retarded children	1. operant	three 20-minute sessions per week for 2 weeks	2 weeks after training	MFFT	yes (for SI groups: younger groups did better)	no
					2. self-instruction					
					3. extended self-instruction			PMT	no (for PMT)	
					4. control			Teacher rating Classroom behavior	yes (rating for experimental groups)	
Horn et al. (1983)	US*	1	9	a black boy referred to an inpatient psychiatric unit	psycho-stimulant (Dexedrine); self-control (SC) training; and direct reinforcement	11 weeks	immediately after every training session	MFFT	yes (direct reinforcement) starting week 8	no
								Behavioral rating (teacher)	yes (drug and SC training for on-task behavior)	

(continued)

TABLE 7.2 (*continued*)

Authors	Country	Sample Size	Age (years)	Nature of Sample	Type of Training	Intensity of Training	Time for Post Test	Selected Outcome Variables	Significant Improvement	Follow Up	Significant Improvement at Follow-Up
Isakson & Isakson (1978)	US	22/119	second grade boys	screened impulsive children	1. training in analysis 2. control group	4–5 20-minute sessions	second day after training	MFFT	yes (E)		
Kappes & Thompson (1985)	US	12	15–18	felonious juvenile resident in a highly restricted environment	1. biofeedback 2. video games	ten 30-minute sessions over 8 weeks	immediate	MFFT PAI	yes (both training methods) yes (both training methods)	no	
Karoly & Briggs (1978)	US	90	5–7	kindergarten through second-grade children	9 groups resulted in 3 rule structuring (RS) conditions by 3 directed delay patterns (DDP): 3 RS groups: 1) general-positive; 2) specific-arbitrary; and 3) specific-negative 3 DDP groups: 1) increasing; 2) decreasing; and 3) fixed	one session #	1 week after training	MFFT	yes (rule provision for L) general and positive RS superior to arbitrary rule or no rule	no	
Kendall (1981)	US	17	11 (average)	non-self-controlled problem children	1. conceptual training 2. concrete training 3. attention control	twelve 45- to 55-minute sessions (biweekly)	13-month follow-up study	MFFT (E) ICCI SCRS	yes (E for all three groups) yes (for all three groups) yes (for all three groups)	3 months after termination of all treatment	yes (cognitive therapy only)

210

Kendall & Braswell (1982)	US	27	8–12	non-self-controlled problem children	1. conceptual training 2. concrete training 3. attention control	twelve 45- to 55-minute sessions (biweekly)	immediate	MFFT WRAT (math)	L&E for all groups for all groups	10 weeks and 1 year	yes (10 weeks) L&E for all groups – compared with pre-treatment no for 1 year yes (10 weeks) for all groups – comparing with both pre-treatment and the first post-test
Kendall & Finch (1976)	US	1	9	an impulsive boy	self-instructions and response cost	six 50-minute sessions	immediate	MFFT School behaviors	yes (L & E) yes	6 months	yes yes
Kendall & Wilcox (1980)	US	33	8–12	non-self-controlled problem children	1. conceptual training 2. concrete training 3. placebo	six 30-minute sessions (twice a week for 3 weeks)	1 week after training	MFFT PMT	yes, all three groups yes, all three groups	1 month	yes, all three groups yes, all three groups
Mcmillian & Janzen (1984)	Canada	44	7	elementary school students	1. self-verbalization (SV) 2. attention control	six 40-minute sessions over 2 weeks	2 weeks after training	MFFT PMT	yes (SV group) yes (SV group)	no	

(*continued*)

TABLE 7.2 (continued)

Authors	Country	Sample Size	Age (years)	Nature of Sample	Type of Training	Intensity of Training	Time for Post Test	Selected Outcome Variables	Significant Improvement	Follow Up	Significant Improvement at Follow-Up
Orbach (1977)	Israel	55/140	8–11	screened impulsive boys	1. modeling and instruction (latency)	15–20 minute session	1 day after training	MFFT	yes (L only) (for 1)	no	
					2. visual detailing (accuracy)				yes (L & E) – 2		
					3. visual discrimination (accuracy)				yes (L & E) – 3		
Porter & Omizo (1984)	US	34	first and second graders	hyperactive boys	1. relaxation training involving parents	3 once-weekly sessions	1 week after training	MFFT	yes (L&E for treatment groups)	no	
					2. relaxation training not involving parents				yes (for treatment groups)		
					3. control			Attention to task			
Rupert & Baird (1979)	US	60/151	first and second graders	screened slow responders (SR) and fast responders (FR)	8 conditions formed by SRs and FRs exposed to models depicting reflective or impulsive strategies that were either success or failure	brief training (video) #	immediate	MFFT	yes (L for viewers of reflective-success model, especially slow responders)	no	
									yes (E for viewers of reflective model – success or failure)		
					control group						
Schleser et al. (1984)	US	112/176	first and second graders	screened children at preoperational and concrete Piagetian levels	1. fading self-instruction	2 hours and 15 minutes over 3 sessions	immediate	MFFT	yes (groups 1 and 2 over groups 3 and 4)	no	
					2. directed discovery self-instruction			A generalization perceptual perspective-taking task	yes (only concrete operational children in group 2)		
					3. didactic instruction						
					4. control group						

Schleser et al. (1981)	US	140	first and second graders	regular school students	1. specific self-instruction (SSI)	brief training #	immediate	MFFT	yes (treatment groups outperformed control groups)
					2. general self-instruction (GSI)				GSI group outperformed all other groups
					3. specific didactic control				
					4. general didactic control				
					5. no-training control				
Schleser et al. (1983)	US	48/72	8–10	screened non-self-controlled children	1. task-specific faded rehearsal self-instruction	one 45-minute session weekly for 4 weeks	immediate	MFFT	yes (E for the 3 training groups) yes (L for Groups 1 and 2)
					2. general problem-solving faded rehearsal self-instruction			PIAT	no
					3. directed discovery				group 1 on spelling and general information
					4. control				group 3 on spelling, reading, and general information
Sousley & Gargiulo (1981)	US	33/104	6	screened impulsive children	1. experimental group (visual discrimination activities)	three 15-minute lessons weekly for 3 weeks	immediate	MFFT	yes (L)
					2. control group				no

(*continued*)

TABLE 7.2 (*continued*)

Authors	Country	Sample Size[@]	Age (years)	Nature of Sample	Type of Training	Intensity of Training	Time for Post Test	Selected Outcome Variables	Significant Improvement	Follow Up	Significant Improvement at Follow-Up
Williams & Akamatsu (2001)	US	30	Unspecified	juvenile delinquents	1. self-guidance 2. attention control 3. assessment control	one session #	immediate	MFFT WISC (picture arrangement)	yes (E only: groups 1 and 2 outperformed group 3) yes (Group 1 outperformed groups 2 and 3)	no	
Zakay et al. (1984)	Israel	74	10	teacher-nominated impulsive children	1. belief treatment (BT) 2. plan training (PT) 3. combined treatment (CT) 4. control	one hour weekly for 8 weeks	8 weeks after training	MFFT Behavioral Measures of Adjustment	yes (groups 1, 2, and 3 more than group 4) yes (9 out of 10 measures)	no	
Zieffle & Romney (1985)	Canada	30	8–12	children with special learning needs	1. self-instruction 2. progressive muscle relaxation 3. control	10 half-hour sessions over 4 weeks	immediate	MFFT PMT	yes (for 2 treatment groups) yes (for 2 treatment groups)	no	

Notes:

CDI: Children's Depression Inventory
CMAS: Children's Manifest Anxiety Scale
ADD: Attention Deficit Disorder
CCT: Children's Checking Task
HMT: Haptic Matching Task
BVRT: Benton Visual Retention Test
OR: Therapist
PAI: Personal Attribute Inventory (assessing self-concept)

* inferred from authors' affiliations
\# training duration not reported
L: latency
E: error
Immediate: immediately after training
[@] Sample size: x/y stands for x selected from y

ICCI: Impulse Control Categorization Instrument
SCRS: Self-Control Rating Scale
PIAT: Peabody Individual Achievement Test
PMT: Porteus Maze Test
WISC: Wechsler Intelligence Scale for Children
WISC-R: Wechsler Intelligence Scale for Children- Revised
WRAT: Wide Range Achievement Test

Although none of the 39 studies reported the effect sizes of the interventions, almost all of them concluded that at least one of the treatment conditions was effective in reducing impulsivity or in developing reflectivity. Such consistent statistically significant findings obtained in various studies conducted in different contexts should provide strong support for the argument that conceptual tempo can be changed through purposeful interventions. However, not all intervention methods can serve as equally efficacious treatments for all populations, or even for different samples of the same population. On the contrary, individuals may respond differently to the same intervention method. In what follows, a wide range of contingencies/factors that may affect the efficacy of particular interventions is discussed.

Generally speaking, these contingencies/factors can be classified into three types. The first type is *presage* in nature and includes factors that people (both research participants and experimenters) bring into the research context. The second type is *process* in nature and concerns the experimental designs (or treatment procedures) of the studies. The final type of contingencies is *product* in nature and pertains to the ways in which treatment outcomes are reported.

Presage Variables and Treatment Effects. Generally referred to as presage variables, the personal characteristics and attributes that research participants (including primary target groups and secondary/assisting groups) and researchers (experimenters) possess may play a critical role in the treatment effects of interventions. Primary target research participants in these studies were the individuals who were trained to reduce their own impulsivity or to increase reflectivity. The secondary/assisting research participants were individuals who helped carry out the experiments. These individuals may have been models of reflective thinking or behavior, and they may have been parents and/or teachers who were involved in the experiments to enhance the treatment effects.

To begin with, the characteristics of the primary research participants made a difference in the experimental outcomes. For example, children's Piagetian cognitive levels played a critical role. Schleser, Meyers, and Cohen (1981) rendered five experimental conditions (non-training, specific self-instruction, specific didactic control, general self-instruction, and general didactic control groups) to 70 pre-operational and 70 concrete-operational first- and second-grade school children in the United States. Although the patterns of improvement following the training were identical, children at the concrete-operational Piagetian level made more overall correct responses on the *Matching Familiar Figures Test* (MFFT, Kagan, Rosman, Day, Albert, & Philips, 1964) than did those at the pre-operational cognitive level. Three years later, Schleser, Cohen, Meyers, and Rodick (1984) conducted an experiment with a sample of 176 children from the same population, this time using four experimental conditions: no-training control, didactic instruction control, fading self-instructions, and directed discovery self-instructions. Once again, the researchers found that children's cognitive-developmental levels made a difference in the experimental outcomes. Although both training groups improved on the training task (i.e., MFFT), only children at the concrete-operational cognitive level in the directed discovery self-instruction group improved on the generalization task – a perceptual perspective-taking task.

Apart from their Piagetian cognitive levels, primary research participants' initial levels of conceptual tempo were also shown to contribute to the experimental outcomes. For example, Gow and Ward (1980) attempted to modify the impulsive cognitive style of 30 mildly retarded adolescents (aged 15 to 20 years) who were engaged in work preparation training in Australia. An interaction effect was noted: for the impulsive adolescents, there was a significant reduction in errors, but not in the case of the reflective ones. This finding could very well be indicative of a possible ceiling on the scores of the reflective research participants. At the same time, this potential ceiling effect was manifested in response latency. For instance, Glenwick and Barocas's (1979) study of impulsive fifth and sixth graders over a period of four weeks in the United States revealed that there was general across-the-board improvement on the MFFT for the control group as well as for the experimental groups. The researchers attributed the lack of differential treatment effects to the possible ceiling on the latency score. As stated by the researchers, there might exist an "upper limit for latency beyond which there was little additional room for improvement" (Glenwick & Barocas, 1979, p. 396).

Age is another personal characteristic of primary research participants that made a significant difference in treatment outcomes. For example, in a study carried out by Holmes (1981), 13 young (aged between 11 and 14 years) and 17 older (aged between 13 and 18 years) mildly retarded students were randomly assigned to four experimental conditions: control, operant treatment, limited self-instruction, and extended self-instruction groups. Although students in the two self-instruction conditions generally performed better on the MFFT than did the other two groups, performance effects within the two self-instruction groups were found to be related to age: younger children outperformed older children in both self-instruction groups.

These examples demonstrate the difference that the characteristics of primary target research participants can make in the efficacy of intervention methods. Research further indicated that the involvement of secondary research participants such as teachers and parents also played an important role in the treatment effects of interventions. For example, Glenwick and

Barocas's (1979) study involved some of the 40 impulsive children's parents and teachers in addition to the children themselves. Among the five treatment conditions used in Glenwick and Barocas's study, three involved parents and/or teachers as the secondary research participants: one involved teachers, a second involved parents, and a third involved both teachers and parents. Results showed that all five groups (the other two being an experimenter-trained group and a no-training group) significantly improved in terms of both latency (i.e., lengthened latency) and errors (i.e., reduced errors) from pre-test to immediate post-test and from pre-test to follow-up test conducted five weeks after the training had stopped. Furthermore, groups with parental and teacher involvement also showed significant improvement with respect to MFFT errors from post-test to follow-up test.

Not only the involvement but also the characteristics of the secondary research participants can influence the experimental outcome. For example, within the context of using the "modeling" technique, the racial background of the models can be an important factor. Using self-instruction and modeling techniques, Genshaft and Hirt (1979) attempted to train 30 black children and 30 white children (aged 7 to 8 years) to become more reflective through learning from "peer group" models. These models were 10 black children and 10 white students (aged 13 to 14 years) from a similar socioeconomic class. The results demonstrated inconsistent support for the effectiveness of the said intervention. Although significant improvement was identified in both black and white children, the improvement was limited to the cases where children were trained by models of their own race. Age of the models can also affect the training effects of particular intervention methods. Cohen and Przybycien (1974) used modeling techniques to increase the level of reflectivity among fourth- and sixth-grade boys and girls and contended that age-appropriate models of similar status may be more effective in changing children's impulsive style, especially with regard to reducing errors.

Moreover, the attributes of the experimenters, often the researchers themselves, can also influence the treatment effects. For instance, in a study on treating impulsivity among non-self-controlled children, Kendall and Wilcox (1980) found that the level of the experimenter's empathy was significantly related to the level of children's improvement on the MFFT.

Process Variables and Treatment Effects. Generally speaking, three major process variables – factors that are related to the experimental procedures themselves – can play a critical role in determining the level of efficacy of the interventions rendered. These include (1) the nature of the sample (in particular, the criteria and procedures used for selecting research participants), (2) methods of training, and (3) intensity of training.

Aside from the aforementioned fact that the existing studies tended to involve special populations, the participants who were ultimately selected to participate in the experiments varied to a large extent, depending on the different selection procedures applied. While the experiments in a great number of studies were carried out on a subsample of impulsive research participants chosen on the basis of their MFFT scores,[1] some studies applied additional measures in the selection process. For example, in addition to taking into account students' MFFT scores, Glenwick and Barocas (1979) used teachers' ratings on the *Classroom Adjustment Rating Scale*.

Other studies used quite different methods to select experimental participants. For example, in Rupert and Baird's (1979) study, the researchers selected 60 first and second graders from a pretested group of 151 students studying in a public school in the United States. The selection was based on students' response latency to the 10 items on Form A of the haptic-visual matching test. As another example, Feindler, Marriott, and Iwata (1980) selected 36 adolescents (aged 12 to 15 years) from a specialized program for 100 disruptive students in a metropolitan area in the United States to be the treatment receivers. The primary selection criterion for participating in this particular study was high rates of classroom and/or community disruption as documented in school records. As a final example, Schleser et al. (1984) selected their research participants through evaluating their cognitive-developmental levels. Children who were at either the Piagetian pre-operational level (i.e., those who failed in conserving on both tasks given) or the concrete-operational level (i.e., those who were successful in conserving on both tasks) were selected to participate in the experiment.

A careful reading of the literature shows that almost every study ultimately administered its treatment conditions to a very unique group of participants, not only because of the varying nature of the initial populations and samples, but also because of the varying screening procedures applied. As such, one naturally wonders if the treatment effects would have been different had the experimentees been different.

In addition to the unique composition of experimental participants in each study, which was largely associated with sampling procedures, the specific training methods used in the experimental studies also played a pivotal role as a process variable in researchers' declaration of the level of their success in modifying conceptual tempo. Early in 1976, Bender classified the various training methods into three broad approaches, and this classification is largely valid today as shown in the existing literature. The first general approach is

---

[1] Most studies used the criteria of above-median error scores and below-median response times.

to slow down the response of the test respondent by (1) enforcing delay, (2) reinforcing increased latency, and (3) modeling reflective behavior. The second approach is to train participants to use specific attention deployment strategies to enhance task performance. The third approach is to employ verbal self-instructional training (i.e., to verbalize strategies to oneself). Based on the review of the literature, I would add a fourth approach – the biological one. The *biological approach* aims at modifying impulsivity through rendering medication and/or facilitating physical/mental exercises (e.g., relaxation training, muscle exercise).

A closer examination of these training methods shows that they tended to differ along one fundamental dimension: the level of empowerment on the part of the primary research participants, with some possessing less (or none) empowerment and others possessing more. Two factors contributed to the level of empowerment of a treatment condition. The first concerned the level of specificity of the training contents: some training contents tended to be more concrete and specific, whereas others tended to be more conceptual and general. The concrete and specific training involved instructions/directions that were worded to apply only to the task at hand, whereas the conceptual and general training, deemed to be more empowering, used instructions/directions that were worded more abstractly and globally so as to apply to a wide range of tasks and situations. The second factor pertained to the mode of delivering the training contents: self-directed versus other-directed instructions. Self-directed instructions involved the primary research participants' use of self-regulating speech to direct themselves through the task, whereas other-directed instructions involved experimenters giving instructions to the primary research participants. Obviously, the former is more empowering than the latter.

Undoubtedly, the efficacy of different training methods varied according to different populations. However, across the board, almost regardless of the nature of the research samples, where the same study adopted multiple intervention methods, treatment conditions that were more empowering tended to be more effective than those that were less so. This claim can be substantiated by much empirical evidence. For example, after studying 60 school children who were at the Piagetian pre-operational or concrete-operational levels, Cohen, Schleser, and Meyers (1981) concluded that "self-instruction interventions seem particularly well suited for modifying performance on the MFFT regardless of the child's cognitive level" (p. 75; see also Brown, Meyers, & Cohen, 1984; Schleser et al., 1984). Similarly, when Williams and Akamatsu (1978) experimented with 30 juvenile delinquents using three different treatment conditions (cognitive self-guidance, attention control, and assessment control), the cognitive self-guidance intervention demonstrated its superiority over the other two conditions in treatment outcomes.

In another study, Holmes (1981) examined the differential effects of four experimental conditions (control, operant treatment, limited self-instruction, and extended instruction) in modifying impulsivity among mildly retarded children. Again, self-instruction training demonstrated significant effects, and these effects were maintained even two weeks after the training had stopped. On the other hand, operant treatment as operationalized by social reinforcement did not show its efficacy in improving children's conceptual tempo.

As a final example, Kendall and Wilcox (1980) created a placebo condition and two treatment conditions for 33 non-self-controlled problem children (aged 8 to 12 years): concrete self-instructional training and conceptual self-instructional training. Again, it was concluded that the treatment had stronger effects for the conceptual training group than for the concrete training group.

Apart from variations in the selection of research participants and in the methods of training, the intensity of training involved in the existing studies also tended to differ. As noted earlier, while 14 of the 40 studies reviewed here each provided a one-off training session, the remaining studies involved a number of training sessions that lasted anywhere between one week and one year. Moreover, the duration of each training session across studies also varied, with some lasting for merely several minutes (e.g., Cole & Hartley, 1978; Denney, 1981–1982) and others lasting for more than one hour (e.g., Genshaft & Hirt, 1979; Schleser et al., 1984) (see also Table 7.2 for details in other studies). Such variations in training intensity, along with variations in other factors concerning other aspects of the studies, are bound to produce differential treatment effects.

Product Variables and Treatment Effects. Product variables refer to the specific ways in which treatment outcomes were ascertained. These include the specific points in time at which treatment effects were examined and the types of data gathered.

One critical factor that conceivably influenced researchers' claims for the success (or failure) of their experiments was the timing for examining the treatment effects. As summarized earlier, while the majority of the studies (27 out of 40) involved immediate post-tests, several studies included follow-up assessment in addition to immediate post-training evaluation or delayed post-tests, and several others used delayed post-tests. Moreover, the timing of these follow-up assessments or delayed post-tests varied from study to study. For example, Egeland (1974) conducted a 2-month follow-up test; Kendall and Finch (1976) tested their research participants in a 6-month follow-up procedure; Kendall and Braswell (1982) not only carried out a 10-week follow-up, but also assessed their research participants in a one-year follow-up; Bell, Mundy, and Quay (1983) administered a delayed post-test two weeks after the training had been completed; and Zieffle and Romney (1985) conducted their post-test four weeks after the training had stopped.

Another product variable that could have modulated the conclusion regarding the efficacy of a particular intervention concerns the type of data collected. While the great majority of the studies relied principally on primary research participants' performance on the MFFT, several studies also supplemented research participants' scores on the MFFT with results generated from classroom behavioral observations, therapist ratings, and teacher ratings of impulsivity (e.g., Brown, Wynne, Borden, Clingerman, Geniesse, & Spunt, 1986; Zakay, Bar-El, & Kreitler, 1984). In one such study (Kendall & Wilcox, 1980), although no significant improvement was shown either on the MFFT latency scores or on the MFFT error scores, both teacher ratings and therapist ratings indicated some significant changes.

In summary, across the existing studies, many contingencies at different stages (presage, process, and product) of each of the studies could have led to different conclusions concerning the efficacy of the interventions aimed at altering conceptual tempo. Despite these contingencies, virtually every study documented in the literature claimed some success.

One could argue that it is possible that studies that report non-significant effects are rarely, if ever, accepted for publication. However, this argument may not be sound. As readers will see, almost half of the experimental studies published that were aimed at developing the *deep* approach did not yield anticipated training effects. In fact, a number of studies suggested that students developed their *surface* approach to learn after participating in the training programs (see the section entitled "Modifying Approaches to Learning" for a full consideration). Returning to the experimental studies of conceptual tempo, whether or not studies reporting non-significant effects were published, there is sufficient evidence to assert that conceptual tempo is dynamic rather than static.

Nevertheless, four obvious limitations with the existing research on modifying conceptual tempo should be noted. To begin with, the literature is quite outdated. With the exception of one study (Barrickman, Perry, Allen, Kuperman, Arndt, Herrmann, & Schumacher, 1995), all the studies were published between the 1960s and the 1980s. New research evidence would strengthen the claim that conceptual tempo is modifiable.

The second limitation concerns the research populations and thus the primary objective of the research. As noted earlier, very few studies were conducted among "normal" populations (as opposed to the special populations described earlier in the chapter). The great majority of the existing studies were aimed at decreasing impulsivity among people who had problems of one kind or another; very few studies were designed with a developmental perspective, that is, to develop reflectivity among normal populations.

Third, although some studies used delayed post-tests and/or rendered follow-up procedures so that the actual treatment effects, rather than practice effects, could be claimed, very few studies involved a long-term follow-up. As such, one naturally questions whether or not the treatment effects would show temporal stability over a longer period of time.

Finally, practically none of the studies reported effect sizes in any format, and some studies did not even provide enough data for effect sizes to be calculated. The availability of effect sizes of the studies would have enabled a better understanding of the degree to which conceptual tempo is modifiable among particular populations.

Modifying Perceptual Styles

As discussed in Chapter 1, the malleability (or stability) of Witkin's field dependence/independence (FDI) construct became a focus for discussion almost from the moment that the construct was proposed. Some scholars strongly advocated the x-linked heritability hypothesis (e.g., Hartlage, 1970; Stafford, 1961) and hormonal explanations (e.g., Broverman, Klaiber, Kobayashi, & Vogel, 1968), whereas others were adamant proponents of sociocultural theories (e.g., Goldstein & Chance, 1965; Nash, 1975; Sherman, 1978). Subsequently, several reviewers (e.g., Burstein et al., 1980; Vandenberg & Kuse, 1979) generally concluded that biological and environmental factors interact to create the development of perceptual styles. Regardless of the theoretical perspective one takes, the question of whether or not the FDI construct can be developed must be answered by results from experimental studies. Experimental studies based on the FDI construct are discussed next.

In spite of the massive body of literature on the FDI construct, there are not many publications that deal with intervention studies involving the FDI construct. Although two book chapters (Kogan, 1983; Kogan & Saarini, 1990) and one article (Witkin, 1965) discuss FDI modification in passing, there is literally no review article that specially focuses on FDI modification. Early in 1965, in the context of discussing psychological differentiation and forms of pathology, Witkin cited several studies (e.g., Pollack, Kahn, Karp, & Fink, 1960; Witkin, 1948) conducted between 1948 and 1965. Interventions in these studies included drug administration, electro-convulsive shock, and stress stemming from anticipated heart surgery. None of the studies showed any training effect. Indeed, it was largely results from studies like these and from those that were unsuccessful in developing field independence among alcoholics (e.g., Karp & Konstadt, 1965; Karp, Witkin, & Goodenough, 1965) that had once made Witkin and his colleagues believe that FDI is a stable and unalterable characteristic (see Witkin, 1962). Nonetheless, the results from several studies of alcoholics conducted during the same period of time and findings from other studies led to a different conclusion: FI can be developed and FD can be reduced. In discussing stylistic variation in childhood and adolescence, Kogan (1983) devoted 1.5 pages to the issue of FDI training, citing several studies to portray the status quo of FDI training effects at the time. He concluded that results revealing significant training effects (e.g., Connor, Serbin, & Schackman, 1977; Connor, Schackman, & Serbin, 1978) were "quite damaging to the view that FDI represents an individual-difference dimension that is highly stable across most of the lifespan" (p. 670). Indeed, the current literature search resulted in 20 intervention studies, of which only three (Goulet, Talbot, Drouin, & Trudel, 1988; Leithwood & Fowler, 1971; Morell, 1976) did not obtain significant training effects.

Across the 17 studies that demonstrated significant training effects, several intervention methods were used. These included alcoholism treatment (to alcoholics in relevant studies), spatial training, cognitive modeling, restructuring skills training, meditation, and musical rhythm training. The duration of training ranged from 5–10 minutes to five years (where the effects of a college curriculum were assessed). Although all these studies generally aimed at developing FI and reducing FD, from some of them, two specific research objectives emerged. One was to correct FD among alcoholics and the other was to narrow the gender gap in FDI (see also Chapter 3). Studies that had these two objectives are reviewed first here, followed by a review of the remaining studies.

With respect to the first of these two objectives, perhaps partially stemming from the fact that Witkin and his colleagues' initial claim for the stability of FDI was based on studies of alcoholism, a number of experimental studies were conducted among alcoholics to examine the stability or malleability of FDI. Four such studies yielded results that challenged the then long-held view that FDI was stable and unalterable. All four studies were conducted in the United States.

A first study was conducted by Goldstein and Chotlos (1966) among 62 alcoholic patients (aged 29 to 57 years) participating in a hospital's alcoholism treatment program. Participants were assessed on their FD/FI levels at pre- and post-treatment (about an 8–10-week interval). It was concluded that the great majority of participants changed in the direction of FI at a level that was greater than could have been expected by statistical chance.

Results from the second study (Jacabson, 1968) can be said to be more provocative because style change was successfully induced among alcoholics of the experimental group by merely providing a one-hour perceptual isolation treatment session. In this study, 30 chronic male alcoholics were randomly divided into experimental and control groups after having been pre-assessed on their levels of FDI. Post-test indicated a significant reduction in FD among participants in the experimental group, but not in the control group.

Equally challenging to the FDI stability proposition are findings from studies indicating that intervention programs have not only developed participants' FI, but also facilitated parallel gains in the correlates of FDI. One set of such results was obtained in the third study, that of Chess, Neuringer, and Goldstein (1971), which compared the change in FDI between 13 alcoholics in a hospital's alcoholism treatment program and 13 non-alcoholics who were employees in the hospital. The experiment involved weekly assessment of participants' FDI levels and measurement of their arousal level by various objective tests (e.g., skin resistance and heart rate) and by an *Internal-External Locus of Control Scale* (I-E scale) for seven weeks. Results indicated changes in both the alcoholic and non-alcoholic groups, with the former having changed in the direction of FI significantly more than the latter. Moreover, the alcoholic group showed a significant change in the direction of internal locus of control on the I-E scale.

Similar results were obtained from the fourth study, a 6-week-long training program reported by O'Leary, Donovan, and Kasner (1975). The research was conducted among 50 male alcoholic inpatients (average age 46 years). The participants' FDI levels were measured by the *Group Embedded Figures Test* (GEFT, Oltman, Raskin, & Karp, 1971), and the participants were also tested on the *Defense Mechanism Inventory* (DMI, Gleser & Ihilivech, 1969) on pre- and post-treatment. Results indicated that the research participants became significantly more field independent regardless of their initial levels of FDI. Furthermore, participants' defense mechanisms also changed in a favorable direction.

The second specific focus of FDI intervention studies seemed to have arisen from the perpetual gender gap in FDI, a gap that is consistently in favor of males, with males scoring significantly higher on FI than females (see Chapter 3 for details). In this respect, several studies (all conducted in the United States) were targeted at reducing/closing the gender gap, and all met with success.

A first study was conducted among a group of 133 first, third, and fifth graders (aged between 6 and 10 years) by Connor, Serbin, and Schackman (1977). Participants were randomly assigned to three conditions: two treatment groups (the overlay group and the flat-figures group) and one control group. A brief training session of 5–10 minutes was rendered to each of the three groups, with children in the overlay group receiving a more sophisticated disembedding training procedure than those in the flat-figures group, and with children in the control group receiving no training. Although there was no obvious training effect for boys, girls in the overlay group performed significantly better on *Children's Embedded Figures Test* (CEFT) than did those in the other two conditions. Moreover, training generally reduced the gender gap, and it did so differently within each condition: (1) in the control condition, boys scored slightly better than did girls on the CEFT; (2) in the flat-figures condition, boys' superior performance to that of girls was reduced; and (3) in the overlay condition (the most sophisticated condition), girls outperformed boys on the CEFT.

A second study, by Connor, Schackman, and Serbin (1978), was carried out among 93 first graders. Children were randomly assigned to either a brief disembedding training or the control condition. In addition to the CEFT, the participants were also given a generalization task of a spatial character. Results suggested that there was a significant training effect beyond practice effect. More importantly, while there was a tendency for boys to score higher than girls on the pre-test, the direction of the difference between boys and girls was reversed on the post-test. That is to say, while training certainly developed FI in both boys and girls, girls benefited more from the training.

Both of the aforementioned studies were conducted among school children. Would training make a difference in an older population? Two studies were conducted among university students. Results from the first study (Johnson, Flinn, & Tyer, 1979) indicated a practice effect for all participants, but a training effect only for female students. The research was conducted among 82 university students studying in three academic disciplines: drafting, liberal arts, and mathematics. The students studying drafting received six weeks of training in spatial abilities between pre-test and post-test, while the students in the other two majors did not. Results revealed that the female students who received training improved more than the females who did not. Moreover, while there was no overall gender difference, liberal arts students performed significantly less well than did the math and drafting students. This result led the researchers to speculate that it might not be gender per se that mattered in the development of FDI. Rather, the academic discipline in which the students were studying might have made a difference (see also Chapter 5).

From the vantage point of this book, it can be argued that regardless of which of the two factors – gender or academic discipline – contributed to the change in participants' FDI scores, FDI is amenable to modification. Moreover, FI can be developed through deliberate training, as shown in this and other studies.

The other study conducted among university students was that by Stericker and Le Vesconte (1982). Participants were 83 introductory psychology students. Students in the experimental group received three 1-hour training sessions in spatial tasks featured in three different tests. Results suggested that both male and female students in the training group performed substantially better on all tests of spatial character than did students in the control group. Moreover, when female students in the experimental group were compared with males in the control group on the post-tests, the gender-related pre-test difference in favor of males disappeared. These results led the researchers to conclude that training can equalize the differential prior exposure to spatial tasks between males and females. That is to say, FI can be cultivated through purposeful training.

Apart from the mentioned studies that aimed at either developing FI among alcoholics or closing the gender gap in FDI, nine other intervention studies were identified. With the exception of one study that was conducted among immigrant Korean adults in the United States, the studies were carried out among school children and university students. The interventions included cognitive restructuring, cognitive modeling, depth perception training, meditation, musical rhythm training, and differentiation furthering training.

Two studies involved cognitive restructuring. In a first study, after having applied a series of selection procedures, Collings (1985) conducted an experimental study with 52 (selected from 270) elementary school students in a rural comprehensive school in the United Kingdom. Participants from both the control group and the experimental group took science lessons for 12 weeks. While all 12 lessons for the control group were normal lessons using the usual materials, for the experimental group, two-thirds of each lesson was a normal science lesson and one-third was conducted using the training materials. The training materials (e.g., random pictures, pattern, shape in shape, word search) were designed to enhance the cognitive restructuring aspect of the FI. Results suggested that students in the experimental group not only outperformed the control group in the GEFT, but also demonstrated superiority in the development of formal operations.

The other study (Rush & Moore, 1991) that adopted cognitive restructuring training was different from the aforementioned study in the sense that it was conducted among university students (n=115) in the United States and the training was brief, involving only 75 minutes of training over two nonconsecutive days. Nevertheless, results suggested that the training enhanced the performance of FD students on the GEFT and on two other dependent measure tasks: verbal disambiguating (*Scrambled Word*) and visual perspectivism (*Paper Fold Test*).

Cognitive modeling was used in Welkowitz and Calkins's (1984) study of 71 university students enrolled in introductory-level psychology classes. Students were randomly assigned to three conditions: cognitive modeling, exemplar modeling, and control. The cognitive modeling group watched a videotape in which examples of embedded figures were presented, accompanied by verbalization of strategies associated with task performance. The exemplar-modeling group observed the same examples of embedded figures, but without verbalization of strategies. Results suggested that cognitive modeling was superior to exemplar modeling and control conditions in improving performance on the GEFT and on one of the two parallel tasks – recognition of strategies modeled. This result resonated with the findings of studies aimed at improving reflectivity and reducing impulsivity that were reviewed in the previous section.

Depth picture perception (DPP) training was adopted in Mshelia and Lapidus's (1990) study of 172 fourth graders in Nigeria. Participants were divided into four groups based on their initial levels of FDI. Groups 1 and 2 received DPP training with Mshelia's Sets A and B, respectively, Group 3 received training with the odd items in the GEFT, and group 4 served as a control group. Each child received a 6-minute training session, in which each child in the control group spent the 6 minutes on a general conversation with the experimenter. Post-tests were administered immediately after the training and, again, one week after the training. Results indicated that participants who were more field independent outperformed FD participants on the depth picture perception test. Moreover, the FI participants gained more from training than did the FD participants. It was further discovered that the effects of perceptual training on the pictures were generalized to performance on the GEFT and that GEFT training led to improved performance on both the depth picture perception and the GEFT post-tests. The researchers concluded that non-Western children's difficulty with pictorially presented depth stimuli can be overcome through brief training. At the same time, they noted several child-rearing practices that may affect the development of FDI.

As in studies aimed at improving reflectivity, meditation was used as a method of intervention in studies whose purpose was to enhance research participants' level of field independence. Three such studies were located. A first study (Linden, 1973) was conducted among a group of third graders in a school in an economically disadvantaged neighborhood composed of blacks and Puerto Ricans in the United States. Children were randomly assigned to three groups: meditation, guidance, and control. The meditation group received 36 20–25-minute meditation training sessions over 18 weeks. The guidance group received a 45-minute guidance session of an information-giving nature once a week for 18 weeks. The control group received no training. Results indicated that relative to the participants in the guidance and control groups, those in the meditation group became more field independent. Moreover, participants in the meditation group showed significantly less test anxiety.

A second study (Pelletier, 1974) was conducted among 40 volunteers (25 years being the average age) recruited from a group of people attending an introductory lecture on transcendental meditation (TM) in the United States. The experiment lasted for three months, during which time the experimental group practiced TM and the participants in the control group were instructed merely to "sit quietly" for 20 minutes every morning. To control for a possible interaction effect between the perceptual measures and meditation, half of the participants in each group were not given pre-tests on the perceptual measures. Post-tests were administered to all participants. Results indicated that participants in the TM group significantly outperformed the control group on all five perceptual tests, including the *Embedded Figures Test* (EFT) and the *Rod-and-Frame Test* (RFT).

The third of the studies that adopted meditation as an intervention was conducted by Dillbeck et al. (1986). The researchers administered the GEFT and the *Culture Fair Intelligence Test* to 50 university students practicing TM. The average number of months of practice was 60 at pre-test and 103 at post-test. Results indicated that practices of TM significantly increased students' levels of FI as well as their fluid intelligence. The researchers attributed the increased levels of FI and fluid intelligence to the nature of the curriculum featured by practices of TM.

Musical rhythm training was used as a technique to increase children's (5- to 9-year-olds) levels of field independence by Parente and O'Malley (1975) in the United States. Twenty-four children selected out of 40 based on their pre-test scores on the CEFT and RFT were assigned to experimental and control groups in such a way that the mean scores of the CEFT for the two groups were roughly equal. The experimental group received eight sessions of musical rhythm training over a period of one month, with each session lasting for 1 hour. Post-test involved administering the CEFT and RFT to the 24 children. Data indicated that training in musical rhythm significantly improved children's performance on the two perceptual style tests.

Finally, the most recent study (Lapidus, Shin, & Hutton, 2001) that reported significant training effects was conducted among 40 community-dwelling immigrant Korean adults who were receiving treatment at an outpatient clinic in New York City for their chronic mental illness. Participants were randomly assigned either to the treatment group or to the control group. Participants in the treatment group received (individually) six weekly 1.5-hour sessions of differentiation training that was designed to provide them with the ability to cope with a wide variety of stressors (physical, psychological, and social) in all phases: anticipation, impact, and post-impact. The whole training process adopted a continuingly self-correcting and self-empowering model. On the other hand, participants in the control group received a directed problem-solving program. Post-tests included an immediate test and a 3-month follow-up test. On the immediate post-test, the experimental group scored significantly higher on the GEFT and on six of 10 mental health subscales. Moreover, on the follow-up test, the experimental group also demonstrated their improved attitude toward mental health.

To sum up, although several of the earlier studies supported the view that FDI is a deep-seated psychological trait that is unalterable, the great majority of the studies consistently suggested that FI can be developed through training. As shown in the studies reviewed, both children and adults can be trained to improve their performance on perceptual tasks. Moreover, various training methods have led not only to enhanced levels of field independence and reduced levels of field dependence, but also to better performance on related tasks of different types (e.g., perceptual, analytical, and affective). Certainly, as has been pointed out earlier, relative to the large body of literature on the FDI construct, the existing experimental studies are far from adequate. Furthermore, as with experimental studies of reflectivity-impulsivity, future studies of FDI must adopt more rigorous research methods and must report long-term training effects with a wider range of populations. These qualifications notwithstanding, the available research on FDI supports the argument that intellectual styles can be modified.

Modifying Approaches to Learning
Research on the general concept of learning approaches has essentially indicated that the deep (or meaning-oriented/directed) approach to learning is more conducive to effective student learning and positive developmental outcomes than the surface (or reproduction-oriented/directed) approach to learning (Zhang & Sternberg, 2005). For this reason, all experimental studies have aimed at developing the deep approach to learning. As noted earlier, research on the development of the deep learning approach is a relatively new

venture in the field of intellectual styles. All but one of the 12 studies found were published in 2002 or later, the exception being one published in 1997. Six studies adopted the *Study Process Questionnaire* (SPQ, Biggs, 1987) or the revised *Two-Factor Study Process Questionnaire* (R-SPQ-2F, Biggs, Kember, & Leung, 2001) as the dependent measure, while the rest of the studies used other inventories that originated from the same family of learning approaches (see Chapter 2). All the studies were carried out in higher education institutions in seven cultures (Australia, Belgium, Finland, Hong Kong, the Netherlands, the United Kingdom, and the United States), with the majority of the studies having been carried out in Australia and the European countries.

In trying to induce the deep approach to learning, each of the studies implemented an intervention that is educationally innovative in nature. Some examples are: action learning-based course, case-based assessment, collaborative examination (featuring students' active participation), hands-on experience with a formative mode of assessment, and reflective learning. Underlying all these interventions is the notion of a constructivist learning environment. Given the nature of the interventions, each of the experiments in these studies lasted for at least one academic semester. Although all studies predicted that students would change in the direction of the deep approach to learning, only six studies lent full support to the prediction. As for the remaining six studies, five showed the exact opposite of what was expected (i.e., students changed in the direction of the surface approach to learning) and one study did not show any significant effect. In the remainder of this section, studies that resulted in the expected training effects will be illustrated first. This will be followed by an analysis of the rest of the studies.

Of the six studies that successfully developed a deep learning approach among students, three adopted the SPQ as the criterion measure. The first of these (Kember, Charlesworth, Davies, McKay, & Scott, 1997) was conducted among Hong Kong university students. The researchers used three case studies. The first was an entirely innovative course on the subject of design aimed at encouraging a wide range of student responses and allowing for individual differences in abilities and aptitudes, rather than at delivering a body of knowledge. The second was a course on radiography designed to replace a previous course that had been highly dominated by lectures and written examinations. The new course put greater weight on tutorials and practical classes and adopted team teaching, with lectures being used to define topics and provide appropriate emphasis. The third study was a program developed for students in their first year of business studies. Its main objective was to promote reflective learning. In all three cases, the effects of the educational innovations on students' learning approaches were assessed by administering the SPQ to the students before and after the courses. Results indicated that all three cases achieved success in promoting students' deep approach to learning.

The second study (Gordon & Debus, 2002) using the SPQ was conducted among three cohorts of students (n=134) studying in a pre-service teacher education degree program at a university in Australia. The educational innovation involved contextual modifications in teaching methods, task requirements, and assessment processes. The first cohort of students (enrolled in the course in 1995) served as the control group, while the second (enrolled in 1996) and the third (enrolled in 1997) cohorts of students received the treatment. The SPQ was administered to each cohort on three occasions: one month after students' enrollment at the university, one year after the first administration, and at the end of their final year of study. Results indicated that the intervention resulted in changes in students' learning approaches by first reducing their use of the surface approach to learning and later increasing their deep approach to learning.

The third study that examined the effects of educational innovation on students' learning approaches using the SPQ was carried out among 90 third-year university students in Australia (Wilson & Fowler, 2005). The participants were concurrently enrolled in two courses designed differently, with one being characterized by a conventional lecture/tutorial design and the other by an action learning design. The experiment lasted for one semester. Results indicated that although there was no difference in the levels of surface learning approach (both the motive and strategy components) between students in the two courses, students in the action learning course reported a significantly higher level of the deep learning approach (both motive and strategy). It should be noted, however, that further analysis revealed that students' initial learning approach made a difference in the effects of the courses. Specifically, the students classified as "typically deep" in their learning approach were consistently deep in their learning approach across the two courses. At the same time, the students classified as "typically surface" in their learning approach adopted the deep learning strategy (although not deep motive) in the action learning course more often than did the students in the conventional course. Regardless of these fine-grained patterns in learning approaches, the action learning course showed superiority in promoting a deep learning approach.

Apart from the aforementioned three studies that adopted the SPQ to identify significant treatment effects of educational innovations on cultivating the deep approach to learning, three studies that used other measures of learning approaches/orientations also resulted in significant findings. Two of these assessed the effects of one particular type of educational innovation on the development of the deep learning approach by using a questionnaire survey that evaluates the general construct of learning approach (in one case, teaching approach), while the third adopted an action research procedure.

The first of these studies was conducted among university students in the United States (Shen, Hiltz, & Bieber, 2008). A total of 1,071 students registered in 22 course sections participated in the research. The aim of the research was to investigate the effects of different modes of examination on students' learning approaches and their levels of social engagement. Although random assignment was not possible, a balancing technique was used to assign sections with similar features to different modes of examinations: collaborative, traditional, and participatory. Both the collaborative and the participatory conditions allowed students to take the examinations online. However, the collaborative condition was designed based on the constructivist approach, whereby high levels of interactions with others were required, whereas students in the participatory test condition participated in the online examination processes individually. The online examination lasted for about two and a half weeks. Students responded to self-designed measures of learning styles and social engagement before and after the examinations. The researchers concluded that collaborative examinations significantly reduced students' surface approach to learning and enhanced their sense of an online learning community.

The second study, by van Der Veken, Valcke De Maeseneer, and Derese (2009), examined the impact of the transition from a conventional (i.e., discipline-based) to an integrated contextual medical curriculum on students' learning patterns/approaches. The participants were enrolled in the matriculating classes of 1998 and 1999 at Ghent University in Belgium. The conventional medical curriculum (CMC) was implemented with the 1998 class, whereas the integrated contextual medical curriculum (ICMC) was implemented with the 1999 class. The experiment lasted for the first four years of the students' medical education. The *Inventory of Learning Styles* (Vermunt, 1998) was administered to students eight weeks after the start of the academic year within three consecutive years from the second to the fourth year. Although not all predictions were supported, compared with students studying the CMC, students who studied the ICMC demonstrated a significant reduction in their use of the reproduction-oriented learning approach.

Finally, in the United Kingdom, Bold (2008) carried out an action research to examine the impact of peer support groups on students' changes in learning approaches. Participants were 20 part-time first-year foundation degree students and two tutors. The students and tutors were guided to engage in reflective practice weekly for 10 weeks. Peer group discussions were centered on students developing understanding and use of each of the 10 principles of reflective practice described by Ghaye and Ghaye (1998). Critical analysis through reflection on all participants' responses to learning and teaching events enabled the researcher to conclude that regular peer group activities "appeared to support deeper learning approaches and increase in students' reflective capacity" (Bold, 2008, p. 257).

In contrast to the preceding six studies that obtained the predicted findings, five studies designed to promote students' deep approach to learning through educational innovations yielded results that were completely opposite to what was expected. Of the five studies, one study (Segers, Nijhuis, & Gijselaers, 2006) was conducted in the Netherlands, and the rest (Baeten, Dochy, & Struyven, 2008; Gijbels & Dochy, 2006; Gijbels, Segers, & Struyf, 2008; Struyven, Dochy, Janssens, & Gielen, 2006) were carried out by essentially the same team of investigators in Belgium.

In the Netherlands, Segers et al. (2006) examined the effects of a redesigned learning and assessment environment on students' perceptions of assessment demands and on their learning approaches. Two successive cohorts of second-year business students attending a required International Business Strategy course participated in the experiment. The first cohort of students (n = 406) studied under the assessment-based learning (ABL) condition, while the second (n = 312) studied under the problem-based learning (PBL) condition. Students responded to a modified version of the SPQ (Biggs, 1987) twice – once at the beginning of the course and once in the last section of the course. In addition, the students were assessed on the *Scouller Perceptions of the Assessment Demands Questionnaire* (Scouller & Prosser, 1994). Results suggested that students in the two different learning conditions did not differ in their perceptions of assessment demands. Furthermore, contrary to expectations, the students in the PBL course adopted a less deep learning approach and a more surface learning approach than did students in the ABL course. In searching for explanations about the unexpected findings, the researchers interviewed selected participants. The results from the interviews showed that students considered the PBL environment to be overloaded, thus leaving no opportunity to exercise the higher levels of cognitive skills demanded by PBL. Instead, they were forced to adopt a surface learning approach.

In Belgium, a series of four studies (Baeten et al., 2008; Gijbels & Dochy, 2006; Gijbels et al, 2008; Struyven et al., 2006) obtained results identical to those in the study in the Netherlands. Data from the first study (Gijbels & Dochy, 2006) were collected from 108 first-year university students studying criminology. The experiment involved the use of formative assessment over the course of one semester. The experiment was based on the premise that formative assessment would promote students' deep approach to learning. Students' learning approaches were assessed by the *Revised Two-Factor Study Process Questionnaire* (R-SPQ-2F, Biggs et al., 2001). Contrary to the prediction, students changed in the direction of a more surface approach to learning. The researchers postulated that the unexpected results could be attributed to other contextual elements together with the students' familiarity with formative assessment. Such elements could include the lack of clarity in course objectives, inappropriateness of workload, and irrelevance of the literature dealt with.

The second study (Baeten et al., 2008) also involved evaluating the influence of an assessment format (i.e., portfolio-based assessment) on students' learning approaches. Participants in this study were 138 first-year university students majoring in office management. Students' learning approaches were also measured by the R-SPQ-2F (Biggs et al., 2001) at the beginning and then again at the end of the semester. Consistent with Gijbels and Dochy's (2006) study, this study concluded that students' deep learning approach was not enhanced as anticipated. On the contrary, their surface learning approach significantly increased. Apart from agreeing with the possible reasons put forward by Gijbels and Dochy (2006), Baeten et al. (2008) raised the possibility that insufficient motivation on the part of students might also have contributed to the unexpected experimental outcomes.

The third study (Struyven et al., 2006) examined the impact of different teaching/learning environments on students' learning approaches. Participants were 790 students from eight teacher education institutions, all studying in their first year of an elementary teacher training program. Students from each institution were assigned to learn in two conditions: a lecture-based learning environment or a student-activating learning environment. Students' learning approaches were evaluated by the *Learning and Studying Questionnaire* (Entwistle, McCune, & Hounsell, 2002) in the first lesson (pretest) and the 10th lesson (post-test). Moreover, two focus group interviews (each containing 8–10 students) were conducted in each of the eight participating institutions after the final lesson. Results indicated that although students' learning approaches were similar at the beginning of the course, a clear distinction was found between the two groups of students after experiencing the two types of learning environments. However, contrary to expectations, participants in the student-activating learning environment developed a more surface approach to learning. Results from the interviews offered some possible explanations for the failure to achieve the intended experimental outcomes. It seems that some inherent problems existed with the student-activating learning environments, including heavy workload, lack of feedback and structure, fragmented knowledge, and the fact that fellow students profited from group work.

Finally, Gijbels et al. (2008) also investigated the effect of a constructivist learning environment on students' perceptions of assessment demands and on their learning approaches. The participants were students taking the course "Education and Psychology" in the teacher training program at the University of Antwerp. The course lasted seven weeks. The data obtained from 67 students consisted of learning approaches assessed in the first session of the course, perceptions of assessment demands in the second session, and actual learning approaches and perceptions of assessment demands at the end of the course. Learning approaches were assessed by the R-SPQ-2F. Results lent full support to Segers et al.'s (2006) finding that although students changed their perceptions of assessment demands toward more deep-level demands, they did not change toward the direction of a deep learning approach. Instead, students appeared to have developed a surface approach to learning during the course. Further analyses suggested that students' initial learning approach made a more significant difference in the degree to which students changed their learning approach than how they perceived the demands of the assessment of the course. In other words, students' changes in learning approaches could be the result of the complex interaction among several variables such as students' initial characteristics, the learning environments, and their perceptions of the learning environments.

It is, perhaps, partially because of such complexity as described in the preceding studies that Reid, Duvall, and Evans (2005) did not obtain any significant finding in their study. Reid and colleagues' experiment involved teaching a medical course with its learning objectives based on Biggs and Collis's (1982) Structure of the Observed Learning Outcome (SOLO) taxonomy, which provides a systematic way of describing how a learner's performance increases in complexity in learning. Instruction was mainly conducted with problem-based learning, and assessment was carried out essentially through constructively aligned assignments and examinations. Participants were three cohorts of second-year students. Each cohort completed the *Approaches and Study Skills Inventory for Students* (ASSIST, Tait, Entwistle, & McCune, 1998) during the early period of their second year of studies, and again at the end of it, with eight months being the time interval. Complete data were collected from 157 (out of 213) students. Results indicated no change in students' learning approaches. The researchers offered several explanations for the lack of significant training effects. First, it was possible that the strategies used to encourage a deep learning approach were insufficient to bring about desired changes. Second, the duration of the experiment was not long enough. Third, students in the course had already displayed high scores on the deep learning approach on entry to such a highly competitive program, and therefore there was limited room for further development of the deep learning approach.

To summarize, this section has reviewed 12 studies that aimed to promote the deep approach to learning among university students. Half of the studies obtained the desired outcome. The majority of the remaining studies (five out of six) found that students became more surface and reproduction oriented in their learning approach. As has been repeatedly explained in the studies that yielded unexpected outcomes, several factors in the educational innovations – all centered on building a constructivist learning environment – might have worked against students' using a deep approach to learning. These factors include, among others, heavy workload, lack of clarity, lack of guidance and structure, insufficient length of the experiments, and students' initial learning approaches. Certainly, these explanations should serve as useful guidelines for designing and implementing future experimental research so as to produce desired outcomes. Regardless, all but one of the available studies indicate that learning approaches can be changed by interventions.

Styles Training Based on Six Other Models
As previously mentioned, in addition to the studies reviewed in the preceding three sections, which were based on the constructs of reflectivity-impulsivity, FDI, and learning approach, respectively, studies based on other style models, although small in number, do exist. Moreover, all but one of these studies demonstrated significant training effects on the development of intellectual styles and, clearly in almost all cases, Type I intellectual styles.

There are 10 such studies in all. These include four studies based on Guilford's (1950) construct of divergent-convergent thinking, two on Torrance's (1988) construct of mode of thinking, one on Kolb's (1976) learning style construct, one on Honey and Mumford's (1992) notion of learning style, one on Jung's (1923) construct of personality style, and one on Kirton's (1961) construct of decision-making and problem-solving style.

Developing Divergent Thinking Style. A series of four studies that attempted to enhance participants' divergent thinking (a Type I style) were conducted by essentially the same research team led by Basadur in Canada, with the other investigators in the research team being from either Canada or the United States. All four studies were conducted in business settings.

In the first study (Basadur, Graen, & Green, 1982), participants were 45 people selected from 220 engineers, engineering managers, and technicians. Among the 45 participants, 32 were randomly assigned to the experimental and placebo groups and another 13 were added at a later stage of the research as a convenient totally untreated non-placebo group. The treatment involved two days of intensive training in creative problem solving. Participants in the treatment group were trained with a series of diverse tasks that encouraged them to attempt to discover concepts such as ideation[2] and the value of divergence in thinking – concepts that they had not considered before.

Several methods were used to assess participants' divergent thinking, including questionnaire, tape recording, and interview. The researchers (Basadur et al., 1982) concluded that there were significant training effects: the participants in the experimental group demonstrated a stronger preference for ideation in problem solving and for the practice of ideation in both problem finding and problem solving, and they outperformed the other two groups in actual problem solving. Moreover, this conclusion was drawn twice – once immediately after the training and again two weeks later at work.

The second study (Basadur, Graen, & Scandura, 1986) was carried out among 112 manufacturing engineers. The experiment was conducted in two phases. In the first phase, the first group (n=65 from eight different locations) received the treatment, while the second group (n=47 from the same location) served as the control group. In the second phase, the two groups switched their roles in terms of serving as the experimental group or as the control group. Each phase of the experiment involved a three-day (24 hours in all) training program in creative problem solving based on divergent thinking. The participants were assessed on their attitudes toward divergent thinking at three points in time: baseline, following the completion of the first phase of the experiment, and following the completion of the second phase of the experiment. Results suggested that the training program had a significantly positive impact on the engineers' attitudes toward divergent thinking in problem solving.

The third study (Basadur, Wakabayashi, & Graen, 1990) was different from the previous two in that the training was heavily geared toward intensive practice of techniques and processes of divergent thinking as opposed to abstract discussion. The study also aimed to determine if the training program would have a stronger effect on individuals whose predominant problem-solving style (i.e., the optimizer style[3]) was the opposite of what was emphasized in the training. Participants were 90 managers and 66 non-managers from

---

[2] Ideation is defined as idea generation without evaluation; the core of ideation is divergent thinking.
[3] The optimizer style is characterized by a preference for thinking-evaluation. The other three styles assessed were generator (experiencing-ideation), conceptualizer (thinking-ideation), and implementor (experiencing-evaluation).

various functional specialties and organizations. The participants were trained in different sessions, each typically involving 15 to 30 participants. Each training session lasted for three days (eight hours per day), with participants being involved in intense practice in synchronizing divergent and convergent thinking in all aspects of the three phases of training: (1) problem sensing and anticipation, fact finding, and problem defining; (2) idea generating, evaluating, and selecting; and (3) planning for implementation, gaining acceptance, and action taking. As anticipated, participants with the optimizer problem-solving style improved on measures of divergent thinking more than did those with the other three styles.

Finally, Basadur, Pringle, and Kirkland (2002) conducted their experimental study with 217 Spanish-speaking South American managers and professionals from business, industry, and government organizations covering a wide range of hierarchical levels and functional specialties. The initial experiment began with 149 participants who constituted an experimental group and a placebo control group. Participants in the experimental group received a half-day training, while the placebo control group received a half-day placebo treatment. In encouraging the participants to value both divergent and convergent thinking, the training was experiential and practice oriented. These participants were assessed on their attitude toward divergent thinking before and after the training. In addition, another 68 participants (who were not exposed to any training) also responded to the same questionnaire (once). Results suggested significant gains in attitude toward divergent thinking in the experimental group as compared with the initial placebo group and the additional control group.

In summary, all four studies grounded in Guilford's construct of divergent-convergent thinking showed that divergent thinking style can be developed. The number of studies is certainly small. Furthermore, all studies were conducted by the same team of investigators in business settings. Nevertheless, the findings were consistent not only across all four studies, but also with the general findings of studies based on other style models previously discussed and those to be introduced.

Developing Holistic and Integrative Modes of Thinking. Two studies, both carried out in the United States, were based on Torrance's (1988) construct of mode of thinking. The first study (Reynolds & Torrance, 1978) was conducted with two different groups of students. The first group comprised 200 gifted and talented high school students participating in the 1977 Career Awareness Component of the Georgia Governor's Honors Program (GHP). The second group consisted of 68 graduate students from a variety of academic disciplines enrolled in a course in creative thinking. The training for the first group involved exposing students to a variety of styles and experiences. Students spent two hours each day for six weeks working in their area of specialization (e.g., communication, French, music, and so forth). For the rest of each day, students were engaged in interdisciplinary activities emphasizing career education, current issues, and futurism, and they were involved in special interest groups. It was predicted that being exposed to diverse styles and experiences would enhance students' use of the integrative style. The training for the second group (four hours each week for 11 weeks) was focused on developing the holistic (right-brain dominance) style of thinking. In addition to receiving lectures and readings on creative thinking, the participants received extensive and intensive training in creative problem solving based on different models, and they were engaged in frequent creative thinking techniques such as brainstorming and imagining.

Both groups of students took the *Your Style of Learning and Thinking inventory* (SOLAT, Torrance, Riegel, & Reynolds, 1976) on the first day and during the last week of their respective training sessions. Significant changes in classification based on the SOLAT scores occurred for both groups. As anticipated, a significantly larger number of GHP students were classified as using the integrative style at the post-test, while significantly more students were classified as demonstrating a preference for the holistic thinking style in the creative thinking class.

However, the second study on modes of thinking, an experimental study conducted among a group of 73 gifted children (Masten & Morse, 1987), did not yield significant training effects on the development of the holistic style of thinking. There are at least two plausible reasons why the training did not work. To begin with, the participants were a highly selected group. To participate in this study, one had to have an IQ of at least 120. As such, the students might have already scored very high on the holistic (right-brain dominance) thinking scale of the SOLAT. As a result, it was difficult to train this group of students to score higher on the holistic scale. In other words, there might have been a ceiling effect. Furthermore, this possible ceiling effect was compounded by the fact that the training constituted of only two 1-hour sessions. Obviously, for such a select group of students, two 1-hour training sessions were insufficient to produce any significant treatment effect. More substantial training might have promoted students' changes in the direction of holistic thinking.

Modifying Learning Styles in Kolb's Model. The study based on Kolb's (1976) learning style construct was conducted among 152 undergraduate students from six management classes in Canada (Loo, 1997). The intervention involved a 30-minute feedback session after the first administration of the *Learning*

Styles Inventory (LSI-1985) at the beginning of the semester. The aim of the feedback session was to explain the effectiveness of Kolb's experiential learning model in improving their learning experiences and in assisting their reflection on their academic and career choices. At the feedback session, students were also given an eight-page handout so that they could refer to the learning styles material throughout the semester. The students were again tested on the LSI-1985 at the end of the semester, 10 weeks later. When t-tests were used to identify the mean differences between pre-test and post-test, no significant result was obtained. However, an examination of the change/stability in style categories revealed several significant experimental effects. While roughly half of the participants maintained the same predominant learning style between pre-test and post-test, approximately half of them changed their styles. Moreover, 13 percent of the students changed dramatically to styles that were opposite to their initial styles. In addition, more male students changed to the opposite styles than did female students.

Modifying Learning Styles in Honey and Mumford's Model. The study (Broad, Matthews, & McDonald, 2004) that examined Honey and Mumford's (1992) concept of learning style was an experiment on a group of 60 university second-year accounting students enrolled in a management accounting unit in the United Kingdom. The intervention involved integrating an online-supported virtual learning environment into regular teaching. Students responded to the *Learning Styles Questionnaire* (Honey & Mumford, 1992) at the beginning of their second-year studies and again six months later. Results indicated that there was a sharp decline in the pragmatist learning style. At the same time, students' reflective learning preference remained the strongest of all four learning styles. The researchers concluded that the way in which the styles changed was in agreement with what had been expected given the nature of the accounting degree.

Modifying Personality Styles. The experimental study grounded in Jung's (1923) construct of personality style was conducted among 61 undergraduate volunteers for research on meditation in a state university in Texas (Fling, Thomas, & Gallaher, 1981). Students were pre-tested on the *Myers-Briggs Type Indicator* (Myers, 1962) and subsequently randomly assigned to four groups: (1) clinically standardized meditation (CSM), (2) quiet sitting (SIT), (3) open focus (OF), and (4) waiting list (no training). Each type of training lasted for eight weeks (the amount of time spent in training each week was not clearly indicated in the research report). Although all groups became more intuitive at post-test, only the scores for the CSM group – the group that received the most intensive training – approached statistical significance. The OF group became more extraverted than did both the CSM and the SIT groups.

Modifying Decision-Making and Problem-Solving Styles. Finally, one study (Murdock, Isaksen, & Lauer, 1993) was conducted based on Kirton's (1961) model of decision-making and problem-solving styles – styles believed by many scholars (Clapp & De Ciantis, 1989; Kirton, 1976; Tullett, 1997) to be unalterable. The participants were 143 students enrolled in eight sections of an introductory creativity course in a mideastern college in the United States. The aim of the training, which happened to be the aim of the creativity course itself, was to promote awareness and enhance understanding of creativity in four broad areas: the creative process, the creative person, the creative press or environment, and the creative product. The classes met twice weekly for 75 minutes. Students were administered the *Kirton Adaption-Innovation Inventory* (KAI, 1982) twice, with 14 weeks between pre- and post-tests. As in the case of Loo's (1997) study based on Kolb's construct of learning styles, although an initial analysis did not result in any significant finding, further analysis indicated that there was a significant gender effect. That is, while female students exhibited stability in their KAI scores, male students became significantly more innovative in their problem-solving style at post-test.

In summary, experimental studies based on the aforementioned six models are certainly very limited in number. However, much more often than not, the available research suggests that styles can be modified through training. Furthermore, this group of studies, like some of the studies reviewed earlier, indicated that the effects of the training programs could be contingent on several critical variables, including specific training techniques, lengths of experiments, and statistical methods used to analyze the data.

Modifying Thinking Styles
As indicated in Chapter 2, Sternberg's (1988, 1997) model of thinking styles is the latest individual style model and has thus far generated hundreds of studies. However, longitudinal intervention investigations are still rare. For the past several years, inducing changes in thinking styles through interventions in the classroom has been the focus of four doctoral dissertations at The University of Hong Kong. While the first two dissertations (Fan, 2008; Yu, 2012) have been completed, the remaining two (Lau; Tai) are still in progress. With the permission of the doctoral candidates, partial results from their dissertations (i.e., data relevant to style changes) are reported here along with the data on style changes in the studies of Fan (2008) and Yu (2012).

Fan's (2008) intervention was conducted among 238 university students in Shanghai, mainland China. The intervention involved students in a general psychology course taught by the same instructor in two types of instructional conditions: traditional and hypermedia. The traditional instructional environment was equipped with conventional teaching aids such as blackboard, overhead projector, and textbook. Teaching was predominantly teacher-centered, whereby the teacher mainly lectured and the students listened. The hypermedia instructional condition adopted a hypermedia system known as the Skyxp-GP that ran under the Web browser of Internet Explorer. All textbook chapters were built into the Skyxp-GP. In addition, the hypermedia instructional environment also provided students with teaching tools (i.e., blackboard, overhead projector, textbook, and so forth) available to students in the traditional learning environment. Teaching was mainly student-centered, with the teacher serving as facilitator, resource provider, and motivator.

The students were studying in four different majors: mathematics, physics, the Chinese language, and history. For practical reasons, the students were divided into four instructional groups: two hypermedia groups and two traditional groups. The first hypermedia group comprised 53 mathematics students, and the second consisted of 72 students majoring in the Chinese language. The first traditional group was composed of 29 mathematics and 25 physics students, while the second was made up of 35 Chinese language students and 24 students majoring in history. Each group attended an 80-minute class session weekly for a period of 18 weeks.

The *Thinking Styles Inventory-Revised* (Sternberg, Wagner, & Zhang, 2003) was administered before and after the instructional experiment. Although their changes of styles were not always in the predicted directions, thinking styles were found to be dynamic in both the traditional and hypermedia learning environments. Within the traditional learning environment, as predicted, students showed a significant increase in three of the four Type II styles: executive, conservative, and monarchic styles. In particular, the significant increase in the conservative style was mainly identified among the social science students, while that in the monarchic style was more obvious among the science students. However, contrary to predictions, the traditional learning environment enhanced the use of the hierarchical thinking style among science students and reduced the use of the local style among the social science students. Moreover, the local thinking style was unexpectedly reduced among the social science students.

Within the hypermedia learning environment, as predicted, students significantly increased their use of two of the Type I (judicial and liberal) styles. Contrary to expectations, however, students decreased their use of the legislative thinking style after the instructional experiment. In addition, students in both learning conditions became significantly more internal in their thinking style after the experiment.

A second experimental study (Yu, 2012) was carried out in a private girls' school in Hong Kong. The school offered a Diploma in Business at the level equivalent to grade 12 (year one at the participating school) and first-year college (year two at the participating school). Participants were five teachers (each teaching one class) and their students (n=139; 84 studying in year one and 55 in year two). The aim of the experiment was to induce students' changes in thinking styles in learning (i.e., learning styles) through teaching with particular interpersonal styles. The underlying assumption of the experiment was that teachers' interpersonal styles are related to their thinking styles in teaching (i.e., teaching styles), and both interpersonal styles and teaching styles would affect students' learning styles.

Prior to the classroom instruction, the five teachers received two 2-hour training sessions. The first session was devoted to the administration and scoring of the *Questionnaire on Teacher Interaction* (QTI, Wubbels, Créton, & Hooymayers, 1985) and the *Thinking Styles Inventory-Revised* (TSI-R, Sternberg, Wagner, & Zhang, 2003) and to a discussion on teachers' interpersonal styles and thinking styles in teaching, respectively, assessed by the two inventories. The second session was aimed at facilitating the teachers' understanding of their own interpersonal styles and teaching styles. They observed the demonstration of the main teacher interpersonal styles and participated in group discussions on these styles with the assistance of a one-page handout that summarized the main interpersonal styles and teaching styles. The teachers were instructed to teach with their predominant interpersonal styles during the entire period of instruction, which lasted for 32 weeks (eight 40-minute lessons per week).

The first teacher (with a *dominant* style) and the second teacher (*cooperative* style) each taught a course on financial accounting. The third teacher (*cooperative* style) taught a course on English for business. The fourth teacher (*submissive* style) and the fifth teacher (*oppositional* style) each taught a business management course. Each class had either 27 or 28 students. To ensure that the teachers were using the interpersonal styles as expected, the researcher (Yu, 2012) made two observations of each class and had one meeting with each of the five teachers during the period of instruction.

Students were administered the TSI-R before and after the classroom instruction. Mixed findings were obtained. Some changes occurred in the expected directions, whereas others did not. For example, as expected, students taught by the teacher with the dominant interpersonal style had significantly decreased in their judicial thinking style at the end of the instruction. Also, as expected, students taught by the teacher with the oppositional interpersonal style significantly decreased their tendency to perform their tasks hierarchically. However, contrary to expectations, students taught by the teacher with the dominant interpersonal style also significantly decreased their use of the local thinking style. In all, 10 significant changes in styles were identified (through comparing pre- and post-test mean scores) among 65 possible pairs of means (13 styles by five experimental classes). The effect sizes ranged from .37 to .61 by Cohen's d. Based on Cohen's (1988) interpretation of effect sizes, the magnitudes of these effect sizes can be considered to be between median and large.

The third experimental study was conducted by Tai (in progress) among ninth graders in 13 schools in Hong Kong, taking courses in liberal studies. The experimental group was composed of six teachers and their students (n=219), and the control group comprised seven teachers and their students (n=464). The main aim of the study was to induce students' development in Type I thinking styles, while reducing their use of Type II thinking styles, through the use of Type I teaching styles. At the same time, the study aimed to determine if receiving instruction through the use of Type I teaching styles would increase students' scores on career interests as measured by Holland's (1994) *Self-Directed Search* (SDS).

Prior to the classroom instruction, the six teachers in the experimental condition were assessed on their thinking styles based on the *Thinking Styles Inventory-Revised II* (TSI-R2, Sternberg, Wagner, & Zhang, 2007), after which they received a 4-hour training workshop. The principal objective of the workshop was to equip the teachers with the required knowledge and skills to construct a learning environment that would encourage students to learn more creatively (e.g., to use Type I learning styles). Tai developed a training package that included a booklet introducing theory and practice of thinking styles, particularly knowledge about how to promote Type I learning styles; a style profile of each teacher participant; and activities designed to foster Type I learning styles. These materials were employed in the workshop through various activities, group discussions, and reflection.

For both the experimental and control groups, the instruction lasted for 24 weeks (five 35–40-minute lessons per week). During the instruction period, Tai conducted a minimum of one class observation followed by a consultation meeting with each of the teachers in the experimental group to ensure that the teachers were indeed using Type I styles to teach. An initial analysis indicated that the students in the control group significantly increased their use of three styles (liberal, monarchic, and internal), whereas the students in the experimental group significantly unexpectedly decreased their use of the legislative style. However, further analyses that took demographic characteristics into account revealed a more complex picture of their changes in learning styles over the 24 weeks. For the control group, three factors were found to affect students' changes in learning styles: gender, engagement in extracurricular activities, and parental educational levels. The analyses revealed significant changes that involved nine thinking styles: Type I teaching increased students' use of Type II (conservative and local) styles (unexpectedly) and Type III (internal and external) styles; promoted the expected Type I styles (judicial, liberal, global, and hierarchical); and in one case, reduced the use of the monarchic style (as expected).

For the experimental group, an even more complicated picture emerged. Apart from gender, engagement in extracurricular activities, and parental educational levels, four other factors also played a significant role in the instructional effects on students' learning styles. These included the school banding,[4] students' preferred subject matter, their satisfaction with their learning environment, and their perceptions of teachers' teaching ability and attitude. Across these variables, changes involved eight styles, although on a number of occasions, changes occurred in unexpected directions for the legislative, conservative, and local styles. It should be noted, however, that the effect sizes for all findings were rather small (all below .2 by Cohen's d).

At the end of the intervention, all participants responded to Holland's (1994) *Self-Directed Search* (SDS). Results showed that compared with the control group, the experimental group scored significantly higher on three SDS scales: social, enterprising, and conventional, with the effect sizes (Cohen's d) being .17, .39, and .27, respectively.

The final study that attempted to stimulate changes in thinking styles was carried out among Hong Kong Chinese school students (eighth, ninth, and 11th graders) by Lau (in progress). The aim of the experiment was to promote the use of Type I thinking styles in learning physics and to enhance students' more adaptive motivational orientations through the use of Type I teaching styles. Participants were 11 physics teachers and their 28 classes of students (n=846) from 11 secondary schools. Among these participants, five teachers and their students (n=499) participated in the experiment, while the remaining six teachers and their students (n=347) served as the control group.

Prior to carrying out the instructions, the five teachers in the experimental group attended a 4-hour training workshop. The workshop involved introducing the teachers to basic knowledge about styles, particularly practices

---

[4] In Hong Kong, schools are classified into three bands (i.e., Band 1, Band 2, and Band 3) based on students' academic achievement levels as indicated by standardized scores of internal assessment, with Band 1 schools admitting students with the highest achievement scores (top 33.3%) and band 3 accepting students with the lowest scores (bottom 33.3%).

that would promote Type I learning styles among students. A booklet containing this information was distributed to each of the teachers to help them understand and apply Type I teaching styles.

The classroom instruction lasted for 13 weeks for both the experimental and control groups. Because the research participants were from different schools, although the standard duration of each lesson was 40 minutes, the number of lessons in each school varied. Therefore, the actual amount of time for instruction at each school was different, ranging from 17.6 hours to 86.8 hours.

All students responded to the TSI-R2 and Nolen's (2003) *Motivational Orientation Scale for Science Classrooms* (MOSSC) at the beginning and at the end of the instructional period. Initial data analyses indicated that there was a significant decrease in the experimental group's scores on five of the 13 thinking styles (global, conservative, oligarchic, anarchic, and internal), while the control group decreased their use of the anarchic style. Meanwhile, in both the experimental and control groups, students' scores on ego-orientation (a maladaptive motivational orientation that is oriented toward a narrow or instrumental focus on tasks) in learning significantly decreased.

However, after further analyzing the data, taking into account such factors as gender, school class level, and the number of hours of class instruction, Lau obtained more specific results. Across the board, while the experiment significantly reduced students' use of Type II styles, which was in line with the objective of the experiment, it also significantly decreased students' use of Type I (especially the judicial, global, and hierarchical) styles, which was contrary to what was expected. More style changes occurred among female students studying in lower school class levels. In the control group, the general trend was for the conservative style to decrease among female students. Moreover, vis-à-vis Type I styles, students changed the most with respect to the liberal style. However, there was a significant gender effect. Whereas male students increased their scores on the liberal style, which supported the prediction, female students unexpectedly decreased their use of the liberal style. Moreover, the decrease in ego orientation occurred primarily in the case of female students.

To summarize, it is clear that the findings obtained in the aforementioned experimental studies on the malleability of thinking styles are largely mixed. While particular thinking styles were developed as intended, each of the studies resulted in unintended outcomes: there was a significant decrease in the use of Type I styles after the experiment. In particular, these unexpected changes occurred more often in the experimental groups than in the control groups. Such unexpected results coincide with the ones obtained in studies that aimed to promote the deep approach to learning. The possible reasons for the unexpected changes in thinking styles that were found have yet to be explored with the research participants in the two ongoing dissertation projects (Lau, in progress; Tai, in progress), each of which will conduct focus group interviews with selected research participants. Nevertheless, for the moment, a preliminary premise about these unexpected findings can be made as follows.

Based on the previously discussed studies that obtained unexpected findings with regard to changes in learning approaches (see section "Modifying Approaches to Learning"), constructivist learning environments such as the ones created in Lau's and Tai's studies tend to be intimidating to students because such learning environments often demand that students work much harder. Unable to deal with such new ways of teaching, students may at times resort more to less creative thinking styles. This retreat to a more comfortable zone of information processing is in line with Perry's (1970) articulation of the trajectory of cognitive development, whereby students deal with the environments they perceive as challenging by seeking such alternatives to forward progression as "temporizing," "escaping," and "retreating" (see also Perry, 1999 for details). Clearly, changes in thinking styles were not straightforward. As previously mentioned, across the studies described here, several factors – both students' demographic characteristics and learning environmental factors – played a significant role in the changing of thinking styles.

One may argue that considering the number of styles assessed by the *Thinking Styles Inventory* and the many dimensions and data sets that have been explored, the number of significant changes obtained from the previously introduced studies is less than impressive. This is true. However, the changes that occurred were statistically significant (although with varying effect sizes), and they were found in all studies. Moreover, in all the previously discussed studies, the test-retest reliability coefficients obviously suggested that thinking styles can be changed (see Table 7.3).

Limitations and Conclusions

It is evident that given the long history of the field of styles, the existing longitudinal intervention studies of style malleability are insufficient. By the same token, considering the large number of style constructs that exist, far too few have generated intervention investigations. Moreover, where a style construct did generate intervention studies, the studies tended to be limited in at least one of three ways. First, most of the studies reported style training programs that did not involve a follow-up study. As such, there is no way of

TABLE 7.3. Test-Retest Reliability Correlation Coefficients in Studies of Changes in Thinking Styles

	Fan (2008)		Lau (in progress)		Tai (in progress)		Yu (2012)
TSI-R1 (TSI-R2)	Traditional (n=113)	Hypermedia (n=125)	Control (n=347)	Experimental (n=499)	Control (n=464)	Experimental (n=219)	Experimental (n=139)
Legislative	.58	.60	.50	.45	.47	.48	.51
Judicial	.49	.64	.34	.40	.41	.49	.55
Global	.60	.42	.23	.25	.34	.42	.51
Hierarchical	.67	.64	.39	.44	.51	.58	.62
Liberal	.74	.64	.36	.35	.40	.51	.61
Executive	.65	.47	.37	.35	.41	.39	.55
Local	.62	.49	.40	.43	.49	.54	.49
Conservative	.70	.48	.32	.32	.38	.50	.59
Monarchic	.33	.55	.22	.22	.43	.42	.54
Oligarchic	.69	.42	.25	.26	Not assessed	Not assessed	.49
Anarchic	.44	.54	.31	.31	Not assessed	Not assessed	.51
Internal	.65	.61	.44	.40	.51	.48	.68
External	.64	.61	.33	.41	.49	.60	.63

248

knowing whether or not the training effects reported in the studies were long term. Second, the majority of the studies did not report effect sizes. Thus, the strength of the efficacy claimed for styles training cannot be determined. Finally, for almost all the style constructs examined so far, research tended to be confined to the study of particular populations, which makes it impossible for the findings to be generalized to other populations. One could continue to pinpoint the limitations of the existing research, and all of these limitations should be taken into consideration in future research.

In spite of the fact that the existing studies are inadequate in many ways, the convergent evidence for the efficacy of styles training – not only concerning the changes in the targeted styles, but also in terms of parallel gains in other types of performance demonstrated by studies based on 10 style models, spanning several decades, and conducted among different populations in various cultures – cannot be regarded as coincidental. Rather, research evidence supports the contention that styles can be developed through training.

8

Longitudinal Studies without Interventions

One of the major contentions of Jean Piaget (1952) in his theory of cognitive development was that people's cognitive structures (i.e., rules for processing information or for connecting experienced events) change as a function of age. This cognitive structural change, according to Piaget, is largely attributable to individuals' active interpretation of their own experiences through interaction with their environments. One may naturally ask: If individuals' general cognitive structure changes over time, do their intellectual styles also change over time? Theoretically, one would expect that individuals' intellectual styles also change as a function of time, without any intervention, for the following reasoning: it has long been conceptually envisaged (Cronbach, 1957; Reuchlin, 1962) and has been empirically proved in various studies (e.g., Longeot, 1969; Globerson & Zelniker, 1989; Zhang, 2002a) that there is a strong association between cognitive development and intellectual styles. Therefore, it is reasonable to suppose that people's intellectual styles are adaptable, as are their cognitive structures.

This chapter documents longitudinal studies without interventions that investigated the changeability (or stability for that matter) of people's intellectual styles. The chapter is divided into three parts. The first part sets the boundaries for this review. The second part introduces studies based on each of the individual style models concerned and, in particular, points out some key factors that are likely to have played important roles in the studies that have shown style change, or lack of style change. The final part draws conclusions and discusses the limitations of the existing literature and their implications for future research.

Setting Boundaries: Literature Search Procedures and Results

In the previous chapter, details were provided regarding the general search procedures for longitudinal investigations, with or without interventions.

Of the 129 articles mentioned in the previous chapter, 39 were identified as longitudinal studies without interventions. Among these, 14 publications concerned studies based on Holland's (1973) construct of career interest/personality type/style; nine on Kolb's (1976) construct of learning style; 10 on the general construct of learning approach (Biggs, 1978) and its related constructs such as learning conception, learning orientation, and learning pattern (Ramsden & Entwistle, 1981; Vermunt, 1994); one on Witkin's (1954) construct of field dependence/independence (FDI); two on Kagan's (1965) construct of reflectivity-impulsivity; two on Jung's (1923) construct of personality type/style; and one on Kirton's (1976) model of adaption-innovation styles.

It is noticeable that the first three style models played a major role in generating nonintervention longitudinal studies of style malleability. Each of the three models falls into one of the three layers of Curry's (1983, 1987) "onion" model: Holland's model falls into the innermost layer of the onion, Kolb's falls into the middle layer, and Biggs's model and its related models fall into the outermost layer of the "onion."

Certainly, in view of the long history of research in the field of intellectual styles, the number of existing nonintervention longitudinal studies is very small. Nonetheless, the scope of the study of temporal changes in styles can be said to be fairly extensive, with studies adopting a decent number of style models and with the three predominant models being situated within each of the three different layers of Curry's (1983) "onion" model. More importantly, the studies that are available for this review are telling, all pointing to the conclusion that although people's intellectual styles can be largely stable, they are susceptible to change over time, as detailed in the next part.

Research Findings

What is the general picture painted by the research findings based on each of the style constructs? Do people's styles change over time in the absence of purposeful interventions? If so, in what directions do they change? Do styles that belong to different layers of Curry's model change in varying degrees? What are some of the factors that moderate and/or mediate style changes from one point in time to another? This part addresses these questions by reviewing the details of the studies based on each of the seven style models mentioned earlier. It first focuses on reviewing studies that were based on each of the three models that generated the majority of nonintervention longitudinal studies, moving from the innermost layer of the "onion" model (i.e., Holland's model of career interest/personality types/styles) to the middle layer (i.e., Kolb's model of learning styles), and to the outermost layer (i.e., Biggs' model of learning approaches and its related learning style constructs). Following that, the small number of studies generated by the other four style models are reviewed.

Malleability of Career Personality Types
Research on the malleability of career personality types has a long history, and broadly speaking, researchers have taken two perspectives on this issue: some have focused on the stability of career personality styles, whereas others have emphasized their development. The stability perspective views career personality types as trait-like, thus being stable, whereas the developmental view (i.e., that styles are changeable) is that career personality types change and crystallize. Changes of career personality types can be regarded as errors from the stability perspective, but as actual change from the development perspective (Tracey & Robbins, 2005).

As mentioned previously, several inventories have been used to assess the six career personality types. The present review primarily included studies that employed the *Self-Directed Search* (Holland, 1973, 1994) and the *Strong Interest Inventory* (Strong, 1927; Strong, Jr., Donnay, Morris, Schaubhut, & Thompson, 2004), as well as its various versions of the *Strong* inventories such as the *Strong-Campbell Interest Inventory* and the *Strong Vocational Interest Blank*. There were two major reasons for including the studies based on the *Strong* inventories. First, although the original objective of studies using the Strong inventories was to examine the stability and/or change of interests, the conceptualization and organization of the *Strong* scales are based on the Holland typology. Moreover, if one looks at the definition of interest, one would realize that the construct of interest (in this case, career interest) is being used the same way as career personality style, which in turn is conceptualized as a personality-centered style construct. For example, Rounds (1995) defined interests as individuals' preferences for behaviors, situations, the contexts in which activities occur, and the outcomes that are associated with their preferred activities. Likewise, Tracey (2002; see also Lent, Brown, & Hackett, 1994) pointed out: "Although the definition of interests varies (Savickas, 1999), the prevailing view is that interests are coherent and enduring cognitive structures that, minimally, are characterized by patterns of likes and dislikes of activities" (p. 148). Such a definition of interests, which is in accord with that of styles, places a strong emphasis on the notion of preference. Among the 14 publications concerning career personality types, three are literature reviews (with one being a chapter and two being journal articles) and the remaining 11 are articles that report empirical studies. Below, major findings of the three review articles are summarized first, followed by an analysis of what the individual studies say about style malleability.

For a long time, the question of whether or not career personality types are modifiable has attracted the attention of many scholars, and work in this area has been systematically reviewed by several researchers. A first review was conducted by David Campbell and his colleagues (Campbell, Borgen, Eastes, Johansson, & Peterson, 1968). This team of researchers examined a variety of statistics, including the test-retest statistics obtained from 22 occupational groups who responded to the *Strong Vocational Interest Blank* twice, respectively, over two weeks, 30 days, 3 years, 22 years, and 30 years. What is so impressive about this set of data is that for all occupational groups, as the test-retest intervals became longer and longer, the test-retest coefficients became lower and lower. One could argue that this trend of decreasing test-retest reliability coefficients is likely to be indicative of the diminishing practice effects. At the same time, it is also possible that, as time went by, the research participants' career personality styles changed. In one table (table 32 in Campbell et al., 1968) of their review article, the authors provided data on these samples over the aforementioned varying periods. In Table 8.1 of this chapter, table 32 in Campbell et al.'s (1968) work is reproduced.

In another review of the malleability of career interest types in 1999, Swanson, in her chapter entitled "Stability and change in vocational interests," examined the findings of 30 studies that directly addressed the long-term stability of vocational interests as assessed by Holland's *Self-Directed Search*, the *Strong* inventories, as well as by a third inventory – *The Kuder Interest Scales* (Kuder, 1939). Although Swanson concluded that career interests were remarkably stable over a long period of time, she also clearly articulated the substantial changes that individuals experienced over time with respect to their career interests. Specifically, for 11 studies that were conducted among samples ranging from ninth graders to working adults and that had test-retest intervals between 8 weeks and 30 years, Swanson (1999) reported median test-retest coefficients (which embody the changes in the relative position of individuals within a group) varying from .54 to .91 (see Table 8.2).

At the same time, Swanson (1999) reviewed 18 studies that investigated the career personality styles of research participants ranging from 13-year-old children to college seniors. The test-retest intervals of these studies covered a range of three weeks to 22 years. Swanson noted that the intra-individual stability median coefficients (i.e., the consistency of prominent career interest dimensions for the same individual at different time points) were between .51 and .88 (see Table 8.3).

TABLE 8.1. *Basic Scale Means, Standard Deviations, and Test-Retest Correlations for Several Samples over Varying Time Periods*

Scale	University of Minnesota Sophomore 2-wk. Sample Test M	Test SD	Retest M	Retest SD	r	Army Reserve Group 30-Day Sample Test M	Test SD	Retest M	Retest SD	r	Harvard Students 3-yr. Sample Test M	Test SD	Retest M	Retest SD	r	YMCA Secretaries 22-yr. Sample Test M	Test SD	Retest M	Retest SD	r	Bankers 30-yr. Sample Test M	Test SD	Retest M	Retest SD	r
Public Speaking	54.6	9.9	55.3	10.0	.89	58.0	9.4	58.7	9.5	.89	57.1	10.3	57.9	10.2	.71	59.6	7.8	62.3	6.5	.40	49.0	7.8	49.5	8.8	.30
Law/Politics	54.6	9.3	55.7	9.7	.88	57.1	10.2	57.2	10.1	.90	58.1	10.1	60.6	9.4	.50	52.6	8.1	55.7	9.3	.67	51.0	7.2	49.8	9.7	.59
Business Management	50.8	10.7	51.5	10.9	.90	52.8	9.5	54.1	9.3	.88	45.6	11.3	47.2	11.7	.72	58.1	7.4	58.2	8.6	.32	52.5	6.6	49.3	8.8	.35
Sales	49.9	9.5	50.6	9.8	.89	50.8	10.5	52.4	11.0	.89	45.3	8.9	45.2	8.8	.57	55.1	9.5	56.3	9.2	.63	52.8	9.0	51.5	9.6	.62
Merchandising	52.1	10.1	52.7	10.1	.89	52.7	10.6	53.8	10.6	.88	44.7	10.2	45.2	11.3	.66	55.3	7.5	55.4	8.2	.40	51.4	7.8	48.6	9.4	.24
Office Practices	50.3	9.7	52.2	10.5	.83	47.5	10.6	49.2	10.7	.87	42.9	10.1	42.6	10.4	.58	54.1	10.4	56.3	9.5	.50	60.2	8.3	58.9	9.4	.42
Military Activities	49.1	9.7	49.0	9.6	.91	50.5	9.3	50.7	9.6	.86	45.3	8.0	45.8	7.7	.52	50.6	9.7	50.1	8.7	.66	51.2	10.1	48.3	9.1	.59
Technical Supervision	49.2	9.6	49.6	10.1	.74	45.1	10.0	46.0	9.7	.71	43.2	10.9	45.0	12.4	.52	47.1	11.8	49.1	11.7	.61	45.0	10.1	42.4	10.5	.26
Mathematics	50.1	10.0	50.6	11.1	.94	47.5	11.3	47.9	10.8	.88	53.3	9.2	52.4	10.2	.71	49.1	10.5	49.3	10.1	.82	49.9	9.3	49.9	9.7	.58
Science	51.0	10.0	51.5	10.4	.94	47.1	9.6	47.4	10.3	.91	53.4	10.4	52.0	11.2	.70	49.3	9.1	47.1	9.2	.78	44.2	8.3	42.3	10.3	.67
Mechanical	47.2	10.0	48.3	10.7	.94	42.5	10.7	42.3	11.3	.94	42.4	9.7	45.1	10.9	.67	47.0	11.3	46.8	10.4	.79	45.1	11.2	42.9	11.0	.72
Nature	45.7	9.0	46.9	9.3	.90	42.2	10.0	42.5	10.1	.90	42.2	10.0	44.4	10.1	.68	51.1	9.7	52.3	8.5	.75	51.5	7.9	49.7	10.6	.61
Agriculture	46.3	9.9	47.1	10.2	.88	40.7	9.8	41.3	10.6	.89	40.2	10.2	43.7	10.2	.71	47.7	9.6	49.0	9.7	.73	49.2	7.8	49.0	8.6	.39
Adventure	58.1	8.5	59.4	9.1	.80	53.9	10.6	54.4	10.5	.81	56.0	11.5	57.2	12.2	.64	46.2	10.2	45.1	9.7	.53	43.8	9.3	39.3	7.3	.42
Recreational Leadership	51.8	9.6	53.1	9.6	.90	49.7	10.4	50.8	9.8	.92	47.2	10.8	48.9	11.3	.81	51.7	9.1	51.1	7.9	.72	46.4	8.3	42.8	9.1	.55
Medical Service	55.2	9.8	56.7	9.8	.89	50.7	9.5	51.1	9.3	.76	51.6	10.5	52.4	11.1	.67	53.6	8.7	52.1	8.2	.65	45.7	8.6	44.6	9.5	.38
Social Service	57.0	9.8	57.6	11.3	.83	55.6	9.7	54.7	9.5	.83	51.1	10.4	53.4	10.8	.54	70.3	5.4	71.7	3.9	.14	50.8	8.3	52.7	8.9	.51
Religious Activities	55.0	11.3	57.4	11.1	.83	53.5	10.8	54.3	10.1	.72	50.6	11.3	49.5	11.2	.51	70.6	6.8	72.2	6.5	.32	49.8	9.6	52.4	10.7	.51
Teaching	55.0	9.4	55.7	9.1	.88	54.2	8.4	55.1	8.3	.77	53.9	9.7	56.6	9.8	.63	55.6	8.6	58.1	8.0	.62	42.4	8.4	43.1	8.8	.41
Music	52.7	10.3	54.0	10.0	.89	53.5	8.5	54.0	8.7	.76	55.6	10.0	58.1	9.0	.60	53.8	7.9	53.5	8.6	.68	49.0	10.6	46.9	9.6	.66
Art	52.2	10.0	53.3	10.1	.93	51.8	9.3	54.4	10.2	.89	52.9	8.6	55.6	8.7	.56	53.9	8.1	51.8	7.9	.12	47.1	8.9	45.3	9.6	.56
Writing	53.4	9.3	54.7	9.5	.92	57.5	8.3	57.6	8.9	.85	59.7	8.0	61.7	7.5	.65	57.0	7.5	57.6	7.7	.72	46.5	8.1	46.1	8.2	.60
Mdn test-retest r for 22 basic scales					.89					.88					.65					.66					.53
Mdn test-retest r for 53 regular SVIB scales					.91					.91					.68					.61					.56

Notes: 2-wk. sample N = 140, 30-day sample N = 102, 3-yr. sample N = 189, 22-yr. sample N = 47, 30-yr. sample N = 48.
Table 32 on page 23 in Campbell, D. P., Borgen, F. H., Eastes, S. H., Johansson, C. B., & Peterson, R. A. (1968). A set of basic interest scales for the Strong Vocational Interest Blank for men. *Journal of Applied Psychology Monograph*, 52 (6), 1–54. Published by the American Psychological Association. Reproduced with the permission of the American Psychological Association.

TABLE 8.2. *Studies Examining Interest Stability via Strong's (1943) Method 1: Test-Retest Correlations of Scale Scores*

Study	Scales	Sample	Time of First Testing	Interval	Range	Median
Strong (1935)	23 SVIB Occupational Scales	223 men	College seniors	5 years	.59 to .84	.76
Van Dusen (1940)	5 SVIB Occupational Scales	76 men	College freshmen	3 years	.50 to .85	.59
Canning, Taylor, & Carter (1941)	7 SVIB Occupational Scales	64 boys	10th grade	3 years	.48 to .65	.57
Fox (1947)	9 Kuder Interest Scales	58 boys	9th grade	8 weeks	.42 to .85	.71
		76 girls			.54 to .85	.81
Strong (1952a)[a]	SVIB Engineer Occupational Scale	247 men	College freshmen	1 year	Not reported	.91
		185 men	College freshmen	9 years		.77
		203 men	College freshmen	19 years		.76
		223 men	College seniors	5 years		.84
		168 men	College seniors	10 years		.83
Rosenberg (1953)	9 Kuder Interest Scales	91 boys	9th grade	3 years	.47 to .75	.61
		86 girls			.50 to .69	.61
Herzberg, Bouton, & Steiner (1954)	10 Kuder Interest Scales	101 college-bound boys	High school	23–42 mos.	.59 to .75	.67
		48 college-bound girls			.59 to .82	.70
		49 work-bound boys		15–49 mos.	.51 to .86	.70
		74 work-bound girls			.65 to .83	.74
Herzberg & Bouton (1954)	10 Kuder Interest Scales	62 college-bound boys	High schools	4 years	.51 to .84	.63
		68 college-bound girls			.61 to .79	.68
Stordahl (1954b)	44 SVIB Occupational Scales	111 urban boys	12th grade	2 years	.54 to .85	.72
		70 rural boys			.45 to .81	.67
Campbell (1966a)	SVIB Banker Occupational Scale	48 bankers	Various	30 years	Not reported	.56
Johansson & Campbell (1971)[a]	59 SVIB Scales	1,306 men	Age 19	5 years	Not reported	.75
				10 years		.61
				20 years		.54
			Age 25	5 years		.82
				18 years		.75
				23 years		.75
			Age 33	12 years		.80

Notes: [a] Coefficients reported in the table are selected samples of more extensive data reported in the study. SVIB = Strong Vocational Interest Blank; Table 6.1 in Swanson (1999), published by Davies-Black Press.

TABLE 8.3. *Studies Examining Interest Stability via Strong's (1943) Method 4: Intra-Individual Stability Coefficients*

Study	Coefficient	Scales	Sample	Time of First Testing	Interval	Range	Median
Finch (1935)	rho	20 SVIB Occupational Scales	112 high school students	11th and 12th grades	3 weeks to 3 years	Not reported	Not reported
Taylor & Carter (1942)	rho	12 SVIB Occupational Scales	58 girls	11th grade	1 year	−.65 to .99	.74
Strong (1951, 1951, 1955)[a]	rho	34 SVIB Occupational Scales	50 men	College freshmen	1 year	Not reported	.88
					9 years		.67
					19 years		.72
			50 men	College seniors	5 years		.84
					10 years		.82
					22 years		.75
Powers (1954)	rho	44 SVIB Occupational Scales	Unemployed men	Age 16 to 63 years	10 years	−.38 to .96	.80
Stordahl (1954a)	Kendall's W	44 SVIB Occupational Scales	181 men	12th grade	2 years	.42 to .98	.74
King (1956)	rho	44 SVIB Occupational Scales	242 men	College freshmen	6 months	.26 to .95	.85
Hoyt, Smith, & Levy (1957)	rho	SVIB Occupational Scales	116 boys and girls	12th grade	2 years	Not reported	Not reported
Hoyt (1960)	rho	SVIB Occupational Scales	121 men	12th grade	4 years	−.48 to .95	Not reported
Dunkleberger & Tyler (1961)	rho	SVIB Occupational Scales	141 boys and girls	11th grade	1 year	Not reported	Not reported
Sprinkle (1961)	Pearson	44 SVIB Occupational Scales	143 men	College freshmen and sophomores	1–11 years	.11 to .92	.69

Joselyn (1968)	Pearson	SVIB Occupational Scales	923 boys, 918 girls	11th grade	5 months	.20 to .99	.92
Zytowski (1976)	rho	Kuder Male Occupational Scales	729 students (5 samples)	Age 13 Age 15 Age 15 Age 17 Age 20	12 years 12 years 18 years 12 years 12 years	Not reported	.58 .70 .58 .69 .76
Hansen & Stocco (1980)	Pearson	124 SCII Occupational Scales	31 boys, 39 girls 262 men, 353 women	9th grade College freshmen	3 years 3-5 years	−.31 to .96 .17 to .97	.72 .80
Hansen & Swanson (1983)	Pearson	162 SCII Occupational Scales	261 men 354 women	College freshmen	3-5 years	−.23 to .96 −.23 to .97	.77 .79
Swanson & Hansen (1988)[a]	Pearson	207 SCII Occupational Scales	79 men, 125 women, 167 men, 242 women	College freshmen College seniors College freshmen	4 years 8 years 12 years	.23 to .98 .25 to .98 −.11 to .96	.81 .83 .72
Lubinski, Benbow, & Ryan (1995)	Pearson	6 SCII GOT 23 SCII BIS	Mathematically gifted (114 boys, 48 girls)	Age 13	15 years	−.71 to .99 −.02 to .91	.57 .51

Notes: [a] Coefficients reported in the table are selected samples of more extensive data reported in the study.
SVIB = Strong Vocational Interest Blank, SCII = Strong-Campbell Interest Inventory, GOT = General Occupational Themes, BIS = Basic Interests Scales; Table 6.2 in Swanson (1999) published by Davies-Black Press.

Consistent with the findings of Campbell et al.'s (1968) review, results in Swanson's (1999) review showed a prominent trend in the magnitudes for both the test-retest scale coefficients and the intra-individual stability coefficients: as the test-retest intervals became progressively longer, the magnitudes of test-retest scale coefficients and those of the intra-individual coefficients became progressively smaller. In other words, the participants' career interests were likely to have changed over time.

To date, the most comprehensive review of studies on the stability/change of career interest styles has been conducted by Low, Yoon, Roberts, and Rounds (2005). The researchers performed a meta-analysis of 66 studies (including nine studies reviewed by Swanson, 1999) that involved groups of participants who were between their early adolescence and middle adulthood. Data were collected between the 1930s and the 1980s, and all except eight studies were published before 1980. Apart from the *Self-Directed Search*, the *Strong* inventories, and the *Kuder Interest Scales*, a number of other career interest inventories were used across these studies. Low and his team reported the effect sizes (using Fisher's Z-to-r transformed stability coefficients) for all 66 studies. The stability coefficients for the majority of the studies fell between .50 and .79, with the stability coefficients for 15 studies being below .50 and those for six studies being above .80. Key statistics in Low et al.'s (2005) article are reproduced in Table 8.4.

Upon examining the stability data, the researchers observed that the results generally supported the argument that career interests represent stable dispositional attributes. At the same time, however, the authors asserted that within the period from early adolescence to middle adulthood, the trajectory of career interest type stability pointed to a marked increase between the ages of 18 and 21 years. In other words, a great deal of the change in career interest styles occurred between the ages of 18 and 21. Moreover, the researchers alluded to the modifiability of career interest types by stating: "It appears that vocational interests are highly stable past college years, with some indication that they retain a dynamic quality" (Low et al., 2005, p. 727).

Based on the aforementioned reviews, it should be safe to conclude that, to a large extent, people's career personality types are stable. At the same time, however, it is correct to say that they can be changed to some extent. Indeed, apart from examining the previous reviews, I surveyed the individual studies that either had not been included in the previous reviews or were not available at the time when the previous reviews were conducted. Eleven articles were found, each describing a longitudinal study of the malleability of career personality styles. Of the 11 studies, one was published in 1973, one in 1988, two in the 1990s, and the remaining seven articles were published between

TABLE 8.4. *Longitudinal Studies of Vocational Interest Stability*

Authors	N^a	Stability Coefficient	Interval	Age Category	Cohort Standing	Measure	Gender	Sample Description
Adams (1957)	57	.63	3.00	2	1940s	KPR	M and F	9th graders
Allen (1991)	32	.71	4.00	4	1960s	SCII	F	College freshmen
Athelstan & Paul (1971)	1,583	.70	4.00	5	1930s	SVIB	M and F	Medical school students
Barak & Meir (1974)	223	.40	7.00	3	1940s	RAMAK	F	High school students
	160	.54	7.00	3	1940s	RAMAK	M	High school students
Benjamin (1968)	229	.42	31.00	4	<1930s	SVIB	M and F	College freshmen
Burnham (1942)	144	.71	3.00	4	<1930s	SVIB	M and F	College freshmen
Campbell (1966)	48	.65	30.00	8	<1930s	SVIB	M and F	Bankers
Campbell (1971)	56	.58	3.50	3	1940s	SVIB	F	College freshmen
	56	.59	10.00	3	1950s	SVIB	F	College freshmen
	1,214	.44	37.00	3	<1930s	SVIB	M	Adolescents
	38	.66	4.00	4	1950s	SVIB	F	College freshmen
	91	.51	27.50	4	<1930s	SVIB	F	College freshmen
	137	.76	9.67	4	<1930s	SVIB	M	College freshmen
	123	.59	10.00	4	1930s	SVIB	M	College students
	126	.59	3.50	4	1950s	SVIB	M	College students
	130	.69	9.67	4	<1930s	SVIB	M	College students
	91	.73	3.50	5	1930s	SVIB	M	Medical school students
	106	.68	3.50	5	1930s	SVIB	M	Medical school students
	82	.65	3.50	5	1930s	SVIB	M	Medical school students
	98	.48	17.00	7	<1930s	SVIB	M	Veterinarians
Campbell et al. (1968)	189	.68	3.00	4	1950s	SVIB	M	College freshmen
Campbell & Soliman (1968)	138	.65	20.50	8	<1930s	SVIB	F	Psychologists
Canning et al. (1941)	64	.57	2.00	2	<1930s	SVIB	M	10th graders

(*continued*)

TABLE 8.4 (continued)

Authors	N^a	Stability Coefficient	Interval	Age Category	Cohort Standing	Measure	Gender	Sample Description
Cisney (1944, 1945)	77	.49	3.00	2	<1930s	SVIB	F	9th graders
	72	.54	3.00	2	<1930s	SVIB	F	9th graders
	74	.73	2.00	2	<1930s	SVIB	M	9th graders
	58.5	.69	2.00	2	<1930s	SVIB	M	9th graders
	64	.76	1.00	3	<1930s	SVIB	M	11th graders
	47	.69	1.00	3	<1930s	SVIB	M	11th graders
Cooley (1967)	1,590	.51	3.00	2	1940s	TALENT	F	Project TALENT participants
	1,466	.51	3.00	2	1940s	TALENT	M	Project TALENT participants
Dolliver et al. (1975)	163	.47	12.00	4	1950s	SVIB	M and F	College students
Dolliver & Will (1977)	23	.32	10.00	4	1940s	SVIB	M and F	College students
Gehman & Gehman (1968)	93	.58	4.00	4	1950s	KPR	M and F	College students
Hansen & Stocco (1980)	70	.72	3.00	2	1960s	SCII	M and F	9th graders
	479.25	.68	3.50	4	1960s	SCII	M and F	College students
Hawkes (1978)	362	.59	2.00	2	1950s	OVIS	F	Junior high school students
	297	.54	2.00	2	1950s	OVIS	M	Junior high school students
Herzberg & Bouton (1954)	68	.69	4.09	3	1930s	KPR	F	High school students
	62	.64	4.39	3	1930s	KPR	M	High school students
Herzberg et al. (1954)	48	.67	2.86	3	1930s	KPR	F	College-bound high school students
	74	.75	2.40	3	1930s	KPR	F	Work-bound high school students
	101	.67	2.84	3	1930s	KPR	M	College-bound high school students
	49	.69	2.35	3	1930s	KPR	M	Work-bound high school students

Holland (1965)	204	.45	4.00	3	1940s	VPI	F	National Merit finalists
	432	.53	4.00	3	1940s	VPI	M	National Merit finalists
Holland (1979)	26	.78	1.00	4	1940s	VPI	M and F	College freshmen
	52	.75	1.00	5	1950s	SDS	F	Teachers in training
	27	.84	1.00	5	1950s	SDS	M	Teachers in training
Hoyt (1960)	121	.61	4.00	3	1930s	SVIB	M and F	12th graders
Johannson & Campbell (1971)	334	.70	3.00	4	1940s	SVIB	M	College freshmen
Knapp & Knapp (1984)	241	.61	1.00	1	1960s	COPS	F	7th graders
	256	.53	1.00	1	1960s	COPS	M	7th graders
Kuder (1975)	328	.47	4.00	1	1940s	KGIS	F	6th–7th graders
	311	.50	4.00	1	1940s	KGIS	M	6th–7th graders
Long & Perry (1953)	32	.40	3.00	4	1930s	KPR	M and F	College freshmen
Lubinski et al. (1995)	162	.47	15.00	1	1960s	SCII	M and F	Mathematically gifted students
McCoy (1955)	177	.68	1.75	2	1940s	KPR	F	9th graders
	56	.62	3.08	2	1940s	KPR	F	9th graders
	142	.75	1.83	2	1940s	KPR	M	9th graders
	57	.59	3.08	2	1940s	KPR	M	9th graders
	33	.68	2.33	3	1930s	KPR	F	10th graders
	29	.71	2.17	3	1930s	KPR	M	10th graders
Mullis et al. (1998)	271	.62	3.00	2	1970s	SCII	M and F	High school students
Nichols (1967)	204	.50	4.00	3	1940s	VPI	F	National Merit finalists
	432	.55	4.00	3	1940s	VPI	M	National Merit finalists
Nolting (1967)[b]	327	.52	9.00	3	1950s	SVIB	F	College freshmen
O'Brien (1974)	102	.74	2.70	4	1950s	SVIB	M and F	College freshmen
Onischenko (1979)	129	.39	14.00	4	1930s	KOIS	M	College students

(*continued*)

TABLE 8.4 (*continued*)

Authors	N^a	Stability Coefficient	Interval	Age Category	Cohort Standing	Measure	Gender	Sample Description
Petrik (1969)	58	.40	4.00	4	1940s	SVIB	F	College freshmen
	26	.60	4.00	4	1940s	SVIB	F	College freshmen
	56	.59	4.00	4	1940s	SVIB	M	College freshmen
	45	.49	4.00	4	1940s	SVIB	M	College freshmen
Powers (1954, 1956)	109	.78	10.50	7	<1930s	SVIB	M	Unemployed men
Reid (1951)	145	.80	1.25	4	1930s	KPR	M and F	College freshmen
Rhode (1971)[b]	37	.41	11.00	4	1940s	SVIB	M	College freshmen
Rohe & Krause (1998)	96	.77	11.00	7	1940s	SII	M	Spinal injury patients
Rosenberg (1953)	86	.60	2.67	2	1930s	KPR	F	Junior high school students
	91	.59	2.67	2	1930s	KPR	M	Junior high school students
Schletzer (1967)	172	.60	9.00	3	1930s	SVIB	M	High school students
Silvey (1951)	250	.73	2.00	4	1930s	KPR	F	College freshmen
	267	.73	2.00	4	1930s	KPR	M	College freshmen
Sprinkle (1961)	143	.70	6.50	4	1930s	SVIB	M	College freshmen and sophomores
Stordahl (1954)	111	.71	2.25	3	1930s	SVIB	M	High school students
	70	.72	2.25	3	1930s	SVIB	M	High school students
Strong (1951)[b]	183	.82	18.78	4	<1930s	SVIB	M	College students
	93.5	.76	10.00	6	<1930s	SVIB	M	Originally tested in college
	50	.87	11.00	6	<1930s	SVIB	M	Originally tested in college
	50	.88	12.00	7	<1930s	SVIB	M	Originally tested in college
Strong (1955)	194.5	.73	22.00	5	<1930s	SVIB	M	Graduate students
Swanson & Hansen (1988)	242	.68	12.00	3	1950s	SVIB	F	College freshmen
	167	.68	12.00	3	1950s	SVIB	M	College freshmen
Taylor (1942)	62	.90	4.00	2	<1930s	SVIB	F	Middle school seniors
	64	.86	4.00	2	<1930s	SVIB	M	Middle school seniors

Taylor & Carter (1942)	58	.74	1.00	3	<1930s	SVIB	F	11th graders
Thomas (1955)	81	.64	15.00	4	<1930s	SVIB	F	College sophomores
Tracey (2002)	221	.77	1.00	1	1980s	ICA-R	M	5th graders
	126	.49	1.00	1	1980s	ICA-R	M	7th graders
Tracey et al. (2005)	4,000	.54	1.00	2	1980s	UNIACT	M and F	8th graders
	4,000	.65	1.00	3	1980s	UNIACT	M and F	8th graders
Trimble (1965)	152	.51	10.00	3	1940s	SVIB	M	High school seniors
Trinkhaus (1952)	212	.58	14.50	4	<1930s	SVIB	M	College freshmen
Van Dusen (1940)	73	.59	3.50	4	<1930s	SVIB	M	College freshmen
Verburg (1952)[b]	47	.61	22.00	8	<1930s	SVIB	M and F	Secretaries
Williamson & Bordin (1950)[b]	93	.46	26.00	4	<1930s	SVIB	M	College freshmen
Wright & Scarborough (1958)	205	.75	2.00	4	1940s	KPR	F	College freshmen
	174	.73	2.00	4	1940s	KPR	M	College freshmen
	105	.68	4.00	4	1940s	KPR	F	College freshmen
	125	.65	4.00	4	1940s	KPR	M	College freshmen
Zytowski (1976)	163	.52	12.00	1	1960s	KOIS	M	13-year-olds
	173	.63	12.00	2	1960s	KOIS	M	15-year-olds
	110	.57	18.00	2	1960s	KOIS	M	15-year-olds
	175	.65	12.00	3	1950s	KOIS	M	17-year-olds
	108	.73	12.00	4	1950s	KOIS	M	20-year-olds

Notes: Effect sizes are Fisher's Z-transformed correlations. Age category represents age at initiation of wave of longitudinal assessment. Age categories were coded as follows: 1 = 12–13.9 years; 2 = 14–15.9 years; 3 = 16–17.9 years; 4 = 18–21.9 years; 5 = 22–24.9 years; 6 = 25–29.9 years; 7 = 30–34.9 years; 8 = 35–40 years. KPR = Kuder Preference Record; G = general interests; M = male; F = female; R = rank-order correlations; SCII = Strong-Campbell Interest Inventory; SVIB = Strong Vocational Interest Bank; O = occupational interests; RAMAK = Hebrew abbreviation for list of occupations; B = basic interests; P = profile correlations; TALENT = Project TALENT Interest Inventory; OVIS = Ohio Vocational Interest Survey; VPI = Vocational Preference Inventory; SDS = Self-Directed Search; COPS = Career Occupational Preference System Interest Inventory; KGIS = Kuder General Interest Survey; KOIS = Kuder Occupational Interest Survey; SII = Strong Interest Inventory; ICA-R = Inventory of Children's Activities-Revised; UNIACT = Unisex American College Testing Interest Inventory.

[a] Sample sizes may not be whole numbers because of the averaging process across scale generality and/or method. [b] Reported in Campbell (1971); table 1 in Low, K. S. D., Yoon, M., Roberts, B. W., & Rounds, J. (2005). The stability of vocational interests from early adolescence to middle adulthood: A quantitative review of longitudinal studies. *Psychological Bulletin, 131* (5), 713–737. Published by the American Psychological Association. Reproduced with the permission of the American Psychological Association.

2002 and 2007. Among these studies, three took a qualitative approach and eight took a quantitative approach. The studies either adopted Holland's *Self-Directed Search* (or some version of the SDS) or used one of the *Strong* inventories. The time intervals for these studies ranged from two months to 40 years, and the research participants varied from fifth graders to working adults. With the exception of one study that was conducted in France, all the studies were carried out in the United States. Further details concerning these studies are presented in Table 8.5.

As was the case with the three reviews introduced earlier, all of the 11 individual studies concluded that although career interest types were primarily stable, they were subject to temporal change. In addition to such factors as initial test age and length of test-retest interval, which have been previously mentioned, changes in individuals' career interest types can be contingent on several important variables, including: (1) personal variables such as age, gender, and personality; (2) factors that have to do with research methodology, including research design and data analysis procedures such as the method that is used to report stability/modifiability and the unit of analysis (group versus individual); and (3) the specific career interest types being considered.

Personal Variables. The age of research participants, for example, could play an important role in the level of stability and change in career interest types. As discussed earlier, the meta-analysis study conducted by Low et al. (2005) clearly indicated that between early adolescence (beginning at 11.5 years of age) and middle adulthood (ending at 44 years of age), the period in which career interest types undergo the most drastic change is between 18 and 21 years – that is, during college years. Low and his colleagues' conclusion about the critical period for changes in career interest types can be considered a solid one, because while the test-retest intervals in all the studies included in their meta-analysis were at least one year, studies conducted among college students who were evaluated within much shorter test-retest intervals also demonstrated changes in career interest types. For example, Slaney, Hall, and Bieschke (1993) investigated the malleability of self-descriptive Holland types among 295 college students over a two-month period. Results indicated that changes in career interest styles occurred in varying degrees among this group of students, with female students who had more difficulty relating their Holland career personality styles to specific occupations experiencing the most change.

Indeed, much of the literature suggested that individuals' career interest style structures change as a function of age, revealing a positive relationship between age and the fit of the Holland circular model (Swaney & Flojo, 2001; Tracey & Ward, 1998). For instance, in a one-year longitudinal study of the

TABLE 8.5. *Longitudinal Studies Based on Holland's Six Career Personality Types*

Authors	N*	Measure	Sample Description	Country	Time Interval	Indicator for Style Change
Darcy & Tracey (2007)	1,000	UNIACT (ACT, 1995)	School students representing major U.S. ethnic groups	U.S.	4 years, each at Grades 8, 10, and 12	Interest structure changed for males, not for females
Gaudron & Vautier (2007)	1,089	18 activities representing Holland's 6 types	Adults	France	1 month	Stability coefficient: .77 to .93
Helwig (2003)	65	Occupational aspirations classified by Holland's 6 types (interviews)	School students representing major U.S. ethnic groups	U.S.	6 interview points within 10 years	More than 60% of the sample had a least 1 set of opposite Holland types over the 6 measurement times
Hetwig & Myrin (1997)	12	SDS	A three-generation 20-member family	U.S.	Twice over 10 years	Changes occurred in Holland's codes – in the direction of consistency rather than inconsistency
Miller (2002)	1	SDS	1 client aged 16 when first tested	U.S.	10 years over 2-year intervals	Changes occurred in raw scores of the 3-letter code
Schomburg & Tokar (2003)	97	SDS	College students	U.S.	12 weeks	Test-retest reliability: .80 to.88 for high private self-consciousness group and .61 to .89 for low self-consciousness group
Slaney et al. (1993)	295	Self-Descriptive Holland Types	College students	U.S.	2 months	Self-descriptive Holland types changed to varying degrees
Swanson & Hansen (1988)	409	SCII	College students initially	U.S.	3 times over 16 years	Stability coefficients: –.11 to .96
Tracey (2002)	126 221	ICA-R	2 samples of school students	U.S.	1 year	Stability estimate: .35 to .62 for elementary students; .74 to .81 for middle school students
Tracey & Robbins (2005)	1,000	UNIACT	School students representing major U.S. ethnic groups	U.S.	4 years, each at Grades 8, 10, and 12	Congruence and clarity increased in 10th grade, but both decreased in 12th grade
Vinitsky (1973)	42	SVIB	Psychologists	U.S.	40 years	At least one-half standard deviation shifts occurred in 12 of the 54 scales

Notes: N*: the sample size(s) shown for each study here represent(s) the number(s) of participants who provided longitudinal data;

UNIACT = Unisex edition of the ACT Interest Inventory; SDS = Self-Directed Search; SCII = Strong-Campbell Interest Inventory; ICA-R = Inventory of Children's Activity-Revised; SVIB = Strong Vocational Interest Blank.

development of career interests among fifth (elementary school) to eighth grade (middle school) students, Tracey (2002) found that changes occurred in both the structure and the intensity of career interests over time. The participants' responses became more integrated with the passage of time, better approximating the Holland hexagon with increasing age. At the same time, there were substantial changes in almost all scale means over one year, especially for the older group. Finally, it should be noted that changes in career interest types are not linear. Instead, the directions in which career interest types change could fluctuate. For example, in a study of eighth through 12th graders, Tracey and Robbins (2005) found that whereas students' congruence and clarity on the Holland model increased during their 10th grade, both indicators of career interests (i.e., structure and levels of intensity) decreased during their 12th grade, suggesting that students needed to reexamine their career interests during their 12th grade – a time when they were faced with the reality of moving on to another major stage in their lives, receiving university education or entering the world of work.

How career interest types change over time may also be contingent on individuals' gender. For example, in Tracey's (2002) one-year longitudinal study of fifth to eighth graders' development of career interests, girls showed most change (a decrease) in the investigative scale, whereas boys demonstrated most change (a decrease) in the social and artistic scales. In another study, Darcy and Tracey (2007) examined school students' changes in the circumplex structure of career interest types based on Holland's model over three time periods: grades 8, 10, and 12. The concept of circumplex structure, initially described by Guttman (1954), is defined as a circular arrangement of relations among variables. Within the context of Holland's typology of career interest styles, the circumplex structure refers to the relations among the six distinct career interest types that can be represented by an equilateral hexagon. Darcy and Tracey (2007) concluded that while changes in career interests over time occurred among male students, no change was identified among female students.

Apart from being affected by age and gender, the malleability of career interest styles has also been found to be moderated by other personal variables such as personality. For example, private self-consciousness – a tendency to be attentive to or aware of private aspects of the self such as inner feelings, motives, and thoughts (Nasby, 1989) – has been found to be a moderator for the development of career interest styles. In a 12-week longitudinal study of 108 undergraduate students in the United States, Schomburg and Tokar (2003) found that college students with higher levels of private self-consciousness demonstrated higher stable scores on the enterprising scale than did students with lower levels of private self-consciousness. Although contrary to the researchers' hypothesis, private self-consciousness did not moderate the stability of the other five SDS scales, the statistically significant difference found in the enterprising scale suggests that personality could well be a factor that moderates the stability of and change in people's career interest styles. As a matter of fact, Schomburg and Tokar's (2003) study is not alone in having identified the potentially important effects of personality on career interest stability, or modifiability for that matter. Early in 1961, Dunkleberger and Tyler had already concluded that high school juniors who were better adjusted tended to be the ones whose career interest type profiles had gone through changes. Such a finding led the researchers to argue that career interest type change during adolescence should be regarded as an index of development as opposed to that of instability. In other words, the change of career personality styles is a normal part of human development.

Research Methodology Adopted. Research methodology may also affect the levels of stability and modifiability reported by various researchers. This includes, but is not limited to, the method selected for defining and reporting malleability and the unit of analysis adopted. There are several good examples of the influence of the different ways of defining and reporting stability. To begin with, Low and Rounds (2007) articulated five types of longitudinal change and stability in career interest types, and thus five major ways of reporting stability and change: (1) rank-order stability, (2) profile stability, (3) mean-level stability, (4) structural stability, and (5) congruence stability. *Rank-order stability* is typically represented by test-retest correlations, which represent the changes in the relative placement of individuals within a group. *Profile stability* is assessed through the correlations of configurations of salient career interest dimensions for the same individual at different time points, averaged across all members of a particular group. *Mean-level stability* reflects the increase or decrease of career interest types of groups of people over time. *Structural stability* is measured by change in the interest-model structure (e.g., Holland's RIASEC structure) at different time points. Finally, *congruence stability* refers to the goodness of fit between an individual's career interest types and the environment. Results from Low et al.'s (2005) meta-analysis research indicated that rank-order stability was less stable than profile stability.

Likewise, after studying career interest stability using the *Strong-Campbell Interest Inventory* (SCII, Hansen & Campbell, 1985) over 4-year, 8-year, and 12-year intervals, Swanson and Hansen (1988) used five methods to compute stability: (1) the six General Occupational Themes and 23 Basic Interest Scales (GOT-BIS), (2) the same-sex occupational scales, (3) the opposite-sex occupational scales, (4) the entire set of 207 occupational scales, and (5) all 236 scales of the SCII profile. The researchers concluded that the five methods of operationally defining stability produced somewhat different results in terms of the characteristics of the stability coefficient distributions. For instance, the median stability coefficients based on the GOT-BIS were lower than median coefficients based on the other four methods of defining stability.

Similarly, French researchers Gaudron and Vautier (2007) challenged the use of test-retest correlations, stating that "the main problem with the interpretation of the test-retest correlation is that the effect of temporal change in true scores with the time period and the effect of measurement error at each occasion of testing cannot be disentangled" (p. 223). Instead, the researchers advocated for the use of true consistency.

By the same token, when conducting a secondary analysis of a three-wave data set from 1,675 school children (at grades 8, 10, and 12) randomly selected from the American College Testing database with a national sample of 69,987 students, Darcy and Tracey (2007) used structural equation modeling (SEM), the randomization test of hypothesized order relations, constrained multidimensional scaling, and circular unidimensional scaling. The four different methods of data analyses led to different conclusions. That is, whereas the SEM analyses did not lend support to the circumplex structure of Holland's RIASEC model, the other three statistical methods did. One would naturally wonder: If the method of data analysis affects the confirmation of the circumplex structure of Holland's RIASEC model, would different methods of data analysis also show different levels of stability and change in career interest styles manifested by individuals? The obvious answer to the question is affirmative, because different statistical procedures may result in stability coefficients of different magnitudes.

With respect to the unit of analysis as a factor that affects the levels of stability and change reported, several researchers (e.g., Low et al., 2005; Swanson, 1999; Swanson & Hansen, 1988) have pointed out the disjuncture between group-level change and individual-level change. It has been found that although career interest style scores for groups of individuals have shown considerable stability, some individuals' career interest styles have been found to change appreciably over time, as demonstrated by the near-zero or even negative intra-individual correlation coefficients. Swanson and Hansen (1988) asserted that while one may be justified in assuming that career interest styles are stable across groups, one is not justified in assuming that career interest styles are stable for all individuals. Low et al. (2005) argued that the change of individuals' career interest styles can be easily masked by the apparent stability of career interest styles at the group level.

In fact, even an unchanged three-letter Holland code in one individual over a long period of time does not guarantee the absolute stability of one's career interest styles. Miller (2002), for instance, investigated the degree of change in a single client's three-letter Holland code over a 10-year period. Results indicated that although the three-letter code remained stable over time, changes in raw scores and permutations of the code occurred.

Specific Career Interest Type Considered. In discussing the stability and change of career interest types, one should also take into account the specific types of interests being investigated. Swanson (1999) observed three patterns in summarizing the findings of some of the earlier studies. First, higher test-retest coefficients were more frequently reported for scales reflecting mechanical or scientific career interests for males and for scales indicating artistic interests for women than for other scales (e.g., Herzberg & Bouton, 1954; Rosenberg, 1953; Strong, 1955). Second, career interest types were more likely to change toward those that were socially desirable (e.g., Hoyt, Smith, & Levy, 1957; Swanson, 1984). Finally, career interests that were "lukewarm" or "indifferent" were more amenable to change than were strong career interests (e.g., Stordahl, 1954; Trinkaus, 1954).

Malleability of Learning Styles

The malleability of learning styles as assessed by Kolb's (1984, 1985) *Learning Style Inventory* (LSI) became a topic of research almost as soon as the inventory came into being (e.g., Sims, Veres III, Watson, & Buckner, 1986; Geiger & Pinto, 1991; Pinto & Geiger, 1991), and this research interest has been maintained until the first decade of the 21st century (e.g., Salter, Evans, & Forney, 2006). However, the number of longitudinal studies that set out to investigate the malleability of learning styles can only be said to be fair. The literature search produced only nine articles, each reporting one or more sets of longitudinal data. All except two studies were conducted in the 1990s, with the earliest one being carried out in 1986 and the most recent one in 2006. For further details about these studies, see Table 8.6.

Lying in the middle layer of Curry's (1983) "onion" model, the styles in Kolb's experiential learning model are expected to be subject to significant change over time (Kolb, 1984; Loo, 1997). Indeed, although the learning styles in Kolb's model are viewed as relatively stable, they are also considered to be dynamic and cyclic – reflecting the changing challenges individuals have been confronted with and experiences they have had. Kolb believes that ideal learners are those who progress from concrete to reflective observation, to abstract conceptualization, and finally to active experimentation. This theoretical hypothesis has been largely supported by the existing studies.

TABLE 8.6. *Longitudinal Studies Based on Kolb's Model of Learning Styles*

Authors	N*	Measure	Sample Description	Country	Time Interval	Indicator for Style Change
Geiger & Pinto (1991)	40	Kolb's LSI (1985)	College business students	U.S.	4 times over 3 years	Style classification
Hsu (1999)	116	LSI-SD (Marshall & Merritt, 1985)	College hospitality students	U.S.	Entering and graduating the program	39% convergers at entry and 55% convergers when graduating
Loo (1997)	152	Kolb's LSI (1985)	College management students	Canada	10 weeks	Roughly 50% changed learning styles, with 13% changed to the opposite style
Pinto & Geiger (1991)	55	Kolb's LSI (1985)	College management students	U.S.	1 year	No change
Pinto et al. (1994)	178	Kolb's LSI (1985)	College business students	U.S.	3 year	Stability of classification: Kappa = .23, .21, and .35
Rakoczy & Money (1995)	144	Kolb's LSI (1985)	Nursing students	Canada	3 times over 3 years	Little change
Ruble & Stout (1991)	139 (N_1) 253 (N_2)	Kolb's LSI (1985) for N_1 Scrambled version of Kolb's LSI for N_2	College business students	U.S.	5 weeks	Stability of classification: Kappa = .39 for N_1 Kappa = .36 for N_2
Salter et al. (2006)	222	Kolb's LSI (1985)	Graduate students in student affairs administration	U.S.	3 times over 3 years	Change in LSI profiles, with Convergers having changed the most
Sims et al. (1986)	309 (N_1) 132 (N_2) 131 (N_3) 94 (N_4)	Kolb's LSI (1979) Kolb's LSI (1979) Kolb's LSI (1984) Kolb's LSI (1984)	Undergraduate and graduate students	U.S.	Samples 1 and 3: twice over 1 year Samples 2 and 4: 3 times over 15 weeks	Stability of classification: Kappa: .13 to .41

Notes: N*: the sample size(s) shown for each study here represent(s) the number(s) of participants who provided longitudinal data; LSI = Learning Style Inventory; LSI-SD = Learning Style Inventory-Semantic Differential format (Marshall & Merritt, 1985).

Of the nine studies located in the literature, two (Ruble & Stout, 1991; Sims et al., 1986) were originally aimed at examining the reliability and classification stability of the *Learning Style Inventory* (Kolb, 1976, 1985). Both of these studies were conducted among graduate and undergraduate students, and both concluded that the LSI possessed low test-retest reliabilities. However, scholars who place emphasis on the modifiability of learning styles could argue that these low test-retest coefficients could easily be construed as representing real change in individuals' learning styles over time (e.g., Tracey & Robbins, 2005). Indeed, as Geiger and Pinto (1991) pointed out, research over much longer periods than the typical three- to five-week test-retest intervals, as in the case of the aforementioned two studies (Ruble & Stout, 1991; Sims et al., 1986), yielded much higher test-retest reliability data. Moreover, other research (e.g., Christopher, 2005) has also shown that the LSI possesses good internal scale reliabilities, with Cronbach's alphas typically ranging from high .70s to high .80s. In other words, the fluctuation of the learning style scores between two testing occasions is more likely to reflect actual change in styles than to indicate low reliability of the inventory.

As for the seven studies that especially aimed at examining the malleability of learning styles, all but one study (Pinto & Geiger, 1991) revealed significant changes in learning styles. In the case of Pinto and Geiger's (1991) one-year longitudinal study conducted among 55 college students between their sophomore and junior years, the researchers did not identify any significant change in learning styles. However, their follow-up study (forming a 3-year study, Geiger & Pinto, 1991) on 44 of the 55 students who had participated in the original study yielded mixed support for the proposition that students' learning styles change as they progress through their college years. Although results of the Wilks Criterion F tests for the X-dimension and Y-dimension did not show any significant difference in learning styles, the classifications of students' learning styles changed.

There are a minimum of two interpretations for the conflicting findings between Geiger and Pinto's (1991) initial study and their follow-up study. One is that changes in learning styles took time. The other is that the methods adopted to examine the data (more specifically, the types of statistical procedures employed) might have made a difference. These arguments concerning methodological issues have been echoed by findings in other studies. For example, in a study of 152 Canadian college students over a test-retest interval of 10 weeks, Loo (1997) found that there was virtually no difference between Time 1 and Time 2 group means, indicating style stability over time. However, upon examining the percentage for each of the four style categories,

Loo found that although approximately half of the total sample maintained the same learning styles from Time 1 to Time 2, roughly half of the sample changed their learning styles, with 13 percent of the total sample having dramatically changed their styles to the opposite styles.

Changes in the classification of learning styles have also been confirmed by a 3-year longitudinal study conducted among 178 undergraduate business students in the United States (Pinto, Geiger, & Boyle, 1994). Although the Kappa coefficients (ranging from .21 to .35) suggested a level of classification stability greater than chance, changes in learning styles were found. Indeed, Loo (1997) argued that it was not appropriate for such statistics as group mean scores to be reported as style change indicators because they focus on group effects, and as such, could easily mask individual changes in learning styles. Still further, Loo's study also revealed gender difference in style changes: female students were found to be less likely to change to the opposite styles than were male students.

A relatively more recent study by Salter, Evans, and Forney (2006) added yet another interesting dimension to findings on style change. Upon analyzing the data collected from 222 graduate students in a three-wave longitudinal study over two years, the researchers concluded that compared with the other three types of learners (i.e., assimilators, convergers, and divergers), accommodators tended to be significantly more stable in learning styles. The least stable LSI profile was that of convergers – students who had a strong preference for technical tasks and unambiguous solutions to problems.

Finally, the identification of style change can be further complicated by the specific environments in which people work, with some environments being more likely to induce change in learning styles than others. For example, Rakoczy and Money (1995) followed the development of the learning styles of a group of female nursing students for three years (one administration of the LSI per year) and found that throughout these years, the students' dominant learning style was that of assimilator. In other words, little change occurred in the students' learning styles. However, in her analysis of the entering data and exiting data provided by 116 hospitality students, Hsu (1999) found that a significant change in learning styles had occurred over the three years. That is, when students entered the program, 39 percent of them were convergers, and 27.8 percent, 16.5 percent, and 10.4 percent were accommodators, assimilators, and divergers, respectively. By the time they were ready to graduate, however, the proportion of convergers had increased to 55.2 percent, whereas the proportions for the other three learning styles had decreased. Furthermore, results of paired t-tests also suggested that the students' learning styles changed significantly during their course of study in the hospitality major as they moved from being accommodators, assimilators, and divergers to being convergers.

One could certainly contend that factors other than different learning environments – in this case, nursing versus hospitality – could have been responsible for the contrasting findings in the two studies. These other factors include, but are not limited to, the research methodology (especially data analysis procedures) applied, the different durations of the two academic programs, and the different cultural settings (Canada versus the United States) in which the two studies were conducted. However, one could argue even more strongly that the likeliest cause of the differential findings was the two different learning environments created by the two different academic programs. For college students' learning styles, learning environment is one of the most pivotal socialization variables (see Chapter 5).

Malleability of Learning Approaches
As mentioned in Chapter 2, several related concepts (e.g., study process, learning preference, learning orientation, and learning pattern), broadly known as learning approaches, have been studied in the field of intellectual styles. Efforts to investigate temporal changes in learning approaches can be said to be fair given the dearth of noninterventional longitudinal studies based on other style constructs. Although the malleability of learning approaches was initially studied by Watkins and Hattie in 1985, such a research endeavor was not attempted again until the mid-1990s, when three studies appeared. Since the turn of the present century, however, relatively more studies have been conducted. This literature search showed that between 2001 and 2010, six studies were published. Details of all 10 studies can be found in Table 8.7.

All these studies were carried out in higher educational institutions, with the data predominantly obtained from four European countries – Belgium, Finland, the Netherlands, and the United Kingdom – as well as from Australia. With the exception of the study carried out in the United Kingdom (Edmunds & Richardson, 2009), all the studies identified significant changes in learning approaches. Moreover, eight of these nine significant-results-bearing studies revealed that students' learning approaches changed in the direction consistent with the mission of higher education: to cultivate more advanced and independent ways of learning among students. As students progress along their learning in higher-education institutions, they are expected to become more and more reflective and meaning-oriented learners.

The earliest set of longitudinal data was obtained by Watkins and Hattie (1985) from a group of 244 Australian university students, using Ramsden and Entwistle's (1981) *Approaches to Studying Inventory* (ASI). The ASI was

TABLE 8.7. *Longitudinal Studies Based on Models of Learning Approaches*

Authors	N*	Measure	Sample Description	Country	Time Interval	Indicator for Style Change
Busato et al. (1998)	32 (N_1) 26 (N_2)	Vermunt's ILS	College psychology students	The Netherlands	1 year for Sample 1 2 years for Sample 2	More meaning directed: $\delta = .32$
Donche et al. (2010)	254 (N_1) 280 (N_2)	Vermunt's ILS	College students in 8 majors	Belgium	3 times over 3 years for N_1; twice in 3 years for N_2	More meaning directed and less undirected: Cohen's d: .17 to .60
Donche & Van Petegem (2009)	236	Vermunt's ILS	Pre-service teachers	Belgium	3 years	More meaning directed and less undirected: Cohen's d: .15 to .80
Edmunds & Richardson (2009)	1,371	ALS	College students in 15 department	UK	2 years	Little change
Nieminen et al. (2004)	66	Deep/Surface scales from Entwistle & Ramsden; 2 scales from Vermunt's ILS	College pharmacy students	Finland	3 years	Reproducing orientation decreased: partial $\eta^2 = .44$ Meaning orientation increased for above-average achievers
Severiens et al. (2001)	191 (N_1) 271 (N_2)	Vermunt's ILS	Students in adult secondary education and in tertiary technical colleges	The Netherlands	Twice in 6 months for Sample 1; 3 times in 6 months for Sample 2	Surface approach decreased in both samples; Deep approached increased in the tertiary group
Vermetten et al. (1999)	276	Vermunt's ILS	College students in 4 departments	The Netherlands	Twice in 2 semesters	Meaning orientation increased: Cohen's d: .13–.33
Volet et al. (1994)	268 (N_1) 91 (N_2)	Biggs' SPQ	College students: Local Australian and South-east Asian students studying in Australia	Australia	13 weeks	
Watkins & Hattie (1985)	244	Ramsden & Entwistle's ASI	College students	Australia	3 years	Mixed findings
Zeegers (2001)	43 (N_1) 125 (N_2) 60 (N_3)	Biggs's SPQ	College science students	Australia	5 times over 3 years (Sample 1 in all trials; Sample 2 in 1st and 3rd trials; Sample 3 in 1st and 5th trials)	Achieving approach declined; Deep approached declined first, followed by a recovery

Notes: N*: the sample size(s) shown for each study here represent(s) the number(s) of participants who provided longitudinal data;

administered to the students once at the beginning of their first year and once at the end of their third year. Mixed findings were obtained, but in favor of the conclusion that students' learning approaches had become deeper. From the first to the third year, students' scores significantly increased on two (interrelating ideas and comprehension learning) of the eight scales that are related to the more adaptive learning approaches (meaning orientation and holistic orientation). At the same time, however, their scores had significantly decreased on the other scales centered on the meaning-oriented learning approach. Moreover, a decrease in the reproducing orientation was found in only one of the four scales. The researchers postulated that such unfavorable parts of the outcome may be attributed to students' perceptions that deep-level learning approaches were not vital to satisfying examination requirements.

Indeed, change in student' learning approaches can be a far more complex issue than it appears to be. Several researchers have discussed the potential impact of students' perceptions of learning environments on their learning approaches. Moreover, the malleability of learning approaches can be contingent on other factors such as students' level of academic achievement, the learning approaches that students use at the time when they enter higher educational institutions, and the duration of a specific longitudinal study. Findings in each of the eight studies to be described in the following reflect the possible effects of one or more of the factors mentioned here.

Learning environments, be they actual or perceived, have been one of the primary factors that researchers turn to when they seek explanations for students' changes in learning approaches. For example, Busato, Prins, Elshout, and Hamaker (1998) obtained longitudinal data, using Vermunt's (1994) *Inventory of Learning Styles*, from two small samples ($N_1=32$ and $N_2=26$) of university students in the Netherlands, with the test interval being one year and two years, respectively. The researchers found that both groups of students became more meaning directed and application directed in their learning styles and that they scored significantly lower in the post-tests on the reproduction and undirected learning approach scales. In explaining their findings, the researchers placed great emphasis on the power of learning environments. They argued that not only environmental variables, but also students' perceptions of their learning environments, could have influenced the changes in their learning approaches.

The strong emphasis on the role of the learning environment has been echoed by Vermetten, Vermunt, and Lodewijks (1999), who examined the changes in the learning approaches as well as the changes in the perceived learning environments of a sample of 276 Dutch university students from four academic departments (economics, law, language and literature, and social sciences) over the first two years of study. Although the students did not demonstrate a significant decrease in the use of the reproduction-directed learning style, they appeared to become more meaning-oriented learners, and they perceived their teachers' instruction as becoming more directed toward activating students in their learning. In explaining these changes, the researchers focused their discussion on the role of the changes in students' perceptions of their learning environment.

The argument for the role of students' perceptions of their learning environment in the modification of styles was also made by Volet, Renshaw, and Tietzel (1994), who compared the learning approaches of local Australian students with those of students from Southeast Asia enrolled in a first-year Introduction to Economics course at a Western Australian university. Students were tested on the *Study Process Questionnaire* (Biggs, 1987) once at the beginning of the semester and once at the end of the semester. Results showed that by the end of the semester, the differences in learning approaches between the two cultural groups found at the beginning of the semester had disappeared. It was concluded that the similarity in learning approaches between the two groups at the end of the semester was attributable to Southeast Asian students adapting to their perceived demands of the particular academic course and the general learning environment in the process of pursuing their education during the first semester.

Nonetheless, the effects of students' learning environment on the changes in their learning approaches can vary depending on the learning approaches that they acquired in the past. Two studies conducted in Belgium support this argument. In the first study, Donche and van Petegem (2009) administered Vermunt's (1994) *Inventory of Learning Styles* to a group of 236 pre-service teachers twice, once at the beginning of the teacher education program and once at the end of the program. Results indicated that in general, meaning-oriented learning increased over time and undirected learning decreased. Further analyses also suggested that the patterns of change in learning approaches differed in accord with the learning approaches that students were already using in their first year of education. Students who initially learned mainly in a meaning-oriented manner in the first year further progressed in this direction to become even more meaning-oriented learners, whereas students who demonstrated a flexible learning approach generally became more meaning-oriented learners in the third year. At the same time, students who predominantly exhibited the characteristics of a reproductive/undirected learner in the first year showed that they had become more flexible and meaning-oriented learners at the end of pre-service teacher training program. These findings were replicated in an independent study conducted by Donche and his colleagues (Donche, Coertijens, & Van Petegem, 2010) among students studying in eight bachelor's degree programs: business management, communication sciences, electro-mechanics, hotel management, journalism, office management, social work, and teacher education. Again, data were gathered over a three-year period. This time, however, some of the students (N = 254) contributed to all three waves of data collection (at the beginning of each of the first three years of university education), while the others (N = 280) participated only in the first and the third data collection.

Changes in students' learning approaches could be further affected by students' level of academic achievement. For example, in Finland, Nieminen, Lindblom-Ylänne, and Lonka (2004) examined the development of the learning approaches of 66 undergraduate students majoring in pharmacy over a three-year period. For the entire sample, the reproducing orientation generally diminished over the three years. In fact, students' reproducing orientation at the end of the three years became negatively correlated with their academic success. However, when data for above-average achievers and below-average achievers were analyzed separately, the development of favorable learning approaches was only detected in the group of above-average achievers. That is, only the above-average achievers increased their meaning-orientation learning approach and decreased their reproducing-oriented approach to learning.

Moreover, the degree to which students change their learning approaches may also be contingent on the level of schooling or type of schooling they are receiving. For example, in the Netherlands, Severiens, Dam, and Van Hout Wolters (2001) administered the "processing and regulation strategies" part of the *Inventory of Learning Styles* (Vermunt & Van Rijswik, 1987) to two separate groups of students. The first group, consisting of 191 students from five schools of adult secondary education, received the test twice over a six-month interval. The second group, comprising 271 students from five different tertiary technical colleges, received the test twice over a period of three months. Results indicated that although in both groups there was a decrease in the surface approach to learning, an increase in the deep approach to learning was only demonstrated among the students studying in tertiary technical colleges. It is possible that the varying findings concerning the two different groups had to do with other factors. However, based on the information provided in the study, the types and levels of the institutions at which the two groups of students were studying were the most likely influential variables.

Finally, the degree of change in students' learning approaches may be modulated by the different points in time at which students' learning approaches were assessed in different studies. This is because research has shown that changes in learning approaches are not linear. For example, Zeegers (2001) followed the development of the learning approaches of 200 commencing students studying in a science course at an Australian university. Over a period of three years, the *Study Process Questionnaire* (SPQ) was administered five times: at the beginning of the first year and at 4-month, 8-month, 16-month, and 30-month intervals. Of the overall sample of students, 43 participated in all five trials, 125 in the first and the third trials, and 60 in the first and the final trials. Results suggested that in general, there was a decrease in both the achieving approach and the deep approach to learning over the years. However, changes in these learning approaches were not linear. For instance, the deep approach exhibited a small decline in the first year of study, but by the time the SPQ was administered for the fifth time, it had recovered to the initial mean score.

Malleability of Other Intellectual Styles

Apart from the aforementioned nonintervention longitudinal studies that were broadly based on three different style constructs (career personality type, learning style, and learning approach), six studies based on four other style constructs were identified in the literature search. These include, as previously mentioned: (1) one study based on Witkin's (1954) construct of field dependence/independence (FDI), (2) two on Kagan's (1965) construct of reflectivity-impulsivity, (3) two on Jung's (1923) construct of personality type, and (4) one on Kirton's (1976) construct of decision-making and problem-solving style. It should be noted that longitudinal studies that are grounded in the first two style constructs (i.e., FDI and reflectivity-impulsivity) are predominantly experimental ones, and these were reviewed in the previous chapter. However, longitudinal studies based on Jung's and Kirton's models, with or without interventions, are lacking. Nonetheless, results from these six studies based on the four models are in concert with those that have been reviewed so far in this chapter – findings of studies based on Holland's construct of career personality types, Kolb's construct of learning styles, and the family of models that are centered on learning approaches.

Malleability of FDI. The study based on Witkin's (1948) construct of FDI was conducted by Witkin, Goodenough, and Karp (1967), who obtained longitudinal data from two groups of research participants. The first was a group of 60 students who were followed from age 10 to age 24, and the second was a group of 48 students who were followed from age 8 to age 13. To assess the research participants' levels of FDI, the researchers administered the *Rod-and-Frame Test* (Witkin & Asch, 1948), the *Room-Adjustment Test* (Witkin, Dyk, Faterson, Goodenough, & Karp, 1962), and the *Body-Adjustment Test* (Witkin, Lewis, Hertzman, Machover, Meissner, & Wapner, 1954) several times over the specified durations (see p. 294 in Witkin et al., 1967). It was concluded that virtually every research participant changed from being relatively field dependent to being relatively field independent without significant reversal. At the same time, the researchers pointed out that the progressive increase in the extent of field independence was evident up to age 17, with little change being evident from age 17 to age 24, thus indicating that the development of psychological differentiation may approach a plateau in young adulthood. However, it is worth emphasizing that this does not mean that it is impossible to enhance people's level of field independence after a certain age. As shown in the previous chapter, with deliberate training, one could improve one's level of field independence – even at a relatively old age.

Malleability of Reflectivity-Impulsivity. Both of the longitudinal studies grounded in Kagan's reflectivity-impulsivity construct were conducted in the early 1980s. Whereas the first study (Messer & Brodzinsky, 1981) had a clear objective to examine the three-year stability of reflectivity-impulsivity among young adolescents, the second study (Brodzinsky, 1982) focused on changes in the patterns of relationship between reflectivity-impulsivity and cognitive development. Messer and Brodzinsky (1981) assessed 85 children on the *Matching Familiar Figures Test* (MFFT) when the children were 11 years old, and reevaluated their levels of reflectivity-impulsivity when they were 14 years old. The researchers reported stability coefficients ranging from .42 to .51 for the MFFT latency and from .43 to .51 for the MFFT errors. These stability coefficients suggested that at least some change in the level of reflectivity-impulsivity occurred among these children during this period of time.

As one of the aims of his study, Brodzinsky (1982) examined the change in reflectivity-impulsivity among two cohorts of children. The first cohort was composed of 20 children who were aged 4 at the initial testing and aged 6 years and 5 months at the follow-up testing. The second cohort consisted of 20 children who were aged 6 at the initial testing and aged 8 years and 7 months at the follow-up testing. In both cohorts, a significant decrease in MFFT errors was found [$t(19) = 4.17$, $p < .001$ for the first cohort; $t(19) = 2.53$, $p < .05$ for the second cohort]. Moreover, in the first cohort, there was a significant increase in MFFT latency [$t(19) = 3.53$, $p < .01$], although the increase in the latency among the second cohort failed to reach a statistically significant level. Even so, this result essentially lent support to the major argument of this book – that intellectual styles do change.

Malleability of Personality Type. With regard to the longitudinal data obtained for personality styles as assessed by the *Myers-Briggs Type Indicator* (MBTI), a first set of data was located in a doctoral dissertation completed by

Morrison (1994) in Canada. As part of his research, Morrison administered the MBTI to 88 junior high school students twice. The time interval between test and retest varied from three to six weeks. The researcher found that test-retest coefficients fell in a range between .50 and .85. Apart from the data acknowledged in Morrison's study, data on test-retest stability/change of the MBTI scales are also documented in the *MBTI Manual* (Myers, McCaulley, Quenk, & Hammer, 1998). These data are from 22 studies of various populations in the United States. It was concluded that in general, when research participants report a change in personality style, it is most likely to occur in only one preference and in scales where the original preference was weak.

Results of the second set of longitudinal data were reported in Salter, Evans, and Forney's (2006) study of 222 graduate students in the United States. Students completed the MBTI three times over two years. Although the researchers asserted that the MBTI preferences of these students "appeared to be quite stable over the course of 2 years" (p. 181), the scores obtained in the second and third administrations were quite different from those obtained in the first one. Configural frequency analyses revealed five (out of eight) significant unstable patterns.

Malleability of Decision-making and Problem-solving Styles. Finally, the study based on Kirton's (1976) model of adaption-innovation styles was conducted by Clapp (1993) among 69 adults working for an administrative services organization at a multinational company in the United Kingdom. The *Kirton Adaption-Innovation Inventory* was administered twice over three years and seven months. Although the study obtained a test-retest coefficient of .82 (meaning that there was still a good indication that the adaption-innovation styles did not stay the same over the test interval), the researcher argued that the styles concerned could not be changed.

Conclusions, Limitations, and Future Research

Based on Piaget's claim that people's cognitive structure changes as a function of time, this chapter began with the premise that people's intellectual styles also experience temporal change. The intention of the chapter was to ascertain if style constructs that fall within different layers of Curry's "onion" model change to varying degrees. The chapter also aimed to determine if people's styles change in particular directions, and further, to identify some of the key factors that may play a critical role in the malleability of intellectual styles.

An examination of the findings from three existing reviews and of those from the individual studies based on seven different style models that spread across all three layers of Curry's "onion" model strongly supported the position that styles are amendable. Among all the studies reviewed, only two arrived at the conclusion that styles cannot be changed. One was Pinto and Geiger's (1991) study based on Kolb's *Learning Style Inventory*, and the other was Clapp's (1991) study using the *Kirton Adaption-Innovation Inventory*. It should be remembered, however, that irrespective of their assertion that styles cannot be changed, when Geiger and Pinto (1991) extended their original one-year study into a three-year investigation, they did find significant changes in students' learning styles. As for Clapp's (1991) study, even though the stability coefficient was not so high as to warrant the conclusion that no change had occurred in the research participants' styles, the researcher argued in favor of style stability.

Clapp's reasoning in reaching his conclusion about the stability of styles can be understood within the context of Tracey and Robbins's (2005) discussion of the two perspectives with respect to findings based on Holland's construct of career personality styles. To reiterate Tracey and Robbins's (2005) observation, changes in styles are often deemed to be errors from the stability perspective, but to be substance (i.e., actual modification of styles) from the development perspective. As a matter of fact, this dialectal view of change/stability of styles is rather common in the field. In making sense of the findings of the studies reviewed here, one should certainly keep these two perspectives in mind. In addition to the fact that whether styles are perceived to be stable or whether they are considered to be dynamic depends on particular scholars' perspectives, five other types of contingencies, which have emerged from the current literature review on nonintervention longitudinal studies, can make a difference in determining whether or not styles are viewed as going through temporal changes. These are: (1) personological characteristics (e.g., age, gender, personality, academic achievement level, and preexisting styles); (2) factors that have to do with research designs (e.g., initial testing age, retest interval, overall length of a study); (3) environmental factors (e.g., type and level of an educational institution, academic discipline, perceived learning environment); (4) types of data analysis procedures applied (e.g., statistics reported, unit of analysis); and (5) specific style constructs and particular individual styles being investigated (see earlier discussion in this chapter).

Observant readers would have noticed that two of the four questions raised earlier have yet to be answered. These questions concern (1) the directions in which styles change and (2) the degrees to which styles change based on their distances from the center of Curry's "onion" model. In relation to the first question, in the case of some style constructs (e.g., learning approach, FDI, and reflectivity-impulsivity), the general trend is for people to develop more adaptive styles (i.e., Type I intellectual styles) over time. However, in the case of some other styles (e.g., career personality type, Kolb's learning styles), the direction in which styles generally change is not as clear-cut. As for the second question, by and large, scholars who study style constructs that are farther away from the center of Curry's "onion" model put more emphasis on change, while those who study style constructs closer to the center of the "onion" model put more stress on stability. However, the statistics reported in the existing literature do not allow a reliable comparison concerning the degrees of change in styles across models. Nevertheless, again, the literature clearly suggests that styles can develop over time.

Although having asserted that the existing literature bears out the view that styles are dynamic, I am very well aware of the limitations of the work documented here. Interestingly, however, these limitations assist in identifying some future directions for nonintervention longitudinal studies.

To begin with, the aforementioned six types of factors (i.e., stability perspective versus development perspective, personological characteristics, research designs, environments, statistical procedures, and specific styles examined) that may affect one's judgment about the malleability of styles should be taken into account not only when a research project is designed and implemented, but also when data of the research project are analyzed and reported. More careful and more comprehensive considerations must be given to the design of nonintervention longitudinal studies, and multiple approaches must be adopted in analyzing and reporting research data. Beyond this, three other major limitations in the existing literature need to be addressed in future research.

First, in the individual studies reviewed in this chapter, less than a handful of them reported effect sizes, and many others failed to report sufficient statistics for effect sizes to be considered. Although the present results support the argument that styles are changeable, they would be even more convincing if good effect sizes were included.

Second, surely the existing evidence should give us reasonable confidence in asserting that people's intellectual styles go through temporal changes. However, relevant to the large number of style constructs available to be examined in the research area dealt with in this chapter, the amount of existing research is very moderate. Future research should look beyond the particular style constructs on which the longitudinal studies reviewed here were based.

Finally, an obvious limitation in the present literature concerns the sampling of the research participants. To begin with, the available studies have been primarily conducted in the higher-education sector in a small number of countries. This limitation regarding research populations is further escalated by the fact that many of the studies suffered from varying degrees of participant attrition attributable to one reason or another. This twofold limitation with respect to sampling may necessarily present a challenge to the generalizability of the extant research findings.

Ultimately, the current claim for the dynamic nature of intellectual styles must be further upheld by a coherent body of research evidence that overcomes the limitations in the present literature. The next and final chapter makes suggestions for research on the topic of this chapter and those in other chapters.

PART IV

CONCLUDING REMARKS

9

Evaluation, Future Directions, and Implications

When Grigorenko (2009) attempted to review the then-existing work on the genetic etiology of intellectual styles a few years ago, she had to venture into related areas of research such as ability, personality, and coping. Grigorenko's creative undertaking was largely motivated by the fact that

> the only set of heritability estimates readily available in the literature is that on Witkin's field dependence-independence (Witkin, Oltman, Raskin, & Karp, 1971) and Salkind's reflection-impulsivity (Salkind, 1979). The heritability estimates of the former were ~11% and for the latter they were negative (i.e., correlations for monozygotic twins were higher than that for dizygotic twins). However, these correlations were not different from 0. It appears that this study is the only published peer reviewed quantitative-genetic report of intellectual styles. (p. 243)

According to the data shown in Grigorenko's (2009) review, the heritability estimates of intellectual styles based on the limited research mentioned earlier are far lower than the possible degree of heritability of roughly 50 percent for both ability and personality. Would higher levels of heritability estimates have been obtained for intellectual styles if more studies had been conducted? The answer is, possibly yes, but not much higher. Much more research effort has gone into either directly or indirectly investigating the malleability of intellectual styles (as opposed to studying the heritability of styles), most likely because styles scientists believe that people's intellectual styles are largely formed after birth – as a result of being influenced by their environments.

The principal goal of this book is to demonstrate that intellectual styles are more dynamic than static. In Chapter 1, I considered the major works that allude to the issue of style malleability primarily through conceptual arguments, while in Chapters 3 through 8, I presented empirical evidence supporting the argument that styles are modifiable. In the present chapter, I summarize the major findings discussed thus far, systematically evaluate the existing research on style malleability, focusing on its major limitations and suggesting research programs that can overcome these limitations, and make recommendations for the development of intellectual styles in education and beyond.

What the Existing Literature Says

Over the years, my personal view on the issue of style malleability has always been that intellectual styles can be changed. This view is founded on my belief that human beings have the capacity for change, a belief that I have always held steadfastly, and one that was reinforced at the beginning of my graduate studies in the spring of 1989, when I read *Client-Centered Therapy* by Carl Rogers (1951), a major spokesman for humanistic psychology. Since then, my conviction that intellectual styles are modifiable has been borne out by ample empirical evidence.

As has been repeatedly noted in the preceding chapters, given the long history of the field of intellectual styles, research on style malleability has certainly been rather piecemeal. Regardless of its apparent lack of harmony, however, the existing literature on style malleability fundamentally supports the view that styles are much more dynamic than static. At the same time, a by-product of the literature has emerged; that is, as shown in four of the six chapters dealing with empirical work (Chapters 3, 4, 7, and 8), Type I intellectual styles are generally more valued than Type II styles.

It should be noted, however, that when discussing the malleability of intellectual styles, one must keep in mind the following critical points derived from the findings reviewed in this book. First, styles change in varying degrees; to say that styles are modifiable should not be equated with saying that styles constantly change. Instead, changes in styles often take the form of a slow process. In fact, styles may simultaneously change and become stable, then change again under necessary conditions. Second, although each of the chapters in this book has a different focus in examining the malleability of styles, different variables (e.g., gender, culture, academic discipline, and occupation) may interact among themselves and with other variables – individual, institutional, and social in nature – to serve as the catalyst for changes in intellectual styles. Finally, despite the fact that across the board, several individual studies failed to obtain statistically significant results, in each and every single case their findings proved to be inadequate to justify the position that styles cannot be changed.

Given the preceding observation, one can draw the conclusion with great confidence that styles are more dynamic than static. Such confidence arises from the fact that the conclusion is based on converging evidence. This evidence is said to be convergent for at least four reasons. First, it is composed essentially of consistent findings accumulated across several decades. Second, and related to the first reason, it principally reveals discernable trends of style development that make substantive sense. Third, it is grounded in research conducted among relatively diverse populations with regard to such factors as age, gender, culture, educational level, ethnicity, occupation, and socioeconomic status. Fourth and finally, the evidence has been obtained through investigations rooted in multiple theoretical foundations.

Notwithstanding the aforementioned achievements, the existing research on style malleability has considerable room for improvement. In the following, the limitations of the existing research are discussed and recommendations are made for future research.

Limitations and Research Agenda

In his book *Psychology's Ghosts: The Crisis in the Profession and the Way Back*, Jerome Kagan (2012) observed:

> Progress in all scientific domains is facilitated by a candid acknowledgment of fault lines as well as celebration of past victories. It was not until the end of the nineteenth century that some biologists had an initial understanding of why the mixing of female and male seed was followed, after a delay, with a newborn animal. Yet humans had been brooding on this puzzle for thousands of years. The formal discipline of psychology is less than 150 years old, suggesting that current accounts of most phenomena are bound to be crude or simply wrong. (p. xxiii)

While I certainly do not think that the research on style malleability is "simply wrong," I do regard it as largely crude. Limitations specific to each research theme were delineated in each of the relevant chapters in this book. In this concluding chapter, I point out several limitations recurrent throughout the chapters dealing with empirical work. At the same time, I offer possible ways to overcome these limitations in future investigations.

It can be concluded from the foregoing chapters that the limitations of the existing research on style malleability are: (1) the insufficient number of style models involved; (2) the narrow range of research populations covered; (3) the lack of methodological rigor; (4) the inadequate reporting of research findings; and (5) more generally, the limited scope of the existing research.

Insufficient Number of Style Models Involved
The first limitation common to all topics in the relevant preceding chapters is the small number of style models involved in the research. As has been pointed out repeatedly in this book, research on the majority of the topics reviewed

involved only a small number of the large array of existing style models. As such, the generalizability of the research findings is confined to those style models on which the empirical studies were based. Furthermore, although the converging evidence mentioned earlier should give us great confidence in asserting that people's intellectual styles do go through changes, considering the tremendous number of style models that have been proposed in the field of styles, the amount of research (leaving aside the quality of the research for the moment) is far from adequate. Future studies should adopt a much broader range of carefully selected style models and examine more systematically the findings to be generated. In this way, some of the perplexing questions, such as whether or not the style constructs situated within the outermost layer of Curry's (1983) "onion" model are more modifiable than those closer to the innermost layer – a question that was raised in Chapter 8 – may be addressed by evidence beyond that provided by Curry three decades ago when she initially proposed the model.

Narrow Range of Research Populations Covered
Another factor that has limited the generalizability of the extant research findings is the narrow range of research populations. In this respect, there are several points to be made. First, concerning the experimental work described in Chapter 7, although hundreds of intervention studies have been conducted to reduce the research participants' levels of impulsivity and to enhance their levels of reflectivity, they have involved almost exclusively special populations, clinical or nonclinical. Likewise, programs aimed at developing the deep learning approach have primarily been conducted among students studying in higher-education institutions. Could the effects of the styles training programs found among the researched populations be generalized to other populations? Only research conducted among the relevant populations will be able answer this question.

Second, in research on the role of culture in the development of intellectual styles, which was reviewed in Chapter 4, studies rooted in most style models are few, unlike some classic style models (e.g., Witkin's field dependence/independence and Kagan's reflectivity-impulsivity), which have been relatively more widely researched in cross-cultural settings. Not only have these classic models been investigated in different cultural contexts, but they also have been studied in socially, economically, or geographically underprivileged countries such as Guatemala, Sierra Leone, Nigeria, Zambia, and a good number of other countries. However, cross-cultural studies based on some of the more recent style models tend to be confined to a number of developing and/or developed countries. In the case of several models, studies have almost utterly been conducted in the country – without exception, a developed country – in which the particular style model or style measure originated. As such, the notion of styles has become a "luxury" concept that is known only to the privileged "minority." It is my view that a large-scale expansion of styles research in general, and that of research on style malleability more specifically, to include many more cultural groups, particularly disadvantaged groups of many kinds (socially, economically, geographically, or otherwise) would significantly enrich the styles literature.

The third point is that, vis-à-vis nonintervention longitudinal studies, the existing research evidence was predominantly obtained from just a few countries. Specifically, all but one of the individual studies related to Holland's model of career personality types were conducted in the United States, with the exception being the one in France. Studies based on Kolb's construct of learning styles were carried out solely in the United States and Canada, while studies of learning approaches were done in four European countries and Australia. Moreover, of the six studies based on four other models, five were undertaken in the United States and one in Canada. It is clear that the existing nonintervention longitudinal studies also tended to be limited to the particular country in which a particular style model and its associated style measures were established. Future studies should investigate the malleability of intellectual styles in a wider range of countries as this would provide more convincing evidence for the topic under investigation.

Finally, also in the case of nonintervention longitudinal studies, much of the research was carried out in higher-education institutions, apparently because the majority of the style inventories employed in the studies were targeted at university students. However, a good number of style inventories are suitable for studying student populations at other school levels and populations in nonacademic settings. One example of an inventory for school students is the *Learning Process Questionnaire* (Biggs, 1993), companion to the *Study Process Questionnaire* (Biggs, 1992), which is intended for university students (see Chapter 2). An example of an inventory that can be used to measure the thinking styles of a wide range of populations, in both academic and non-academic settings, is the *Thinking Styles Inventory – Revised II* (Sternberg, Wagner, & Zhang, 2007), based on Sternberg's (1997) theory of mental self-government. Data from diverse populations would facilitate a better understanding of the likely changes that occur to people's intellectual styles.

Lack of Methodological Rigor

A third limitation of the existing research on style malleability is its lack of methodological rigor. This weakness manifests itself in such aspects as

(1) research design – particularly the dearth of longitudinal investigations (with or without interventions), (2) the lack of adequate control for confounding variables that either moderate or mediate the variables of research interest, and (3) the measures used to evaluate research participants' styles and style changes. Furthermore, the longitudinal studies that were conducted had many weaknesses.

As has been repeatedly pointed out, the major weakness in the studies reviewed in Chapters 3, 4, 5, and 6 is that they were all cross-sectional. Although convincing cases have been made in all four bodies of literature for the modifiability of intellectual styles, empirical studies would contribute more to our understanding of the nature of the development of styles if they were well-controlled experimental and longitudinal studies, guided by sound theoretical frameworks. Therefore, future studies investigating the impact of gender, culture, academic discipline, and occupation (among other socialization variables) on styles should consider employing experimental and longitudinal designs.

Also, as has been repeatedly noted, many factors may interfere with investigations into if and how intellectual styles change. Such interfering variables must be taken into consideration in future research. In this regard, some of the factors/variables included in Figure 5.1, or their equivalents[1] in the case of research conducted among populations in nonacademic settings, are surely good candidates for consideration.

Like any other research on styles, research on style malleability must go beyond quantitative studies that rely predominantly on self-report measures. Empirical work that incorporates other research methods such as qualitative procedures and the use of behavioral measures would prove to be more informative to styles' practitioners and the general public, as well as to styles' researchers. Moreover, if and when self-report measures have to be used, researchers must ensure their cross-cultural suitability in addition to the reliability and validity of the measures. With respect to the cross-cultural appropriateness of self-report inventories, the primary concept that needs to be understood is that of equivalent usage. There exists a hierarchy of possible uses to which an inventory can be put, ranging from conceptual equivalence (the basic level) to metric/scalar equivalence (the advanced level). Each level of the hierarchy requires that a corresponding hierarchy of assumptions be demonstrated (Hui & Triandis, 1985; Watkins, 2001).

---

[1] For example, in nonacademic settings, factors such as organizational ethos, organizational goals, employees' levels of self-efficacy, employers' leadership style, and so forth should be taken into account.

Finally, to increase the rigor of the research methods used, future researchers must make an effort to overcome the limitations of the existing body of literature on longitudinal studies. Apart from taking into account the wide range of limiting factors that affect the outcomes of the longitudinal studies detailed in Chapters 7 and 8, future researchers must use appropriate procedures to prevent the attrition of research participants. On the whole, as with longitudinal studies in many other fields of inquiry, the sample sizes of the longitudinal studies – with or without interventions – reviewed in this book experienced severe attrition from the original samples to the actual study samples. Consider, for example, two studies reviewed in Chapter 8. In Clapp's (1993) study, the original sample size of 153 for the initial study was reduced to 69 for the follow-up study. Similarly, in Messer and Brodzinsky's (1981) study, the final study sample had decreased to 85 from the original sample size of 127. Attrition rates such as these are quite common in the literature.[2] With such high attrition rates, the final samples may not have accurately represented the original ones because the demographic details of the study samples might have been very different from those of the original ones. Had the attrition rates not been so high, how different would the results have been? The answer to such a question awaits future studies using more effective strategies to prevent high attrition rates. One strategy is to select the participants more carefully. Researchers should take every precaution to ensure that only those people who are highly likely to be available for the duration of the longitudinal studies are recruited at the initial data collection. Another strategy is for researchers to keep track of participants' geographical mobility and find ways of ensuring that their research participants remain motivated to continue to take part in their longitudinal investigations.

Inadequate Reporting of Research Findings
One striking weakness in the data reported in the publications reviewed in the six chapters dealing with empirical studies is that only a minority number of studies included effect sizes, and indeed, many other studies did not even provide adequate statistics for effect sizes to be calculated. It is clear that the results from almost all the existing studies are in favor of the argument that styles are modifiable. However, adequate reporting of effect sizes as part of solid research evidence would enable results from studies of style malleability not only to help the field of styles fortify its credibility but also to assist in translating statistical significance into practical values, thus

---

[2] The sample size(s) documented for each study, both in the text and the tables in Chapters 7 and 8, represent(s) the number of participants who provided longitudinal data.

instilling even greater confidence in practitioners, especially educators, who often work with students in the belief that education changes students' ways of thinking for positive development. Consequently, styles researchers are strongly encouraged to report effect sizes for the statistically significant data that they claim in all types of research on styles.

Limited Scope of the Existing Research
The final, but certainly not the least important, area for improvement in research on style malleability concerns the lack of particular types of investigations such as applied research, updated research in the case of several classic style constructs, authentic cross-cultural and interdisciplinary investigations, and studies that involve the examination of the human brain.

One of the major criticisms of styles work has been that there is a lack of evidence that styles make a difference in real contexts. This criticism is certainly ill-founded because there is abundant research evidence indicating that styles do matter – in academic settings, in the business world, and in many other domains of our life (e.g., Rayner & Cools, 2011; Zhang, Sternberg, & Rayner, 2012a). Nonetheless, it is likely that critics would be less inclined to criticize styles work if researchers could provide more solid evidence from applied research. Without a doubt, one important type of research evidence styles researchers need to provide concerns the sustainable effects of their styles training programs. Likewise, researchers need to demonstrate the parallel and generalization effects of styles training programs on various domains of human performance. To be able to do this, they must continue to be engaged in experimental and longitudinal investigations – investigations that avoid the weaknesses of the body of literature previously discussed in this book.

It is commonly acknowledged that all theories are subject to revision, very likely in order to take into account the intricate interaction among many factors, and research on style malleability is no exception. As has been noted several times in the previous chapters, some of the existing literature is quite dated. For example, as argued in Chapter 3, gender differences in the levels of FDI may have been a manifestation of gender-role socialization effects. However, in the contemporary era, females have been increasingly gaining the same opportunities as men in various domains of life. Is there any evidence that the gender gaps in intellectual styles have been decreasing? By the same token, in time, the nature of any academic discipline or of any occupation is subject to change. Would the findings of the research discussed in this book, especially the findings that were based on classic style models and obtained decades ago, such as some of those reviewed in Chapters 5 and 6, hold true today? Answers to these and many other questions that could be asked about any of the research topics dealt with in this book definitely require a tremendous amount of further investigation, particularly in view of advances in science and technology.

Time and again, Rayner and his colleagues (e.g., Rayner, 2011; Rayner & Peterson, 2009; Rayner, Zhang, & Sternberg, 2012) have called for collaborative research efforts among scholars across disciplines. Rayner et al. (2012) contended that a shared research agenda should be one that "facilitates a global aim for international and interdisciplinary cooperation in the study of theory and application in the styles research community" (p. 409). This proposed research agenda is especially timely for the study of style malleability. As it is at this moment, barely any study can be classified as one that is genuinely cross-cultural or interdisciplinary. However, as frequently noted throughout this book, the development of intellectual styles can be contingent on numerous factors. Without well-designed longitudinal experimental studies that are based on a number of theoretical perspectives rooted in various disciplines and that involve well-considered cross-cultural comparisons, the quality of research on style malleability will remain open to criticism.

Finally, an obvious gap in research on style malleability is the association between intellectual styles and the human brain. Of the many possible ways of advancing research on the development of intellectual styles, one would be to study the neurological aspect of intellectual styles to determine the interplay among intellectual styles, brain activities, and behaviors. Well-designed research projects that adopt physiological and information-processing approaches to investigating human behaviors, cognition, and perceptions may well enlighten us on the developmental processes of intellectual styles. However, in pursuing this research agenda, one has to be aware of and guard against the "Voodoo" science of brain imaging (Vul, Harris, Winkielam, & Pashler, 2009).[3] Whether or not the criticism and skepticism concerning the existing literature centered on the reliability and validity of applying brain imaging to social and cognitive sciences are legitimate, research on style malleability that involves the exploration of brain activation must be properly planned and executed, and research data must be correctly dealt with and reported with the highest level of integrity.

General Implications for Education and Beyond

Notwithstanding the limitations stated earlier in this chapter and elsewhere in this book, the literature reviewed throughout this book lends firm support to the position that intellectual styles can be changed. Moreover, this literature

---

[3] Vul et al. (2009) noticed that many research papers in social neuroscience that use brain imaging reported correlations between brain activity and social/emotional behaviors or thoughts that appeared too good to be true or even mathematically possible.

shows that Type I intellectual styles are generally more adaptive than Type II styles. These findings should put at ease the minds of those who are doubtful about the usefulness of intellectual styles in education and beyond. At the same time, the findings imply that there are ways in which people's intellectual styles can be nurtured. Implications of the research findings concerning the relationships between intellectual styles and four major socialization variables – gender, culture, academic discipline, and occupation – were elaborated in Chapters 3, 4, 5, and 6, respectively. On the basis of the fundamental message of this book that intellectual styles are modifiable, I briefly discuss in the following section a general strategy for developing intellectual styles. In addition, given that the findings reveal that Type I intellectual styles are typically more valued than Type II styles, I suggest, in the final section of this chapter, strategies for developing Type I intellectual styles for consideration in education and beyond.

Recognizing and Embracing the Diversity of Intellectual Styles

Whether fostering the development of intellectual styles of other people or developing our own, we can count on one general strategy: recognizing and embracing diverse intellectual styles. Because intellectual styles are largely the result of the interactions between people and their environments, recognizing and allowing for the diversity of intellectual styles attributable to all possible factors (gender, culture, academic discipline, occupation, geographical location, age, socioeconomic status, and so on) would be conducive to both accommodating people's existing styles and challenging people to expand their repertoire of styles. Zhang and Sternberg (2006) have argued that an understanding of the multiplicity of intellectual styles could benefit students' learning and development, teachers' attitudes and practices, and senior managers' approach in educational institutions at all levels. Likewise, Zhang and Sternberg have contended that an awareness of the existence of different intellectual styles could assist business organizations in various essential domains such as human resource management, teamwork, conflict resolution, as well as staff training and development programs. A detailed discussion of how an acceptance of diversity in the use of intellectual styles could positively influence each of the aforementioned aspects in education and business can be found in Zhang and Sternberg's (2006) title, *The Nature of Intellectual Styles*.

In the same publication, Zhang and Sternberg (2006) commented on the potential advantages of recognizing and embracing diverse intellectual styles in facing some of the challenges presented by the continuously globalizing world and in promoting some of the key social values that are considered desirable in many societies: autonomy, choice, democracy, pluralism, respect, and tolerance. These social values are important because they often represent positive forces for effective communication within and across social groups at all levels: family, school, community, organizational, and national. As Zhang and Sternberg (2006) put it, "For any social group to thrive, and indeed, even to survive, effective communication is paramount" (pp. 180–181). To communicate effectively, members of a society must be aware that different people have different intellectual styles, and they must respect other people's intellectual styles. Zhang and Sternberg (2006) provided examples of how these seemingly overly inflated, but in effect highly practical, functions of style awareness could take place. The point that needs to be made clear in the context of this book, however, is this: if recognizing and embracing the diversity of intellectual styles can facilitate effective communication, which, in turn, can lead to positive outcomes, all members of a society could and should make a positive contribution to the development of not only their own styles, but also those of people around them.

Fostering Type I Intellectual Styles

The present literature provides solid empirical evidence supporting the position that has long been held by many scholars in the field – that intellectual styles are changeable. In addition, the desirability of Type I intellectual styles has been shown in a wide range of cross-sectional studies, and there has been a sustained interest in developing Type I intellectual styles, as manifested in the research goals set in nearly all the longitudinal experimental studies. It therefore makes good sense in this closing section (and indeed, closing chapter) to suggest some strategies for fostering Type I intellectual styles.

Zhang and Sternberg (2006) proposed several concrete strategies for promoting Type I intellectual styles in both academic and business settings. These strategies call for strong leadership from both educators and business leaders in serving as role models for creative thinking, allowing mistakes, encouraging risk-taking behaviors, facilitating enrichment experiences, rewarding creative ideas and products, and upholding social values such as autonomy, choice, democracy, pluralism, respect, and tolerance. In particular, educators and business leaders should encourage creative thinking, which they often claim to value, but in reality quite often suppress. At the time of this writing, it has been more than half a dozen years since Zhang and Sternberg proposed the aforementioned strategies for nurturing creative thinking. I certainly hope that by now the strategies proposed then have been tried out by some people and proved to be effective.

In this book, in addition to earnestly endorsing the previously proposed strategies, I put forward some additional ones. These additional strategies are based on the conclusion that has been reached in this book: that people can modify their intellectual styles through receiving specific training and as a function of the experiences they gain, whether these experiences are stemming from their personal characteristics or facilitated by their environments. Taking a step further, I propose strategies based on well-established research evidence revealing that particular human attributes are strongly associated with creativity-generating intellectual styles. Specifically, in the remainder of this closing chapter, I introduce two main strategies for cultivating Type I intellectual styles: (1) styles training in real-life contexts and (2) nurturing styles on a daily basis.

Training for Type I Intellectual Styles in Real-life Contexts. As the reader may recall, hundreds of studies reported in 90 publications were discussed in Chapter 7. These studies, irrespective of their limitations, by providing empirical evidence that styles can be modified through training, should give educators and business leaders enough confidence to begin to think of ways to foster Type I intellectual styles in the classroom and in the workplace, respectively.

I firmly believe that conducting carefully designed experimental training programs in laboratory settings is not only possible but also necessary. However, such programs tend to be very costly in that they are labor-intensive and expensive. In addition to these disadvantages, experimental programs in laboratory settings tend to be remedial (as opposed to developmental) and are likely to be limited to benefiting only minority groups, that is, the so-called special populations (see Chapter 7). Nevertheless, these limitations can be overcome by educators' involvement in training students in the use of Type I intellectual styles in the classroom and by business leaders initiating training programs in work settings. These programs should target more general "research" populations, both academic and nonacademic, be more sustainable, and, in an educational context, allow for the integration of teaching and research. For example, supported by researchers, teachers could develop students' Type I intellectual styles by (1) designing and teaching innovative courses that take into account, as far as possible, individual differences in various domains of learning and development; (2) using diverse teaching methods; (3) encouraging reflective thinking and practice; and (4) initiating educational innovation that involves modifications in teaching methods, task requirements, and assessment processes. By the end of these long-term experiments, researchers could understand more about the nature of style malleability, and teachers could become more adept at promoting Type I intellectual styles among their students.

By the same token, with the support of researchers, business leaders could explore different ways to create work environments that are more conducive to the development of Type I intellectual styles. They could, for example, experiment with a new leadership style that allows for more autonomy, rewards creative ideas, and provides more opportunities for their employees to participate in decision making.

These proposed strategies for training individuals in the use of Type I intellectual styles in real-life contexts have led me to the idea that we should all cultivate Type I intellectual styles on a regular basis. In the following section, I make suggestions by first taking into account the general evidence-based argument that styles can be developed through socialization and then going beyond the literature reviewed in this book to consider the general finding that Type I intellectual styles are positively associated with a whole host of human attributes that are normally considered to be adaptive.

Nurturing Type I Intellectual Styles – Routinely. If one truly believes in the value of Type I intellectual styles in human learning and performance, one could find many ways to nurture them. It has been shown that gender, culture, academic discipline, and occupation are some of the strong candidates that could serve as agents of intellectual style change. Specific strategies, based on findings concerning the association between intellectual styles and the aforesaid socialization variables, have been elaborated in the corresponding chapters in this book and will not be recapitulated here. Instead, I would like to focus on two related critical concepts underlying all strategies for developing Type I intellectual styles, anchored in the relationships between intellectual styles and socialization variables: the concept of global cultural awareness and that of exposure.

One should be aware that people who are socialized in different cultures may exhibit significant differences in intellectual styles. In other words, one must have a global cultural awareness. It should be pointed out that the notion of "culture" within the context of "global cultural awareness" is used as a broad term in line with Hofstede's (1990) proposition that culture can be understood as "the collective programming of the mind that distinguishes the members of one category of people from another" (p. 4). That is to say, the meaning of "culture" here goes far beyond the traditional sense of cultural differences – beliefs and practices of different countries and regions or ethnic groups within countries. Rather, cultural groups can be those distinguished by any socialization variable. Therefore, within the realm of "global cultural awareness," the concept of culture can be pertinent to gender, national/regional/ethnic group, academic discipline, occupation, and so on; and thus, we have gender culture, national/regional/ethnic group culture, academic discipline culture, occupational/organizational culture, and so forth.

Global cultural awareness, however, is only the first of the two necessary conditions for promoting Type I intellectual styles on a routine basis. Global cultural awareness needs to be accompanied by a willingness to be exposed to different cultures. One should seek every opportunity to expose oneself to at least some elements of different cultures, be they gender, nation/ethnicity, academic discipline, occupation, age, religion, or social class. As an individual and as a scholar, I have always held the view that cognitive development is one of the most fundamental types of human growth. Throughout my academic career, my thinking on cognitive development has been heavily influenced by Piaget's (1952) exposition of how cognitive development takes place. According to Piaget and his followers (myself included), cognitive development occurs when an individual works through a state of cognitive dissonance that comes about only when the individual is exposed to new stimuli. In education and business settings alike, teachers and business leaders can use countless ways to create such stimuli – organizing debates over controversial issues, providing opportunities for role playing and perspective taking, and facilitating experiential learning, just to name a few. In fact, we should all be voluntarily seeking these opportunities for the development of our adaptive intellectual styles in our daily lives.

Finally, looking beyond the scope of the literature discussed in this book, I would like to draw this final chapter to a close by reminding the reader (and myself) that developing Type I intellectual styles is highly feasible, be it within ourselves or among others, by stimulating the growth of positive human attributes. It is well established that Type I intellectual styles are positively related to many positive human attributes, including cognitive development, career development, moral maturity, identity development, and the acquisition and strengthening of adaptive personality traits such as conscientiousness, openness, and tolerance of ambiguity. Type I styles are also associated with the development of critical thinking, metacognitive thinking, and emotional intelligence (see Zhang & Sternberg, 2006, 2009b). Conceivably, the development of these and other positive human attributes would set in motion changes in intellectual styles in a positive way. I shall not precisely specify how this could be accomplished as only the length of another book would do justice to such an undertaking.

Epilogue

Many have argued that intellectual styles cannot be changed, in the belief that styles are characteristically habits. However, the underlying assumption of this argument is completely flawed because it rests on the unproven premise that habits are intractable. Drawing on classical behaviorism and citing numerous examples from various domains of human life, Charles Duhigg (2012), in his book *The Power of Habit*, has convincingly made the case that even habits can be changed.

This book has demonstrated that an intellectual style is a learnable human attribute. Admittedly, there are limitations to the literature, such as the limited range and number of models involved in the studies. Likewise, because of space limitations in this book, I had to select studies grounded in particular models only. Also, owing to both the lack of space and an absence of qualitative data, my explanations concerning some of the research findings had to be sketchy and could not go beyond being speculative, particularly in the case of findings from the cross-sectional studies introduced in the four chapters dealing with the relationships of intellectual styles to four socialization variables: gender, culture, academic discipline, and occupation.

Nevertheless, these and other potential limitations are overshadowed by the fact that the case can successfully be made that intellectual styles are more dynamic than static. Such a convincing case, based on several bodies of empirical literature converging on the same conclusion (see Chapter 9), should provide a great incentive for researchers to continue to study the malleability of intellectual styles until it has been resolved. At the same time, the evidence presented throughout the book should give educators and business leaders sufficient confidence to apply the notion of intellectual styles to their work. Above all, the evidence-based conclusion drawn in this book – that styles are modifiable – should encourage all of us to do what we can to contribute to the development of adaptive intellectual styles within ourselves and among others.

I believe that by now I have made my position clear regarding the topic of this book – the issue of style malleability. I should therefore like to end this book by noting three caveats. First, changing an intellectual style is not always easy. Duhigg (2012) has cogently contended that changing a habit takes hard work, and it must start with a conscious decision to make a change, which can then become an automatic behavior. The same can be said about changing an intellectual style. Although intellectual styles change "automatically" as a function of socialization, if one wishes to develop intellectual styles, one needs not only self-awareness of one's existing styles but also the determination to acquire new styles, or to strengthen the styles that one is already using. The development of styles, like the development of many other attributes, may not always occur in a linear fashion. As a matter of fact, these changes quite often follow a curvilinear trajectory. Given this, one needs to be persistent in pursuing the intellectual styles that one wishes to master or strengthen.

Second, changes in intellectual styles, like many other changes in human behavior, most probably happen in a top-down rather than a bottom-up manner. Students cannot be expected to develop Type I intellectual styles if their teachers do not create a learning environment that is conducive to students' use of creativity-generating styles. In turn, teachers cannot design an environment for students to display creative thinking and behaviors unless they work in an academic environment that encourages them to demonstrate innovative thinking and behaviors. An academic environment is naturally affected by institutional policies made by senior managers. Again, a great deal of important institutional decision and policy making is deeply affected by what is going on outside the institution itself. That is to say, changes in individuals' intellectual styles, especially the development of Type I styles, are heavily reliant on support as well as challenges from their environments. Individuals are more prone to modifying their styles when they perceive that their changes in styles are rewarded.

The third caveat is that the information provided in this book is not sufficient by itself to enable us to understand the nature of style malleability in its entirety. There must be many aspects concerning the malleability of intellectual styles that cannot be revealed by the evidence and exposition that I have offered. Advances in science and technology, among others, have truly outpaced our capacity to appreciate fully the dynamic nature of intellectual styles. Regardless, human beings have the power to act creatively, proceeding from a little comprehension to a rich, well articulated, and highly sophisticated body of knowledge concerning the malleability of intellectual styles.

APPENDIX

Further Information on Inventories Based on the Style Constructs in Zhang and Sternberg's (2005) Threefold Model of Intellectual Styles

1. Embedded Figures Test

Samples of Simple Figures:

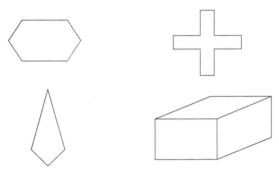

Samples of Complex Figures:

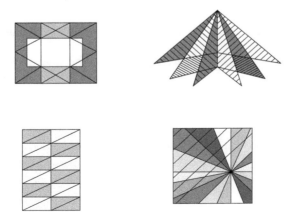

2. Assessment of Divergent-Convergent Thinking

Guilford's (1950) divergent-convergent thinking is usually assessed by a series of tests with open-ended questions. Some of these tests developed by Guilford and his colleagues are introduced as follows.

i) **Fluency Tests** (Christensen & Guilford, 1959).
   This test assesses four kinds of fluency.
   A) *Word Fluency* (divergent symbolic units)
      Anagrams represent one type of tests used to assess Word Fluency.
   B) *Expressional Fluency* (divergent semantic systems)

One type of tests used to assess expressional fluency is vocabulary completion tests. A stimulus word is used in a brief context – enough to indicate its meaning; and participants are asked to provide the word.

   C) *Associational Fluency* (divergent semantic relations)

One type of tests used to assess associational fluency is to ask participants to list as many words as he/she can that are similar in meaning to each given word.
   Sample item: "hard" (participants may respond with "tough," "difficult," "unyielding," and so forth)

   D) *Ideational Fluency* (divergent semantic units)

Participants are asked to list as many objects as they can that satisfy certain given specifications.
   Sample item: "All objects that are white and edible."

ii) **Consequences Test** (Christensen et al., 1958; Guilford & Guilford, 1980).

There are several forms of this test. *Form A-I* is the most commonly used. The test is composed of five items. Each item describes an unusual situation and provides four possible consequences of this situation as examples. Participants are asked to list as many different consequences of the situation as possible. Two minutes are allowed for each item. Each response/consequence participants provide can be classified as *unacceptable, obvious,* or *remote*. The total number of obvious responses is calculated as the score of CQ-O, while the total number of remote responses is calculated as the score of CQ-R. CQ-O is viewed as an indicator for *Ideational Fluency*, while CQ-R is seen as an indicator for *Originality*.

Sample item: "What would be the results if people no longer needed or wanted sleep?"

iii) **Alternate Uses Test** (Christensen et al., 1960; Wilson et al., 1960; Guilford et al., 1978).

This test has three forms with nine items (three items in each form). Each item includes the name of a common object and its ordinary use. Participants are asked to list as many other alternate uses of the object as they possibly can. Four minutes are allowed for each form. The total number of acceptable alternate uses is calculated as the score of *AU*. It is considered to assess *Spontaneous Flexibility* in Guilford's (1956) structure-of-intellect model. In some research, the number of unusual uses that participants provide is also recorded to indicate *Originality* (e.g., Hocevar, 1979).

Sample item: "newspaper"

iv) **Plot Titles Test** (Berger & Guilford, 1969).

Each part presents a short story that potentially has a large number of pertinent titles. Some publications (e.g., Piers et al., 1960) indicated that there are a total of four stories, whereas others (e.g., Hocevar, 1979) recorded that there are a total of two stories. Respondents are asked to list as many titles as they can conceive. All acceptable responses are classified as *clever* or *non-clever*. The number of non-clever responses is used to indicate *Ideational Fluency*, while the number of clever responses is used to indicate *Originality*.

Furthermore, the following table from Guilford's work (1956, p. 277) presents the factors and the relevant tests assessing them.

Production Factors – Divergent Thinking

Type of Result Produced	Type of Content		
	Figural	Structural	Conceptual
Words		*Word fluency*	*Associational fluency*
		Prefixes	Controlled
		Anagrams	Associations II
			Associations III
Ideas			*Ideational fluency*
			Plot Titles
			Consequences

(*continued*)

Production Factors – Divergent Thinking (*continued*)

Type of Result Produced	Type of Content		
	Figural	**Structural**	**Conceptual**
Expressions			*Expressional fluency* Vocabulary Completion Similes
Shifts	*Flexibility of closure* Hidden Pictures Gottschaldt A	*Adaptive flexibility* Match Problems Planning Air Maneuvers	*Spontaneous flexibility* Brick Uses Unusual Uses
Novel responses			*Originality* Plot Titles (cleverness) Symbol Production
Details	*Elaboration** Planning Elaboration Figure Production		*Elaboration** Planning Elaboration Figure Production

* At present regarded as the same factor, but future results may indicate two separate factors.

3. The Kirton Adaption-Innovation Inventory

The *Kirton Adaption-Innovation Inventory* comprises 33 items, with one being an un-scored warm-up item and 32 items contributing to three subscales: *Originality* (13 items), *Efficiency* (9 items), and *Rule/Group Conformity* (10 items). Participants are asked to respond on a 5-point scale (from "*very hard*" to "*very easy*") to indicate the level of ease (or difficulty) that each of the items can describe themselves over a long period of time.

Sample Items:

<u>Originality</u>: "Proliferates ideas"

<u>Efficiency</u>: "is thorough"

<u>Rule/Group Conformity</u>: "fits readily into 'the system'"

4. Matching Familiar Figures Test

Sample Item #1:

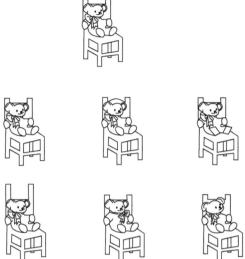

Sample Item #2:

5. Style of Learning and Thinking

Directions: Place a check mark in the blank if the statement is true of you. You may check one or both of the statements in a pair or neither – whatever fits you.

Sample Item #1

_____ I like to learn about things we are sure of.

_____ I like to learn about hidden possibilities.

Sample Item #2

_____ I like to take ideas apart and think about them separately.

_____ I like to put a lot of ideas together.

6. Meyers-Briggs Type Indicator

Part I. Which answer comes closer to telling how you usually feel or act?

Sample Item #1
When you go somewhere for the day, would you rather

(A) plan what you will do and when,
   or
(B) just go?

Sample Item #2
If you were a teacher, would you rather teach

(A) fact course,
   or
(B) courses involving theory?

Part II. Which word in each pair appeals to you more? Think what the words mean, not how they look or how they sound.

Sample Item #1
   (A) Scheduled   unplanned (B)

Sample Item #2
   (A) Firm-minded   warm-hearted (B)

Part III. Which answer comes closer to telling how you usually feel or act?

Sample Item #1
   Would you say you

   (A) get more enthusiastic about things than the average person, or
   (B) get less excited about things than the average person?

Sample Item #2
   When you start a big project that is due in a week, do you

   (A) take time to list the separate things to be done and the order of doing them, or
   (B) plunge in?

7. Self-Directed Search

Sample Items:
Activities: (indicate those activities one would like to do, and those things one would dislike doing or would be indifferent to)

   Fix electrical things (Realistic)
   Read scientific books or magazines (Investigative)
   Sketch, draw, or paint (Artistic)
   Work for a charity (Social)
   Learn strategies for business success (Enterprising)
   Take an accounting course (Conventional)

Competencies: (indicate those activities one can do well or competently, and those one has never performed or performed poorly)

   I can make simple electrical repairs (Realistic)
   I can perform a scientific experiment or survey (Investigative)
   I can play a musical instrument (Artistic)
   I find it easy to talk with all kinds of people (Social)
   I know how to be a successful leader (Enterprising)
   I can do a lot of paperwork in a short time (Conventional)

Occupations: (indicate the occupations one likes or dislikes)

   Airplane mechanic (Realistic)
   Biologist (Investigative)
   Poet (Artistic)
   Career counselor (Social)

Sales manager (Enterprising)
Bookkeeper (Conventional)

Self-Estimates: (Rate oneself on each of the traits as one really thinks when compared with other people one's own age. The respondents are required to rate on a 7-point scale)

Set #1

Mechanical ability (Realistic)
Scientific ability (Investigative)
Artistic ability (Artistic)
Teaching ability (Social)
Sales ability (Enterprising)
Clerical ability (Conventional)

Set #2

Manual skills (Realistic)
Math ability (Investigative)
Musical ability (Artistic)
Understanding of others (Social)
Managerial skills (Enterprising)
Office skills (Conventional)

8. The Gregorc Style Delineator

Sample Item #1:

Aesthetic (Abstract-Random)
Analytical: (Abstract-Sequential)
Experimenting (Concrete-Random)
Persistent (Concrete-Sequential)

Sample Item #2:

Colorful (Abstract-Random)
Research: (Abstract-Sequential)
Risk-taker (Concrete-Random)
Perfectionist (Concrete-Sequential)

9. The Study Process Questionnaire

Sample Items:
  I choose my courses largely with a view to the job situation when I graduate rather than because of how much they interest me. (Surface Motive)

I find that studying gives me a feeling of deep personal satisfaction. (Deep Motive)

I want top grades in most or all of my courses so that I will be able to select from among the best positions available when I graduate. (Achieving Motive)

I think browsing around is a waste of time, so I only study seriously what's given out in class or in the course outlines. (Surface Strategy)

While I am studying, I think of real-life situations to which the material that I am learning would be useful. (Deep Strategy)

I summarize suggested readings and include these as part of my notes on a topic. (Achieving Strategy)

10. Thinking Styles Inventory – Revised II

Sample Items:

When faced with a problem, I use my own ideas and strategies to solve it. (Legislative)

I like to figure out how to solve a problem following certain rules. (Executive)

I like situations where I can compare and rate different ways of doing things. (Judicial)

I like to set priorities for the things I need to do before I start doing them. (Hierarchical)

When talking or writing about ideas, I prefer to focus on one idea at a time. (Monarchic)

When there are several important things to do, I do those most important to me and to my colleagues. (Oligarchic)

I find that when I am engaged in one problem, another comes along that is just as important. (Anarchic)

I care more about the general effect than about the details of a task I have to do. (Global)

I prefer to deal with problems that require me to attend to a lot of details. (Local)

I like to challenge old ideas or ways of doing things and to seek better ones. (Liberal)

I stick to standard rules or ways of doing things. (Conservative)

I like to control all phases of a project, without having to consult with others. (Internal)

When starting a task, I like to brainstorm ideas with friends or peers. (External)

11. Room-Adjustment Test and Body-Adjustment Test

The *Room-Adjustment Test* (Witkin, Dyk, Faterson, Goodenough, & Karp, 1962) and the *Body-Adjustment Test* (Witkin, Lewis, Hertzman, Machover, Meissner, & Wapner, 1954) are two parts of the tilting-room-tilting-chair tests (TRTC). The main equipment for these tests includes a 70 × 71 × 69-inch box-like room that is suspended on ball-bearing pivots so that it can be tilted by any amount to left or right. Inside the room is a chair for the test respondent. The chair can also be tilted to left or right independently of the box-like room. The equipment is shown below:

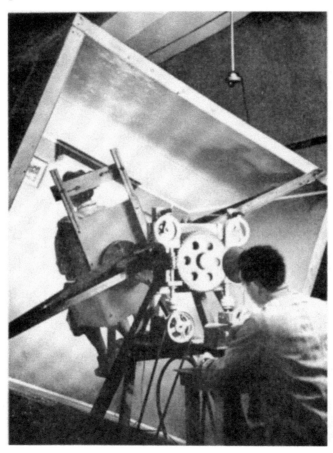

The *Room-Adjustment Test* (RAT) comprises eight trials. In four of the eight trials (i.e., Series la), the room and the chair are initially tilted to opposite sides, while in the remaining four (i.e., Series lb), the room and the chair are tilted to the same side. In the beginning, the room is always tilted 56 degrees and the chair 22 degrees. On each trial, while his/her chair remains in its initial position of tilt, the test respondent instructs the test administrator to move the room to a position in which he/she perceives it as upright.

The *Body-Adjustment Test* (BAT) contains six trials. In half of the trials (i.e., Series 2a), the box-like room and the chair are initially tilted to the same side, while in the other half (Series 2b), the room and the chair are tilted to opposite sides. The initial tilt of the room is 35 degrees and that of the chair is 22 degrees. On each trial, with the room remaining tilted, the test respondent directs the test administrator to move the chair to a position in which he/she views it to be upright.

The raw score for each of the four series of trials (i.e., Series 1a, Series 1b, Series 2a, and Series 2b) is represented by the mean absolute error in degrees from the true upright for the trials in the relevant series. The score for each series is converted to a standard score, using the mean and standard deviation of the test respondent's age and gender groups. The total RAT index is the mean of the standard scores for Series la and lb, while the mean of the standard scores for Series 2a and 2b is that for the BAT. For both tests, a positive index indicates a higher level of field dependence, while a negative index suggests a higher level of field independence.

References

Abdolmohammadi, M. J., Read, W. J., & Scarbrough, D. P. (2003). Does selection-socialization help to explain accounts' weak ethical reasoning? *Journal of Business Ethics, 42*, 71–81.
Abikoff, H. (1979). Cognitive training interventions in children: Review of a new approach. *Journal of Learning Disabilities, 12* (2), 65–77.
Adejumo, D. (1979). Conceptual tempo and visual perceptual ability of some Nigerian children. *Psychological Reports, 45*, 911–916.
Adler, N. J. (2001). *International dimensions of organizational behavior* (4th ed.). Cincinnati, OH: South-Western College Publishing.
Albaili, M. A. (1993). Inferred hemispheric thinking style, gender, and academic major among United Arab Emirates college students. *Perceptual and Motor Skills, 76* (3), 971–977.
Albaili, M. A. (1995). An Arabic version of the Study Process Questionnaire: Reliability and validity. *Psychological Reports, 77* (3), 1083–1089.
Albaili, M. A. (1996). Inferred hemispheric style and problem-solving performance. *Perceptual and Motor Skills, 83*, 427–434.
Albaili, M. A. (1997). Differences among low-, average-, and high-achieving college students on learning and study strategies. *Educational Psychology, 17* (1 & 2), 171–177.
Allinson, C. W., & Hayes, J. (1988). The Learning Styles Questionnaire: An alternative to Kolb's inventory. *Journal of Management Studies, 25* (3), 269–281.
Allport, G. W. (1937). *Structure et dévelopment de la personnalité*. Neuchâtel: Delachaux-Niestlé.
American Association of University Women Education Foundation (1992). *How schools shortchange girls*. Washington, DC.
American Association of University Women Education Foundation (2002). How girls negotiate school. In *The Jossey-Bass reader on gender in education* (pp. 243–276). San Francisco: Jossey-Bass.
Anastasi, A. (1988). *Psychological testing*. New York: Macmillan.
Angrist, S. S. (1969). The study of sex roles. *Journal of Social Issues, 25*, 215–232.
Armstrong, S. J. (1999a). *Cognitive style and dyadic interaction: A study of supervisors and subordinates engaged in working relationships*. Unpublished PhD thesis, University of Leeds, United Kingdom.

Armstrong, S. J. (1999b). The influence of individual cognitive style on performance in management education. *Educational Psychology, 20* (3), 323–339.

Armstrong, S. J., & Cools, E. (2009). Cognitive styles and their relevance for business and management: A review of development over the past two decades. In L. F. Zhang & R. J. Sternberg (Eds.), *Perspectives on the nature of intellectual styles* (pp. 253–290). New York: Springer Publishing Company.

Armstrong, S. J., van der Heijden, B. I. J. M., & Sadler-Smith, E. (2012). Intellectual styles, management of careers, and improved work performance. In L. F. Zhang, R. J. Sternberg, & S. Rayner (Eds.), *Handbook of intellectual styles: Preferences in cognition, learning, and thinking* (pp. 273–294). New York: Springer Publishing Company.

Ausburn, F. B., & Ausburn, L. J. (1983). Visual analysis skills among two populations in Papua New Guinea. *International Review, 31* (2), 112–122.

Baeten, M., Dochy, F., & Struyven, K. (2008). Students' approaches to learning and assessment preferences in a portfolio-based learning environment. *Instructional Science, 36,* 359–374.

Bagley, C., & Mallick, K. (1998). Field independence, cultural context and academic achievement: A commentary. *British Journal of Educational Psychology, 68,* 581–587.

Balkis, M., & Isiker, G. B. (2005). The relationship between thinking styles and personality types. *Social Behavior and Personality, 33* (3), 283–294.

Bandura, A. (1986). *Social foundations of thought and action: A social cognitive theory.* Englewood Cliffs, NJ: Prentice Hall.

Barker, R. G. (1968). *Ecological psychology: Concepts and methods for studying the environment of human behavior.* Stanford, CA: Stanford University Press.

Barrett, G. V., & Thornton, C. L. (1967). Cognitive style differences between engineers and college students. *Perceptual and Motor Skills, 25,* 789–793.

Barrett, G. V., & Trippe, H. R. (1975). Field dependence and physical ability. *Perceptual and Motor Skills, 41,* 216–218.

Barrickman, L. L., Perry, P. J., Allen, A. J., Kuperman, S., Arndt, S. V., Herrmann, K. J., & Schumacher, E. (1995). Bupropion versus methylphenidate in the treatment of attention-deficit hyperactivity disorder. *Journal of the American Academy of Child and Adolescent Psychiatry, 34* (5), 649–657.

Barris, R., Kielhofner, G., & Bauer, D. (1985). Learning preferences, values and satisfaction. *Journal of Allied Health, 14,* 13–20.

Basadur, M., Graen, G. B., & Green, S. G. (1982). Training in creative problem solving: Effects on ideation and problem finding and solving in an industrial research organization. *Organizational Behavior and Human Performance, 30,* 41–70.

Basadur, M., Graen, G. B., & Scandura, T. A. (1986). Training effects on attitudes toward divergent thinking among manufacturing engineers. *Journal of Applied Psychology, 71* (4), 612–617.

Basadur, M., Pringle, P., & Kirkland, D. (2002). Crossing cultures: Training effects on the divergent thinking attitudes of Spanish-speaking South American managers. *Creativity Research Journal, 14* (3 & 4), 395–408.

Basadur, M., Wakabayashi, M., & Graen, G. B. (1990). Individual problem-solving styles and attitudes toward divergent thinking before and after training. *Creativity Research Journal, 3* (1), 22–32.

Batesky, J. A., Malacos, J. A., & Purcell, K. M. (1980). Comparison of personality characteristics of physical education and recreation majors, and factors which affect career choice. *Perceptual and Motor Skills, 51* (3), 1291–1298.

Becher, T. (1994). The significance of disciplinary differences. *Studies in Higher Education*, *19*, 151–161.
Becker, L. D., Bender, N. N., & Morrison, G. (1978). Measuring impulsivity-reflection: A critical review. *Journal of Learning Disabilities*, *11* (10), 626–632.
Bell, C. R., Mundy, P., Quay, H. C. (1983). Modifying impulsive responding in conduct-disordered institutionalized boys. *Psychological Reports*, *52*, 307–310.
Bem, S. (1974). The measurement of psychological androgyny. *Journal of Consulting and Clinical Psychology*, *42*, 155–162.
Bem, S. (1981). *Bem sex-role inventory: Sampler set*. Palo Alto, CA: Mind Garden.
Bem, S., & Lenney, E. (1976). Sex typing and the avoidance of cross-sex behavior. *Journal of Personality and Social Psychology*, *33*, 48–54.
Bender, N. N. (1976). Self-verbalization versus tutor verbalization in modifying impulsivity. *Journal of Educational Psychology*, *68* (3), 347–354.
Bennett, C. I. (2002). *Comprehensive multicultural education: Theory and practice* (5th ed.). Boston: Allyn and Bacon.
Berger, R. M., & Guilford, J. P. (1969). *Plot titles*. Beverly Hills, CA: Sheridan Psychological Services.
Bernardi, R. A. (1993). Group Embedded Figures Test: Psychometric data documenting shifts from prior norms in field independence of accountants. *Perceptual and Motor Skills*, *77*, 579–586.
Bernardo, A. B., Zhang, L. F., & Callueng, C.M. (2002). Thinking styles and academic achievement among Filipino students. *Journal of Genetic Psychology*, *163* (2), 149–163.
Bernstein, B. (1965). A socio-linguistic approach to social learning. In J. Gould (Ed.), *Penguin survey of the social sciences* (pp. 144–168). Harmondsworth: Penguin.
Berry, J. W. (1966). Temne and Eskimo perceptual skills. *International Journal of Psychology*, *1*, 207–229.
Berry, J. W. (1991). Cultural variations in field dependence-independence. In S. Wapner & J. Demick (Eds.), *Field dependence-independence* (pp. 289–307). Hillside, NJ: Lawrence Erlbaum.
Betz, N. E. (1992). Career assessment: A review of critical issues. In N. E. Betz, S. D. Brown, & R. W. Lent (Eds.), *Handbook of counseling psychology* (2nd Ed.) (pp. 453–484). Oxford: John Wiley & Sons.
Biberman, G., & Buchanan, J. (1986). Learning style and study skills differences across business and other academic majors. *Journal of Education for Business*, *65*, 303–307.
Bickham, P. J., Miller, M. J., O'Neal, H., & Clanton, R. (1998). Comparison of error rates on the 1990 and 1994 revised self-directed search. *Perceptual and Motor Skills*, *86* (3, Pt 2), 1168–1170.
Biggs, J. B. (1978). Individual and group differences in study processes. *British Journal of Educational Psychology*, *48*, 266–279.
Biggs, J. B. (1979). Individual differences in study processes and the quality of learning outcomes. *Higher Education*, *8*, 381–394.
Biggs, J. B. (1987). *Student approaches to learning and studying*. Hawthorn: Australian Council for Educational Research.
Biggs, J. B. (1992). *Why and how do Hong Kong students learn? Using the Learning and Study Process Questionnaires*, Education Paper No. 14, Faculty of Education, The University of Hong Kong.
Biggs, J. B. (1993). What do inventories of students' learning process really measure? A theoretical review and clarification. *British Journal of Educational Psychology*, *63*, 3–19.

Biggs, J. B. (1996). Western misconceptions of the Confucian-heritage culture. In D. Watkins & J. Biggs (Eds.), *The Chinese learner: Cultural, psychological and contextual influences* (pp. 45–67). Hong Kong / Melbourne: Comparative Education Research Center / Australian Council for Educational Research.

Biggs, J. B. (2010). Teaching according to how students learn. In L. F. Zhang, J. B. Biggs, & D. Watkins (Eds.), *Learning and development of Asian students: What the 21st century teacher needs to think about* (pp. 245–273). Jurong, Singapore: Pearson Prentice Hall.

Biggs, J. B., & Collis, K. F. (1982). *Evaluating the quality of learning: The SOLO Taxonomy*. New York: Academic Press.

Biggs, J. B., Kember, D., & Leung, D. Y. P. (2001). The revised two-factor Study Process Questionnaire: R-SPQ-2F. *British Journal of Educational Psychology, 71*, 133–149.

Bishop, C., & Foster, C. (2011). Thinking styles: Maximizing online supported learning. *Journal of Educational Computing Research, 44* (2), 121–139.

Bock, R. D., & Kolakowski, D. (1973). Further evidence of sex-linked major-gene influence on human spatial visualizing ability. *American Journal of Human Genetics, 25*, 1–14.

Bold, C. (2008). Peer support groups: Fostering a deeper approach to learning through critical reflection on practice. *Reflective Practice, 9* (3), 257–267.

Booth, P., Luckett, P., & Mladenovic, R. (1999). The quality of learning in accounting education: The impact of approaches to learning on academic performance. *Accounting Education, 8* (4), 77–300.

Borchers, B. J. (2007). Workplace environment fit, commitment, job satisfaction in a nonprofit association. *Dissertation Abstracts International (Section B): Sciences and Engineering, 67*, 4139.

Boreham, B. W., & Watts, J. D. (1998). Personality type in undergraduate education and physics students. *Journal of Psychological Type, 44*, 26–31.

Boyd, R., & Brown, T. (2005). Pilot study of Myers Briggs Type Indicator: Personality profiling in emergency department senior medical staff. *Emergency Medicine Australasia, 17*, 200–203.

Bradley, D., & Bradley, M. (1984). *Problems of Asian students in Australia: Language, culture and education*. Canberra: AGPS.

Brand, M. (2001). Chinese and American music majors: Cross-cultural comparisons in motivation and strategies for learning and studying. *Psychology of Music, 29*, 170–178.

Brislin, R. W., Bochner, S., & Lonner, W. J. (Eds.) (1975). *Cross-cultural perspectives on learning*. New York: Sage Publications.

Broad, M., Matthews, M., & McDonald, A. (2004). Accounting education through an online-supported virtual learning environment. *Active Learning in Higher Education, 5* (2), 135–151.

Brodzinsky, D. M. (1982). Relationship between cognitive style and cognitive development: A 2-year longitudinal study. *Developmental Psychology, 18* (4), 617–626.

Broer, E., & McCarley, N. G. (1999). Using and validating the Myers-Briggs Type Indicator in mainland China. *Journal of Psychological Type, 51*, 5–21.

Broverman, D. M., Klaiber, E. L., Kobayashi, Y., & Vogel, W. (1968). Roles of activation and inhibition in sex differences in cognitive abilities. *Psychological Review, 75*, 23–50.

Brown, C. M., Meyers, A. W., & Cohen, R. (1984). Self-instruction training with preschoolers: Generalization to proximal and distal problem-solving tasks. *Cognitive Therapy and Research, 8* (4), 427–438.

Brown, H. D., & Burke, H. D. (1987). Accounting education: a learning-styles study of professional-technical and future adaptation issues. *Journal of Accounting Education*, 5, 187–206.

Brown, R. T., Wynne, M. E., Borden, K. A., Clingerman, S. R., Geniesse, R., & Spunt, A. (1986). Methylphenidate and cognitive therapy in children with attention deficit disorder: A double-blind trial. *Journal of Developmental and Behavioral Pediatrics*, 7 (3), 163–170.

Buela-Casal, G., Carretero-Dios, H., De-los-Santos-Roig, M., & Bermudez, M. P. (2003). Psychometric properties of a Spanish adaptation of the Matching Familiar Figures Test (MFFT-20). *European Journal of Psychological Assessment*, 19 (2), 151–159.

Buie, E. A. (1988). Psychological type and job satisfaction in scientific computer professionals. *Journal of Psychological Type*, 15, 50–53.

Buriel, R. (1975). Cognitive styles among three generations of Mexican American children. *Journal of Cross-Cultural Psychology*, 6, 417–429.

Buriel, R. (1978). Relationship of three field-dependence measures to the reading and math achievement of Anglo American and Mexican American children. *Journal of Educational Psychology*, 70 (2), 167–174.

Burnett, P. C., & Proctor, R. M. (2002). Elementary school students' learner self-concept, academic self-concepts and approaches to learning. *Educational Psychology in Practice*, 18 (4), 325–333.

Burstein, B., Bank, L., & Jarvik, L. F. (1980). Sex differences in cognitive functioning: Evidence, determinants, implications. *Human Development*, 23, 289–313.

Burstyn, J. N. (1980). *Victorian education and the ideal of womanhood*. London: Groom Helm.

Burton, L. (1996). A socially just pedagogy for the teaching of mathematics. In P. F. Murphy & C. V. Gipps (Eds.) *Equity in the classroom: towards effective pedagogy for girls and boys* (pp. 136–145). London: Falmer Press.

Busato, V. V., Prins, F. J., Elshout, J. J., & Hamaker, C. (1998). Learning styles: A cross-sectional and longitudinal study in higher education. *British Journal of Educational Psychology*, 68, 427–441.

Busch, J. C., Watson, J. A., Brinkley, V., Howard, J., & Nelson, C. (1993). Preschool Embedded Figures Test performance of young children: Age and gender differences. *Perceptual and Motor Skills*, 77, 491–496.

Bush, C. M., Schkade, L. L. (1985). In search of the perfect programmer. *Datamation*, 31 (6), 128–132.

Bussey, K., & Bandura, A. (1999). Social cognitive theory of gender development and differentiation. *Psychological Review*, 106 (4), 676–713.

Cahill, D. J. (2007). Real estate agents and the MBTI: A research note. *Journal of Psychological Type*, 67, 85–88.

Cairns, E. (1977). The reliability of the Matching Familiar Figures Test. *British Journal of Educational Psychology*, 47 (2), 197–198.

Cairns, E., & Cammock, T. (1978). Development of a more reliable version of the Matching Familiar Figures Test. *Developmental Psychology*, 14 (5), 555–560.

Cakan, M. (2003). Psychometric data on the Group Embedded Figures Test for Turkish undergraduate students. *Perceptual and Motor Skills*, 96 (3), 993–1004.

Campbell, D. P., Borgen, F. H., Eastes, S. H., Johansson, C. B., & Peterson, R. A. (1968). A set of basic interest scales for the Strong Vocational Interest Blank for men. *Journal of Applied Psychology Monograph*, 52 (6), 1–54.

Canino, C., & Cicchelli, T. (1988). Cognitive styles, computerized treatments on mathematics achievement and reaction to treatments. *Journal of Educational Computing Research, 4*, 253–264.

Caño, J. E., & Márquez, S. (1995). Field dependence-independence of male and female Spanish athletes. *Perceptual and Motor Skills, 80*, 1155–1161.

Cano-Garcia, F., & Hughes, E. H. (2000). Learning and thinking styles: An analysis of their relationship and influence on academic achievement. *Educational Psychology, 20* (4), 413–430.

Capretz, L. F. (2003). Personality types in software engineering. *International Journal of Human-Computer Studies, 58*, 207–214.

Carlson, R. (1963). Parental identification and personality structure in preadolecents. *Journal of Abnormal and Social Psychology, 67*, 566–573.

Carlson, R. (1965). Stability and change in the adolescent's self image. *Child Development, 36*, 659–666.

Carlson, R., & Levy, N. (1968). Brief method for assessing social-personal orientation. *Psychological Reports, 23*, 911–914.

Case, J. C., & Blackwell, T. L. (2008). Review of strong interest inventory, revised edition. *Rehabilitation Counseling Bulletin, 51* (2), 122–126.

Caspi, A., Roberts, B. W., & Shiner, R. L. (2005). Personality development: stability and change. *The Annual Review of Psychology, 56*, 453–484.

Cattell, R. B. (1973). *Personality and mood by questionnaire.* San Francisco: Jossey-Bass Publishers.

Chan, D., Leung, R., Gow, L., & Hu, S. (1989). Approaches to learning of accountancy students: Some additional evidence. In *Proceedings of the ASAIHL Seminar on University Education in the 1990s,* December 4–7, Kuala Lumpur, pp. 186–193. Bangi, Singapore: Penerbit Universiti Kebangsaan.

Chen, G. H., & Zhang, L. F. (2010). Mental health and thinking styles in Sternberg's theory: An exploratory study. *Psychological Reports, 103* (3), 784–794.

Chess, S. B., Neuringer, C., & Goldstein, G. (1971). Arousal and field dependency in alcoholics. *Journal of Gen. Psychology, 85*, 93–102.

Christensen, P. E., & Guilford, J. P. (1959). *Manual for the Christensen-Guilford fluency tests* (2nd ed.). Beverly Hills, CA: Sheridan Supply.

Christensen, P. E., Guilford, J. P., Merrifield, P. R., & Wilson, R. C. (1960). *Alternate uses. Manual of administration, scoring, and interpretation.* Beverly Hills, CA: Sheridan Supply.

Christensen, P. E., Merrifield, P. R., & Guilford, J. P. (1958). *Consequences. Manual for administration, scoring and interpretation* (2nd Ed.). Beverly Hills, CA: Sheridan Supply.

Christopher, K. D. (2005). Internal validity and reliability of Kolb's learning style inventory version 3 (1999). *Journal of Business and Psychology, 20* (2), 249–257.

Clack, G. B., Allen, J., Cooper, D., & Head, J. O. (2004). Personality differences between doctors and their patients: Implications for the teaching of communication skills. *Medical Education, 38* (2), 177–186.

Clapp, R. G. (1993). Stability of cognitive style in adults and some implications: A longitudinal study of the Kirton Adaption-Innovation Inventory. *Psychological Reports, 73*, 1235–1245.

Clapp, R. G., & De Ciantis, S. M. (1989). Adaptors and innovators in large organizations: Does cognitive style characterize actual behavior of employees at work? An exploratory study. *Psychological Reports, 65* (2), 503–513.
Clark, T. (2003). Review of the book *Culture's consequences: Comparing values, behaviors, institutions and organizations across nations* (2nd ed.). *Journal of Marketing, 67* (2), 151–153.
Clarke, R. M. (1986). Students' approaches to learning in an innovative medical school: A cross-sectional study. *British Journal of Educational Psychology, 56,* 309–321.
Coan, R. (1974). *The optimal personality: An empirical and theoretical analysis.* New York: Columbia University Press.
Coates, S. W. (1972). *Manual for the Preschool Embedded Figures Test.* Palo Alto, CA: Consulting Psychologists Press.
Coffield, F. C., Moseley, D. V. M., Hall, E., & Ecclestone, K. (2004). *Learning styles and pedagogy in post-16 learning: Findings of a systematic and critical review of learning styles models.* London: Learning and Skills Research Center.
Cohen, J. (1988). *Statistical power analysis for the behavioral sciences.* San Diego, CA: Academic Press.
Cohen, R. A. (1967). Primary group structure, conceptual styles and school achievement. Unpublished doctoral dissertation. University of Pittsburg.
Cohen, R., Schleser, R., & Meyers, A. (1981). Self-instructions: Effects of cognitive level and active rehearsal. *Journal of Experimental Child Psychology, 32,* 65–76.
Cohen, S., & Przybycien, C. A. (1974). Some effects of sociometrically selected peer models on the cognitive styles of impulsive children. *Journal of Genetic Psychology, 124,* 213–220.
Cole, P. M., & Hartley, D. G. (1978). The effects of reinforcement and strategy training on impulsive responding. *Child Development, 49,* 381–384.
Collings, J. N. (1985). Scientific thinking through the development of formal operations: Training in the cognitive restructuring aspect of field-independence. *Research in Science & Technological Education, 3* (2), 145–152.
Collins, A. R., White, B. J., & O'Brien, T. P. (1992). The relationship of cognitive style and selected characteristics of vocational education teachers. *College Student Journal, 26* (2), 167–173.
Collins, J. H., & Milliron, V. C. (1987). A measure of professional accountants' learning style. *Issues in Accounting Education, 2,* 193–206.
Connor, J. M., Schackman, M., & Serbin, L. A. (1978). Sex-related differences in response to practice on a visual-spatial test and generalization to a related test. *Child Development, 49,* 24–29.
Connor, J. M., Serbin, L. A., Schackman, M. (1977). Sex differences in children's response to training on a visual-spatial test. *Developmental Psychology, 13* (3), 293–294.
Cools, E. (2012). Understanding styles in organizational behaviors: A summary of insights and implications. In L. F. Zhang, R. J. Sternberg, & S. Rayner (Eds.), *Handbook of intellectual styles: Preferences in cognition, learning, and thinking* (pp. 329–351). New York: Springer Publishing Company.
Crandall, V., Katkovsky, W., & Preston, A. (1962). Motivational and ability determinants of young children's intellectual achievement behaviors. *Child Development, 33,* 643–661.

Cronbach, L. J. (1951). Coefficient alpha and the internal structure of tests. *Psychometrika, 16*, 297–334.
Cronbach, L. J. (1957). The two disciplines of scientific psychology. *American Psychologist, 12*, 671–684.
Cross, T. L., Neumeister, K. L. S., & Cassady, J. C. (2007). Psychological types of academically gifted adolescents. *Gifted Child Quarterly, 51* (3), 285–294.
Curry, L. (1983). An organization of learning styles theory and constructs. *ERIC Document, 235*, 185.
Curry, L. (1987). *Integrating concepts of cognitive or learning style: A review with attention to psychometric standards*. Ottawa: Canadian College of Health Service Executives.
Darcy, M. U. A., & Tracey, T. J. G. (2007). Circumplex structure of Holland's RIASEC interests across gender and time. *Journal of Counseling Psychology, 54* (1), 17–31.
Dart, B., Burnett, P., Boulton-Lewis, G., Campbell, J., Smith, D., & McCrindle, A. (1999). Classroom learning environments and students' approaches to learning. *Learning Environments Research, 2*, 137–156.
Daub, C., Friedman, S. M., Cresci, K., & Keyser, R. (2000). Frequencies of MBTI types among nursing assistants providing care to nursing home eligible individuals. *Journal of Psychological Type, 54*, 12–16.
Dawson, J. L. (1966). Kwashiorkor, gynaecomastia, and feminization processes. *Journal of Tropical Medicine and Hygiene, 69*, 175–179.
Dawson, J. L. (1967). Cultural and physiological influences upon spatial-perceptual processes in West Africa: I. *International Journal of Psychology, 2*, 115–128.
Dawson, J. L. M. (1972). Effects of sex hormones on cognitive style in rats and men. *Behavior Genetics, 2*, 21–42.
De Fruyt, F., & Mervielde, I. (1996). Personality and interests as predictors of educational streaming and achievement. *European Journal of Personality, 10* (5), 405–425.
Debus, R. L. (1970). Effects of brief observation of model behavior on conceptual tempo of impulsive children. *Developmental Psychology, 2*, 22–32.
Delbridge-Parker, L., & Robinson, D. (1989). Type and academically gifted adolescents. *Journal of Psychological Type, 17*, 66–72.
Dember, W. N. (1964). *Visual perception: The nineteenth century*. New York: Wiley.
Denney, N. W. (1981–1982). Attempts to modify cognitive tempo in elderly adults. *International Journal of Aging and Human Development, 14* (4), 239–254.
Dershowitz, A. (1971). Jewish subcultural patterns and psychological differentiation. *International Journal of Psychology, 6* (3), 223–231.
DeRussy, F. A., & Futch, E. (1971). Field-dependence/independence as related to college curricula. *Perceptual and Motor Skills, 33*, 1235–1237.
DeSanctis, G., & Dunikoski, R. (1983). Group Embedded Figures Test: Psychometric data for a sample of business students. *Perceptual and Motor Skills, 56*, 707–710.
Dillbeck, M. C., Assimakis, P. D., Raimondi, D., Orme-Johnson, D. W., & Rowe, R. (1986). Longitudinal effects of the transcendental meditation and TM-Sidhi program on cognitive ability and cognitive style. *Perceptual and Motor Skills, 62*, 731–738.
Donche, V., Coertijens, L., & Van Petegem, P. (2010). Learning pattern development throughout higher education: A longitudinal study. *Learning and Individual Differences, 20*, 256–259.
Donche, V., & Van Petegem, P. (2009). The development of learning patterns of student teachers: A cross-sectional and longitudinal study. *Higher Education, 57*, 463–475.

Doyle Conner, P., Kinicki, A. J., & Keats, B. W. (1994). Integrating organizational and individual information processing perspectives on choice. *Organizational Science, 5* (3), 294–308.

Drysdale, M. T. B., Ross, J. L., Schulz, R. A. (2001). Cognitive learning styles and academic performance in 19 first-year university courses: Successful students versus students at risk. *Journal of Education for Students Placed at Risk, 6* (3), 271–289.

Dubois, T. E., & Cohen, W. (1970). Relationship between measures of psychological differentiation and intellectual ability. *Perceptual and Motor Skills, 31*, 411–416.

Duff, A. (1998). Objective tests, learning to learn and learning styles: A comment. *Accounting Education, 7* (4), 335–345.

Duhigg, C. (2012). *The power of habit: Why we do what we do in life and business*. New York: Random House.

Dunkleberger, C. J., & Tyler, L. E. (1961). Interest stability and personality traits. *Journal of Counseling Psychology, 8*, 70–74.

Eccles, J. S., Jacobs, J. E., & Harold, R. D. (1990). Gender role stereotypes, expectancy effects, and parents' socialization of gender differences. *Journal of Social Issues, 46* (2), 183–201.

Edmunds, R., & Richardson, J. T. E. (2009). Conceptions of learning, approaches to studying and personal development in UK higher education. *British Journal of Educational Psychology, 79*, 295–309.

Egeland, B. (1974). Training impulsive children in the use of more efficient scanning techniques. *Child Development, 45*, 165–171.

Einarsdòttir, S., Rounds, J., Agisòttir, S., & Gerstein, L. H. (2002). The structure of vocational interests in Iceland: Examining Holland's and Gati's RIASEC models. *European Journal of Psychological Assessment, 18* (1), 85–95.

Eklund-Myrskog, G., & Wenestam, C. G. (1999). Students' approaches to learning in Finnish general upper secondary school. *Scandinavian Journal of Educational Research, 43* (1), 5–18.

Elder, R. L. (1989). Relationships between adaption-innovation, experienced control, and state-trait anxiety. *Psychological Reports, 65* (1), 47–54.

Eley, M. G. (1992). Differential adoption of study approaches within individual students. *Higher Education, 23*, 231–254.

Engelbrecht, P., & Natzel, S. G. (1997). Cultural variations in cognitive style: Field dependence vs. field independence. *School Psychology International, 18*, 155–164.

Engle, D. E., Mah, J. J., & Sadri, G. (1997). An empirical comparison of entrepreneurs and employees: Implications for innovation. *Creativity Research Journal, 10* (1), 45–49.

Entwistle, N. J. (1981). *Styles of teaching and learning: An integrated outline of educational psychology for students, teachers, and lecturers*. New York: John Wiley & Sons.

Entwistle, N. J. (1988). Motivational factors in students' approaches to learning. In R. Schmeck (Ed.), *Learning strategies and learning styles* (pp. 21–51). New York: Plenum Press.

Entwistle, N. J., & McCune, V. (2009). The disposition to understand for oneself at university and beyond: Learning processes, the will to learn, and sensitivity to context. In L. F. Zhang & R. J. Sternberg (Eds.), *Perspectives on the nature of intellectual styles* (pp. 29–62). New York: Springer Publishing Company.

Entwistle, N. J., McCune, V., & Hounsell, J. (2002). *Occasional report 1: Approaches to studying and perceptions of university teaching-learning environments: Concepts, measures and preliminary findings*. University of Edinburgh, ETL Project. United Kingdom: Higher and Community Education, The School of Education. Available from: http://www.ed.ac.uk/etl.

Entwistle, N. J., & Ramsden, P. (1983). *Understanding student learning*. London: Croom Helm.

Entwistle, N. J., & Tait, H. (1994). *The revised approaches to studying inventory*. Edinburgh: Center for Research into Learning and Instruction, University of Edinburgh.

Epstein, M. H., Hallahan, D. P., & Kauffman, J. M. (1975). Implications of the reflectivity-impulsivity dimension for special education. *Journal of Special Education, 9* (1), 11–25.

Erikson, E. H. (1950). *Childhood and society*. New York: W. W. Norton and Co.

Evans, C., & Waring, M. (2009). The place of cognitive style in pedagogy: Realizing potential in practice. In L. F. Zhang & R. J. Sternberg (Eds.), *Perspectives on the nature of intellectual styles* (pp. 169–208). New York: Springer Publishing Company.

Fan, W. Q. (2008). Thinking styles among university students in Shanghai: Comparing traditional and hypermedia instructional environments. *Dissertation Abstracts International, Section A: Humanities and Social Sciences, 68* (7A), 2808.

Fan, W. Q., & Ye, S. (2007). Teaching styles among Shanghai teachers in primary and secondary schools. *Educational Psychology, 27* (2), 255–272.

Fan, W. Q., & Zhang, L. F. (2009). Thinking styles and achievement motivations. *Learning and Individual Differences, 19*, 299–303.

Fan, W. Q., Zhang, L. F., & Watkins, D. (2010). Incremental validity of thinking styles in predicting academic achievements: An experimental study in hypermedia learning environments. *Educational Psychology, 30* (5), 605–623.

Feindler, E. L., Marriott, S. A., & Iwata, M. (1980). *An anger control training program for junior high delinquents*. Paper presented at Association for Advancement of Behavior Therapy, New York.

Fer, S. (2005). Validity and reliability of the Thinking Styles Inventory/Düsünme Stilleri Envanterinin Geçerlik ve Güvenirlik Çalismasi. *EDAM Egitim Danismanligi Ve Arastirmalari Merkezi, 5* (1), 33–67.

Fer, S. (2007). What are the thinking styles of Turkish student teachers? *Teachers College Record, 109* (6), 1488–1516.

Ferguson, M. (1992). Is the classroom still a chilly climate for women? *College Student Journal, 26*, 507–511.

Fisher, D. G., & Ott, R. L. (1996). A study of the relationship between accounting students' moral reasoning and cognitive styles. *Research on Accounting Ethics, 2*, 51–71.

Fjell, A. M., & Walhovd, K. B. (2004). Thinking styles in relation to personality traits: An investigation of the Thinking Styles Inventory and NEO-PI-R. *Scandinavian Journal of Psychology, 45* (4), 293–300.

Fling, S., Thomas, A., Gallaher, M. (1981). Participant characteristics and the effects of two types of meditation versus quiet sitting. *Journal of Clinical Psychology, 37* (4), 784–790.

Flynn, J. R. (1984). The mean IQ of Americans: Massive gains 1932 to 1978. *Psychological Bulletin, 95*, 29–51.

Flynn, J. R. (2007). *What is intelligence?: Beyond the Flynn effect*. New York: Cambridge University Press.

Fouad, N. A., & Dancer, L. S. (1992). Cross-cultural structure of interests: Mexico and the United States. *Journal of Vocational Behavior, 40*, 129–143.

Fowler, W. (1980). Cognitive differentiation and developmental learning. In H. Rees & L. Lipsitt (Eds.), *Advances in child development and behavior*, Vol. 15 (pp. 163–206). New York: Academic Press.

Foxall, G. R. (1986). Managers in transition: An empirical test of Kirton's adaption-innovation theory and its implications for the mid-career MBA. *Technovation*, 4, 219–232.

Foxall, G. R. (1990). An empirical analysis of mid-career managers' adaptive-innovative cognitive styles and task orientations in three countries. *Psychological Reports*, 66, 1115–1124.

Foxall, G. R., & Payne, A. F. (1989). Adaptors and innovators in organizations: A cross-cultural study of the cognitive styles of managerial functions and subfunctions. *Human Relations*, 42 (7), 639–649.

Foxall, G. R., Payne, A. F., & Walters, D. A. (1992). Adaptive-innovative cognitive styles of Australian managers. *Australian Psychologist*, 27 (2), 118–122.

Francis, B. (2000). *Boys, girls and achievement: Addressing the classroom issues*. London: Taylor & Francis.

Frank, B. M. (1986). Cognitive styles and teacher education: Field dependence and areas of specialization among teacher education majors. *Journal of Educational Research*, 80 (1), 19–22.

Freud, S. (1962 [1905]). *Three contributions to the theory of sex* (J. Strachey, Trans.). New York: Nervous and Mental Disease.

Friedman, B. (1963). *The feminine mystique*. London: Gollancz.

Fung, Y. H., Ho, A. S. P., & Kwan, K. P. (1993). Reliability and validity of the Learning Styles Questionnaire. *British Journal of Educational Technology*, 24 (1), 12–21.

Furnham, A. (1995). The relationship of personality and intelligence to cognitive learning style and achievement. In D. Saklofske & M. Zeidner (Eds.), *International handbook of personality and intelligence* (pp. 397–413). New York: Plenum.

Furnham, A. (2012). Intelligence and intellectual styles. In L. F. Zhang, R. J. Sternberg, & S. Rayner (Eds.), *Handbook of intellectual styles: Preferences in cognition, learning, and thinking* (pp. 173–192). New York: Springer Publishing Company.

Gade, E. M., Fuqua, D., & Hurlburt, G. (1984). Use of the self-directed search with Native American high school students. *Journal of Counseling Psychology*, 31 (4), 584–587.

Gaudron, J. P., & Vautier, S. (2007). Estimating true short-term consistency in vocational interests: A longitudinal SEM approach. *Journal of Vocational Behavior*, 71, 221–232.

Gebbia, M., & Honigsfeld, A. (2012). Learner developmental outcomes and intellectual styles. In L. F. Zhang, R. J. Sternberg, & S. Rayner (Eds.), *Handbook of intellectual styles: Preferences in cognition, learning, and thinking* (pp. 251–271). New York: Springer Publishing Company.

Geiger, M. A., & Pinto, J. K. (1991). Changes in learning style preference during a three-year longitudinal study. *Psychological Reports*, 69, 755–762.

Genshaft, J. L., Hirt, M. (1979). Race effects in modifying cognitive impulsivity through self-instruction and modeling. *Journal of Experimental Child Psychology*, 27, 185–194.

Ghaye, A., & Ghaye, K. (1998). *Teaching and learning through critical reflective practice*. London: David Fulton.

Ghosh, J. (1980). A comparison of cognitive styles of mathematically, musically, and artistically talented adolescents. *Dissertation Abstracts International*, 40, 578A.

Gijbels, D., & Dochy, F. (2006). Students' assessment preferences and approaches to learning: Can formative assessment make a difference? *Educational Studies, 32* (4), 399–409.

Gijbels, D., Segers, M., & Struyf, E. (2008). Constructivist learning environments and the (im)possibility to change students' perceptions of assessment demands and approaches to learning. *Instructional Science, 36,* 431–443.

Gillespie, B. V. (1999). Is math achievement a matter of personality type? *Journal of Psychological Type, 49,* 37–41.

Gilligan, C. (1982). *In a different voice: Psychological theory and women's development.* Cambridge, MA: Harvard University Press.

Gilmore, G. C., Wenk, H. E., Naylor, L. A., & Stuve, T. A. (1992). Motion picture and aging. *Psychology and Aging, 7* (4), 654–660.

Gledhill, R. F., & van Der Merwe, C. A. (1989). Gender as a factor in student learning: Preliminary findings. *Medical Education, 23,* 201–204.

Glenn, D. (2010). Customized teaching fails a test. *Chronicle of the Higher Education,* (January 8), A6–A8.

Glenwick, D. S., & Barocas, R. (1979). Training impulsive children in verbal self-control by use of natural change agents. *The Journal of Special Education, 13* (4), 387–398.

Gleser, G. C., & Ihilivech, D. (1969). An objective instrument for measuring defense mechanisms. *Journal of Consulting and Clinical Psychology, 33,* 51–60.

Glidden, R. C., & Greenwood, A. K. (1997). A validation study of the Spanish self-directed search using back-translation procedures. *Journal of Career Assessment, 5* (1), 105–113.

Globerson, T., & Zelniker, T. (1989). *Cognitive style and cognitive development.* Norwood, NJ: Ablex Publishing Corporation.

Goldstein, A. G., & Chance, J. E. (1965). Effects of practice on sex-related differences in performance on embedded figures. *Psychonomic Science, 3,* 361–362.

Goldstein, G., & Chotlos, J. W. (1966). Stability of field dependence in chronic alcoholic patients. *Journal of Psychology, 71,* 420.

Goldstein, K. M., & Blackman, S. (1978). *Cognitive style: Five approaches and relevant research.* New York: Wiley Interscience.

Goodenough, D. R., & Eagle, C. J. (1963). A modification of the embedded-figures test for use with young children. *The Journal of Genetic Psychology: Research and Theory on Human Development, 103* (1), 67–94.

Gordon, C., & Debus, R. (2002). Developing deep learning approaches and personal teaching efficacy within a preservice teacher education context. *British Journal of Educational Psychology, 72,* 483–511.

Gottfredson, G. D., & Holland, J. L. (1989). *Dictionary of Holland occupational codes.* Odessa, FL: Psychological Assessment Resources.

Goulet, C., Talbot, S., Drouin, D., & Trudel, P. (1988). Effect of structured ice hockey training on scores on field-dependence/independence. *Perceptual and Motor Skills, 66,* 175–181.

Gow, L., Balla, J., Kember, D., Stokes, M. et al. (1989). *Bulletin of the Hong Kong Psychological Society* (January–July), 22–23, 57–77.

Gow, L., & Kember, D. (1990). Does higher education promote independent learning? *Higher Education, 19,* 307–322.

Gow, L., Kember, D., & Cooper, B. (1994). The teaching context and approaches to study of accountancy students. *Issues in Accounting Education, 9* (1), 118–130.

Gow, L., & Ward, J. (1980). Effects of modification of conceptual tempo on acquisition of work skills. *Perceptual and Motor Skills, 50,* 107–116.
Gregorc, A. F. (1979). Learning/teaching styles: Potent forces behind them. *Educational Leadership, 36* (4), 234–236.
Gregorc, A. F. (1982). *An adult's guide to style.* Columbia, CT: Gregorc Associates.
Gregorc, A. F. (1982). *Gregorc Style Delineator.* Maynard, MA: Gabriel Systems.
Gregorc, A. F. (1984). Style as a symptom: A phenomenological perspective. *Theory into Practice, 23,* 51–55.
Gregorc, A. F. (1985). *Inside styles: Beyond the basics.* Maynard, MA: Gabriel Systems.
Gregorc, A. J. (1979). Learning/teaching styles: Potent forces behind them. *Educational Leadership, 36* (January), 234–236.
Gridley, M. C. (2006a). Concrete and abstract thinking and preferences in a sample of serious art collectors. *Psychological Reports, 98,* 853–857.
Gridley, M. C. (2006b). Thinking styles in a sample of women engineers. *Psychological Reports, 98,* 911–914.
Gridley, M. C. (2006c). Preferred thinking styles of professional fine artists. *Creativity Research Journal, 18* (2), 247–248.
Gridley, M. C. (2007). Differences in thinking styles of artists and engineers. *The Career Development Quarterly, 56* (2), 177–182.
Grigorenko, E. L. (2009). What is so stylish about styles? Comments on the genetic etiology of intellectual styles. In L. F. Zhang & R. J. Sternberg (Eds.), *Perspectives on the nature of intellectual styles* (pp. 233–251). New York: Springer Publishing Company.
Grigorenko, E. L., LaBuda, M. C., & Carter, A. S. (1992). Similarity in general cognitive ability, creativity, and cognitive styles in a sample of adolescent Russian twins. *Acta Geneticae Medicae et Gemellologiae, 41,* 65–72.
Grigorenko, E. L., & Sternberg, R. J. (1993). *Thinking Styles in Teaching Inventory.* Unpublished test, Yale University.
Grigorenko, E. L., & Sternberg, R. J. (1995). Thinking styles. In D. Saklofske & M. Zeidner (Eds.), *International handbook of personality and intelligence* (pp. 205–229). New York: Plenum.
Grigorenko, E. L., & Sternberg, R. J. (1997). Styles of thinking, abilities, and academic performance. *Exceptional Children, 63* (3), 295–312.
Grossman, H., & Grossman, S. H. (1994). *Gender issues in education.* Boston, MA: Allyn & Bacon.
Gruenfeld, L. W., & MacEachron, A. E. (1975). A cross-national study of cognitive style among managers and technicians. *International Journal of Psychology, 10* (1), 27–55.
Guilford, J. P. (1950). Creativity research: Past, present and future. *American Psychologist, 5,* 444–454.
Guilford, J. P. (1956). The structure of intellect. *Psychological Bulletin, 53* (4), 267–293.
Guilford, J. P. (1967). *The nature of human intelligence.* New York: McGraw-Hill.
Guilford, J. P., Christensen, P. E., Merrifield, P. R., & Wilson, R. C. (1978). *Alternate uses Form B and Form C.* Orange, CA: Sheridan Psychological Services.
Guilford, J. P., & Guilford, J. S. (1980). *Consequences Form AI Form AII: Manual of instructions and interpretations.* Orange, CA: Sheridan Psychological Services.
Guttman, L. (1954). A new approach to factor analysis: The radix. In P. F. Lazarsfeld (Ed.), *Mathematical thinking in the social sciences* (pp. 258–348). Glencoe, IL: Free Press.

Hall, C. W. (2001). A measure of executive processing skills in college students. *College Student Journal, 35* (3), 442–450.

Hall, E. T. (1976). *Beyond culture.* Garden City, NY: Anchor Press/Doubleday.

Hall, R. H. (1975). *Occupations and the social structure* (2nd Ed.). Englewood Cliffs, NJ: Prentice Hall.

Halpern, D. F. (2000). *Sex differences in cognitive abilities* (3rd Ed.). Mahwah, NJ: Lawrence Erlbaum Associates.

Hammer, A. L., & Mitchell, W. D. (1996). The distribution of MBTI types in the U.S. by gender and ethnic group. *Journal of Psychological Type, 37,* 2–15.

Hansen, J. C., & Campbell, D. P. (1985). *Manual for the SCII* (4th Ed.). Palo Alto, CA: Stanford University Press.

Harbison, F. H., Maruhnic, J., & Resnick, J. R. (1970). *Quantitative analysis of modernization and development.* Princeton, NJ: Princeton University Press.

Hartlage, L. C. (1970). Sex-linked inheritance of spatial ability. *Perceptual and Motor Skills, 31,* 610.

Hassan, M. M., & Abed, A. S. (1999). Differences in spatial visualization as a function of scores on hemisphericity of mathematics teachers. *Perceptual and Motor Skills, 88,* 387–390.

Hawkins, J. (1997). Giftedness and psychological type. *Journal of Secondary Gifted Education, 9,* 57–67.

Hayes, J., & Allinson, C. W. (1994). Cognitive style and its relevance for management practice. *British Journal of Management, 5,* 53–71.

Hayes, J., & Allinson, C. W. (1998). Cognitive style and the theory and practice of individual and collective learning in organizations. *Human Relations, 51* (7), 847–871.

Hayward, G., & Everett, C. (1983). Adaptors and innovators: Data from the Kirton Adaptor-Innovator Inventory in a local authority setting. *Journal of Occupational Psychology, 56,* 339–342.

Heckel, R. V., Allen, S. S., Andrews, L., Roeder, G., Ryba, P., & Zook, W. (1989). Normative data on the Kagan Matching Familiar Figures test for adult male incarcerates. *Journal of Clinical Psychology, 45* (1), 155–160.

Hedegard, J. M., & Brown, D. R. (1969). Encounters of some Negro and white freshmen with a public university. *Journal of Social Issues, 25,* 131–144.

Heider, E. R. (1971). Information processing and the modification of an "impulsive conceptual tempo." *Child Development, 42,* 1276–1281.

Helson, R., Kwan, V. S. Y., John, O., & Jones, C. (2002). The growing evidence for personality change in adulthood: Findings from research with personality inventories. *Journal of Research in Personality, 36,* 287–306.

Henson, K. T., & Borthwick, P. (1984). Matching styles: A historical look. *Theory Into Practice, 23* (1), 3–9.

Herzberg, F., & Bouton, A. (1954). A further study of the stability of the Kuder Preference Record. *Educational and Psychological Measurement, 14,* 326–331.

Hicks, E., Bagg, R., Doyle, W., & Young, J. D. (2007). Public accountants' field dependence: Canadian evidence. *Perceptual and Motor Skills, 105* (3), 1127–1135.

Higgins, P., & Zhang, L. F. (2009). The thinking styles of human resource practitioners. *The Learning Organization, 16* (4), 276–289.

Hill, J., Puurula, A., Sitko-Lutek, A., & Rakowska, A. (2000). Cognitive style and socialisation: An exploration of learned sources of style in Finland, Poland and the UK. *Educational Psychology, 20* (3), 285–305.

Hocevar, D. (1979). Ideational fluency as a confounding factor in the measurement of originality. *Journal of Educational Psychology, 71* (2), 191–196.

Hofstede, G. H. (1980). *Culture's consequences: International differences in work-related values*. Beverly Hills, CA: Sage.

Hofstede, G. H. (1990). Empirical models of cultural differences. In N. Bleichrodt & P. J. D. Drenth (Eds.). *Contemporary issues in cross-cultural psychology* (pp. 4–20). Amsterdam: Swets & Zeitlinger.

Hofstede, G. H. (1997). *Culture and organization: Software of mind*. New York: McGraw-Hill.

Hofstede, G. H. (2001). *Culture's consequences: Comparing values, behaviors, institutions and organizations across nations* (2nd ed.). Thousand Oaks, CA: Sage.

Holland, J. L. (1966). *The psychology of vocational choice*. Waltham, MA: Blaisdell.

Holland, J. L. (1972). *Professional manual for the self-directed search*. Palo Alto, CA: Consulting Psychologist Press.

Holland, J. L. (1973). *Making vocational choices: A theory of careers*. Englewood Cliffs, NJ: Prentice-Hall.

Holland, J. L. (1975). *Manual for the Vocational Preference Inventory*. Palo Alto, CA: Consulting Psychologist Press.

Holland, J. L. (1985a). *Making vocational choices: A theory of vocational personalities and work environments* (2nd ed.). Englewood Cliffs, NJ: Prentice-Hall.

Holland, J. L. (1985b). *Manual for Vocational Preference Inventory*. Odessa, FL: Psychological Assessment Resources.

Holland, J. L. (1994). *Self-Directed Search*. Odessa, FL: Psychological Assessment Resources.

Holland, J. L., Fritzsche, B. A., & Powell, A. B. (1994). *Self-Directed Search–Technical manual*. Odessa, FL: Psychological Assessment Resources.

Holland, P. A. (1987). Adaptors and innovators: Application of the Kirton Adaption-Innovation Inventory to bank employees. *Psychological Reports, 60*, 263–270.

Holmes, C. S. (1981). Reflective training and causal attributions in impulsive mildly retarded children. *Journal of Clinical Child Psychology, 10* (3), 194–199.

Honey, P., & Mumford, A. (1982, 1986, 1992). *The manual of learning styles*. Maidenhead, Berkshire: Honey Press.

Hood, A. B., & Johnson, R. W. (2002). *Assessment in counseling: A guide to the use of psychological assessment procedures*. Alexandria, VA: American Counseling Association.

Hoyt, D. P., Smith, J. L., Jr., & Levy, S. (1957). A further study in the prediction of interest stability. *Journal of Counseling Psychology, 4*, 228–233.

Hsu, C. H. C. (1999). Learning styles of hospitality students: Nature or nurture? *Hospitality Management, 18*, 17–30.

Huang, C. H., & Huang, C. E. (1991). *Chinese university students on the MBTI*. Garden Grove, CA: InfoMedia, Program D203-CS68.

Huang, J. Y., & Chao, L. (1995). Chinese and American students' perceptual styles of field independence versus field dependence. *Perceptual and Motor Skills, 80* (1), 232–234.

Huang, J. Y., & Chao, L. (1998). A study of reflectivity and impulsivity of Chinese and American university students. *Perceptual and Motor Skills, 86*, 440–442.

Hui, C. H., & Triandis, H. C. (1985). Measurement in cross-cultural psychology: A review and comparison of strategies. *Journal of Cross-cultural Psychology, 16*, 131–152.

Hui, C. H., & Triandis, H. C. (1989). Effects of culture and response format on extreme response style. *Journal of Cross-Cultural Psychology, 20*, 296–309.

Huston, A. (1985). Development of sex typing: Themes from recent research. *Developmental Review, 5*, 1–17.

Huston, A. C. (1983). Sex typing. In E. M. Hetherington (Ed.), P. H. Mussen (Series Ed.), *Handbook of child psychology, Vol. 4. Socialization, personality, and social behavior* (pp. 387–467). New York: Wiley.

Hyde, J. S. (1981). How large are cognitive gender differences? A meta-analysis using ω^2 and d. *American Psychologist, 36* (8), 892–901.

Jablokow, K. W., & Kirton, M. J. (2009). Problem solving, creativity, and the level-style distinction. In L. F. Zhang & R. J. Sternberg (Eds.), *Perspectives on the nature of intellectual styles* (pp. 137–168). New York: Springer Publishing Company.

Jacabson, G. R. (1968). Reduction of field dependence in chronic alcoholics. *Journal of Abnormal Psychology, 73*, 547–549.

Jackson, D. M. (1956). A short form of Witkin's Embedded Figures Test. *Journal of Abnormal and Social Psychology, 53*, 254–255.

Jacobson, C. M. (1993). Cognitive styles of creativity: Relations of scores on the Kirton Adaption-Innovation Inventory and the Myers-Briggs Type Indicator among managers in USA. *Psychological Reports, 72*, 1131–1138.

Jain, V., & Lall, R. (1996). Nurses' personality types based on the Myers-Briggs Type Indicator. *Psychological Reports, 78*, 938.

Jamison, W., & Signorella, M. L. (2001). Relations of masculinity and femininity in self-concept to spatial performance in adolescents. *Journal of Genetic Psychology, 148* (2), 249–251.

Johnson, J., & Kane, K. (1992). Developmental and task factors in LOGO programming. *Journal of Educational Computing Research, 8* (2), 229–253.

Johnson, S., Flinn, J. M., & Tyer, Z. E. (1979). Effect of practice and training in spatial skills on embedded-figures score of males and females. *Perceptual and Motor Skills, 48*, 975–984.

Jones, A. E. (1997a). *Field dependence revisited: An evaluation of issues for education and psychology.* Unpublished doctoral thesis, University of Lancaster, England.

Jones, A. E. (1997b). Reflection-impulsivity and wholist-analytic: Two fledglings? or is R-I a cuckoo? *Educational Psychology, 17* (1 & 2), 65–77.

Jones, C., Reichard, C., & Mokhtari, K. (2003). Are students' learning styles discipline specific. *Community College Journal of Research and Practice, 27* (5), 363–375.

Jones, C. F. N. (2001). Are learning styles subject-area sensitive? *Dissertation Abstracts International Section A: Humanities and Social Sciences, 61* (9-A), 3453.

Jones, G. K., & Herbert, J. (2000). National culture and innovation: Implications for locating global R&D operations. *Management International Review, 40* (1), 11–39.

Joniak, A. J., & Isaken, S. G. (1988). The Gregorc Style Delineator: Internal consistency and its relationship to Kirton's adaptive-innovative distinction. *Educational and Psychological Measurement, 48* (4), 1043–1049.

Juliano, D. B. (1977). Reflection-impulsivity and concept learning in disadvantaged and middle class children. *The Journal of Psychology, 96*, 103–110.
Jung, C. G. (1923). *Psychological types.* New York: Harcourt Brace.
Jung, C. G. (1946 [1924]). *Psychological types* (H. G. Baynes, trans.). New York: Harcourt, Brace.
Jung, C. G. (1958). *Psychology and religion: West and East. Collected Works 11.* (R. R. C. Hull, trans.). Princeton, NJ: Princeton University Press.
Jung, C. G. (1969 [1938]). *Psychology and religion: West and east* (2nd ed.). (R. F. C. Hall, trans.). Princeton, NJ: Princeton University.
Kagan, J. (1964). Acquisition and significance of sex-typing and sex-role identity. In M, L. Hoffman and L. W. Hoffman (Eds.), *Review of child development research, Vol. I* (pp. 137–167). New York: Russell Sage.
Kagan, J. (1965). Individual differences in the resolution of response uncertainty. *Journal of Personality and Social Psychology, 2*, 154–160.
Kagan, J. (1976). Commentary on reflective and impulsive children: Strategies of information processing underlying differences in problem solving. *Monographs of the Society for Research in Child Development, 41* (5, S168), pp. 48–52.
Kagan, J. (2012). *Psychology's ghosts: The crisis in the profession and the way back.* New Haven, CT: Yale University Press.
Kagan, J., & Kogan, N. (1970). Individual variation in cognitive processes. In P. A. Mussen (Ed.), *Carmichael's manual of child psychology (Vol. 1)* (pp. 1273–1365). New York: Wiley.
Kagan, J., & Moss, H. A. (1963). Psychological significance of styles of conceptualization. In J. E. Wright & J. Kagan (Eds.), *Basic cognitive processes in children* (pp. 73–112). Monographs of the Society for Research in Child Development, 28 (2), 73–112.
Kagan, J., Pearson, L., & Welch, L. (1966). Modifiability of an impulsive tempo. *Journal of Educational Psychology, 57*, 359–365.
Kagan, J., Rosman, B. L., Day, D., Albert, J., & Philips, W. (1964). Information processing in the child: Significance of analytic and reflective attitudes. *Psychological Monographs, 78 (1,* W578).
Kalsbeek, D. H. (1989). *Linking learning style theory with retention research: The TRAILS project.* AIR professional file (Report No. 23206–3038). Tallahassee, FL: Association for Institutional Research. (ERIC Document Reproduction Service No. ED 304 964)
Karp, S. A., & Konstadt, N. L. (1963). *Manual for the Children's Embedded Figures Test.* Oxford: Cognitive Tests.
Karp, S. A., & Konstadt, N. L. (1965). Alcoholism and psychological differentiation: Long range effect of heavy drinking. *Journal of Nervous and Mental Disease, 240*, 412–416.
Karp, S. A., Witkin, H. A., & Goodenough, D. R. (1965). Alcoholism and psychological differentiation: Effects on achievement of sobriety on field dependence. *Quarterly Journal of Studies on Alcoholism, 26*, 580–585.
Katz, N., & Heimann, N. (1991). Learning style of students and practitioners in five health professions. *Occupational Therapy Journal of Research. 11* (4), 238–244.
Katz, P. (1987). Variations in family constellation: Effects on gender schemata. In L. Liben & M. Signorella (Eds.), *New directions for child development: Children's gender schemata, 38*, 39–56.
Kaufman, A. S., & Kaufman, N. L. (1993). *Kaufman Adolescent & Adult Intelligence Test.* Circle Pines, MN: American Guidance Service.

Kaufman, A. S., McLean, J. E., & Lincoln, A. (1996). The relationship of the Myers-Briggs Type Indicator to IQ level and the fluid and crystallized IQ discrepancy on the Kaufman Adolescent and Adult Intelligence Test. *Assessment, 3* (3), 225–239.

Kaufman, J. C., & Baer, J. M. (2009). How are intellectual styles related to creativity across multiple domains? In L. F. Zhang & R. J. Sternberg (Eds.), *Perspectives on the nature of intellectual styles* (pp. 87–106). New York: Springer Publishing Company.

Kelleher, W. E. (1997). The Group Embedded Figures Test: Field dependence/independence and undergraduate commerce major. *College Student Journal, 31* (1), 115–120.

Keller, R. T., & Holland, W. E. (1978). A cross-validation study of the Kirton Adaption-Innovation Inventory in three research and development organizations. *Applied Psychological Measurement, 2* (4), 563–570.

Kelly, M. (1995). Turning heads: Changes in the preferred learning styles of school leaders and managers in the 1990s. *School Organization, 15*, 189–201.

Kember, D., Charlesworth, M., Davies, H., McKay, J., & Scott, V. (1997). Evaluating the effectiveness of educational innovations: Using the Study Process Questionnaire to show that meaningful learning occurs. *Studies in Educational Evaluation, 23* (2), 141–157.

Kember, D., Leung, D. Y. P., & McNaught, C. (2008). A workshop activity to demonstrate that approaches to learning are influenced by the teaching and learning environment. *Active Learning in Higher Education, 9* (1), 43–56.

Kendall, P. C., & Braswell, L. (1982). Cognitive-behavioral self-control therapy for children: A components analysis. *Journal of Consulting and Clinical Psychology, 50* (5), 672–689.

Kendall, P. C., & Finch, A. J. (1976). A cognitive-behavioral treatment for impulse control: A case study. *Journal of Consulting and Clinical Psychology, 44* (5), 852–857.

Kendall, P. C., & Wilcox, L. E. (1980). Cognitive-behavioral treatment for impulsivity: Concrete versus conceptual training in non-self-controlled problem children. *Journal of Consulting and Clinical Psychology, 48* (1), 80–91.

Khan, S. B., Alvi, S. A., Shaukat, N., Hussain, M. A., & Baig, T. (1990). A study of the validity of Holland's theory in a non-Western culture. *Journal of Vocational Behavior, 36*, 132–146.

Kienholz, A. & Hritzuk, J. (1986). Comparing students in architecture and medicine: Findings from two new measures of cognitive style. *Psychological Reports, 58*, 823–830.

Kim, D. H. (1993). The link between individual and organizational learning. *Sloan Management Review*, Fall, 37–50.

Kim, M. (2010). The relationship between thinking style differences and career choice for high-achieving high school students. *Dissertation Abstracts International Section A: Humanities and Social Sciences, 70* (8A), 2902

Kirchner-Nebot, T., & Amador-Campos, J. A. (1998). Internal consistency of scores on Matching Familiar Figures Test-20 and correlation of scores with age. *Perceptual and Motor Skills, 86* (3), 803–807.

Kirton, M. J. (1961). *Management initiative.* London: Acton Society Trust.

Kirton, M. J. (1976). Adaptors and innovators: A description and measure. *Journal of Applied Psychology, 61*, 622–629.

Kirton, M. J. (1980). Adaptors and innovators in organizations. *Human Relations*, 33, 213–224.
Kirton, M. J. (1982). *Kirton Adaption-Innovation Inventory (KAI)*. St. Albans: Occupational Research Center, Hatfield Polytechnic.
Kirton, M. J. (1987). *Adaption-Innovation Inventory (KAI). Manual* (2nd ed.). Hatfield, Herts: Occupational Research Center.
Kirton, M. J. (1988). Adaptors and innovators: Problem solvers in organizations. In K. Gronhaug & G. Kaufman (Eds.), *Innovation: A cross-disciplinary perspective* (pp. 65–85). Oslo: Norwegian University Press.
Kirton, M. J. (1994a). *Adaptors and innovators* (2nd ed.). London: Routledge.
Kirton, M. J. (1994b). Adaptors and innovators at work. In M. J. Kirton (Ed.), *Adaptors' and innovators' styles of problem solving* (2nd ed.) (pp. 51–71). London: Routledge.
Kirton, M. J., & McCarthy, R. M. (1988). Cognitive climate and organizations. *Journal of Occupational Psychology*, 61, 175–184.
Kirton, M. J., & Pender, S. R. (1982). The adaption-innovation continuum, occupational type and course selection. *Psychological Reports*, 51, 883–886.
Kloner, A., & Britain, S. (1984). The relation between sex-role adoption and field independence in preschool children. *Journal of Genetic Psychology*, 145, 109–116.
Kogan, N. (1973). Creativity and cognitive style: A life-span perspective. In P. B. Baltes & K. W. Schaie (Eds.), *Life-span developmental psychology: Personality and socialization* (pp. 146–160). New York: Academic Press.
Kogan, N. (1980). A style of life, a life of style – Review of cognitive styles in personal and cultural adaptation. *Contemporary Psychology*, 25, 595–598.
Kogan, N. (1983). Stylistic variation in childhood and adolescence: Creativity, metaphor, and cognitive styles. In P. H. Mussen (Ed.), *Handbook of child development, Vol. III* (4th ed.) (pp. 630–706). New York: John Wiley and Sons.
Kogan, N. (1989). A stylistic perspective on metaphor and aesthetic sensitivity in children. In T. Globerson & T. Zelniker (Eds.), *Cognitive style and cognitive development* (Human Development, Volume 3) (pp. 192–213). Norwood, NJ: Ablex Publishing Corporation.
Kogan, N., & Block, J. (1991). Field dependence-independence from early childhood through adolescence: Personality and socialization aspects. In S. Wapner, & J. Demick (Eds.), *Field dependence-independence: Cognitive style across the life span* (pp. 177–207). Hillsdale, NJ: Lawrence Erlbaum Associates.
Kogan, N., & Saarni, C. (1990). Cognitive style in children: Some evolving trends. In O. N. Saracho (Ed.), *Cognitive style and early education* (pp. 3–31). New York: Gordon & Breach.
Kohlberg, L. (1966). A cognitive-developmental analysis of children's sex-role concepts and attitudes. In E. E. Maccoby (Ed.), *The development of sex differences* (pp. 82–173). Stanford, CA: Stanford University Press.
Kolb, D. A. (1976). *The learning style inventory: Technical manual.* Boston, MA: McBer.
Kolb, D. A. (1984). *Experimental learning: Experience as a source of learning and development.* Englewood Cliffs, NJ: Prentice Hall.
Kolb, D. A. (1985). *The learning style inventory: Technical manual.* Boston, MA: McBer.
Kolb, D. A. (1993). *LSI-IIA Learning Style Inventory.* Boston, MA: McBer.
Kolb, D. A. (1995). *Learning style inventory: Technical specifications.* Boston, MA: McBer.
Kolb, D. A. (1999). *The Learning Style Inventory, Version 3.* Boston, MA: McBer.

Kopper, B. A., & Epperson, D. L. (1996). The experience of expression of anger: Relationships with gender, gender role socialization, depression, and mental health functioning. *Journal of Counseling Psychology, 43* (2), 158–165.

Korchin, S. J. (1982). The legacy of H. A. Witkin. *Contemporary Psychology, 27* (18), 602–604.

Kuder, G. F. (1939). *Kuder Preference Record-Form A*. Chicago: University of Chicago Bookstore.

Kulik, L. (2005). Predicting gender role stereotypes among adolescents in Israel: The impact of background variables, personality traits, and parental factors. *Journal of Youth Studies, 8* (1), 111–129.

LaBarbera, D. M. (2005). Physician assistant self-directed search holland codes. *Journal of Career Assessment, 13* (3), 337–346.

Lapidus, L. B., Shin, S. K., & Hutton, E. M. (2001). An evaluation of a six-week intervention designed to facilitate coping with psychological stress. *Journal of Clinical Psychology, 57* (12), 1381–1401.

Laschinger, H. K. S. (1992). Impact of nursing learning environments on adaptive competency development in baccalaureate nursing students. *Journal of Professional Nursing, 8* (2), 105–114.

Lau, C. H. (in progress). *Thinking styles, motivational orientations, and achievements in physics: Do teachers' teaching styles make a difference?* Doctoral thesis. The University of Hong Kong.

Lavach, J. F. (1991). Cerebral hemispherecity, college major and occupational choices. *Journal of Creative Behavior, 25* (3), 218–222.

Lawrence, G. (1993). *People types and tiger stripes* (3rd ed.). Gainesville, FL: Center for Applications of Psychological Type.

Lee, A. (1996). *Gender, literacy, curriculum: Rewriting school geography*. London: Taylor & Francis.

Leithwood, K. A., & Fowler, W. (1971). Complex motor learning in four-year-old. *Child Development, 42*, 781–792.

Lent, R. W., Brown, S. D., & Hackett, G. (1994). Toward a unifying social cognitive theory of career and academic interest, choice, and performance. *Journal of Vocational Behavior, 45*, 79–122.

Leo-Rhynie, L. (1985). Field independence, academic orientation, and achievement. *Current Psychological Research & Reviews* (Spring), 22–27.

Leung, S. A., & Hou, Z. J. (2001). Concurrent validity of the 1994 Self-Directed Search for Chinese high school students in Hong Kong. *Journal of Career Assessment, 9* (3), 283–296.

Levy, N., Murphy, C., & Carlson, R. (1972). Personality type among Negro college students. *Educational and Psychological Measurement, 32*, 641–653.

Lewin, K. (1936). *Principles of topological psychology*. New York: McGraw-Hill.

Lewin, Z. G. (1983). A study about the validity of the Group Embedded Figures Test. *Arquivos Brasileiros de Psicologia, 35* (2), 11–35.

Li, J. (2002). A cultural model of learning: Chinese "heart and mind for wanting to learn." *Journal of Cross-Cultural Psychology, 33* (3), 248–269.

Linden, W. (1973). Practicing of meditation by school children and their levels of field dependence-independence, test anxiety, and reading achievement. *Journal of Consulting and Clinical Psychology, 41* (1), 139–143.

Linton, H. (1952). *Relations between mode of perception and the tendency to conform.* Unpublished doctoral dissertation. Yale University.

Longeot, F. (1969). *Psychologie différentielle et théorie opératoire de l'intelligence.* Paris: Dunod.

Lonka, K., & Lindblom-Ylänne, S. (1996). Epistemologies, conceptions of learning, and study practices in medicine and psychology. *Higher Education, 31,* 5–24.

Lonner, W. J. (1968). Cross-cultural measurement of vocational interests. *Dissertation Abstracts International (Section A): Humanities and Social Sciences, 28,* 5226–5227A.

Loo, R. (1997). Evaluating change and stability in learning style scores: A methodological concern. *Educational Psychology, 17* (1/2), 95–100.

Lorber, J. (1994). *Paradoxes of gender.* New Haven, CT: Yale University Press.

Losh, C. L. (1983). *The relationship of student hemisphericity to performance in a computer programming course.* Unpublished doctoral dissertation. Georgia State University.

Low, K. S. D., & Rounds, J. (2007). Interest change and continuity from early adolescence to middle adulthood. *International Journal of Educational and Vocational Guidance, 7,* 23–36.

Low, K. S. D., Yoon, M., Roberts, B. W., & Rounds, J. (2005). The stability of vocational interests from early adolescence to middle adulthood: A quantitative review of longitudinal studies. *Psychological Bulletin, 131* (5), 713–737.

Lowe, E. A., & Taylor, W. G. K. (1986). The management of research in the life sciences: The characteristics of researchers. *R & D Management, 16,* 45–61.

Lusk, E. J., & Wright, H. (1981a). Differences in sex and curricula on learning the Group Embedded Figures Test. *Perceptual and Motor Skills, 53,* 8–10.

Lusk, E. J., & Wright, H. (1981b). Note on learning the Group Embedded Figures Test. *Perceptual and Motor Skills, 53,* 370.

MacArthur, R. S. (1970). *Cognition and psychosocial influences of Eastern Eskimos and Nsenga Africans: Some preliminaries.* Paper presented at Memorial University of Newfoundland Symposium on Cross-cultural Research, St. John's.

Maccoby, E. E., & Jacklin, C. N. (1974). *The psychology of sex differences.* Stanford, CA: Stanford University Press.

MacDonald, D. A., Anderson, P. E., Tsagarakis, C. I., & Holland, C. J. (1994). Examination of the relationship between the Myers-Briggs Type Indicator and the NEO Personality Inventory. *Psychological Reports, 74,* 339–344.

Marambe, K. N., Vermunt, J. D., & Boshuizen, H. P. A. (2012). A cross-cultural comparison of student learning patterns in higher education. *Higher Education, 64,* 299–316.

Markus, H., Crane, M, Bernstein, S., & Siladi, M. (1982). Self-schemas and gender. *Journal of Personality and Social Psychology, 42,* 38–50.

Markus, H. R., & Kitayama, S. (1991). Culture and the self: Implications for cognition, emotion, and motivation. *Psychological Review, 98,* 224–253.

Marton, F. (1976). What does it take to learn? Some implications on an alternative view of learning. In N. J. Entwistle (Ed.), *Strategies for research and development in higher education* (pp. 200–222). Amsterdam: Swets & Zeitlinger.

Marton, F., & Säljö, R. (1976). On qualitative differences in learning, I – Outcome and process. *British Journal of Educational Psychology, 46,* 4–11.

Mason, E. S., & Mudrack, P. E. (1996). Gender and ethical orientation: A test of gender and occupational socialization theories. *Journal of Business Ethics, 15* (6), 599–604.

Massa, L. J., Mayer, R. E., & Bohon, L. M. (2005). Individual differences in gender role beliefs influence spatial test performance. *Learning and Individual Differences*, 15, 99–111.

Masten, W. G., & Morse, D. T. (1987). Effects of training gifted children in creative imagination on "Your Style of Learning and Thinking." *Psychological Reports*, 61, 107–109.

Matsumoto, D. R. (2002). *The new Japan: Debunking seven cultural stereotypes*. Yarmouth, ME: Intercultural Press.

Mayer, R. E. (2009). Another valiant attempt to resuscitate intellectual styles as a field of study: A review of "Perspectives on the nature of intellectual styles." *PsycCRITIQUES, Number 4*, Vol. 54, Release 1, Article 1.

McCarthy, R. (1993). *The relationship between work pressure, cognitive style, sex role attitudes and coping behavior in women managers and secretaries*. Unpublished PhD thesis, University of Hertfordshire, UK.

McCarthy, S. V. (1975). Differential V-Q ability: Twenty years later. *Review of Educational Research*, 45, 263–282.

McCaulley, M. H. (1990). The Myers-Briggs Type Indicator in counseling. In C. E. Watkins, Jr., & V. L. Campbell (Ed.), *Testing in counseling practice* (pp. 91–134). Hillsdale, NJ: Lawrence Erlbaum.

McCaulley, M. H., & Moody, R. A. (2001). Multicultural applications of the Myers-Briggs Type Indicator. In L. A. Suzuki, J. G. Ponterotto, & P. J. Meller (Eds.), *Handbook of multicultural assessment: Clinical, psychological, and educational applications* (pp. 279–305). San Francisco: Jossey-Bass.

McCune, V., & Hounsell, D. (2005). The development of students' ways of thinking and practicing in three final-year biology courses. *Higher Education*, 49, 255–289.

McHale, S. M., Crouter, A. C., & Tucker, C. J. (1999). Family context and gender role socialization in middle childhood: Comparing girls to boys and sisters to brothers. *Child Development*, 70 (4), 990–1004.

McLeod, B. (1987). Sex, structured sport activity, and measurement of field dependence. *Perceptual and Motor Skills*, 64, 452–454.

McMillan, B., & Janzen, H. L. (1984). Peter parrot: Evaluation of a classroom self-instructional training program to increase reflectivity in children. *School Psychology International*, 5, 71–76.

Melancon, J. G., & Thompson, B. (1989). Measurement characteristics of the Finding Embedded Figures Test. *Psychology in the Schools*, 26 (1), 69–78.

Messer, S. B. (1976). Reflectivity-impulsivity: A review. *Psychological Bulletin*, 83 (6), 1026–1052.

Messer, S. B., & Brodzinsky, D. M. (1981). Three-year stability of reflection-impulsivity in young adolescents. *Developmental Psychology*, 17 (6), 848–850.

Messick, S. (1976). *Individuality in learning*. London: Jossey-Bass.

Messick, S. (1984). The nature of cognitive styles: Problems and promise in educational practice. *Educational Psychologist*, 19, 59–74.

Messick, S. (1994). The matter of style: Manifestations of personality in cognition, learning, and teaching. *Educational Psychologist*, 29, 121–136.

Messick, S. (1996). Bridging cognition and personality in education: the role of style in performance and development. *European Journal of Personality*, 10, 353–376.

Meyer, J. H. F., Dunne, T., & Richardson, J. T. E. (1994). A gender comparison of contextualized study behavior in higher education. *Higher Education, 27,* 469–485.

Miller, A. (1987). Cognitive styles: An integrated model. *Educational Psychology, 7* (4), 251–268.

Miller, M. J. (2002). Longitudinal examination of a three-letter Holland code. *Journal of Employment Counseling, 39,* 43–48.

Mills, C. (2003). Characteristics of effective teachers of gifted students: Teacher backgrounds and personality styles of students. *Gifted Child Quarterly, 47,* 272–281.

Mills, C. J., & Parker, W. D. (1998). Cognitive-psychological profiles of gifted adolescents from Ireland and the U.S.: Cross-societal comparisons. *International Journal of Intercultural Relations, 22,* 1–16.

Mills, T. Y. (1995). Mobility-fixity: Further psychometric data on the field independence of accountants. *Perceptual and Motor Skills, 80,* 515–521.

Mills, T. Y. (1997). An examination of the relationship between accountants scores on field independence and use of and attitude toward computers. *Perceptual and Motor Skills, 84,* 715–720.

Mishra, J. (1998). Learning styles in relation to information processing modes and multiple talents. *Psycho-Lingua, 28,* 7–18.

Mitchell, C. W. (2006). Relationships between MBTI personality types and coping styles: A pilot study. *Journal of Psychological Type, 66* (6), 49–57.

Mitchell, T., & Cahill, A. M. (2005). Cognitive style and plebe turnover at the U.S. Naval Academy. *Perceptual and Motor Skills, 101* (1), 55–62.

Monfort, M., Martin, S. A., & Frederickson, W. (1990). Information-processing differences and laterality of students from different colleges and disciplines. *Perceptual and Motor Skills, 70,* 163–172.

Morell, J. A. (1976). Age, sex, training, and the measurement of field dependence. *Journal of Experimental Child Psychology, 22,* 100–112.

Morgan, H. (1997). *Cognitive styles and classroom learning.* Westport, CT: Praeger Publishers.

Morris, T. L., & Bergum, B. O. (1978). A note on the relationship between field-independence and creativity. *Perceptual and Motor Skills, 46* (3), 1114.

Morrison, W. B. (1994). *Psychological types: Implications for teacher student relationships.* Unpublished doctoral dissertation, University of Alberta, Canada.

Moskvina, V., & & Kozhevnikov, M. (2011). Determining cognitive style: Historical perspective and directions for future research. In S. Rayner & E. Cools (Eds.), *Style differences in cognition, learning, and management: Theory, research, and practice* (pp. 19–31). New York: Taylor & Francis Group.

Most, R., & Zeidner, M. (1995). Constructing personality and intelligence instruments. In D. Saklofske & M. Zeidner (Eds.), *International handbook of personality and intelligence* (pp. 475–503). New York and London: Plenum Press.

Mpofu, E., & Oakland, T. (2001). Predicting school achievement in Zimbabwean multiracial schools using Biggs' Learning Process Questionnaire. *South African Journal of Psychology, 31* (3), 20–29.

Mshelia, A. Y., & Lapidus, L. B. (1990). Depth picture perception in relation to cognitive style and training in non-Western children. *Journal of Cross-Cultural Psychology, 21* (4), 414–433.

Mumbauer, C. C., & Miller, J. O. (1970). Socioeconomic background and cognitive functioning in preschool children. *Child Development, 41*, 471–480.

Murdock, M. C., Isaksen, S. G., & Lauer, K. J. (1993). Creativity training and the stability and internal consistency of the Kirton Adaption-Innovation Inventory. *Psychological Reports, 72* (3), 1123–1130.

Murphy, A., & Janeke, H. C. (2009). The relationship between thinking styles and emotional intelligence: An exploratory study. *South African Journal of Psychology, 39* (3), 357–375.

Murphy, H. J., Casey, B., Day, D. A., & Young, J. D. (1997). Scores on the Group Embedded Figures Test by undergraduates in information management. *Perceptual and Motor Skills, 84* (3), 1135–1138.

Myers, B., McCaulley, M., Quenk, N., & Hammer, A. (1998). *Manual: A guide to the development and use of the Myers-Briggs Type Indicator* (3rd Ed.). Palo Alto, CA: Consulting Psychologists Press.

Myers, I. B. (1962). *The Myers-Briggs Type Indicator: Manual.* Palo Alto, CA: Consulting Psychologists Press.

Myers, I. B., & McCaulley, M. H. (1985, 1989, 1993). *Manual: A guide to the development and use of the Myers-Briggs Type Indicator.* Palo Alto, CA: Consulting Psychologists Press.

Myers, P. L. (1988). Paranoid pseudocommunity beliefs in a sect milieu. *Social Psychiatry and Psychiatric Epidemiology, 23* (4), 252–255.

Nachmias, R., & Shany, N. (2002). Learning in virtual courses and its relationship to thinking styles. *Journal of Educational Computing Research, 27* (3), 315–329.

Nasby, W. (1989). Private self-consciousness, self-awareness, and the reliability of self-reports. *Journal of Personality and Social Psychology, 56*, 950–957.

Nash, S. C. (1975). The relationship among sex-role stereotyping, sex-role preference, and the sex difference in spatial visualization. *Sex Roles, 1*, 15–32.

Nash, S. C. (1979). Sex role as a mediator of intellectual functioning. In M. A. Wittig & A.C. Peterson (Eds.), *Sex-related differences in cognitive functioning: Developmental issues* (pp. 263–302). New York: Academic Press.

Nielsen, T. (2012). A historical review of the styles literature. In L. F. Zhang, R. J. Sternberg, & S. Rayner (Eds.), *Handbook of intellectual styles: Preferences in cognition, learning, and thinking* (pp. 21–46). New York: Springer Publishing Company.

Nieminen, J., Lindblom-Ylänne, S., & Lonka, K. (2004). The development of study orientations and study success in students of pharmacy. *Instructional Science, 32*, 387–417.

Nijhuis, J. F. H., Segers, M. S. R., & Gijselaers, W. H. (2005). Influence of redesigning a learning environment on student perceptions and learning strategies. *Learning Environment Research, 8*, 67–93.

Niles, F. S. (1995). Cultural differences in learning motivation and learning strategies: A comparison of overseas and Australian students at an Australian university. *International Journal of Intercultural Relations, 19* (3), 369–385.

Nolen, S. B. (2003). Learning environment, motivation, and achievement in high school science. *Journal of Research in Science Teaching, 40* (4), 347–368.

O'Brien, T. P. (1990). Construct validation of the Gregorc Style Delineator: An application of LISREL 7. *Educational and Psychological Measurement, 50* (3), 631–636.

O'Brien, T. P. (1992). Relationships among selected characteristics of college students and cognitive style preference. *College Student Journal, 26*, 492–500.
O'Leary, M. R., Donovan, D. M., & Kasner, K. H. (1975). Shifts in perceptual differentiation and defense mechanisms in alcoholics. *Journal of Clinical Psychology, 31* (3), 565–567.
Okonji, M. (1969). The differential effects of rural and urban upbringing on the development of cognitive styles. *International Journal of Psychology, 4*, 293–305.
Oltman, P. R. (1968). The portable rod-and-frame apparatus. *Perceptual and Motor Skills, 26*, 503–506.
Panek, P. E., Funk, L. G., & Nelson, P. K. (1980). Reliability and validity of the Group Embedded Figures Test across the life span. *Perceptual and Motor Skills, 50* (3), 1171–1174.
Parente, J. A., & O'Malley, J. J. (1975). Training in musical rhythm and field dependence of children. *Perceptual and Motor Skills, 40*, 392–394.
Pargman, D. (1977). Perceptual cognitive ability as a function of race, sex, and academic achievement in college athletes. *International Journal of Sport Psychology, 8*, 79–91.
Park, S. K., Park, K. H., & Choe, H. S. (2005). Relationship between thinking styles and scientific giftedness in Korea. *Journal of Secondary Gifted Education, 16* (2–3), 87–97.
Pascale, R. T., & Athos, A. G. (1981). *The art of Japanese management.* New York: Simon & Schuster.
Pask, G. (1976). Styles and strategies of learning. *British Journal of Educational Psychology, 46*, 128–148.
Pask, G., & Scott, B. C. E. (1972). Learning strategies and individual competence. *International Journal of Man-Machine Studies, 4*, 217–253.
Passmore, J., Holloway, M., & Rawle-Cope, M. (2010). Using MBTI type to explore differences and the implications for practice for therapists and coaches: Are executive coaches really like counsellors? *Counselling Psychology Quarterly, 23* (1), 1–16.
Payne, M. A., & Sabaroche, H. F. (1985). Personality type and occupational preference: Testing Holland's theory in the Caribbean. *International Journal for the Advancement of Counseling, 8*, 147–156.
Pelletier, K. R. (1974). Influence of transcendental meditation upon autokinetic perception. *Perceptual and Motor Skills, 39*, 1031–1034.
Perry, W. G. (1970). *Forms of intellectual and ethical development in the college years: A scheme.* (2nd Ed.). New York: Holt, Rinehart and Winston.
Perry, W. G. (1999). *Forms of intellectual and ethical development in the college years: A scheme.* (3rd Ed). San Francisco: Jossey-Bass.
Peterson, J. M., & Sweitzer, G. (1973). Field-independent architecture students. *Perceptual and Motor Skills, 36*, 195–198.
Petrakis, E. (1981). Cognitive styles of physical education majors. *Perceptual and Motor Skills, 53* (2), 74.
Pettigrew, A. C., & King, M. O. (1993). A comparison between scores on Kirton's inventory for nursing students and a general student population. *Psychological Reports, 73* (1), 339–345.
Pettigrew, A. C., & King, M. O. (1997). Adaptors and innovators: A description of staff nurses. *Psychological Reports, 81*, 16–18.

Piaget, J. (1952). *The origins of intelligence in children.* New York: International Universities Press.
Piers, E. V., Daniels, J. M., & Quackenbush, J. F. (1960). The identification of creativity in adolescents. *Journal of Educational Psychology, 51* (6), 346–351.
Pierson, J. S. (1965). *Cognitive styles and measured vocational interests of college men.* Doctoral dissertation, University of Texas. University Microfilms, No. 65–8082.
Pincus, K. V. (1985). Group Embedded Figures Test: Psychometric data for a sample of accountants compared with student norms. *Perceptual and Motor Skills, 60,* 707–712.
Pinker, S. (1997). *How the mind works.* New York: W. W. Norton & Company.
Pinto, J. K., & Geiger, M. A. (1991). Changes in learning style preferences: A prefatory report of longitudinal findings. *Psychological Reports, 68,* 195–201.
Pinto, J. K., Geiger, M. A., & Boyle, E. (1994). A three-year longitudinal study of changes in student learning styles. *Journal of College Student Development, 35* (2), 113–119.
Pollack, M., Kahn, R. L., Karp, E., & Fink, M. (1960). *Individual differences in the perception of the upright in hospitalized psychiatric patients.* Paper read at Eastern Psychological Association, New York.
Prato-Previde, G. (1991). Italian adaptors and innovators: Is cognitive style underlying culture? *Personality and Individual Differences, 12* (1), 1–10.
Raina, M. K., & Vats, A. (1983). Style of learning and thinking (hemisphericity), openness to inner experience, sex and subject choice. *Psychological Studies, 28* (2), 85–89.
Raiszadeh, A. D. (1999). Relationship between personality type, learning style preference, and mathematics achievement in college developmental mathematics. *Dissertation Abstracts International (Section A): Humanities and Social Sciences, 59* (7A), 2407.
Rakoczy, M., & Money, S. (1995). Learning styles of nursing students: A 3-year cohort longitudinal study. *Journal of Professional Nursing, 11* (3), 170–174.
Ramirez, M., Castaneda, A., & Herold, P. L. (1974). The relationship of acculturation to cognitive style among Mexican Americans. *Journal of Cross-Cultural Psychology, 5* (4), 424–433.
Ramsden, P., & Entwistle, N. J. (1981). Effects of academic departments on students' approaches to studying. *British Journal of Educational Psychology, 51,* 368–383.
Rayner, S. (2011). Researching style: Epistemology, paradigm shifts and research interest groups. *Learning and Individual Differences, 21* (2), 255–262.
Rayner, S., & Cools, E. (Eds.) (2011). *Style differences in cognition, learning, and management: Theory, research, and practice.* New York: Taylor & Francis.
Rayner, S., & Peterson, E. R. (2009). Reaffirming style as an individual difference: Toward a global paradigm or knowledge diaspora? In L. F. Zhang & R. J. Sternberg (Eds.), *Perspectives on the nature of intellectual styles* (pp. 107–134). New York: Springer Publishing Company.
Rayner, S., & Riding, R. (1997). Towards a categorization of cognitive styles and learning styles. *Educational Psychology, 17* (1 & 2), 5–27.
Rayner, S., Zhang, L. F., & Sternberg, R. J. (2012). Conclusion: Back to the future. In L. F. Zhang, R. J. Sternberg, & S. Rayner (Eds.), *Handbook of intellectual styles: Preferences in cognition, learning, and thinking* (pp. 395–413). New York: Springer Publishing Company.
Readence, J. E., & Bean, T. W. (1978). Modification of impulsive cognitive style: A survey of the literature. *Psychological Reports, 43,* 327–337.

Reid, W. A., Duvall, E., & Evans, P. (2005). Can we influence medical students' approaches to learning? *Medical Teacher, 27* (5), 401–407.
Renner, V. (1970). Effects of modification of cognitive style on creative behavior. *Journal of Personality and Social Psychology, 14* (3), 257–262.
Reuchlin, M. (1962). *Les méthodes quantitatives en psychologie*. Paris: PUF.
Reynolds, C. R., & Torrance, E. P. (1978). Perceived changes in styles of learning and thinking (hemisphericity) through direct and indirect training. *Journal of Creative Behavior, 12*, 247–252.
Rezler, A. G., & French, R. M. (1975). Personality types and learning preferences of students in six allied health professions. *Journal of Allied Health, 4*, 20–26.
Rezler, A. G., & Rezmovick, V. (1981). The learning preference inventory. *Journal of Allied Health, 10*, 28–34.
Richardson, A. G., & Cuffie, J. C. (1997). University students' approaches to studying: Some Caribbean findings. *Journal of Psychology in Africa, 1*, 68–75.
Richardson, J. A., & Turner, T. E. (2000). Field dependence revisited I: Intelligence. *Educational Psychology, 20* (3), 255–270.
Richardson, J. T. E. (1990). Reliability and replicability of the Approaches to Studying Questionnaire. *Studies in Higher Education, 15*, 155–168.
Richardson, J. T. E., & King, E. (1991). Gender differences in the experience of higher education: Quantitative and qualitative approaches. *Educational Psychology, 11* (3/4), 363–383.
Riding, R. J. (1997). On the nature of cognitive style. *Educational Psychology, 17* (1 & 2), 29–49.
Riding, R. J., & Cheema, I. (1991). Cognitive styles – an overview and integration. *Educational Psychology, 11* (3 & 4), 193–215.
Roach, B. (1996). Organizational decision makers: Different types for different levels. *Journal of Psychological Type, 12*, 16–24.
Rogers, C. (1951). *Client-centered therapy*. Boston: Houghton Mifflin.
Rogers, J. C., & Hill, D. J. (1980). Learning style preferences of bachelor's and master's students in occupational therapy. *American Journal of Occupational Therapy, 34*, 789–793.
Roodenburg, J., Roodenburg, E., & Rayner, S. (2012). Personality and intellectual styles. In L. F. Zhang, R. J. Sternberg, & S. Rayner (Eds.), *Handbook of intellectual styles: Preferences in cognition, learning, and thinking* (pp. 209–231). New York: Springer Publishing Company.
Rosati, P. (1997). Psychological types of Canadian engineering students. *Journal of Psychological Type, 41*, 33–37.
Rosenberg, N. (1953). Stability and maturation of Kuder interest patterns during high school. *Educational and Psychological Measurement, 13*, 449–458.
Rosenfeld, R. B., Winger-Bearskin, M., Marcic, D., & Braun, C. L. (1993). Delineating entrepreneurs' styles: Application of adaption-innovation subscales. *Psychological Reports, 72*, 287–298.
Rotter, J. B. (1966). Generalized expectancies for internal versus external control of reinforcement. *Psychological Monographs, 80* (I, W600).
Rounds, J. B. (1995). Vocational interests: Evaluating structural hypotheses. In D. Lubinski & R. V. Dawis (Eds.), *Assessing individual differences in human behavior: New concepts, methods and findings* (pp. 177–232). Palo Alto, CA: Davies-Black.

Rounds, J. B., & Tracey, T. J. (1996). Cross-cultural structural equivalence of the RIASEC models and measures. *Journal of Counseling Psychology, 43* (3), 310–329.

Royce, J. R. (1973). The conceptual framework for a multi-factor theory of individuality. In J. R. Royce (Ed.), *Contributions of multivariate analysis to psychological theory* (pp. 305–497). London: Academic Press.

Ruble, T. L., & Stout, D. E. (1991). Reliability, classification stability, and response-set bias of alternate forms of the Learning Style Inventory (LSI-1985). *Educational and Psychological Measurement, 51* (2), 481–489.

Rupert, P. A., & Baird, R. (1979). Modification of cognitive tempo on a haptic-visual matching task. *The Journal of Genetic Psychology, 135*, 165–174.

Rush, G. M., & Moore, D. M. (1991). Effects of restructuring training and cognitive style. *Educational Psychology, 11* (3/4) 309–321.

Sadler-Smith, E. (1996). Approaches to studying: Age, gender and academic performance. *Educational Studies, 22* (3), 367–379.

Sadler-Smith, E. (2009). A duplex model of cognitive style. In L. F. Zhang & R. J. Sternberg (Eds.), *Perspectives on the nature of intellectual styles* (pp. 3–28). New York: Springer Publishing Company.

Sadler-Smith, E., & Tsang, F. (1998). A comparative study of approaches to studying in Hong Kong and the United Kingdom. *British Journal of Educational Psychology, 68*, 81–93.

Sak, U. (2004). A synthesis of research on psychological types of gifted adolescents. *The Journal of Secondary Gifted Education, 15* (2), 70–79.

Salkind, N. J. (1979). *The development of norms for the Matching Familiar Figures Test.* Unpublished manuscript.

Salter, D. W. (2003). Exploring the "chilly classroom" phenomenon as interactions between psychological and environmental types. *Journal of College Student Development, 44* (1), 110–120.

Salter, D. W., Evans, N. J., & Forney, D. S. (2006). A longitudinal study of learning style preferences on the Myers-Briggs Type Indicator and Learning Style Inventory. *Journal of College Student Development, 47* (2), 173–184.

Samuelowicz, K. (1987). Learning problems of overseas students: Two sides of a story. *Higher Education in Research and Development, 6*, 121–133.

Sanders, M., Scholz, J. P., & Kagan, S. (1976). Three social motives and field independence-dependence in Anglo American and Mexican American children. *Journal of Cross-Cultural Psychology, 7*, 451–462.

Satterly, D. (1976). Cognitive styles, spatial ability, and school achievement. *Journal of Educational Psychology, 68*, 36–42.

Saucier, D. M., McCreary, D. R., & Saxberg, J. K. J. (2002). Does gender role socialization mediate sex differences in mental rotations? *Personality and Individual Differences, 32*, 1101–1111.

Savickas, M. L. (1999). The psychology of interests. In M. L. Savickas & A. R. Spokane (Eds.), *Vocational interests: Meaning, measurement, and counseling use* (pp. 19–56). Palo Alto, CA: Davies-Black.

Schleser, R., Cohen, R., Meyers, A. W., & Rodick, J. D. (1984). The effects of cognitive level and training procedures on the generalization of self-instructions. *Cognitive Therapy and Research, 8* (2), 187–200.

Schleser, R., Meyers, A. W., & Cohen, R. (1981). Generalization of self-instructions: Effects of general versus specific content, active rehearsal, and cognitive level. *Child Development, 52*, 335–340.

Schomburg, A. M., & Tokar, D. M. (2003). The moderating effect of private self-consciousness on the stability of vocational interests. *Journal of Vocational Behavior, 63*, 368–378.

Schurr, K. T., Ruble, V. E., & Henriksen, L. W. (1988). Relationships of Myers-Briggs Type Indicator personality characteristics and self-reported academic problems and skill ratings with scholastic aptitude test scores. *Educational and Psychological Measurement, 48*, 187–196.

Scouller, K., & Prosser, M. (1994). Students' experiences in studying for multiple choice question examinations. *Studies in Higher Education, 19*, 267–279.

Segers, M., Martens, R., & Van den Bossche, P. (2008). Understanding how a case-based assessment instrument influences student teachers' learning approaches. *Teacher and Teacher Education, 24*, 1751–1764.

Segers, M., Nijhuis, J., & Gijselaers, W. (2006). Redesigning a learning and assessment environment: The influence on students' perceptions of assessment demands and their learning strategies. *Studies in Educational Evaluation, 32*, 223–242.

Seidel, L. E., & England, E. M. (1999). Gregorc's cognitive styles: College students' preferences for teaching methods and testing techniques. *Perceptual and Motor Skills, 88* (3), 859–875.

Severiens, S., Dam, G. T., & Van Hout Wolters, B. (2001). Stability of processing and regulation strategies: Two longitudinal studies on student learning. *Higher Education, 42*, 437–453.

Seymour, R., & West-Burnham, J. (1989). Learning styles and education management: Part 1. *International Journal of Educational Management, 3*, 19–25.

Shade, B. J. (1983). *Afro-American patterns of cognition*. Final report to the Wisconsin Center for Education Research, Madison, WI.

Shade, B. J. (1986). Is there an Afro-American cognitive style? An exploratory study. *The Journal of Black Psychology, 13* (1), 13–16.

Shade, B. J. (1997). African American cognitive patterns: A review of the research. In B. J. Shade (Eds.), *Culture, style, and the educative process: Making schools work for racially diverse students* (2nd ed., pp. 79–91). Springfield, IL: Charles C. Thomas.

Sharma, G., & Kolb, D. A. (2011). The learning flexibility index: Assessing contextual flexibility in learning style. In S. Rayner & E. Cools (Eds.), *Style differences in cognition, learning, and management: Theory, research, and practice* (pp. 60–77). New York/London: Taylor & Francis Group.

Shen, J., Hiltz, S. R., & Bieber, M. (2008). Learning strategies in online collaborative examinations. *IEEE Transactions on Professional Communication, 51* (1), 63–78.

Sherman, J. A. (1967). Problems of sex differences in space perception and aspects of psychological functioning. *Psychological Review, 74*, 290–299.

Sherman, J. A. (1978). *Sex-related cognitive differences: An essay on theory and evidence*. Springfield, IL: Charles C. Thomas.

Shewchuk, R. M., & O'Connor, S. J. (1995). Health care executives: Subjective well-being as a function of psychological type. *Journal of Psychological Type, 32*, 23–29.

Shipman, S. L. (1989). Limitations of applying cognitive styles to early childhood education. *Early Childhood Development and Care, 51*, 3–12.

Shokri, O., Kadivar, P., Farzad, V., Sangari, A. A., & Ghana-ei, Z. (2006). The role of personality traits and thinking styles in academic achievement: Introducing casual models. *Journal of Iranian Psychologists, 2* (7) [NP].

Siann, G. (1970). Measuring field-independence in Zambia. *International Journal of Psychology, 7*, 87–96.

Signorella, M. L., & Jamison, W. (1978). Sex differences in the correlations among field dependence, spatial ability, sex-role orientation, and performance on Piaget's water-level task. *Developmental Psychology, 14*, 689–690.

Signorella, M. L., & Jamison, W. (1986). Masculinity, femininity, androgyny, and cognitive performance: A meta-analysis. *Psychological Bulletin, 100*, 207–228.

Silbey, V. (1980). *Hemispherity and performance on the Myers-Briggs*. Unpublished paper, Ball State University, Muncie, IN.

Sims, R. R., Veres, G. G., & Shake, I. G. (1989). An exploratory examination of the convergence between the LSQ and the Learning Style Inventory II. *Educational and Psychological Measurement, 49*, 227–233.

Sims, R. R., Veres III, J. G., Watson, P., & Buckner, K. E. (1986). The reliability and classification stability of the Learning Style Inventory. *Educational and Psychological Measurement, 46*, 753–760.

Sinha, D., & Shrestha, A. B. (1992). Ecocultural factors in cognitive style among children from hills and plains of Nepal. *International Journal of Psychology, 27* (1), 49–59.

Skogsberg, K., & Clump, M. (2003). Do psychology and biology majors differ in their study processes and learning styles? *College Student Journal, 37* (1), 27–33.

Slaney, R. B., Hall, M. E., & Bieschke, K. J. (1993). Stability of self-descriptive Holland types and career indecision. *Journal of Career Assessment, 1* (1), 83–92.

Smith, D. C. (1989). The personality of the systems analyst: An investigation. *ACM Computer Personnel, 12* (2), 12–14.

Smith, S. N., & Miller, R. J. (2005). Learning approaches: Examination type, discipline of study, and gender. *Educational Psychology, 25* (1), 43–53.

Smith, T. P., & Ribordy, S. C. (1980). Correlates of reflection-impulsivity in kindergarten males: Intelligence, socioeconomic status, race, fathers' absence, and teachers' ratings. *Psychological Reports, 47*, 1187–1191.

Snyder, R. P. (1998). An assessment of the reliability and validity of scores obtained by six popular learning styles instruments. *Dissertation Abstracts International (Section B): The Sciences and Engineering, 58* (11B), 6275.

Sofman, R. J., Hajosy, R. C., & Vojtisek, J. E. (1976). Psychology of scientist: XXXIII. Cognitive style differences between science and non-science faculty and students. *Perceptual and Motor Skills, 43* (3), 851–854.

Solis-Cámara, R. P., & Fox, R. A. (1985). Reflection-impulsivity in Mexican children: Cross-cultural relationships. *The Journal of General Psychology, 112* (3), 285–290.

Sousley, S. A., & Gargiulo, R. M. (1981). Effect of conceptual tempo on kindergarten reading readiness. *Perceptual and Motor Skills, 53*, 127–134.

Spotts, J. X. V., & Mackler, B. (1967). Relationship of field-dependent and field-independent cognitive styles to creative tests performance. *Perceptual and Motor Skills, 24*, 239–268.

Stafford, R. E. (1961). Sex differences in spatial visualization as evidence of sex-linked inheritance. *Perceptual and Motor Skills, 13*, 428.

Steele, A. L., & Young, S. (2008). A comparison of music education and music therapy majors: Personality types as described by the Myers-Briggs Type Indicator and demographic profiles. *Journal of Music Therapy, 45* (1), 2–20.

Stericker, A., & Le Vesconte (1982). Effect of brief training on sex-related differences in visual-spatial skill. *Journal of Personality and Social Psychology, 43* (5), 1018–1029.

Stern, G. G. (1970). *People in context.* New York: Wiley.

Sternberg, R. J. (1988). Mental self-government: A theory of intellectual styles and their development. *Human Development, 31*, 197–224.

Sternberg, R. J. (1996). Styles of thinking. In P. B. Baltes & U. M. Staudinger (Eds.), *Interactive minds: Life span perspectives on the social foundation of cognition* (pp. 347–365). New York: Cambridge University Press.

Sternberg, R. J. (1997). *Thinking styles.* New York: Cambridge University Press.

Sternberg, R. J. (2001). Epilogue: Another mysterious affair at styles. In R. J. Sternberg & L. F. Zhang (Eds.), *Perspectives on thinking, learning, and cognitive styles* (pp. 249–252). Mahwah, NJ: Lawrence Erlbaum.

Sternberg, R. J., & Grigorenko, E. L. (1995). Styles of thinking in the school. *European Journal for High Ability, 6*, 201–219.

Sternberg, R. J., Grigorenko, E. L., & Zhang, L. F. (2008). Styles of learning and thinking matter in instruction and assessment. *Perspectives on Psychological Science, 3* (6), 486–506.

Sternberg, R. J., & Wagner, R. K. (1992). *Thinking Styles Inventory.* Unpublished test, Yale University.

Sternberg, R. J., Wagner, R. K., & Zhang, L. F. (2003). *Thinking Styles Inventory – Revised.* Unpublished test, Yale University.

Sternberg, R. J., Wagner, R. K., & Zhang, L. F. (2007). *Thinking Styles Inventory – Revised II.* Unpublished test, Tufts University.

Sternberg, R. J., & Zhang, L. F. (1995). What do we mean by giftedness? – A pentagon implicit theory. *Gifted Child Quarterly, 39* (2), 88–94.

Sternberg, R. J., & Zhang, L. F. (Eds.). (2001). *Perspectives on thinking, learning and cognitive styles.* Mahwah, NJ: Lawrence Erlbaum Associates.

Stetson, T. E. (2007). Rules versus principles: Accountants' cognitive styles and professional penalties. *Journal of Psychological Type, 67* (12), 115–128.

Stever, G. S. (1995). Gender by type interaction effects in mass media subcultures. *Journal of Psychological Type, 32*, 3–12.

Stewart, K. L., & Felicetti, L. A. (1992). Learning styles of marketing majors. *Educational Research Quarterly, 15*, 15–23.

Stilwell, N. A., Wallick, M. M., Thal, S. E., & Burleson, J. A. (2000). Myers-Briggs type and medical specialty choice: A new look at an old question. *Teaching and Learning in Medicine, 12* (1), 14–20.

Stordahl, K. E. (1954). Permanence of Strong Vocational Interest Blank scores. *Journal of Applied Psychology, 38*, 423–427.

Stricker, L. J., & Ross, J. (1963). Intercorrelations and reliability of the Myers-Briggs Type Indicators scales. *Psychological Reports, 12*, 287–293.

Strong, E. K., Jr. (1927). Vocational Interest Test. *Educational Record, 8*, 107–121.

Strong, E. K., Jr. (1943). *The vocational interests of men and women*. Palo Alto, CA: Stanford University.
Strong, E. K., Jr. (1955). *Vocational interests 18 years after college*. Minneapolis: University of Minnesota Press.
Strong, E. K., Jr., Donnay, D. A. C., Morris, M. L., Schaubhut, N. A., & Thompson, R. C. (2004). *Strong Interest Inventory, Revised Edition*. Mountain View, CA: Consulting Psychologists Press.
Struyven, K., Dochy, F., Janssens, S., & Gielen, S. (2006). On the dynamics of students' approaches to learning: The effects of the teaching/learning environment. *Learning and Instruction, 16*, 279–294.
Stuart, I. R. (1967). Perceptual style and reading ability: Implications for an instructional approach. *Perceptual and Motor Skills, 24*, 135–138.
Swan, K. C. (2005). Vocational interests (the Self-Directed Search) of female carpenters. *Journal of Counseling Psychology, 52* (4), 655–657.
Swaney, K., & Flojo, J. (2001). *Age differences in vocational interest structure and clarity*. Paper presented at the annual meeting of the American Psychological Society, Toronto.
Swanson, J. L. (1984). *Can stability of interests be empirically predicted?* Paper presented at the annual meeting of the American Psychological Association, Toronto.
Swanson, J. L. (1992). The structure of vocational interests for African-American college students. *Journal of Vocational Behavior, 40*, 144–157.
Swanson, J. L. (1999). Stability and change in vocational interests. In M. L. Savickas & A. R. Spokane (Eds.), *Vocational interests: Meaning, measurement, and counseling use* (pp. 135–158). Palo Alto, CA: Davies-Black.
Swanson, J. L., & Hansen, J. C. (1988). Stability of vocational interests over 4-year, 8-year, and 12-year intervals. *Journal of Vocational Behavior, 33*, 185–202.
Swiatek, M. A., & Cross, T. L. (2007). Construct validity of the Social Coping Questionnaire. *Journal for the Education of the Gifted, 30* (4), 427–449.
Szirony, G. M., Pearson, L. C., Burgin, J. S., Murray, G. C., & Elrod, L. M. (2007). Brain hemisphere dominance and vocational preference: A preliminary analysis. *Work: Journal of Prevention, Assessment & Rehabilitation, 29* (4), 323–329.
Tabernero, B., & Márquez, S. (1999). Field dependence-independence of basketball referees. *Perceptual and Motor Skills, 88* (3), 929–934.
Tai, R. (in progress). *The impact of teaching styles on students' learning styles and career interests*. PhD thesis. The University of Hong Kong.
Tait, H., Entwistle, N., & McCune, V. (1998). ASSIST: A reconceptualization of the approaches to studying inventory. In C. Rust (Ed.), *Improving student learning: Improving students as learners* (pp. 262–271). Oxford: Oxford Center for Staff and Learning Development.
Taylor, J. (1994). The stability of school-children's cognitive style: A longitudinal study of the Kirton Adaption-Innovation Inventory. *Psychological Reports, 74* (3), 1008–1010.
Taylor, R. N., & Benbasat, I. (1980). A critique of cognitive styles theory and research. *Proceedings of the First International Conference on Systems*.
Tennant, M. (1997). *Psychology and adult learning* (2nd ed.). London: Routledge.
Terman, L. M., & Miles, C. C. (1936). *Sex and personality: Studies in masculinity and femininity*. New York: Russell & Russell.
The Jossey-Bass Reader (2002). *Gender in education*. San Francisco: Jossey-Bass.

Thomas, K. (1988). Gender and the arts/science divide in higher education. *Studies in Higher Education, 13*, 123–137.

Thomson, D. (1980). Adaptors-innovators: A replication study of managers in Singapore and Malaysia. *Psychological Reports, 47*, 383–387.

Tinajero, C., & Páramo, M. F. (1997). Field dependence–independence and academic achievement: A re-examination of their relationship. *British Journal of Educational Psychology, 67* (2), 199–212.

Tobacyk, J., & Cieslicka, A. (2000). Compatibility between psychological type and academic major in Polish university students. *Journal of Psychological Type, 54*, 22–30.

Torrance, E. P. (1984). *Human Information Processing Survey, Research Edition*. Athens, GA: HIP Systems.

Torrance, E. P. (1988). *SOLAT (Style of learning and thinking) manual*. Bensenville, IL: Scholastic Testing Service.

Torrance, E. P. (1988). *Style of learning and thinking: Administrator's manual*. Bensenville, IL: Scholastic Testing Service.

Torrance, E. P., McCarthy, B., & Kolesinski, M. T. (1988). *Style of learning and thinking*. Bensenville, IL: Scholastic Testing Service.

Torrance, E. P., & Reynolds, C. R. (1980). *Preliminary norms technical manual for Your Style of Learning and Thinking – Form C*. Athens: Department of Educational Psychology, The University of Georgia.

Torrance, E. P., Reynolds, C. R., Ball, O. E., & Riegel, T. (1978). *Revised norms – technical manual for Your Style of Learning and Thinking*. Athens: Department of Educational Psychology, The University of Georgia.

Torrance, E. P., Riegel, T. R., & Reynolds, C. R. (1976). *Preliminary norms: Technical manual for your style of learning and thinking*. Athens: Georgia Studies of Creative Behavior, The University of Georgia.

Torrance, E. P., Riegel, T., Reynolds, C. R., & Ball, O. (1976). *Preliminary manual: Your Style of Learning and Thinking*. Athens: Department of Educational Psychology, The University of Georgia.

Tracey, T. J. G. (2002). Development of interests and competency beliefs: A 1-year longitudinal study of fifth- to eighth-grade students using the ICA-R and structural equation modeling. *Journal of Counseling Psychology, 49* (2), 148–163.

Tracey, T. J. G., & Robbins, S. B. (2005). Stability of interests across ethnicity and gender: A longitudinal examination of grades 8 through 12. *Journal of Vocational Behavior, 67*, 335–364.

Tracey, T. J. G., & Ward, C. C. (1998). The structure of children's interests and competence perceptions. *Journal of Counseling Psychology, 45*, 290–303.

Trinkaus, W. K. (1954). The permanence of vocational interests of college freshmen. *Educational and Psychological Measurement, 14*, 641–647.

Tucker, R. W. (1999). An examination of accounting students' thinking styles. *Dissertation Abstracts International (Section B): The Sciences and Engineering, 60* (6B), 2977.

Tullett, A. D. (1995). The adaptive-innovative (A-I) cognitive styles of male and female project managers: Some implications for the management of change. *Journal of Occupational and Organizational Psychology, 68*, 359–365.

Tullett, A. D. (1997). Cognitive style: Not culture's consequence. *European Psychologist, 2* (3), 258–267.

Tylor, E. B. (1958 [1871]). *Primitive culture*. New York: Harper & Row.

Unger, R. K., & Denmark, F. L. (Eds.) 1975. *Woman: Dependent or independent variable.* New York: Psychological Dimensions.

Utz, P. H., & Hartman, B. (1978). An analysis of the discriminatory power of Holland's types for business majors in three concentration areas. *Measurement & Evaluation in Guidance, 11* (3), 175–182.

Van Der Veken, J., Valcke, M., De Maeseneer, J., & Derese, A. (2009). Impact of the transition from a conventional to an integrated contextual medical curriculum on students' learning patterns: A longitudinal study. *Medical Teacher, 31,* 433–441.

Van Leeuwen, M. S. (1978). A cross-cultural examination of psychological differentiation in males and females. *International Journal of Psychology, 13* (2), 87–122.

Van Rossum, E.J., & Schenk, S. M. (1984). The relationship between learning conception, study strategy and learning outcome. *British Journal of Educational Psychology, 54,* 73–83.

Vandenberg, S. G., & Kuse, A. R. (1979). Spatial ability: A critical review of the sex-linked major gene hypothesis. In M. A. Wittig & A. C. Petersen (Eds.), *Sex-related differences in cognitive functioning: Developmental issues* (pp. 67–95). New York: Academic Press.

Verbeke, W. J., Belschak, F. D., Bakker, A. B., & & Dietz, B. (2008). When intelligence is (dys)functional for achieving sales performance. *Journal of Marketing, 72,* 44–57.

Vermetten, Y. J., Vermunt, J. D., & Lodewijks, H. G. (1999). A longitudinal perspective on learning strategies in higher education – different view-points towards development. *British Journal of Educational Psychology, 69* (2), 221–242.

Vermunt, J. D. (1992). *Learning styles and regulation of learning in higher education – toward process-oriented instruction in autonomous thinking.* Amsterdam/Lisse: Swets & Zeilinger.

Vermunt, J. D. (1994). *Inventory of Learning Styles in Higher Education: Scoring key for the Inventory of Learning Styles in Higher Education.* Department of Educational Psychology, Tilburg University.

Vermunt, J. D. (1998). The regulation of constructive learning processes. *British Journal of Educational Psychology, 58,* 149–171.

Vermunt, J. D. (2011). Patterns in student learning and teacher learning: Similarities and differences. In S. Rayner & E. Cools (Eds.), *Style differences in cognition, learning, and management: Theory, research, and practice* (pp. 173–187). New York: Routledge.

Vermunt, J. D., & Van Rijswijk, F. A. W. M. (1987). *Inventaris Leerstijlen voor het Hoger Onderwijs [Inventory of Learning Styles for Higher Education].* Tilburg, Netherlands: Katholieke Universiteit Brabant.

Vermunt, J. D., & Vermetten, Y. J. (2004). Patterns in student learning: Relationships between learning strategies, conceptions of learning, and learning orientations. *Educational Psychology Review, 16,* 359–384.

Vernon, M. D. (1963). *The psychology of perception.* Harmondsworth: Penguin Books.

Vernon, P. E. (1973). Multivariate approaches to the study of cognitive styles. In J. R. Royce (Ed.) *Multivariate analysis and psychological theory* (pp. 125–148). London: Academic Press.

Vigeland, K. (1973). Cognitive style among rural Norwegian children. *Scandinavian Journal of Psychology, 14,* 305–309.

Volet, S. E., Renshaw, P. D., & Tietzel, K. (1994). A short-term longitudinal investigation of cross-cultural differences in study approaches using Biggs' SPQ questionnaire. *British Journal of Educational Psychology, 64,* 301–318.

Vul, E., Harris, C., Winkielam, P., & Pashler, H. (2009). Puzzling high correlations in fMRI studies of emotion, personality, and social cognition. *Perspectives on Psychological Science, 4* (3), 274–290.

Waldo, C., & Reschetz, S. (1988). Psychological type and real estate sales. *Journal of Psychological Type, 16*, 67–70.

Walsh, W. B., Bingham, R., Horton, J. A., & Spokane, A. (1979). Holland's theory and college-degreed working black and white women. *Journal of Vocational Behavior, 15*, 217–223.

Walsh, W. B., Hildebrand, J. O., Ward, C. M., & Matthews, D. F. (1983). Holland's theory and non-college-degreed working black and white women. *Journal of Vocational Behavior, 22*, 182–190.

Walsh, W. B., Horton, J. A., & Gaffey, R. L. (1977). Holland's theory and college degreed working men and women. *Journal of Vocational Behavior, 10*, 180–186.

Watkins, D. (1996). The influence of social desirability on learning process questionnaires: A neglected possibility? *Contemporary Educational Psychology, 21*, 80–82.

Watkins, D. (1998). Assessing approaches to learning: A cross-cultural perspective on the Study Process Questionnaire. In B. Dart & G. Boulton-Lewis (Eds.), *Teaching and learning in higher education* (pp. 124–144). Melbourne: Australian Council for Educational Research.

Watkins, D., & Hattie, J. (1981). The learning processes of Australian university students: Investigations of contextual and personological factors. *British Journal of Educational Psychology, 51*, 384–393.

Watkins, D., & Hattie, J. (1985). A longitudinal study of the approaches to learning of Australian tertiary students. *Human Learning, 4*, 127–142.

Watkins, D., Hattie, J., & Astilla, E. (1986). Approaches to studying in Filipino students: A longitudinal investigation. *British Journal of Educational Psychology, 56*, 357–362.

Watkins, D., & Mboya, M. (1997). Assessing the learning processes of Black South African students. *Journal of Psychology, 131*, 623–640.

Watkins, D., & Murphy, J. (1994). Modifying the Study Process Questionnaire for students learning English as a second language: Comparisons of reliability and factor structure. *Psychological Reports, 74* (3), 1023–1026.

Watkins, D., Reghi, M., & Astilla, E. (1991). The Asian-learner as a rote learner stereotype: Myth or reality. *Educational Psychology, 11*, 21–24.

Watkins, D. A. (2001). Correlates of approaches to learning: A cross-cultural meta-analysis. In R. J. Sternberg and L. F. Zhang (Eds.), *Perspectives on thinking, learning, and cognitive styles* (pp. 165–198). Mahwah, NJ: Lawrence Erlbaum Associates.

Weisz, J. R., O'Neill, P., & O'Neill, P. C. (1975). Field-dependence-independence on the Children's Embedded Figures Test: Cognitive style or cognitive level? *Developmental Psychology, 11*, 539–540.

Welkowitz, L. A., & Calkins, R. P. (1984). Effects of cognitive and exemplar modeling on field dependence-independence. *Perceptual and Motor Skills, 58*, 439–442.

Wenham, C., & Alie, R. E. (1992). Learning styles and corporate training. *Mid-American Journal of Business, 7* (1), 3–10.

Wertheimer, M. (1945). *Productive thinking.* New York: Harper.

Westwood, R., & Low, D. R. (2003). The multicultural muse: Culture, creativity, and innovation. *International Journal of Cross-Cultural Management, 3* (2), 235–259.

Williams, D. Y., & Akamatsu, T. J. (1978). Cognitive self-guidance training with juvenile delinquents: Applicability and generalization. *Cognitive Therapy and Research, 2* (3), 285–288.

Williams, M. E. (2001). The effects of conceptual model provision and cognitive style on problem-solving performance of learners engaged in an exploratory learning environment. *Dissertation Abstracts International (Section A): Humanities and Social Sciences, 62* (3A), 983.

Willing, D. C., Guest, K., & Morford, J. (2001). Who is entering the teaching profession? MBTI profiles of 525 master in teaching students. *Journal of Psychological Type, 59,* 36–44.

Wilson, D. J., Mundy-Castle, A., & Sibanda, P. (1990). Field differentiation and LOGO performance among Zimbabwean school girls. *Journal of Social Psychology, 130* (2), 277–279.

Wilson, K., & Fowler, J. (2005). Assessing the impact of learning environments on students' approaches to learning: Comparing conventional and action learning designs. *Assessment & Evaluation in Higher Education, 30* (1), 87–101.

Wilson, K. L., Smart, R. M., & Watson, R. J. (1996). Gender differences in approaches to learning in first year psychology students. *British Journal of Educational Psychology, 66,* 59–71.

Wilson, R. C., Christensen, P. E., Merrifield, P. R., & Guilford, J. P. (1960). *Alternate Uses Form A. Manual of Administration, Scoring and Interpretation* (2nd prelim. Ed.). Beverly Hills, CA: Sheridan Supply.

Wilson, R. M. S., & Hill, A. P. (1994). Learning styles – A literature guide. *Accounting Education, 3* (4), 349–358.

Witkin, H. A. (1948). The effect of training of structural aids on performance in three tests of space orientation. *CAA Div. Research Report,* No. 80.

Witkin, H. A. (1954). *Personality through perception: An experimental and clinical study.* New York: Harper.

Witkin, H. A. (1959). The perception of the upright. *Science American, 200,* 50–56.

Witkin, H. A. (1962). *Psychological differentiation; studies of development.* New York: Wiley.

Witkin, H. A. (1965). Psychological differentiation and forms of pathology. *Journal of Abnormal Psychology, 70* (5), 317–336.

Witkin, H. A. (1971). *A manual for the Embedded Figures Test.* Palo Alto, CA: Consulting Psychologists Press.

Witkin, H. A. (1976). Cognitive style in academic performance and in teacher-student relations. In S. Messick, et al. (Eds.), *Individuality in learning* (pp. 38–72). San Francisco: Jossey-Bass.

Witkin, H. A. (1978). *Cognitive styles in personal and cultural adaptation: The 1977 Heinz Werner lectures.* Worcester, MA: Clark University Press.

Witkin, H. A., & Asch, S. E. (1948). Studies in space orientation: IV. Further experiments on perception of the upright with displaced visual fields. *Journal of Experimental Psychology, 38,* 762–782.

Witkin, H. A., & Berry, J. W. (1975). Psychological differentiation in cross-cultural perspective. *Journal of Cross-Cultural Psychology, 6* (1), 4–87.

Witkin, H. A., Dyk, R. B., Faterson, H. F., Goodenough, D. R., & Karp, S. A. (1962). *Psychological differentiation: Studies of development.* Hoboken, NJ: John Wiley & Sons.

Witkin, H. A., & Goodenough, D. R. (1977). Field dependence and interpersonal behavior. *Psychological Bulletin, 84* (4), 661–689.

Witkin, H. A., & Goodenough, D. R. (1981). *Cognitive styles: Essence and origins: Field dependence and field independence.* New York: International Universities Press.

Witkin, H. A., Goodenough, D. R., & Karp, S. A. (1967). Stability of cognitive style from childhood to young adulthood. *Journal of Personality and Social Psychology, 7* (3), 291–300.

Witkin, H. A., Karp, S. A., & Goodenough, S. A. (1959). Dependence in alcoholics. *Quarterly Journal of Studies on Alcoholism, 20,* 493–504.

Witkin, H. A., Lewis, H. B., Hertzman, M., Machover, K., Meissner, P. B., & Wapner, S. (1954). *Personality through perception: An experimental and clinical study.* New York: Harper & Brothers.

Witkin, H. A., Moore, C. A., Oltman, P. K., Donald R., Goodenough, D. R., Friedman, F., Owen, D. R., & Raskin, E. (1977). Role of the field-dependent and field-independent cognitive styles in academic evolution: A longitudinal study. *Journal of Educational Psychology, 69* (3), 197–211.

Witkin, H. A., Oltman, P. K., Raskin, E., & Karp, S. A. (1971). *Embedded Figures Test, Children's Embedded Figures Test: Manual.* Palo Alto, CA: Consulting Psychologists Press.

Wittig, M. A. (1976). Sex differences in intellectual functioning: How much difference do genes make? *Sex Roles, 2,* 63–74.

Wober, M. (1966). Sensotypes. *Journal of Social Psychology, 70,* 181–189.

Wubbels, T., Créton, H. A., & Hooymayers, H. P. (1985). *Discipline problems of beginning teachers.* Paper presented at the Annual Conference of The American Educational Research Association, Chicago (April). ERIC Document Reproduction Services No. ED 260040.

Yao, Y. P. (1993). *Analyses of the MBTI personality types of Chinese female school administrators in Liaoning Province, the People's Republic of China.* Unpublished doctoral dissertation, Mississippi State University, Mississippi, MS.

Yelland, N., & Lloyd, M. (2001). Virtual kids of the 21st century: Understanding the children in schools today. *Information Technology in Childhood Education Annual, 13,* 175–192.

Young, J. B., & Shoemaker, E. (1928). Selection of college majors as a personality expression. *School and Society, 27,* 119–120.

Young, J. D., Kelleher, W. E., & McRae, L. E. (1989). Field independence and business students' achievement: A note. *Perceptual and Motor Skills, 69,* 997–998.

Yu, T. M. (2012). *Do teachers' interaction styles affect secondary school students' thinking styles and academic performance?* Unpublished doctoral dissertation. The University of Hong Kong.

Zakay, D., Bar-El, Z., & Kreitler, S. (1984). Cognitive orientation and changing the impulsivity of children. *British Journal of Educational Psychology, 54,* 40–50.

Zakrajsek, D. B., Johnson, R. L., & Walker, D. B. (1984). Comparison of learning styles between physical education and dance majors. *Perceptual and Motor Skills, 58,* 583–588.

Zeegers, P. (2001). Approaches to learning in science: A longitudinal study. *British Journal of Educational Psychology, 71,* 115–132.

Zelniker, T., & Jeffrey, W. E. (1976). Reflective and impulsive children: Strategies of information processing underlying differences in problem solving. *Monographs of the Society for Research in Child Development, 41* (5), 1–59.

Zhang, L. F. (2000). University students' learning approaches in three cultures: An investigation of Biggs's 3P model. *The Journal of Psychology, 134* (1), 37–55.
Zhang, L. F. (2001). Do thinking styles contribute to academic achievement beyond abilities? *The Journal of Psychology, 135* (6), 621–637.
Zhang, L. F. (2002a). Thinking styles and cognitive development. *The Journal of Genetic Psychology, 163* (2), 179–195.
Zhang, L. F. (2002b). Thinking styles and modes of thinking: Implications for education and research. *The Journal of Psychology, 136* (3), 245–261.
Zhang, L. F. (2002c). Thinking styles: Their relationships with modes of thinking and academic performance. *Educational Psychology, 22* (3), 331–348.
Zhang, L. F. (2003). Contributions of thinking styles to critical thinking dispositions. *The Journal of Psychology, 137* (6), 517–544.
Zhang, L. F. (2004a). Do university students' thinking styles matter in their preferred teaching approaches? *Personality and Individual Differences, 37,* 1551–1564.
Zhang, L. F. (2004b). Field-dependence/independence: Cognitive style or perceptual ability? – Validating against thinking styles and academic achievement. *Personality and Individual Differences, 37,* 1295–1311.
Zhang, L. F. (2004c). Revisiting the predictive power of thinking styles for academic performance. *The Journal of Psychology, 138* (4), 351–370.
Zhang, L. F. (2004d). Thinking styles: University students' preferred teaching styles and their conceptions of effective teachers. *Journal of Psychology, 138* (3), 233–252.
Zhang, L. F. (2007). Intellectual styles and academic achievement among senior school students in rural China. *Educational Psychology, 27* (5), 675–692.
Zhang, L. F. (2008). Thinking styles and identity development among Chinese university students. *The American Journal of Psychology, 121* (2), 255–271.
Zhang, L. F. (2009). Anxiety and thinking styles. *Personality and Individual Differences, 47,* 347–351.
Zhang, L. F. (2010). Further investigating thinking styles and psychosocial development in the Chinese higher education context. *Learning and Individual Differences, 20,* 593–603.
Zhang, L. F. (2011). The developing field of intellectual styles: Four recent endeavours. *Learning and Individual Differences, 21,* 311–318.
Zhang, L. F., Fu, H., & Jiao, B. (2008). Accounting for Tibetan university students' and teachers' intellectual styles. *Educational Review, 60* (1), 21–37.
Zhang, L. F., & He, Y. F. (2003). Do thinking styles matter in the use of and attitudes toward computing and information technology among Hong Kong university students? *Journal of Educational Computing Research, 29* (4), 471–493.
Zhang, L. F., & Higgins, P. (2008). The predictive power of socialization variables for thinking styles among adults in the workplace. *Learning and Individual Differences, 18* (1), 11–18.
Zhang, L. F., Postiglione, G. A., & Jiao, B. (2012). Thinking styles, culture, and economy: Comparing Tibetan minority students with Han Chinese majority students. In W. R. Allen, R. T. Teranishi, & M. Bonous-Hammarth (Eds.), *As the world turns: Implications of global shifts in higher eudcation for theory, research, and practice* (pp. 239–259). United Kingdom: Emerald Group Publishing.
Zhang, L. F., & Sachs, J. (1997). Assessing thinking styles in the theory of mental self-government: A Hong Kong validity study. *Psychological Reports, 81,* 915–928.

Zhang, L. F., & Sternberg, R. J. (1998a). The pentagonal implicit theory of giftedness revisited: A cross validation in Hong Kong. *Roeper Review, 21* (2), 149–153.

Zhang, L. F., & Sternberg, R. J. (1998b). Thinking styles, abilities, and academic achievement among Hong Kong university students. *Educational Research Journal, 13* (1), 41–62.

Zhang, L. F., & Sternberg, R. J. (2000). Are learning approaches and thinking styles related? A study in two Chinese populations. *The Journal of Psychology, 134* (5), 469–489.

Zhang, L. F. & Sternberg, R. J. (2002). Thinking styles and teacher characteristics. *International Journal of Psychology, 37* (1), 3–12.

Zhang, L. F., & Sternberg, R. J. (2005). A threefold model of intellectual styles. *Educational Psychology Review, 17* (1), 1–53.

Zhang, L. F., & Sternberg, R. J. (2006). *The nature of intellectual styles.* Mahwah, NJ: Lawrence Erlbaum.

Zhang, L. F., & Sternberg, R. J. (Eds.) (2009). *Perspectives on the nature of intellectual styles.* New York: Springer Publishing Company.

Zhang, L. F., & Sternberg, R. J. (2011). Revisiting the investment theory of creativity. *Creativity Research Journal, 23* (3), 229–238.

Zhang, L. F., Sternberg, R. J., & Rayner, S. (Eds.) (2012a). *Handbook of intellectual styles: Preferences in cognition, learning, and thinking.* New York: Springer Publishing Company.

Zhang, L. F., Sternberg, R. J., & Rayner, S. (2012b). Intellectual styles: Challenges, milestones, and agenda. In L. F. Zhang, R. J. Sternberg, & S. Rayner (Eds.), *Handbook of intellectual styles: Preferences in cognition, learning, and thinking* (pp. 1–20). New York: Springer Publishing Company.

Zhu, C., & Zhang, L. F. (2011). Thinking styles and conceptions of creativity among university students. *Educational Psychology, 31* (3), 361–375.

Zieffle, T. H., & Romney, D. M. (1985). Comparison of self-instruction and relaxation training in reducing impulsive and inattentive behavior of learning disabled children on cognitive tasks. *Psychological Reports, 57,* 271–274.

Zigler, E. (1963). A measure in search of a theory. *Contemporary Psychology, 8,* 133–135.

Zucker, J. S., & Stricker, G. (1968). Impulsivity-reflectivity in preschool headstart and middle class children. *Journal of Learning Disabilities, 1* (10), 578–584.

Zytowski, D. G., Mills, D. H., & Paepe, C. (1969). Psychological differentiation and the Strong Vocational Interest Blank. *Journal of Counseling Psychology, 16,* 41–44.

Author Index

Abdolmohammadi, M. J., 175, 180, 183
Abed, A. S., 31
Abikoff, H., 192, 194
Adejumo, D., 104
Adler, N. J., 87
Agisòttir, S., 107
Akamatsu, T. J., 219
Albaili, M. A., 31, 40, 134
Albert, J., 30, 215
Alie, R. E., 178
Allen, A. J., 221
Allen, J., 170
Allen, S. S., 104
Allinson, C. W., 8, 39, 183, 184
Alvi, S. A., 107, 108
Amador-Campos, J. A., 31
Anastasi, A., 11
Anderson, P. E., 67
Andrews, L., 104
Angrist, S. S., 51
Armstrong, S. J., 8, 10
Arndt, S. V., 221
Asch, S. E., 279
Astilla, E., 41, 111
Ausburn, F. B., 103
Ausburn, L. J., 103

Baer, J. M., 82
Baeten, M., 233, 234
Bagg, R., 164
Bagley, C., 101
Baig, T., 107, 108
Bakker, A. B., 182
Balkis, M., 77, 152
Ball, O., 31, 134

Balla, J., 111
Bandura, A., 51, 52
Bar-El, Z., 221
Barker, R. G., 127, 184
Barocas, R., 216, 217, 218
Barrett, G. V., 159, 161
Barrickman, L. L., 221
Barris, R., 42, 151
Basadur, M., 236, 237, 238
Batesky, J. A., 141
Bauer, D., 42, 151
Bean, T. W., 192, 193
Becher, T., 148
Becker, L. D., 31
Bell, C. R., 221
Belschak, F. D., 182
Bem, S., 51, 53, 64, 65
Bender, N. N., 31
Bennett, C. I., 101
Bergum, B. O., 128
Bermudez, M. P., 31
Bernardi, R. A., 62, 163, 164
Bernardo, A. B., 114
Bernstein, B., 103
Bernstein, S., 51
Berry, J. W., 49, 59, 61, 62, 80, 88, 100
Betz, N. E., 72
Biberman, G., 150
Bickham, P. J., 35
Bieber, M., 232
Bieschke, K. J., 264
Biggs, J. B., 21, 25, 39, 40, 41, 50, 74, 75, 93, 110, 123, 124, 148, 149, 159, 191, 230, 233, 234, 235, 251, 276, 291
Bingham, R., 176
Bishop, C., 45

Blackman, S., 15
Blackwell, T. L., 36
Block, J., 7
Bock, R. D., 15
Bohon, L. M., 65
Bold, C., 232, 233
Booth, P., 147
Borchers, B. J., 140
Borden, K. A., 221
Boreham, B. W., 136
Borgen, F. H., 253
Borthwick, P., 14
Boshuizen, H. P. A., 43
Boulton-Lewis, G., 74, 75
Bouton, A., 269
Boyd, R., 171
Boyle, E., 272
Bradley, D., 111
Bradley, M., 111
Brand, M., 111
Braswell, L., 202, 221
Braun, C. L., 167
Brinkley, V., 61
Brislin, R. W., 87
Britain, S., 61
Broad, M., 240
Brodzinsky, D. M., 279, 293
Broer, E., 105, 106
Broverman, D. M., 222
Brown, C. M., 194, 219
Brown, D. R., 105, 146
Brown, H. D., 145
Brown, R. T., 221
Brown, S. D., 252
Brown, T., 171
Buchanan, J., 150
Buckner, K. E., 269
Buela-Casal, G., 31
Buie, E. A., 173
Burgin, J. S., 32
Buriel, R., 102, 116
Burke, H. D., 145, 146
Burleson, J. A., 137
Burnett, P. C., 74, 75, 76
Burstein, B., 222
Burstyn, J. N., 49
Burton, L., 72
Busato, V. V., 275
Busch, J. C., 61
Bush, C. M., 173
Bussey, K., 51, 52

Cahill, A. M., 133
Cahill, D. J., 174
Cairns, E., 31
Cakan, M., 28
Calkins, R. P., 227
Callueng, C. M., 114
Cammock, T., 31
Campbell, D. P., 253, 258
Campbell, J., 74, 75
Canino, C., 84, 164
Caño, J. E., 63, 162
Cano-Garcia, F., 45, 114, 155
Capretz, L. F., 173
Carlson, R., 70, 105
Carretero-Dios, H., 31
Carter, A. S., 49
Case, J. C., 36
Casey, B., 28
Caspi, A., 14, 71
Cassady, J. C., 67, 68
Castaneda, A., 101
Cattell, R. B., 7
Chan, D., 148
Chance, J. E., 222
Chao, L., 104, 127, 155
Charlesworth, M., 191, 230
Cheema, I., 7, 8, 9, 29, 121, 190
Chen, G. H., 45
Chess, S. B., 224
Choe, H. S., 45
Chotlos, J. W., 223
Christopher, K. D., 271
Cicchelli, T., 84, 164
Cieslicka, A., 105
Clack, G. B., 170, 171, 183
Clanton, R., 35
Clapp, R. G., 15, 30, 241, 280, 281, 293
Clark, T., 116
Clarke, R. M., 76
Clingerman, S. R., 221
Clump, M., 148
Coan, R., 11
Coerrtijens, L., 277
Coffield, F. C., 9, 17
Cohen, J., 244
Cohen, R., 194, 215, 219
Cohen, S., 217
Cohen, W., 6
Cole, P. M., 220
Collings, J. N., 226
Collins, A. R., 130

Author Index

Collins, J. H., 179, 180
Collis, K. F., 235
Connor, J. M., 15, 223, 225
Cools, E., 10, 294
Cooper, B., 148
Cooper, D., 170
Crandall, V., 103
Crane, M., 51
Cresci, K., 170
Créton, H. A., 243
Cross, T. L., 66, 67, 68
Crouter, A. C., 53, 86
Cuffie, J. C., 41, 147
Curry, L., 9, 18, 20, 21, 251

Dam, G. T., 277
Dancer, L. S., 107, 109
Darcy, M. U. A., 266, 268
Dart, B., 74, 75
Daub, C., 170
Davies, H., 191, 230
Dawson, J. L., 49, 100
Day, D. A., 28, 30, 215
De Ciantis, S. M., 241
De Fruyt, F., 141
De Maeseneer, J., 232
Debus, R. L., 193, 231
Delbridge-Parker, L., 67
De-los-Santos-Roig, M., 31
Dember, W. N., 4
Denmark, F. L., 51
Denney, N. W., 220
Derese, A., 232
Dershowitz, A., 101
DeRussy, F. A., 126
DeSanctis, G., 62, 163
Dietz, B., 182
Dillbeck, M. C., 228
Dochy, F., 233, 234
Donche, V., 276, 277
Donnay, D. A. C., 34, 36, 252
Donovan, D. M., 224
Doyle Conner, P., 184
Doyle, W., 164
Drouin. 223
Drysdale, M. T. B., 143
Dubois, T. E., 6, 28
Duff, A., 39
Dunikoski, R., 62, 163
Dunkleberger, C. J., 267
Dunne, T., 73

Duvall, E., 41, 235
Dyk, R. B., 25, 100, 279

Eagle, C. G., 27
Eastes. S. H., 253
Eccles, J. S., 53, 86
Ecclestone, K., 9
Edmunds, R., 273
Egeland, B., 220
Einarsdòttir, S., 107
Eklund-Myrskog, G., 75
Elder, R. L., 132, 155
Eley, M. G., 149
Elrod, L. M., 32
Elshout, J. J., 275
Engelbrecht, P., 101
England, E. M., 142
Engle, D. E., 167, 168
Entwistle, N., 16, 21, 25, 39, 41, 54, 74, 120, 123, 124, 147, 191, 234, 235, 251, 273
Epperson, D. L., 53
Epstein, M. H., 192, 193
Erickson, R., 37
Evans, C., 8, 9
Evans, N. J., 272
Evans, P., 41, 235
Everett, C., 168, 169

Fan, W. Q., 241
Farzad, V., 45
Faterson, H. F., 25, 100, 279
Feindler, E. L., 218
Felicetti, L. A., 142
Fer, S., 45, 152
Ferguson, M., 71
Finch, A. J., 221
Fisher, D. G., 175
Fjell, A. M., 45
Fling, S., 14, 15, 240
Flinn, J. M., 225
Flynn, J. R., 101
Forney, D. S., 272
Foshter, C., 45
Fouad, N. A., 107, 109
Fowler, J., 231
Fowler, W., 11, 223
Fox, R. A., 103
Foxall, G. R., 165, 166, 167, 182
Francis, B., 72
Frank, B. M., 130
Frederickson, W., 134

French, R. M., 41, 42, 123, 137, 147, 150
Freud, S., 51
Friedman, B., 49, 85
Friedman, S. M., 170
Fung, Y. H., 39
Funk, L. G., 28
Fuqua, D., 107, 110
Furnham, A., 7, 8
Futch, E., 126

Gade, E. M., 107, 110
Gaffey, R. L., 176
Gallaher, M., 14, 240
Gaudron, J. P., 268
Gebbia, M., 10
Geiger, M. A., 269, 271, 272, 281
Geniesse, R., 221
Genshaft, J. L., 217, 220
Gerstein, L. H., 107
Ghana-ei, Z., 45
Ghaye, A., 233
Ghaye, K., 233
Ghosh, J., 136
Gielen, S., 233
Gijbels, D., 233, 234, 235
Gijselaers, W. H., 155, 233
Gillespie, B. V., 66, 70
Gilligan, C., 71
Gilmore, G. C., 62
Gledhill, R. F., 74, 75
Glenwick, D. S., 216, 217, 218
Glesner, G. C., 224
Glidden, R. C., 35
Globerson, T., 250
Goldstein, A. G., 222
Goldstein, G., 223, 224
Goldstein, K. M., 15
Goodenough, D. R., 7, 25, 27, 131, 223, 278, 279
Goodenough, S. A., 6, 15
Gordon, C., 231
Gottfredson, G. D., 158, 175
Goulet, C., 223
Gow, L., 111, 148, 216
Graen, G. B., 236, 237
Green, S. G., 236
Greenwood, A. K., 35
Gregorc, A. F., 11, 24, 37, 122, 124, 142, 159, 161, 178, 179, 190
Gridley, M. C., 37, 78, 179, 181, 182
Grigorenko, E. L., ix, 8, 9, 16, 17, 18, 20, 21, 22, 24, 45, 49, 50, 78, 160, 180, 287

Grossman, H., 53
Grossman, S. H., 53
Gruenfeld, L. W., 100
Guest, K., 138, 139
Guilford, J. P., 24, 29, 236
Guttman, L., 266

Hackett, G., 252
Hajosy, R. C., 131
Hall, E., 9, 88
Hall, M. E., 264
Hall, R. H., 107
Hallahan, D. P., 192
Halpern, D. F., 52, 53
Hamaker, C., 275
Hammer, A. L., 33, 66, 70, 105, 280
Hansen, J. C., 268
Harbison, F. H., 100
Harold, R. D., 53, 86
Hartlage, L. C., 222
Hartley, D. G., 220
Hartman, B., 140
Hassan, M. M., 31
Hattie, J., 41, 75, 273
Hawkins, J., 67
Hayes, J., 8, 39, 183, 184
Hayward, G., 168, 169
He, Y. F., 84
Head, J. O., 170
Heckel, R. V., 104
Hedegard, J. M., 105
Heider, E. R., 193
Heimann, N., 145
Helson, R., 14, 71
Henriksen, L. W., 66, 69
Henson, K. T., 14
Herbert, J., 88
Herold, P. L., 101
Herrmann, K. J., 221
Hertzman, M., 6, 279
Herzberg, F., 269
Hicks, E., 164
Higgins, P., 46, 160, 182
Hildebrand, J. O., 176
Hill, A. P., 39
Hill, D. J., 42, 147, 150
Hill, J., 104
Hiltz, S. R., 232
Hirt, M., 217, 220
Ho, A. S. P., 39
Hofstede, G. H., 71, 87, 88, 89, 92

Holland, C. J., 67, 93, 124, 161
Holland, J. L., x, 21, 24, 34, 35, 36, 140, 158, 159, 175, 176, 244, 251, 252
Holland, P. A., 169
Holland, W. E., 165
Holloway, M., 170, 172
Holmes, C. S., 216, 220
Honey, P., 24, 38, 39, 190, 192, 236, 240
Hongsfeld, A., 10
Hood, A. B., 36
Hooymayers, H. P., 243
Horton, J. A., 176
Hou, Z. J., 107, 141
Hounsell, D., 120, 234
Howard, J., 61
Hoyt, D. P., 269
Hritzuk, J., 135
Hsu, C. H. C., 272
Hu, S., 148
Huang, C. E., 106
Huang, C. H., 106
Huang, J. Y., 104, 127, 155
Hughes, E. H., 45, 114, 155
Hui, C. H., 75, 111, 293
Hurlburt, G., 107, 110
Hussain, M. A., 107, 108
Huston, A., 52, 86
Hutton, E. M., 229
Hyde, J. S., 49

Ihilivech, D., 224
Isaksen, S. G., 30, 37, 241
Isiker, G. B., 77, 152

Jablokow, K. W., 8, 16
Jacabson, G. R., 224
Jacklin, C. N., 49, 52
Jackson, D. M., 131
Jacobs, J. E., 53, 86
Jacobson, C. M., 63, 165
Jain, V., 170, 183
Jamison, W., 53, 64
Janeke, H. C., 45
Janzen, H. L., 194
Jeffrey, W. E., 31
Johansson, C. B., 253
John, O., 14, 71
Johnson, R. L., 144
Johnson, R. W., 36
Johnson, S., 225
Jones, A. E., 6, 7, 9, 28

Jones, C., 14, 71, 145, 149, 151
Jones, C. F. N., 155
Jones, G. K., 88
Joniak, A. J., 30, 37
Juliano, D. B., 103
Jung, C. G., x, 9, 10, 15, 21, 24, 32, 34, 50, 92, 93, 105, 159, 161, 180, 190, 236, 240, 251

Kadivar, P., 45
Kagan, J., 3, 4, 6, 7, 9, 21, 24, 30, 93, 102, 159, 190, 191, 215, 251, 278, 289
Kagan, S., 102
Kalsbeek, D. H., 69
Karp, S. A., 6, 25, 27, 28, 101, 161, 191, 223, 224, 278, 279, 287
Kasner, K. H., 224
Katkovsky, W., 103
Katz, N., 145
Katz, P., 86
Kauffman, J. M., 192
Kaufman, A. S., 66, 69
Kaufman, J. C., 82
Kaufman, N. L., 69
Keats, B. W., 184
Keilhofner, G., 42
Kelleher, W. E., 62, 128
Keller, R. T., 165
Kelly, M., 39
Kember, D., 40, 111, 148, 155, 191, 230
Kendall, P. C., 202, 217, 220, 221
Keyser, R., 170
Khan, S. B., 107, 108
Kielhofner, G., 151
Kienholz, A., 135
Kim, M., 123, 152, 184
King, M. O., 132, 133, 167, 168
King, T. E., 73, 76
Kinicki, A. J., 184
Kirchner-Nebot, T., 31
Kirkland, D., 238
Kirton, M. J., 8, 10, 15, 16, 24, 29, 30, 63, 124, 132, 159, 161, 165, 166, 167, 168, 182, 183, 190, 192, 236, 241, 251, 278
Kitayama, S., 88
Klaiber, E. L., 222
Kloner, A., 61
Kobayashi, Y., 222
Kogan, N., 4, 6, 7, 9, 12, 13, 61, 72, 222, 223
Kohlberg, L., 51
Kolakowski, D., 15

Kolb, D. A., 14, 24, 25, 38, 39, 121, 122, 124, 144, 159, 161, 179, 180, 190, 192, 236, 239, 251, 269, 271
Kolesinski, M. T., 31
Konstadt, N. L., 28, 223
Kopper, B. A., 53
Korchin, S. J., 7
Kozhevnikov, M., 4
Kreitler, S., 221
Kuder, G. F., 253
Kulik, L., 53, 86
Kuperman, S., 221
Kuse, A. R., 222
Kwan, K. P., 39
Kwan, V. S. Y., 14, 71

LaBarbera, D. M., 177
LaBuda, M. C., 49
Lall, R., 170, 183
Lapidus, L. B., 227, 229
Laschinger, H. K. S., 155
Lauer, K. J., 241
Lavach, J. F., 134
Lawrence, G., 72
Le Vesconte, 226
Lee, A., 72
Leithwood, K. A., 223
Lenney, E., 53, 64
Lent, R. W., 252
Leo-Rhynie, L., 123, 127
Leung, D. Y. P., 40, 148, 155
Leung, R., 148
Leung, S. A., 107, 123, 141
Levy, N., 70, 105
Levy, S., 269
Lewin, K., 37
Lewin, Z. G., 28
Lewis, H. B., 6, 279
Li, J., 111
Lincoln, A., 66, 69
Lindblom-Ylänne, S., 41, 150, 277
Linden, W., 227
Linton, H., 122
Lloyd, M., 84
Lodewijks, H. G., 275
Lonka, K., 41, 150, 277
Lonner, W. J., 87, 109
Loo, R., 239, 241, 269, 271, 272
Lorber, J., 51
Losh, C. L., 136
Low, D. R., 92

Low, K. S. D., 258, 264, 267, 268
Lowe, E. A., 165
Luckett, P., 147
Lusk, E. J., 163

MacArthur, R. S., 100
Maccoby, E. E., 49, 52
MacDonald, D. A., 67
MacEachron, A. E., 100
Machover, K., 6, 279
Mackler, B., 6, 28
Mah, J. J., 167
Malacos, J. A., 141
Mallick, K., 101
Marambe, K. N., 43
Marcic, D., 167
Markus, H., 51, 88
Márquez, S., 63, 162, 183
Martin, S. A., 134
Marton, F., 39, 41
Maruhnic, J., 100
Mason, E. S., 52
Massa, L. J., 65
Masten, W. G., 239
Matsumoto, D. R., 92
Matthews, D. F., 176, 240
Mayer, R. E., 65
Mboya, M., 111
McCarley, N. G., 105, 106
McCarthy, B., 31
McCarthy, R., 63
McCarthy, R. M., 183
McCarthy, S. V., 67
McCaulley, M. H., 33, 34, 69, 70, 169, 170, 280
McCreary, D. R., 51
McCrindle, A., 74, 75
McCune, V., 16, 41, 120, 234, 235
McDonald, A., 240
McHale, S. M., 53, 86
McKay, J., 191, 230
McLean, J. E., 66, 69
McMillan, B., 194
McRae, L. E., 62
Meissner, P. B., 6, 279
Melancon, J. G., 28
Mervielde, I., 141
Messer, S. B., 31, 279, 293
Messick, S., 4, 7, 8, 9, 13
Meyer, J. H. F., 73, 74, 76
Meyers, A. W., 194, 215, 219
Miles, C. C., 52

Miller, A., 8, 9, 11
Miller, J. O., 103
Miller, M. J., 35, 269
Miller, R. J., 147, 148, 149, 151
Milliron, V. C., 179, 180
Mills, C., 68
Mills, C. J., 68
Mills, D. H., 122
Mills, T. Y., 163, 164
Mishra, J., 135, 144
Mitchell, T., 133
Mitchell, W. D., 66, 105
Mladenovic, R., 147
Mokhtari, K., 145
Money, S., 272
Monfort, M., 134, 136
Moody, R, A., 34
Moore, D. M., 226
Morell, J. A., 223
Morford, J., 138, 139
Morgan, H., 9
Morris, M. L., 34, 36
Morris, T. L., 128
Morrison, G., 31
Morrison, W. B., 280
Morse, D. T., 239
Moseley, D. V. M., 9
Moskvina, V., 4
Most, R., 8
Mpofu, E., 111, 112
Mshelia, A. Y., 227
Mudrack, P. E., 52
Mumbauer, C. C., 103
Mumford, A., 24, 38, 39, 190, 192, 236, 240
Mundy, P., 221
Muray, G. C., 32
Murdock, M. C., 241
Murphy, A., 45
Murphy, C., 105
Murphy, H. J., 28
Myers, B., 70
Myers, I. B., 33, 69, 169, 170, 192, 240, 280
Myers, P. L., 7

Nachmias, R., 114
Nasby, W., 266
Nash, S. C., 51, 52, 71, 83, 222
Natzel, S. G., 101
Naylor, L. A., 62
Nelson, C., 61
Nelson, P. K., 28

Neumeister, K. L. S., 67, 68
Neuringer, C., 224
Nielsen, T., 4
Nieminen, J., 277
Nijhuis, J. F. H., 155, 233
Niles, F. S., 111
Nolen, S. B., 246

Oakland, T., 111, 112
O'Brien, T. P., 37, 130, 143
O'Connor, S. J., 171
Okonji, M., 100
O'Leary, M. R., 224
Oltman, P. R., 25, 27, 101, 161, 224, 287
O'Malley, J. J., 228
O'Neal, H., 35
O'Neill, P., 6, 28
O'Neill, P. C., 6, 28
Ott, R. L., 175

Paepe, C., 122
Panek, P. E., 28
Páramo, M. F., 155
Parente, J. A., 228
Pargman, D., 63
Park, K. H., 45
Park, S. K., 45
Parker, W. D., 68
Pascale, R. T., 92
Pask, G., 41
Passmore, J., 170, 172
Payne, A. F., 165, 166, 167, 182
Payne, M. A., 107, 109
Pearson, L. C., 32, 191
Pelletier, K. R., 228
Pender, S. R., 166, 182
Perry, P. J., 221
Perry, W. G., 247
Peterson, E. R., 16, 128, 295
Peterson, J. M., 128, 158
Peterson, R. A., 253
Petrakis, E., 129
Pettigrew, A. C., 132, 133, 167, 168
Philips, W., 30, 215
Piaget, J., 38, 139, 250
Pierson, J. S., 122
Pincus, K. V., 62, 163
Pinker, S., 78
Pinto, J. K., 269, 271, 272, 281
Pollack, M., 222
Prato-Previde, G., 63

Preston, A., 103
Pringle, P., 238
Prins, F. J., 275
Proctor, R. M., 74, 76
Prosser, M., 233
Przybycien, C. A., 217
Purcell, K. M., 141
Puurula, A., 104

Quay, H. C., 221
Quenk, N. L., 33, 70, 280

Raina, M. K., 134, 135
Raiszadeh, A. D., 70
Rakoczy, M., 272
Rakowska, A., 104
Ramirez, M., 101
Ramsden, P., 25, 39, 41, 147, 251, 273
Raskin, E., 25, 27, 101, 161, 224, 287
Rawle-Cope, M., 170, 172
Rayner, S., 4, 5, 8, 9, 11, 16, 87, 294, 295
Read, W. J., 175
Readence, J. E., 192, 193
Reghi, M., 111
Reichard, C., 145
Reid, W. A., 41, 235
Renner, V., 15
Renshaw, P. D., 276
Reschetz, S., 174
Resnick, J. R., 100
Reynolds, C. R., 31, 134, 135, 238, 239
Rezler, A. G., 41, 42, 123, 124, 137, 147, 150
Rezmovick, V., 42
Ribordy, S. C., 104
Richardson, A. G., 41, 73, 147
Richardson, J. A., 6, 28
Richardson, J. T. E., 41, 73, 76, 273
Riding, R., 4, 7, 8, 9, 11, 29, 121, 190
Riegel, T. R., 31, 134, 239
Roach, B., 172
Robbins, S. B., 252, 266, 271, 281
Roberts, B. W., 14, 71, 258
Robinson, D., 67
Rodick, J. D., 194, 215
Roeder, G., 104
Rogers, C., 288
Rogers, J. C., 42, 147, 150
Romney, D. M., 221
Roodenburg, E., 8
Roodenburg, J., 8
Rosati, P., 138, 139

Rosenberg, N., 269
Rosenfeld, R. B., 167, 183
Rosman, B. L., 30, 215
Ross, J. L., 143
Rotter, J. B., 103
Rounds, J. B., 107, 108, 252, 258, 267
Royce, J. R., 14
Ruble, T. L., 271
Ruble, V. E., 66, 69
Rush, G. M., 226
Ryba, P., 104

Saarni, C., 12, 222
Sabaroche, H. F., 107, 109
Sachs, J., 45
Sadler-Smith, E., 9, 10, 17, 73, 74, 75, 82, 84
Sadri, G. 167
Sak, U., 67
Säljö, R., 39, 41
Salkind, N. J., 49, 287
Salter, D. W., 272
Samuelowicz, K., 111
Sanders, M., 102
Sangari, A. A., 45
Satterly, D., 6, 28
Saucier, D. M., 51, 52
Savickas, M. L., 252
Saxberg, J. K. J., 51
Scabrough, D. P., 175
Scandura, T. A., 237
Schackman, M., 15, 223, 225
Schaubhut, N. A., 34, 36, 252
Schenk, S. M., 76
Schkade, L. L., 173
Schleser, R., 194, 215, 218, 219, 220
Scholz, J. P., 102
Schomburg, A. M., 266, 267
Schulz, R. A., 143
Schumacher, E., 221
Schurr, K. T., 66, 69
Scott, V., 191, 230
Scouller, K., 233
Segers, M. S. R., 155, 233, 235
Seidel, L. E., 142
Serbin, L. A., 15, 223, 225
Severiens, S., 277
Seymour, R., 39
Shade, B. J., 101, 105, 106
Shake, I. G., 39
Shany, N., 114
Sharma, G., 14

Author Index

Shaukat, N., 107, 108
Shen, J., 232
Sherman, J. A., 15, 222
Shewchuck, R. M., 171
Shin, S. K., 229
Shiner, R. L., 14, 71
Shipman, S. L., 13
Shoemaker, E., 122
Shokri, O., 45
Shrestha, A. B., 102
Signorella, M. L., 53, 64
Siladi, M., 51
Silbey, V., 136
Sims, R. R., 39, 269, 271
Sinha, D., 102
Sitko-Lutek, A., 104
Skogsberg, K., 148
Slaney, R. B., 264
Smart, R. M., 73
Smith, D., 74, 75
Smith, D. C., 173
Smith, J. L., 269
Smith, S. N., 147, 148, 149, 151
Smith, T. P., 104
Snyder, R. P., 28
Sofman, R. J., 131
Solis-Cámara, R. P., 103
Spokane, A., 176
Spotts, J. X. V., 6, 28
Spunt, A., 221
Stafford, R. E., 222
Steele, A. L., 138
Stericker, A., 226
Stern, G. G., 127
Sternberg, R. J., ix, 3, 4, 5, 7, 8, 9, 11, 13, 14, 16, 17, 18, 20, 21, 22, 23, 24, 25, 26, 29, 34, 40, 44, 45, 50, 53, 77, 78, 80, 82, 83, 87, 92, 93, 103, 110, 112, 113, 114, 121, 123, 124, 139, 151, 159, 160, 161, 165, 167, 180, 182, 190, 192, 229, 241, 242, 243, 244, 291, 294, 295, 296, 297, 300
Stetson, T. E., 175, 180
Stever, G. S., 66
Stewart, K. L., 142
Stilwell, N. A., 137
Stokes, M., 111
Stordahl, K. E., 269
Stout, D. E., 271
Stricker, G., 103
Strong, E. K., Jr., 34, 36, 159, 252, 269
Struyf, F., 233
Struyven, K., 233

Stuart, I. R., 6, 28
Stuve, T. A., 62
Swan, K. C., 35, 177, 178
Swanson, J. L., 107, 109, 253, 258, 268, 269
Sweitzer, G., 128, 158
Swiatek, M. A., 66, 67, 68
Szirony, G. M., 32

Tabernero, B., 162, 183
Tait, H., 41, 74, 235
Talbot, S., 223
Taylor, J., 30
Taylor, W. G. K., 165
Tennant, M., 11
Terman, L. M., 52
Thal, S. E., 137
Thomas, A., 14, 76, 240
Thomas, K., 76
Thompson, B., 28
Thompson, R. C., 34, 36, 252
Thomson, D., 165
Thornton, C. L., 159, 161
Tietzel, K., 276
Tinajero, C., 155
Tobacyk, J., 105
Tokar, D. M., 266, 267
Torrance, E. P., 24, 31, 32, 124, 134, 135, 159, 236, 238, 239
Tracey, T. J. G., 16, 107, 108, 252, 266, 268, 271, 281
Triandis, H. C., 75, 111, 293
Trinkaus, W. K., 269
Trudel, P., 223
Tsagarakis, C. I., 67
Tsang, F., 75
Tucker, C. J., 53, 86
Tucker, R. W., 77
Tullett, A. D., 16, 62, 63, 83, 104, 106, 167, 168, 183, 241
Turner, T. E., 6, 28
Tyer, Z. E., 225
Tyler, L. E., 267
Tylor, E. B., 87

Unger, R. K., 51
Utz, P. H., 140

Valcke, M., 232
van de Heijden, B. I. J. M., 10
van Der Merwe, C. A., 74, 75
Van Der Veken, J., 232

Van Hout Wolters, B., 277
Van Leeuwen, M. S., 49, 61, 62, 80
Van Petegem, P., 276, 277
Van Rijswik, F. A. W. M., 277
van Rossum, E. J., 76
Vandenberg, S. G., 222
Vats, A., 134, 135
Vautier, S., 268
Verbeke, W. J., 182
Veres, G. G., 39, 269
Vermetten, Y. J., 43, 275
Vermunt, J. D., 16, 42, 43, 147, 190, 191, 232, 251, 275, 276, 277
Vernon M. D., 8
Vernon, P. E., 4, 9
Vigeland, K., 102
Vogel, W., 222
Vojtisek, J. E., 131
Volet, S. E., 116, 276
Vul, E., 295

Wagner, R. K., 45, 113, 180, 242, 243, 244, 291
Wakabayashi, M., 237
Waldo, C., 174
Walhovd, K. B., 45
Walker, D. B., 144
Wallick, M. M., 137
Walsh, W. B., 176, 177
Walters, D. A., 166
Wapner, S., 6, 279
Ward, C. C., 16
Ward, C. M., 176
Ward, J., 216
Waring, M., 8, 9
Watkins, D., 40, 41, 75, 111, 112, 273, 293
Watson, J. A., 61
Watson, P., 269
Watson, R. J., 73
Watts, J. D., 136
Weisz, J. R., 6, 28
Welch, L., 191
Welkowitz, L. A., 227
Wenestam, C. G., 75
Wenham, C., 178

Wenk, H. E., 62
Wertheimer, M., 15
West-Burnham, J., 39
Westwood, R., 92
White, B. J., 130
Wilcox, L. E., 217, 220, 221
Williams, D. Y., 219
Willing, D. C., 138, 139
Wilson, K. L., 73, 75, 81, 231
Wilson, R. M. S., 39
Winger-Bearskin, M., 167
Witkin, H. A., 6, 7, 15, 21, 24, 25, 27, 49, 59, 61, 62, 80, 92, 93, 100, 101, 122, 124, 125, 126, 161, 190, 191, 222, 223, 251, 278, 279, 287
Wittig, M. A., 15
Wober, M., 100
Wright, H., 163
Wubbels, T., 243
Wynne, M. E., 221

Yao, Y. P., 106
Yelland, N., 84
Yoon, M., 258
Young, J. B., 122
Young, J. D., 28, 62, 164
Young, S., 138
Yu, T. M., 241, 243

Zakay, D., 221
Zakrajsek, D. B., 144, 155
Zeegers, P., 73, 278
Zeidner, M., 8
Zelniker, T., 31, 250
Zhang, L. F., ix, 4, 5, 8, 9, 11, 13, 16, 17, 20, 22, 23, 24, 25, 26, 28, 29, 31, 32, 40, 44, 45, 46, 53, 73, 74, 77, 78, 80, 82, 83, 84, 87, 92, 100, 103, 110, 112, 113, 114, 115, 121, 139, 151, 159, 160, 165, 167, 180, 182, 190, 229, 242, 243, 244, 250, 291, 294, 295, 296, 297, 300
Zhou, Z. J., 123
Zieffle, T. H., 221
Zigler, E., 6
Zook, W., 104
Zucker, J. S., 103
Zytowski, D. G., 122

Subject Index

ability/intelligence, distinguishing intellectual style from, 5–8
academic discipline
 career personality type and, 140–142
 conclusions and implications, 153, 155
 decision-making and problem-solving style and, 132–133
 field dependence/independence (FDI) and, 124–131
 general literature search procedures, 121–122
 history of studies on, 122–123
 intellectual styles and, 120–121
 Kolb's construct of learning style and, 143–147
 learning approach and, 147–151
 mind style and, 142–143
 mode of thinking and, 133–136
 personality type and, 136–140
 research findings, 123–124
 summary of studies, 152–155
 thinking style and, 151–152
accountants, personality type and, 175
achieving learning approach, 39
acting impulsively, 3
acting reflectively, 3
adaption-innovation decision-making and problem-solving styles (A-I construct), 15–16

brain dominance. *See* mode of thinking

career personality types, 34
 academic discipline and, 140–142
 culture and, empirical evidence, 106–110
 inventories for assessing, 34–36
 occupation and, 175–178
 research on malleability of, 252–269
Children's Embedded Figures Test (CHEF), 27–28
Clinton, Bill, 3
cognitive climate, 183
collectivism, individualism verus, 89
computer professionals, personality type and, 173
conceptual tempo, modifying, 192–222. *See also* reflectivity-impulsivity
culture
 defined, 87–88
 Hofstede's dimensions of, 88–90
 hypothesis for conceptual links between intellectual styles and, 90–92
 intellectual styles, empirical evidence, 93–115
 limitations and implications of studies, 116–119
 literature search procedures and results for hypothesis of, 92–93
 summary of findings across models, 115–116
 theories of, 88
Curry's, 20–21

decision makers, personality type and, 172–173
decision-making and problem-solving style
 academic discipline and, 132–133
 modifying, 241
 occupation and, 165–169
 research on malleability of, 280
deep learning approach, 39
divergent-convergent thinking, 29
 developing, 236–238

Embedded Figures Test (EFT), 27–28

365

FDI. *See* field dependence/independence (FDI)
femininity, masculinity *versus*, 89–90
field dependence/independence (FDI), 6–7, 28
  academic discipline and, 124–131
  culture and, empirical evidence, 93–102
  gender differences in, research on, 58–65
  literature results for gender socialization and, 55
  occupation and, 161–165
  research on malleability of, 278–279

gender differences
  conclusions, 80
  dependent/independent styles and, research on, 58–65
  implications for education, 82–86
  implications for research on, 81–82
  in intellectual styles, research evidence on, 56–79
  in learning approaches, research on, 72–76
  in personality types, research on, 65–72
  in thinking styles, research on, 76–79
  intellectual styles and, 49–51
  limitations of findings on, 81
  summary of general findings, 79
gender roles
  defined, 51
  research on appropriate, 53
gender-role socialization
  defined, 51
  intellectual styles and, 53
  literature results for, 54–56
  literature search procedures, 53–54
  research evidence, 52–53
  theoretical perspectives, 51–52
gender-role stereotypes
  defined, 52
  research evidence, 52–53
Gregorc Style Delineator, 37
Grigorenko and Sternberg's model of style traditions, 21–22
Group Embedded Figures Test (GEFT), 28

hemispheric specificity. *See* mode of thinking

individualism, collectivism *versus*, 89
integrative style models
  Curry's, 20–21
  Grigorenko and Sternberg's model of style traditions, 21–22
  Zhang and Sternberg's threefold model of intellectual styles, 22–24

intellectual styles, 4. *See also* style malleability
  academic discipline and, 120–121
  difficulty of distinguishing ability/intellegence and personality, 5–8
  difficulty of linking field of styles with other fields, 9–10
  difficulty of searching for common language and conceptual framework, 8–9
  gender differences and, 49–51
  hypothesis for conceptual links between culture and, 90–92
  identity issues of, 5–10
  malleability of, 4
  research on malleability of, 278–280
  style malleability controversy of, 14–16
  style overlap controversy of, 10–11
  style value controversy of, 11–14
intelligence/ability, distinguishing intellectual style from, 5–8
Inventory of Learning Styles (ILS), 42–43

Kirton Adaption–Innovation Inventory (KAI), 29–30
Kirton's theory of styles for decision making, problem solving, and creativity, 29

learning approaches, 39
  academic discipline and, 147–151
  culture and, empirical evidence, 110–112
  gender differences in, research on, 72–76
  limitations of findings on, 81
  literature results for gender socialization and, 56
  modifying, 229–236
  research on malleability of, 273–278
  research tools for assessing, 39–43
  summary of general findings, 79
learning orientation, 40–41
learning pattern, 42–43
learning preference, 41–42
Learning Preferences Inventory (LPI), 41–42
Learning Process Questionnaire (LPQ), 39–40
Learning Style Inventory (LSI), 38
learning style, Kolb's construct of, 37–39
  academic discipline and, 143–147
  modifying, 239–240
  occupation and, 179–180
learning styles
  modifying Honey and Mumford's model, 240
  research on malleability of, 269–273

Learning Styles Questionnaire (LSQ), 38–39
longitudinal studies with interventions
   approaches to learning, modifying, 229–236
   conceptual tempo, modifying, 192–222
   general literature search procedures, 189–191
   limitations and conclusions, 247–249
   literature search results, 191–192
   research findings, 192
   styles training, six other models, 236–241
longitudinal studies without interventions
   career personalities types, malleability of, 252–269
   conclusions, 280–283
   future research, 280–283
   learning approaches, malleability of, 273–278
   learning styles, malleability of, 269–273
   limitations, 280–283
   literature search procedures and results, 250–251
   other intellectual sttyles, malleability of, 278–280

malleability. *See* style malleability
masculinity, femininity *versus*, 89–90
Matching Familiar Figures Test (MFFT), 30–31
McCain, John, 3–4
medical personnel, personality type and, 170–171
mental self-government, theory of, 3–4
   assessment of, 44–45
mind style, 37
   academic discipline and, 142–143
   occupation and, 178–179
mode of thinking, 31
   academic discipline and, 133–136
   developing holistic and interactive, 238–239
monarchic thinking, 3–4
Myers-Briggs Type Indicator (MBTI), 33–34
Myers-Briggs Type Indicator (MBTI) *Manual*, 33–34

Obama, Barack, 3–4
occupation
   career personality type and, 175–178
   decision-making and problem-solving style and, 165–169
   field dependence/independence (FDI) and, 161–165
   general literature search procedures, 158–159
   implications of findings, 184–185
   intellectual styles and, 158
   Kolb's construct of learning style and, 179–180
   literature search results, 159
   mind style and, 178–179
   personality type and, 169–175
   research findings, 159–160
   summary, 183–184
   thinking style and, 180–183
organizational advisers, personality type and, 172–173

perceptual styles, modifying, 222–229
personality styles, modifying, 240–241
personality types, 32–33
   academic discipline and, 136–140
   accountants and, 175
   computer professionals and, 173
   culture and, empirical evidence, 105–106
   gender differences in, research on, 65–72
   literature results for gender socialization and, 56
   medical personnel and, 170–171
   occupation and, 169–175
   real estate agents and, 173–175
   research on malleability of, 279–280
personality, distinguishing intellectual style from, 5–8
power distance, 88–89
Preschool embedded Figures Test (PEFT), 27–28
psychological differentiation. *See* field dependence/independence (FDI)

real estate agents, personality type and, 173–175
reflectivity-impulsivity, 30
   culture and, empirical evidence, 102–104
   research on malleability of, 279
Revised Two-Factor Study Process Questionnaire (R-SPQ-2F), 40
Rod-and-Frame Test (RFT), 25–27

Self-Directed Search (SDS), 34–35
   Form-R of, 34–35
Self-Directed Search (SDS) *Manual*, 34–35
Strong Interest Inventory (SII), 36
Strong Vocational Interest Blank (SVIB), 36
Study Process Questionnaire (SPQ), 39–40
style malleability. *See also* intellectual styles
   controversy of, 14–16
   existing literature on, 288–289
   general implications for education, 295–300
   research limitations, 295
Style of Learning and Thinking (SOLAT), 31–32

Style of Learning and Thinking (SOLAT)
    Administrator's Manual, 31–32
style overlap, 10–11
style traditions, Grigorenko and Sternberg's model of, 21–22
styles for decision making, problem solving, and creativity, Kirton's theory of, 29
surface learning approach, 39

thinking styles, 43–44
    academic discipline and, 151–152
    culture and, empirical evidence, 112–115
    gender differences in, research on, 76–79
    literature results for gender socialization and, 56
    modifying, 241–247
    occupation and, 180–183

Thinking Styles Inventory (TSI), 44–45
Thinking Styles Inventory-Revised (TSI-R), 44–45
Thinking Styles Inventory-Revised II (TSI-R2), 44–45
threefold model of intellectual styles, Zhang and Sternberg's, 22–24
Type I intellectual styles, 12, 22–24
    fostering, 297–300
Type II intellectual styles, 12, 22–24
Type III intellectual styles, 12, 22–24

uncertainty avoidance, 89

Vocational Preference Inventory (VPI), 35–36
Vocational Preference Inventory (VPI) *Manual*, 35–36

For EU product safety concerns, contact us at Calle de José Abascal, 56–1°, 28003 Madrid, Spain or eugpsr@cambridge.org.

www.ingramcontent.com/pod-product-compliance
Ingram Content Group UK Ltd.
Pitfield, Milton Keynes, MK11 3LW, UK
UKHW011326060825
461487UK00005B/379